To Susan,

We hope you enjoy Tante Lutie's story and find the murder and mayhem of the Cocoune as compelling as we did!

Gayle K. Brunelle

MURDER IN THE MÉTRO

MURDER
IN THE MÉTRO

LAETITIA TOUREAUX AND THE CAGOULE IN 1930S FRANCE

GAYLE K. BRUNELLE AND
ANNETTE FINLEY-CROSWHITE

LOUISIANA STATE UNIVERSITY PRESS BATON ROUGE

Published by Louisiana State University Press
Copyright © 2010 by Louisiana State University Press
All rights reserved
Manufactured in the United States of America
First printing

Designer: Michelle A. Neustrom
Typefaces: Warnock Pro, text; Market Deco, display
Printer and binder: Thomson-Shore, Inc.

Portions of chapters 2 and 3 were first published as "Murder in the Métro: Masking and
Unmasking Laetitia Toureaux in 1930s France," *French Cultural Studies* 14 (February 2003):
53–80, and are reproduced by permission.

LIBRARY OF CONGRESS CATALOGING-IN-PUBLICATION DATA

Brunelle, Gayle K., 1959–
    Murder in the métro : Laetitia Toureaux and the Cagoule in 1930s France / Gayle K. Brunelle
and Annette Finley-Croswhite.
        p. cm.
    Includes bibliographical references and index.
    ISBN 978-0-8071-3616-4 (cloth : alk. paper) 1. Murder—France—Paris—Case studies
2. Murder investigation—France—Paris—Case studies. 3. Toureaux, Laetitia, 1907–1937.
4. Comité secret d'action révolutionnaire. 5. Right-wing extremists—France—History—20th
century. 6. France—History—1914–1940. 7. France—Politics and government—1914–1940.
I. Finley-Croswhite, S. Annette. II. Title.
    HV6535.F6B786 2010
    364.152'3092—dc22
                                                                    2010000716

The paper in this book meets the guidelines for permanence and durability of the Committee
on Production Guidelines for Book Longevity of the Council on Library Resources. ∞

For Yolande

CONTENTS

Illustrations follow page 98.

PREFACE

Laetitia Toureaux came into our lives quite by happenstance—a serendipitous moment that began when we both purchased the same travel book in different airports to read on separate transatlantic flights to France. The book, Lawrence Osborne's *Paris Dreambook: An Unconventional Guide to the Splendor and Squalor of the City* (1990), contained a small section on the first murder ever to occur on the Paris Métro, which took place in 1937. The story was intriguing, and although we were in France researching other projects, we decided to take some time to investigate the murder. In the summer of 1997, therefore, we set off to the archives to try to unravel the mystery behind the assassination of a beautiful, twenty-nine-year-old Italian immigrant named Laetitia Toureaux. The further we advanced in our research, the more interesting and mysterious Toureaux's story became, and before too long we were hooked. What began as an amusing diversion soon turned into a spectacular obsession.

Very quickly, however, we discovered we had chanced upon a subject that made many people in France profoundly uncomfortable, even fearful. Friends and acquaintances with whom we discussed the project discouraged us from continuing our research and warned us that persisting in it might not be good for our careers. At one point, we asked a French friend to photocopy some material and mail it to us. The friend complied but only with great trepidation, as she feared that by doing so she would suffer negative repercussions in her career or even become the subject of a police inquiry. Paranoia? Perhaps; but if so, it seemed to be widespread. Another very good French friend bought a book on the right-wing political organization connected to Toureaux in order to converse more seriously with us on the subject. After making her purchase, she wrapped the book carefully in brown paper so that no one would know what she was reading. At first we did not understand these reactions, but clearly Laetitia Toureaux and the right-wing terrorist organization to which her name was linked, the Cagoule, represented a minefield in both popular and scholarly culture in France in the late 1990s. The reason, we came to realize, was the connection between the Cagoule and the deep political divisions in interwar France over whether to oppose the rising tide of the extreme right in Europe. Reinterpretations of recent history seemed in the eyes of many people to pose a serious threat to the carefully crafted postwar construction of modern memory in France. This constructed memory had papered over the reality of the strong support for fascism in France before World War II and the deep divisions between the right and the left that persisted into the postwar period. In this context, resurrecting and reexamining the memory of the terrorist organization known as the Cagoule struck many with whom we discussed the project as a risky transgression. Even serious scholars warned us away from the topic as "too controversial." It did not help that we were trained as early modern Europeanists and were thus considered outsiders to the scholarly field of modern French history.

It was precisely because we were outsiders, used to researching subjects who had been safely dead for centuries, that we were surprised at the evasion and, at times, outright resistance we often encountered in the archives as we sought access to documents on Toureaux's murder and the Cagoule. After doing some general background reading on the subject and the times, we went into the Archives Nationales late one afternoon as seasoned tenured professors with a good deal of research experience and numerous publications under our belts, sure that we knew what we were doing. We happened upon a young woman at the information desk in the Salle des Répertoires. After conversing a short while about our research, the woman left and came back with a handwritten inventory of documents, a sort of annex to the judicial files housed in the Series B. In the inventory we found codes for the investigation of Toureaux's murder that the French judicial authorities had conducted. The archivist pointed out various files that she thought might be helpful, but before we could write anything down, an older man and woman, her senior colleagues, came up to the information desk, motioned our helpful young documents specialist aside, and began to have a heated discussion with her about the inventory lying in front of us. Rather than rifling surreptitiously through the inventory while the trio had their discussion, as we were sorely tempted to do, we waited for them to finish. By then it was too late. The younger woman left, looking red in the face, as the man positioned himself at the information counter and the inventory disappeared beneath the desk. He told us that formal written permission known as a *dérogation* would be necessary to see any of the documents in question but reassured us that we would be able to apply for one the next day, as it was closing time and thus too late to do the paperwork that afternoon.

Meanwhile another researcher in the salle who had overheard our conversation came up to the desk, expressed interest in our topic, and even offered a couple of suggestions about secondary sources we might consult. The three of us had a brief but friendly conversation, and the older male archivist joined in. We left buoyed by the feeling that we had made significant progress. We knew the documents existed and we saw no reason why we would not be able to get permission to see them, given that our interest was at that time narrowly focused on what seemed to us to be nothing more than a good murder mystery. But when we came back, the handwritten inventory was gone, the young documentaliste was nowhere to be found, and from that day to this the Archives Nationales has firmly denied that any such handwritten inventory—much less a supplement to the Series B—exists or ever has existed. One rather strongly worded written exchange with archive management dashed any hopes we ever had of recovering the inventory. Had we not been there and seen it together, we might have even questioned our own story. Before going home that summer, therefore, we well understood that we had stumbled onto a troubled story that many French men and women preferred to forget.

These hurdles of course piqued our interest—we are historians, after all. But as early modernists we were quite unprepared for the obstacles and the sometimes emotional resistance to our topic we would encounter. Difficulty accessing documents repeatedly cropped up, slowing the progress of our research significantly as we refused to give up and archivists refused to yield a single document more than absolutely necessary. We eventually became somewhat obsessed with the enigmatic Laetitia Toureaux and her adventurous life, which was so tragically cut short. And it did not lessen our determination that indexes, documents, and even whole sub-series went missing or became unavailable, elevators giving access to document collections mysteriously broke down and thus became another excuse as to why we could not see certain documents, and nobody who could answer any of our questions was ever available. Waiting on the dérogations—formal permission from the French Ministry of Culture to examine sensitive or sealed documents—meant that legal roadblocks frequently derailed our research plans. After World War II, the files concerning Toureaux's murder were sealed for 101 years. That means we will be seventy-seven years old when the documents are publicly released. Thus the pursuit of the precious dérogations was obligatory.

Conducting research on 1930s France was no easy matter. One memorable archival story concerns our first trip to the Archives de Paris on the boulevard Sérurier, in the 19th arrondissement of Paris. It was again the summer of 1997 when we arrived at this depository and asked to see an archivist. We explained that we had come to see the huge file on the Comité Secret d'Action Révolutionnaire, also known as the Cagoule. The otherwise pleasant archivist with whom we spoke became increasingly upset when we persisted in our request to see these documents. At first she tried to discourage us by stating that there were "over six meters" of material on the Cagoule in the archives and moreover that she had personally perused the contents of every carton and could assure us that not one contained so much as a mention of Laetitia Toureaux. We informed her that, however large the file, we had made a career studying thousands of horribly written sixteenth-century documents and were willing to try our luck rummaging around in some of those cartons of extremely legible and typewritten CSAR-related materials. She became visibly distraught at our persistence, vehemently insisting there was nothing in the documents on Laetitia Toureaux and we shouldn't waste our time searching further. When that failed to dissuade us, she pointed out with obvious relief that we needed our dérogations before we could see the file. So the checkmate went to the anxious archivist, at least for the time being. Reluctantly, she let us fill out the paperwork, and to our surprise we received the necessary permissions six months later. Yet because of the delay, we were unable to view the documents until we could make another trip to France.

Obstacles that prevented us from getting at Toureaux popped up over and over during our early years of work on the project. For example, not too long after we started our research we went to the archives of the Préfecture de Police in Paris. This is a much smaller depository than the formidable Archives Nationales or the Archives de Paris. The police archives are housed on the second floor of the actual Préfecture. At first we had little luck: once again, no dérogations meant no documents. But while we were informed that we had reached a dead end and no documents on Laetitia Toureaux had survived World War II, we were given a file of newspaper clippings the Préfecture had kept. With that, we wrote our first scholarly article on Laetitia Toureaux, which appeared in 2003 in *French Cultural Studies*. If we couldn't write about the investigation of her murder, we could at least explore journalists' interpretations of her life and Toureaux's role in 1930s popular culture.

After the year 2000 attitudes began to loosen somewhat in the archives regarding our topic, and our persistence won out when we made a great discovery in the spring of 2002. We were sitting in the Bibliothèque Nationale, conflicted over indications in books and articles published as late as 1965 that a huge police file existed on Toureaux's murder. But where was it now? We had exhausted every angle and irritated (or scared) every archivist we met. We screwed up our courage one last time and went to the president of the Salle des Lectures, a man whose name we never learned, but to whom we owe a great deal of thanks. We were in the "old" Bibliothèque on the rue de Richelieu with its domed reading room, creaky wooden floors, and dim lighting. Much to our surprise, the man with whom we spoke seemed undisturbed and even mildly interested when we described our quest. We showed him a passage from a book that discussed the documents related to Toureaux's murder, demonstrating that they had indeed existed at one time, and told him we were at a loss about where to look next. He tugged on his long mustache and said, "The archives can't be here, Mesdames, they have to be at the Préfecture." "But we've been there," we insisted. "They say nothing exists." "I don't know," he replied sympathetically. "It's a very sensitive subject. All I can suggest is to try again."

We went back to the Préfecture de Police. But this time a regime change had occurred at the archives of the Préfecture. The former employees of the reading room must have retired, and a new, younger, less apprehensive group of men and women seemed to have taken over. The change probably coincided as well with a law passed in 1999 that made many formerly classified documents accessible to researchers with specific dérogations. We met an archivist named Grégory d'Auda who proved to be extremely helpful and, most important, who knew exactly where the file on Toureaux was housed. By this point, our hearts were pounding, full of the exhilaration that only a researcher understands when a longed-for cache of documents dangles within reach. D'Auda explained that the documents had been lost for some time but had resurfaced in a recent move and were downstairs. He also informed us that we had to have a dérogation. Crestfallen, we explained that our trip ended the following week. As a result d'Auda took us to the police commissaire to see if she could help.

Commissaire Françoise Gicquel was incredible. Instead of expressing dismay, she found our research topic fascinating and said she would do her best to expedite the dérogations. We got them three weeks later, two weeks too late for that particular research trip but certainly the quickest we ever received a dérogation in the history of our project. Planning for the next research trip began immediately. Thus, on July 17, 2002, on a day prearranged with the archives, we walked into the reading room at the Préfecture de Police, and the boxes housing the documents concerning the investigation into the murder of Laetitia Nourrissat Toureaux were lined up and waiting for us. It had been five years since we began searching for Laetitia. Our hands shook with anticipation of discovery as we opened the boxes. It was the kind of quintessential moment that historians dream about but seldom experience.

Our greatest thanks, therefore, go to Grégory d'Auda and Françoise Gicquel, who first placed the archives on Laetitia Toureaux in our hands. Without their help, it is quite clear that we never could have written this book. We also owe debts to several friends in France who undertook research for us when we could not be there. Hélène Teisseire and Anne-Marie Chevais searched out information for us on numerous occasions, and Anne-Marie in particular arranged for one of us to meet Jean-Pierre Rioux, a specialist on the Popular Front. Philippe Andrau helped with copyright questions and general information on French perceptions of the 1930s and offered much enthusiasm along the way.

Many historians and scholars have also played a key part in the production of this book, both through the helpful insights they offered us and by listening to us rattle on about Laetitia Toureaux's story. A generous colleague, Maura Hametz, and a former colleague, Roshanna P. Sylvester, offered critical advice on many occasions. Deans Karen Gould, Janet Katz, and Chandra de Silva of Old Dominion University and colleagues Nancy Fitch, Mona Danner, Douglas Greene, Stephen Foster, Lee Slater, and Peter Schulman especially encouraged the publication of this book. Friends Chris and Laura Mackail gave much appreciated beach-related support. Alonzo Brandon from Old Dominion University provided numerous public venues where Toureaux's story could be told. Old Dominion University and California State University, Fullerton, generously provided funds on more than one occasion that helped to pay for research in French archives and supported the publication of the book with subventions for photographic expenses. The interlibrary loan divisions at our universities were also helpful in securing materials for us, in particular Stuart Frazer, who tracked down a hard-to-find photograph of Toureaux. Bob Jones from ODU's graphics division was also quite helpful. Old Dominion University also featured our research on Toureaux in the publication *Quest,* a magazine published by the university to highlight faculty research. This resulted in numerous people from around the world contacting us for more information about our work. Robin Walz and Michael Wilson gave many suggestions for improvement of the manuscript and remained steadfastly enthusiastic about the project. John Sweets and Julian Jackson offered useful critical remarks. Kim Mulholland also encouraged our endeavor into modern history and supplied helpful insights into a period with which we were less familiar than our own. We thank Jim Tracy for putting us in touch with him. We are also indebted to two researchers in Italy, Alessandro Celi in Aosta and Giorgio Guzzetta in Rome, who conducted research for us, and we thank Matthew Vester for introducing us to Alessandro. We also thank Pierre Jeantet for meeting with us and sharing his memories of his father. And we are especially grateful for the photograph he graciously provided us. A huge debt of gratitude goes to Natalie Zemon Davis, who eased our fears about tackling the 1930s instead of the 1590s and recognized right away that the mystery of Laetitia Toureaux was another one of those great stories that needed to be told. Alisa Plant at Louisiana State University Press was a tremendous and patient editor and deserves much credit for finding us and shaping the book. Special thanks go to the anonymous readers that the Press secured to review critically the manuscript. Their suggestions for improvement have been studied and appreciated.

A debt of a particular nature goes to the late J. Russell Major. We (the authors) met in graduate school at Emory University and there began a marvelous friendship while we both became Russell Major's dissertation students. Given Russell's broad vision of history and his personal role in liberating the city of Reims in 1944, we believe he would be quite proud of this book and not mind so much that two of his early modernists tackled a project on the 1930s.

But one's greatest debts are always to family members, who all too frequently have to sacrifice shared time because of a book project and research demands. Our parents and brothers have always been a great source of support, as well as Chip Croswhite, Annette's most devoted and understanding spouse. Annette's cousin, Kim Thomas, showed keen interest in the project and promoted it enthusiastically in Europe with her social networking expertise. Her generosity is much appreciated. During the production of this book our families grew significantly with the arrival of Annette's sons and two of Gayle's nieces. A book project is so overwhelming at times that it is easy to overlook the needs of others, but the beautiful faces of Alex, Matthew, Sarah, Geneva, and Antonia kept us grounded in the present even while consumed by the past.

This book is dedicated to the memory of Laetitia Nourrissat Toureaux, the mysterious Yolande, who broadened our historical vision and understanding while taking us on a splendid and completely unexpected adventure through 1930s France.

ABBREVIATIONS

ADP	Archives de Paris
AF	*L'Action Française*
AN	Archives Nationales
APP	Archives de la Préfecture de la Police
BN	Bibliothèque Nationale
CF	Croix de Feu
CGQJ	Commissariat Général aux Questions Juives
CGT	Confédération Général du Travail
CR	Camelots du Roi
CSAR	Comité Secret d'Action Révolutionnaire
FN	Front National
FP	Front Populaire
LVF	Légion des Volontaires Français contre le Bolchévisme
MSR	Mouvement Social Révolutionnaire
OSAR	Organisation Secrète d'Action Révolutionnaire
OVRA	Opera Vigilanza Repressione Antifascista (also known as the Organizzaziione per la Vigilanza e la Repressiione dell' Antifascismo)
PCF	Parti Communiste Français
PRNS	Parti Républicain, Nationale, et Social (Jeunesses Patriotes)
PSF	Parti Social Français
RNP	Rassemblement National Populaire
RP	Rassemblement Populaire
SFIO	Section Française de l'Internationale Ouvrière
SPF	Syndicats Professionnels Français (Croix de Feu–Parti Social Français)
UCAD	Union des Comités d'Action Défensive

MURDER IN THE MÉTRO

INTRODUCTION
MURDER IN THE MÉTRO

The Parisian press called the assassination of the twenty-nine-year-old Italian widow Laetitia Toureaux a perfect crime. At 6:00 P.M. on Pentecost Sunday, May 16, 1937, Toureaux left L'Ermitage, a dance hall, or *bal musette*, located in the Paris suburb of Charentonneau. Approximately twenty-four minutes later she entered a Métro station and took a seat in an empty first-class car on a train headed in the direction of central Paris, towards the République station. At 6:27 P.M. the train left the station. When it arrived less than sixty seconds later at its next stop, Toureaux was dying, an eight-inch dagger buried to its hilt in her neck. She expired before she could identify her killer, who had managed to enter the car, attack her, and flee unseen from the Métro station. Just as the disappearance of Amelia Earhart in 1937 mesmerized America, the mystery of Laetitia Toureaux's murder in that same year enthralled the French reading public and continues to fascinate to the present day. Toureaux's murder on the Métro remains a mystery, an unsolved and seemingly unsolvable crime.

The Enigma of Laetitia Toureaux

Laetitia Toureaux's tale in many ways encapsulates the cultural upheavals and political struggles of interwar France. By day Toureaux, an Italian immigrant, labored in a wax polish factory; at night she escaped into the Parisian underworld, where she danced for money and love in the bals musette and found work as a sleuth and a spy. As a young girl, the ambitious Laetitia Nourrissat had secretly married Jules Toureaux, the son of a wealthy industrialist, and had become a naturalized French citizen as a result. Jules's premature death in 1935 and his family's subsequent rejection of her, however, caused Laetitia to return to her dangerous life as a private detective and undercover agent. In so doing, the young widow calling herself "Yolande" became entangled with her executioners—French right-wing extremists and Italian fascists as infatuated with action and intrigue as she was. In the end,

1

the violent reality of the 1930s caught up with her personal fantasies of adventure and romance and her overly simplistic understanding of right-wing politics. After her death, Toureaux was portrayed in the press and popular culture as a lascivious and scheming adventuress who paid a high price for her ambitions, and the French came to see her life as the ultimate morality tale.

While Laetitia Toureaux's story has been told in France in many popular formats, including radio shows and television documentaries, this is the first book to use comprehensive archival research to unravel her complicated and mysterious life, offer the most probable solution to her murder, and assess her complex, multiple identities in the cultural context of the 1930s. It encompasses two separate but closely related issues. The first is the story of the beautiful, enigmatic, and frenetically ambitious Laetitia "Yolande" Toureaux, who resembled the 1930s French film star Simone Simon. We grapple with her identities and allow her to guide the reader into the streets, back alleys, and dance halls of 1930s Paris. The second is the story of the Cagoule, a secret, extreme-right political action society formally known as the Comité Secret d'Action Révolutionnaire, or CSAR. In the right-wing paper *L'Action Française,* the contemporary French journalist Maurice Pujo gave the CSAR the moniker La Cagoule, translated as "the hood" or "the hooded ones," asserting that at their meetings members wore hooded masks over their faces to hide their identities.[1] Newspaper renderings of these hooded men from the 1930s made them look something like Ku Klux Klansmen. The CSAR has also been known as the Organization Secrète d'Action Révolutionnaire or OSARN, often shortened to OSAR, but in this book we have chosen to stay with CSAR and the more popular Cagoule. We investigate the strange mélange of brilliant and daring journalists and engineers (often from prosperous, upper-class families), callow young adventurers, political opportunists, and outright thugs that comprised the membership of the CSAR, and we explore their motives behind the waves of violence they unleashed in the mid-1930s and again during the Vichy years. In the conclusion, we consider the legacy of Toureaux's murder and the Cagoule and their respective places in the historical context of Vichy and the post-Vichy era.

This is also the first book in English to address Toureaux and her association with the Cagoule. In doing so, it calls for a reassessment of the CSAR, a small terrorist organization that many historians of modern France have never taken seriously.[2] Most scholars dismiss the Cagoule as a group of half-hearted, often comical street thugs whose inexperience doomed their far-fetched plan to overthrow the French government and bring Mussolini-style fascism to France. As a result, no serious scholarly monograph has ever been written on the CSAR in either French or English. This book is not a history of the Cagoule, although the Toureaux-CSAR connection means that the organization and its members play a prominent role in the narrative. We contend that historians have underestimated the significance of Cagoulard violence and as a result have failed to perceive the group's purposeful terrorist action for what it was—a form of public discourse that quite successfully engaged the French populace in a dialogue about the fate of the Third Republic and in the process left a chilling trail of bloodshed.

In the police reports and legal files associated with their activities, members of the Cagoule were identified as "terrorists."[3] The terms "terrorist" and "terrorism," however, have proven extremely difficult for scholars to define, resulting in a multitude of possible definitions that the events in the United States on September 11, 2001, and the resulting outpouring of literature on terrorism have complicated and problematized even more. "Terrorism" is a pejorative, but one with a long history. Terrorist acts inspiring widespread fear have been written about since at least the time of Xenophon, but ironically the word "terrorism" was coined in the French Revolution and is specifically associated with governance through intimidation. The first terrorists were the Jacobins, who sought to influence political behavior through terror, and their instrument of execution, the guillotine, became a symbol of terrorism or at least a method of behavior control. "Terrorism" was introduced into the English language in 1794.[4]

When we contend that the Cagoulards perpetrated terrorism, we are basing our assertion on the 1937 League of Nations' definition of the term: "All criminal acts directed against a State and intended or calculated to create a state of terror in the minds of particular persons or groups of persons in the general public."[5] The Cagoule fits this definition, as its members unquestionably used violent acts to incite widespread fear in the hopes of bringing about the fall of the Third Republic. The fact that they did not succeed does not negate their importance as terrorists either in their aims or in the means they employed to achieve those ends. Nor does the fact that they were political terrorists as opposed to religious fundamentalists invalidate their status as terrorists. The Cagoulards focused on rather limited targets, as opposed to the hyperterrorists of today who operate globally to kill as many people as possible. Still, in their effort to influence French society and change the governing hierarchy of their day, the Cagoulards practiced many techniques commonly associated with all terrorists. They engaged in arms trafficking, sabotage, assassinations, and bombings, and they directed violence toward noncombatants, although their targets were specific rather than indiscriminate, at least during the period 1936–37.[6]

We trace the Cagoule's history through its various incarnations during and after World War II. We also connect the historiographical literature on the CSAR with postwar scholarship on Vichy. A complete understanding of Vichy, we argue, must incorporate into the historical narrative the political pressures after the war that led to the legal and scholarly dismissal of the threat of the prewar French right and an enduring discourse denigrating or dismissing the significance of the Cagoule. As such, *Murder in the Métro* contributes to a growing post-revisionist literature on the nature of the extreme right in pre–World War II France, one that calls for a more nuanced understanding of the complex political realities and competing ideologies that deeply divided the French population in the 1930s.[7]

We never intended to plunge into the ferocious scholarly debates about French fascism, which have subsided somewhat since we first began this project. We were trained in a less politicized field, where historical memories are not so fresh and thus engender less passion among researchers. By the same token, we began our research with a very small, albeit intriguing problem—an unsolved murder—and only expanded our scope to the Cagoule and Vichy and postwar France as our digging in the archives led us ineluctably in those directions. We have purposely tried to broaden our historical vision as part of this project, breaking free of subdisciplinary boundaries imposed by the historical profession.

First and foremost, the evidence—rather than any theoretical constructs, political stances, or preconceived ideas about the period—guided us in the directions we have taken in this book. We argue, for example, that the Cagoulards were terrorists in part because that is how they described themselves and their activities on more than one occasion. Terrorism is certainly what they thought they were doing. We contend that the Cagoule posed a real danger to the stability of the French state in part because people who were in a good position to know, such as Léon Blum and Marx Dormoy, clearly firmly believed as much.[8] Of course, one cannot simply take the statements of historical actors such as Blum and Dormoy at face value, any more than one can rely uncritically on police reports or trial statements. But neither can we dismiss such evidence without very good cause, and we found more reasons to be distrustful of the rhetoric of contemporaries such as Pozzo di Borgo and Maurice Pujo, who derided the Cagoule, than that of those who took it seriously. After extensive research, including work with restricted documents that required special permissions or dérogations to access, this book comes as close to cracking Laetitia Toureaux's case as the surviving evidence permits. Our work also explores the public face of Toureaux as the French press molded and presented it, as well as the ways in which class, gender, and ethnicity shaped both how she was viewed and her own identity. The enigma of Toureaux herself proved more difficult to resolve. She was a fascinating person whose life raises interesting questions about gender roles and their transgression in 1930s France. She seemed deliberately to cultivate different personas and identities and to wear various masks for different audiences. She carefully guarded her double life and took many of her secrets to her grave. Beautiful, charming, a flirtatious dancer and a regular client (*habitué*) of Paris's bals musette who enjoyed an adventurous sex life, Toureaux was also a cheerful, well-liked, and hardworking immigrant factory worker ensconced in the Italian milieu of Paris. She inhabited an unpretentious apartment in the heart of the Italian immigrant community, was a loving daughter and sister, and wore modest widows' weeds after her husband's untimely death. Yet she was during this same period a daring private detective who worked as a spy for both the French police and the Italian consulate and was rumored to have been the mistress of at least one member of the CSAR.

How to reconcile these vastly different—in many ways, contradictory—roles proved to be the most difficult problem of this book. Laetitia "Yolande" Nourrissat Toureaux was complex and conflicted, and she presented a wide variety of faces to her many different circles of friends, lovers, and colleagues. Nevertheless, breathing life back into her story offers critical insight into France in 1937. The significance of this book lies in its analysis of two interwoven investigations, one of the way one woman stretched the limits of gender, class, and ethnicity in the explosive atmosphere of 1930s Paris, and the other of the role of violent elements of the extreme right in France in shaping the political and cultural discourse during the period from 1935 to 1948.

What follows retraces Toureaux's life through the streets of Paris to the places where she lived, worked, sleuthed, and danced, and ultimately to the site where she is buried in the outskirts of the capital in the Cimetière de Thiais. This cemetery is home to the graves of Paris's less prosperous citizens, immigrants, and members of the working classes, people like Laetitia Toureaux.

The Political Environment of the 1930s: A Climate of Fear

In many ways, the last year of Laetitia Toureaux's life was one of the most complex in French history. The period of the Front Populaire (FP), or Popular Front (an alliance of left-wing Socialists, Radicals, and Communists in the face of a perceived fascist threat), witnessed a struggle between the French left and right that approached a civil war. World War I had taken a great toll on France; nearly 1.4 million men perished, the highest proportion of the population lost by any belligerent country in Western Europe.[9] The immense loss in terms of mortality and destruction fostered both staunch pacifism and a penchant toward using violence to reform a government and society that seemed to most French people sterile and increasingly mired in corruption. The Great Depression, while not as severe in France as in other European nations, nevertheless sapped French confidence and the self-satisfaction born of victory in 1919. It also spawned growing ranks of unemployed and desperate young men and women, who were open to the seduction of political extremism on the right and left and who supported any legislation to expel foreign workers from the labor force. Total French unemployment never rose above 1 million, but production levels from 1929 were not reached again until after World War II.[10] The success of the Russian Revolution in 1917 created a kind of paranoia about the spread of Bolshevism among most French citizens except the Communists, many of whom took their orders from Moscow. Fears of a communist-style putsch sent a shiver down the spines of French industrialists and spurred to action the extreme right antiparliamentary leagues and militias they bankrolled, such as Colonel François de La Rocque's Croix de Feu and Marcel Bucard's Francistes.[11]

Scandals rocked the French state in the 1930s. One, the Stavisky affair, brought about massive violent antigovernment demonstrations led by right-wing activists; these protests helped bring the Popular Front into existence. In 1933, a Ukrainian-born Jew, Serge Stavisky, managed despite his checkered past to obtain a job with the Crédit Municipale de Bayonne and, using the bank's capital, to launch a bond-selling scheme involving tens of millions of francs. Once the scandal broke, it quickly emerged that members of the Chamber of Deputies (i.e., the French House of Representatives), most of them from the Radical Party, were implicated in the scheme. No sooner had the initial scandal begun to die down than, on January 8, 1934, Stavisky, cornered by police, killed himself. Antigovernment newspapers seized on the story and insisted that the government had "suicided him," or ordered his assassination to keep him from revealing more damaging information about leading politicians. In the massive antigovernment protests that followed, right-wing leagues (including the Ligue d'Action Française, the Jeunesses Patriotes, and the Solidarité Française) as well as veterans' organizations (the aforementioned Croix de Feu and the Union Nationale de Combattants) played an active role.

The most important of these demonstrations took place on February 6, 1934. When the protest began to turn violent, the police, struggling to control the thousands of demonstrators, opened fire on the crowd. Seventeen people died, including one policeman, and 2,329 were injured, of whom 1,764 were policemen. The riots ended one government led by Édouard Daladier and brought about another based on the idea of right-wing National Unity, headed first by Gaston Doumergue and then by Pierre-Étienne Flandin and Pierre Laval.[12] Trotsky described this regime as "senile bonapartism," and indeed, the Third Republic seemed mired in a paralysis with an antiparliamentarian bent.[13] To many people, especially the young, it appeared that only the radical medicine of revolution, communist or fascist, could possibly provide a remedy for its impotence. Despite the new government, violent left-wing counter-demonstrations continued, including one on February 9 in which nine more people died, followed by a general strike on February 12. Worse, the Stavisky affair took on new life when, on February 22, the mangled body of Albert Prince, a councillor in the office of the Parisian public prosecutor, was found near Dijon. Prince, who had been delegated the task of following up on the Stavisky affair, had come under a cloud of suspicion for going too lightly on Stavisky, and despite the official verdict of suicide, people again assumed that he too had been "suicided," silenced before he could reveal all he knew about the full reach of the scandal in the government.[14]

The most significant ramification to come out of the February 6 riots was the temporary unification of the left. The Communists, or the Parti Communiste Français (PCF), who had previously denounced the Socialists as too bourgeois, reversed their stance and joined with the Section Française de l'Internationale Ouvrière (SFIO) to fight the threat of fascism. On July 27, 1934, the two groups signed a pact pledging joint action, and in 1936 the majority of Radicals joined them in an alliance known as the Rassemblement Populaire (RP). This Rassemblement was the precursor of the Popular Front, which rallied people with the campaign slogan, "For bread, peace, and liberty." As historian Julian Jackson notes, "The Popular Front was both a social response to the Depression and a political response to the fear of fascism. Its vast demonstrations brought huge numbers of people into the streets, showing that when it came to mass politics, the left could mobilize larger forces than the right."[15] The result was a spectacular victory in the elections of 1936 that gave the left-wing alliance 380 seats and their opponents only 237 seats in the Chamber of Deputies.[16]

With the Socialists as the real victors of the elections, the SFIO's leader Léon Blum formed a government on June 4, 1936, and Blum outlawed the right-wing leagues only fourteen days later. Blum's ascent to the position of prime minister was extraordinary: he was the first Socialist and the first Jew to achieve that office. He moved cautiously in governing, however, and hoped to broaden support for the left by showing moderation instead of pushing an agenda for social change. He also wanted to rearm France in anticipation for the inevitable war that lay on the horizon while strengthening democratic institutions and restoring economic prosperity. His government devoted itself to the problem of leisure for industrial workers and is noted for legislating a forty-hour workweek as well as the creation of the first paid vacations in France in the summer of 1936.

The jubilation that accompanied Blum's arrival in office did not last long, for a wave of strikes broke out a few weeks later. Julian Jackson notes that these strikes were unprecedented and included about 1.8 million workers in June 1936.[17] Many of these strikes turned into factory occupations, where a spirit of festival and celebration dominated the events. Food was brought in to the strikers, and songs were written to commemorate the event. "Against the workers, the army won't be sent in vain. Soldiers, break the Nazi swastika! Give us your hand comrades! Give us your hand!" strikers sang.[18] The strikes ended in July 1936 as a result of the Matignon Accords, which temporarily gave workers wage increases of between 7 and 15 percent. The accords were not well enforced, however, and in general the strikes sapped the energy of Blum's government right from the start.

Although Europeans during the interwar years were without doubt subject to rising anxieties related to fears of a second world war breaking out, as it ultimately did, much of the arms smuggling during this period appears to have derived from anxieties of a different kind. To many Europeans, including many French men and women, the danger appeared to come from within, with civil war seemingly on the verge of eruption in their own country as extreme right and left groups battled over the ideals of their nation.[19]

Most French people, aware of the larger events taking place on the international stage—the rearmament of Germany, Germany's aggression toward its neighbors, and the Spanish Civil War—perceived them as symptoms of communist or fascist conspiracies to foment revolutions and civil wars that sooner or later would erupt in France as well. The French polity suffered from deep political divisions, and conspiracy theories were rife; socialists and conservatives alike suspected each other of dark plots to overthrow the Third Republic and persecute their enemies. As Eugen Weber puts it, "The problems of nation might have looked clearer if the nation had been more clearly one. Unfortunately, as Daniel Halévy wrote in 1931 . . . two nations faced each other the country over, 'each with its great men, slogans, books, newspapers, soon with its own language and syntax too.'"[20]

Especially in the mid-1930s, massive strikes and demonstrations were common. When the Matignon Accords of June 1936 failed, employers looked to the government to use the police to force the strikers out of idled factories. As the gains for workers embodied in the Matignon Accords were lost, strikers turned a deaf ear to the pleas of Popular Front and union representatives to rein in their activities. Blum and his successor (as well as his predecessor) as prime minister, Camille Chautemps, found themselves obliged to resort to the police to restore order and reopen factories, whose production was desperately needed for the rearmament of France. As a result, the tone of these strikes, and employer retaliation against strikers now that they had the police to help them break the workers' resolve, became increasingly ugly. Blum attempted to pacify the left by accusing the Paris police chief of favoring right-wing demonstrators over leftists when using police forces to disperse demonstrations in Paris, forcing him to resign. The gambit failed, however, and the demonstrations became more violent. One of the worst took place on March 16, 1937. Despite Blum's dissolution of the right-wing leagues the previous year, the government permitted Colonel de La Rocque to call a meeting at a theater in Clichy, the heart of the communist district in Paris, of the reconstituted Croix de Feu, a right-wing veteran's league founded in 1920 that had become increasingly violent in the 1930s and was further legitimized in 1936 as the Parti Social Français (PSF). The Socialists and Communists organized a counter-demonstration, which Marx Dormoy, Blum's interior minister, and André Blumel, head of Blum's cabinet, attended. The counter-demonstration degenerated into violence, most likely as a result of the work of *agents provocateurs* from the Cagoule who had infiltrated the crowd disguised as Socialists and Communists. The police—or the Cagoule—opened fire, and five deaths resulted while at least nine thousands demonstrators attacked the police barricades. Three hundred and sixty-four others were injured, among them Blumel. The Clichy incident played a significant role in weakening Blum's support within his own party and especially among the Communists, while the right accused him of trying to persecute the PSF. A new strike called by the Confédération Général du Travail (CGT) on March 18 further weakened his government. By June 1937 Laetitia Toureaux was dead, but the Popular Front to which she had been a witness also ended when Blum resigned on June 22 after he proved unable to fix France's economic and financial problems.[21] In the meantime, the Popular Front experiment had radicalized the entire far right and had led to the creation of the extreme right-wing group known as the CSAR.[22]

In 1937 the dangers faced by France appeared to lie as much within—in the hearts of one's fellow citizens, even neighbors and co-workers—as outside the borders of the nation. On Tuesday, May 25, 1937, just nine days after the murder of Laetitia Toureaux, the right-wing newspaper *Le Matin*, in the same section where it published a report on the seemingly fruitless efforts of the police to get to the bottom of Toureaux's murder, also published reports of three violent incidents during various strikes that had broken out. Among them was an episode in which fifteen strikers beat up an accountant who, it turned out, was not even affiliated with their company. Several other short articles also focused on strikes that threatened to become violent, including one in Toulouse in which the 540 workers in a single factory were divided between opponents of the strike and strike supporters, who prevented their opponents from going to work. On the same page was a brief report about a political argument in a café on the boulevard de la Madeleine in Paris that resulted in one of the disputants shooting at the other with a revolver. Luckily, the shooter's aim was off and his adversary escaped unharmed. According to the report, M. Auguste Mariaud, the intended victim, did not even know the fellow who tried to shoot him. Mariaud claimed the man walked up to him while he was enjoying a peaceful drink in the café, started an argument with him related to a politically themed button the stranger was wearing, and then pulled a revolver on him when, evidently, it became apparent that Mariaud did not share his political views.[23]

French people in the 1930s were continuously buffeted with news reports such as these, which seemed to demonstrate that the world in which they lived was becoming increasingly violent and that extremists threatened their society's stability. Mysterious assassinations, real or rumored (like those alleged in the Stavisky affair and linked to political scandals), grabbed the headlines and hung on tenaciously as journalists fed the already firm conviction of many French people that their government was both corrupt and incompetent.[24] Laetitia Toureaux's murder in May 1937 was only one of a series of violent and mysterious deaths that made headlines in the 1930s.[25]

It is no accident, then, that the 1920s and 1930s were a heyday for tales of espionage and intrigue. Many "true life" spy dramas were published in newspapers or as books, rivaling the best stories that fiction writers could conceive (not that the line between fiction and nonfiction was all that closely respected in this genre anyway).[26] Much of this intrigue was related to arms smuggling and the clandestine accumulation of arms among civilian militias such as the Cagoule. The years 1936–1937, the period in which the Popular Front was in power in France, and which Julian Jackson has dubbed a time of "guerilla war," were also the time in which the Cagoule was most active prior to the German invasion of France.[27] This headline of the socialist paper *Le Populaire* in September 1936 seemed to say it all: "The Fascists Are Preparing a Civil War with Foreign Arms." The cache of arms announced in the article was in fact the first of many the police would uncover in and around Paris, the fruits of arms smuggling on the part of the Cagoule.[28] Moreover, one motive for Cagoulards to assassinate political figures appears to have been the arms they expected to obtain from the Italians in payment for services rendered. It was this world of right- and left-wing politics, arms smuggling, intrigue, espionage, and assassinations that Italian-born beauty Laetitia Toureaux infiltrated sometime in 1936. As a result, she lost her life.

The Valle d'Aosta in Paris

By 1930, over 3 million foreigners resided in France, making up 7 percent of the total population, and nearly 1 million of them were Italian. Toureaux and her family—her mother, sister, and brothers, but, interestingly, not her father—had participated in the mass migration from all over Europe to France that had occurred in the 1920s, and they were part of an ongoing influx of Italian immigrants who had been heading to France to work in French factories, as well as in urban construction and agriculture, since the mid-nineteenth century.[29] World War I and the debilitating toll it took on the French male population created a serious labor shortage in the postwar period, to the extent that the French government developed policies to stimulate immigration. During the war France lost over 10 percent of its active male population as war casualties and suffered well over another million losses to its male workforce in the form of mutilated and otherwise injured soldiers. Nor did the French population recover well from these losses. The numbers of economically active French workers continued to shrink in the twenties and thirties, even as the Italian population expanded considerably. Italians had been coming to France to find work since the Middle Ages, as crossing the border was easy, and the French seemed eager for them to fill the more dangerous and/or low-paying jobs that the they themselves no longer wanted.[30]

Toureaux's family was not at all unusual in the trajectory they followed in their migration into France. Laetitia Toureaux hailed from a particular part of Italy known as the "Valle d'Aosta" in Italian or the "Vallée d'Aoste" (also "Val d'Aoste") in French. Originally a small corner of Savoy, the identity of denizens of the Valle d'Aosta had long been fluid. Like Savoy itself, during the centuries preceding the creation of a united Italy in the mid-nineteenth century, control of the Valle d'Aosta passed back and forth between France and the Holy Roman Empire, both of which claimed the region. The Valle d'Aosta was an alpine valley on the eastern side of the Alps; most of its valleys, however, led downward toward France. The largely peasant population of the Valle engaged in fabricating such products as butter, cheese, and wine, in herding cattle and sheep, and in exploiting the limited iron deposits in the region. Like many mountainous regions, the Valle d'Aosta was poor and rural, and out-migration was constant as the Valdôtains crossed the Alps into surrounding regions searching for work. Given the linguistic, historical, cultural and geographical ties linking the Valle d'Aosta with the area around Lyon, it is unsurprising that many emigrants from the Valle d'Aosta migrated first to Lyon and from there to Paris. The vibrancy of the French economy after World War I, and its higher level of industrialization compared to that of Italy, guaranteed that most emigrants from the Valle would head toward France. As was true of other Italian emigrants, the numbers of Valdôtains in France swelled enormously between 1920 and 1930.[31]

Yet in some ways immigrants from the Valle d'Aosta differed from those who came from elsewhere in Italy. History and geography conspired to create a mixed identity for the Valdôtains because their valley was one of the main routes through the Alps linking France with Italy. This fluidity meant that many Valdôtains were unsure about their own identities and felt that their fellow Italians viewed them with suspicion as insufficiently patriotic.[32] It did not help that many Valdôtains spoke French at least as well as they spoke Italian, albeit with a distinct accent. In fact, there were three main languages in the Valle: French, Italian, and a local dialect, Franco-Provençal, which was a synthesis of French and the southern French language of Provençal. Auguste Petigat, a prominent Valdôtain priest who immigrated to Paris, wrote in 1938 that "we Valdôtains have to put up with plenty of claptrap about our Italian identity."[33] He remarked that his Italian acquaintances were often surprised at how well he spoke Italian, and that many Italians treated Valdôtains like "savages" who had to be taught how to be patriotic Italians. Yet even those who emigrated in search of work, Petigat argued, maintained their Italian loyalty and identity. Who, after all, had been more patriotic during the Great War than the humble, steadfast, uncomplaining Valdôtains, many of whom returned or sent their sons to fight for Italy? Still, the Italian government distrusted them, Petigat complained, and functionaries from Rome sent to oversee the region disdained its citizens.[34] In his role as spokesman for his compatriots, Petigat's complaints reflect the difficulty that Valdôtains encountered in trying to navigate between French and Italian identities. Too Italian to be fully French, they were in the eyes of the Italian government too French to be fully trustworthy.

By 1897, Valdôtains had drifted to Paris in sufficient numbers to form a group called Des Sociétés Valdôtaines à l'Étranger, which eventually became L'Union Valdôtaine et Mont-Cervin Réunies. Their numbers in France swelled further during the interwar period, when lack of work opportunities in Italy, combined with plentiful work in France (ironically, among other things laboring on the Maginot Line and other defense projects), drew even more of them across the Alps. During the 1930s, many Valdôtains in Paris seemed out of step with their Italian compatriots who adhered to the growing fascist party, in part because the fascists were unpopular in the Valle d'Aosta itself. In fact, due to the resistance against fascism in the Valle d'Aosta, Mussolini's government facilitated and encouraged the migration into the valley of thousands of Italians from other regions of Italy more favorable to the fascists. This led to an out-migration of people from Valle d'Aosta in the 1920s and 1930s that clearly in part was economically motivated. It was also political, not only because some migrants were actually dissidents or agitators, but also in that the migration into the Valle of outsiders only exacerbated the scarcity of jobs there. By the same token, Mussolini's fascist government played a role in the bankruptcy of two important financial institutions based in the Valle d'Aosta. Hence it is unsurprising that on an almost weekly basis beginning in 1929, the Tribunal of Aosta tried and convicted Valdôtains for the crime of "clandestine expatriation," as people sought both work and political refuge in France despite the strenuous efforts of the fascists to limit and control emigration from Italy.[35]

Within France too, the Italian government sought to control the ideology and political affiliations of Italian emigrants, in part through the creation of *fasci* within France beginning in 1922. These organizations devoted themselves to instructing people in fascism and to increasing and maintaining the loyalty of Italians in France to both Italy and fascism through the creation of schools, adult education classes, holiday camps for children, mutual aid, and job placement assistance. The fasci also sponsored cultural programs that made use of language classes and concerts in Italian, and they published books, reviews, and journals.[36] Much of the French working class was dechristianized by the 1920s. Despite the implantation of Catholic missions—such as the famous Opera Bonomelli in France, which was staffed with Italian priests expressly to arrest this decline in religious fidelity in part through offering economic aid and assistance in finding work—most Italian immigrants soon became less devout. Many of those who did take part in the activities of either the Opera Bonomelli (which the fascists took over and then persuaded the pope to eliminate in 1928) or the fasci seem to have done so for opportunistic reasons that signified little in the way of their ideological orientation.[37]

The majority of Italian immigrants seem to have been cautious about political involvement in France, despite the reputation they developed of enacting their political struggles between pro- and antifascists rather violently on French soil, although in the 1930s they did become more involved in labor unions than they had been previously.[38] Emigrants from the Valle d'Aosta tended to adopt a decidedly antifascist stance in Paris that mirrored the resistance to fascism in the Valle d'Aosta. In 1938, for example, when the Federal Association of Italians in France ordered all the Italian organizations in France to transfer their allegiance to the Casa del Fascio, L'Union Valdôtaine refused, thus isolating its members further from their compatriots.[39] It is important to be cautious in this regard, however. Organizations such as L'Union Valdôtaine had a relatively low membership that comprised only a small portion of the total numbers of Italian immigrants in France. At the end of the 1920s, the thirty-odd Italian associations in the Paris region, including L'Union Valdôtaine, had a membership of only about four thousand people, even though there were more than 100,000 Italian migrants in Paris and its suburbs at that time. It is likely that members of L'Union Valdôtaine represented more prominent and possibly the wealthier and more politically active members of the Valdôtaine community in Paris. By the same token, Italians in France were increasingly adopting the same sort of leisure activities, including films and music, as their working-class French counterparts—and thus drifting away from organizations that reinforced their Italian identity. Even the Abbé Petigat, in many ways the unofficial *curé* of the Parisian Valdôtaine community in Paris in the 1930s, seems to have flirted with fascist sympathies despite his ultimate firm rejection of the movement.[40] In the aggregate, however, people from the Valle d'Aosta in France appear to have been more opposed to fascism than most other Italians, whether in Italy or in France.

By all accounts Laetitia Toureaux lived in a community in Paris noted for its numbers of Italian immigrants. Her apartment in the 20th arrondissement was not far from the part of Paris where the 11th touched the 20th. Her mother and other relatives lived nearby, in the 12th arrondissement. Her personal Italian world centered around the rue Pierre Bayle (just off the Boulevard de Ménilmontant), the rue St. Maur (more squarely in the 11th), and the rue d'Avron (not too far from the Place de la Nation in the 12th). As late as 1993, the last known address of a Nourrissat relative of Toureaux was on the boulevard de Ménilmontant, within sight of Toureaux's former apartment. But even in this Italian enclave there were many other immigrants assimilated into what native Parisians viewed as an undifferentiated band of working-class people, many of whom were French by birth and had ventured to Paris from the provinces in search of work. The section of Paris where Toureaux lived was populated by many first- and second-generation emigrants who came from Brittany, Alsace, and Auvergne from within France, as well as from Russia and Italy; this mix of people lived in the triangle of the 11th, 12th, and 20th arrondissements and shared a similar lifestyle.[41] "No one was a foreigner," Liliane Riou, the daughter of one of Toureaux's friends, recalled of the area, but of course to native bourgeois Parisians, everyone was.[42]

Given the particularly strong cultural and linguistic ties between the Valle d'Aosta and France, Valdôtains were likely to have adapted to French society somewhat more easily than their counterparts from other regions of Italy. Moreover, Valdôtains often had lighter skin and hair color, and thus blended in more easily with the French, than Italians from the central and southern regions of the peninsula. Yet while the Valdôtains may have assimilated easily in France, back in Italy the Italian Ministry of the Interior tracked emigrants deemed politically suspect from the Valle d'Aosta who resided in France and even considered them politically more suspect than emigrants leaving other parts of Italy.[43] The Italian government clearly felt it necessary to keep a close eye on its Valdôtain emigrants.

The influx of immigrants was a source of real concern on the part of the French public and its government as well, especially after France began to experience the effects of the global economic depression in the 1930s, and French angst about immigrants was further compounded by a growing sense that another war was on the horizon. Right-wing journalists played upon the fears of ordinary French citizens that immigrants were criminals, while government officials fretted about the political intrigue and social agitation that they believed immigrants, and especially the Italians, fomented in France. The papers portrayed Italians as a *classe dangereuse*, ready to fight fascist versus antifascist battles in the streets of France. Xenophobia reached an all-time interwar high in 1937, as Italians became increasingly associated with violence.[44] This characterization was not entirely incorrect, although it should also be pointed out that many of the "provocations" that the French press blamed on foreign immigrants and spies were actually the work of home-grown terrorists, and especially the Cagoule. Of the fourteen most notable violent incidents that occurred in France between January and September 1937, and which greatly heightened French anti-immigrant sentiment, the Cagoule either carried out or played a part in eight of them, even though neither the French press nor the French authorities recognized this fact at the time.[45] There is no doubt that the rising influx of political refugees from Italy into France in the 1920s and 1930s, and the equally swelling numbers of Italian profascist spies and infiltrators in France, led to an expansion in the number of confrontations between them in the newspapers, cafés, and streets of Paris. These refugees, agitators, and spies blended easily into the mass of immigrants.[46] Even though most Italian immigrants in France were not overtly involved in these political struggles, fears that Italian strife would spill over into France echoed the deepening conflict between the right and the left within France and the growing sense that French national unity was itself fragile, menaced both from within and without.

Laetitia Toureaux's World of the Bal Musette

Within her immigrant community, Laetitia Toureaux was also immersed in a vibrant social milieu centered on the world of the bal musette. She began attending these popular dance halls as a teenager, not long after coming to Paris. In the bals Toureaux felt at ease and able to "live her life" (*"vivre sa vie"*), a catchphrase used in the 1930s to describe self-willed, independent men and women who were intent on pursuing nonconformist lifestyles.[47] The bals offered a kind of nonjudgmental space, a temporary freedom from prevailing upper-class morality, at least on the part of the regular, working-class types who brought into the bals their various backgrounds and accents and gave them their local flavor. Toureaux was drawn to the bals because she loved to dance, but she also found friends and lovers there in an atmosphere that was reminiscent of her village life back in Italy. The bals' working-class clientele included a large immigrant population, and it was not uncommon to hear Italian spoken there, as well as other languages and a variety of French dialects. The bals offered Toureaux a life-affirming sense of community that connected her past in Italy with her present in France.[48] Indeed, Ginette Vincendeau argues that the accordion, the key instrument found in all bals musette, was a metaphor itself for the larger social environment surrounding the bals.[49] For Toureaux the bals had a homey feel that she clearly enjoyed, and they enhanced her natural sociability even after she began working in them as a hat-check girl and professional private detective.[50]

Nevertheless, the bals musette had a sordid reputation. They were linked to the Paris underworld and associated with gangs, prostitution, homosexuality, and drugs. Located mostly in the 5th, 11th, and 12th arrondissements, by Toureaux's day many bals were congregated in some of the worst sections of the city, in Les Halles and the Quartier Latin, on Montmartre, in the faubourg Saint-Antoine, around the place de la Bastille, and particularly on the notorious rue de Lappe and a disreputable street that led from it called le passage Thiéré.[51] In the 1930s all of these sections were known for prostitution. Even today, after the recent gentrification of the area around the Bastille, the reputation of the rue de Lappe has not been entirely rehabilitated.

In the eighteenth century, people coming from central France, an area known as the Auvergne, settled in the area around the Bastille. It was these Auvergnat immigrants who brought to Paris their traditional music and dance and created the first bals around 1750, noted for the music of bagpipes known as the *cabrette*. But Parisians viewed the Auvergnats as provincials and held them in the same negative light as the Jews. This disdain rubbed off on La Bastoche, the area around the Bastille section of the city, where one found many of the bals musette. The rue de Lappe, home of many of the oldest bals, including some dating to the nineteenth century, has existed since 1652, although it did not acquire its present name until 1848. In Toureaux's day it was known as a squalid street of hardware stores, coppersmiths, knife sharpeners, food merchants, small cafés, brothels, and bals musette. One of the oldest bals was named Le Bal Vernet, but Toureaux would have recognized it as Vrai de Vrai. It is still in existence today, operating continuously under the name Le Balajo since late 1937. Other bals on the rue de Lappe were Des Barreaux-Verte, Le Boule Rouge, Le Bal des Trois Colonnes, Le Bal Bouscatel, and Le Musette, as well as the notorious Le Petit-Balcon on the nearby passage Thiéré, a favorite haunt of both Toureaux and members of the Cagoule. Most of the bals were small venues with a bar, wooden tables, and a dance floor, which was usually strung with electric lights and framed by mirrors. They were known to be dark and smoke-filled, and anyone who spent much time in the bals ultimately reeked of cigarette and cigar smoke. By the 1930s, many of the bals had become quite large to cater to a growing clientele. Le Balajo could accommodate five hundred customers; L'Ermitage, which Toureaux frequented, was a multi-level establishment with room for over eight hundred revelers. These larger bals were more prosperous, brighter inside, and often featured neon signs and well-nickeled bars.[52]

The bals were renowned for seduction and intrigue and were often associated with *guinguettes*—smaller, generally seedier, dance locales. The music centered on the plaintive wails of the accordion, which had supplanted the cabrette by 1900; it was often accompanied by violins, drums, cymbals, and *grelottières*, bracelets with bells that musicians wore on their ankles to enhance the music. The dances were waltzes, tangos, foxtrots, beguines, polkas, mazurkas, javas, and something known in Paris as the *toupie*, in which the dance couple resembled a spinning top and often performed atop the round bistro tables found in the bals. Dancers in the bals held each other tight, dancing cheek to cheek, and when dancing scandalous javas partners placed their hands on each other's buttocks. Couples often kissed, although prolonged kissing was discouraged; patrons referred offenders to nearby hotels. Breaks from dancing offered customers opportunities to talk, drink, mingle, and even order food, often some kind of Spanish tapas or more traditional French hors d'oeuvres. Alcohol flowed liberally. Patrons usually ordered a Picon-Curaçao-Citron, Pernod or Pastis, a P'tit Blanc or P'tit Beaujolais, or even a special delight of cherries soaked in eau-de-vie.[53] Parisians perceived the bals as venues of the night, and they stayed open until the wee hours of the morning, but many bals also operated at lunchtime, when they catered to a clientele of married women who sought handsome young lovers for afternoon trysts. Gangs operated out of the bals, and some gang-lords even owned and operated a number of them or worked with pimp-prostitute couples who catered to the sex trade.

Fights were common. One journalist wrote in 1937, "It isn't far for certain men to go from the musette to prison, and from there to a penal sentence of over five years."[54] Even given this unsavory ambiance, by the 1930s the bals were becoming more respectable. They were closed during World War I, and when they reopened after the war, they attracted a more upscale crowd of bourgeois voyeurs who came in search of adventure. The bals became a popular nightspot for the young; in the interwar period, they even became a tourist attraction, noted for fake police raids staged to enhance tourist appeal with manufactured thrills. Édith Piaf added to the bals' newfound allure with her popular song "L'Accordeoniste," which told of a prostitute who falls in love with an accordion player in a bal musette but goes mad when he is killed in the war.[55]

Laetitia Toureaux's love of the bal musette, however, suggests a picture of a conflicted woman. Right after her death one acquaintance described her as "a brave girl, not stupid but a little twisted, someone who always grumbled if slang was spoken."[56] It seems odd that Toureaux, a habitué of bals musette who regularly worked as a hat-check girl and met her lovers in the unsavory venues, would object to slang when it was so commonly spoken in that setting. This is just one of the many inconsistencies about Laetitia Toureaux that will be disclosed in the pages to follow. Morganatic wife of an industrialist's son, hard-working and cheerful immigrant factory worker, ambitious mistress of dangerous men, private detective and spy—Toureaux's life and identities ran the gamut of female characters that populated French popular fiction and news reports in the 1930s. People all over Paris seemed to be acquainted with Toureaux, and she had the knack of charming most people she encountered in part by becoming what they wanted her to be (or what she believed they wanted)—yet not even her closest relatives and friends seemed really to have known everything about her. We do not pretend to comprehend Toureaux in all her complexities either, but we do think we have correctly analyzed the significance of her life and death, both of which epitomized the political, social, and cultural struggles taking place in 1930s France.

For years, the story of Laetitia Toureaux's murder has floated on the margins of scholarly literature about sensational stories from the 1930s without ever attracting a serious study. It is hoped that what is offered here will engage the reader on multiple levels: as a good story and a perplexing mystery; as a work focused on identity and how individuals shape their personal identities: as an exploration uncovering aspects of the long-neglected Cagoule; and, finally, as a book contributing to a growing discussion about current French historiography and how fictions are maintained in French memory over decades with a persistence that appears almost sacrosanct.[57]

LAETITIA TOUREAUX

LE CRIME DU MÉTRO

A PERFECT CRIME

On Sunday, May 16, 1937, a striking, twenty-nine-year-old woman, elegantly dressed in a tightly fitted green suit, walked out of a bal musette called L'Ermitage. The squeals of lively accordion music and the murmur of laughter and conversation quite probably escorted her into the street that day. She would have been familiar to any passers-by because she was a handsome woman and often drew the gazes of men, young and old. She regularly danced at L'Ermitage, one of the largest dance establishments in the city, which catered to the working classes and accommodated over eight hundred clients on this particular Sunday afternoon. The heavy wooden door, known to regulars as "le Tambour" slammed behind her. It was a hot, cloying afternoon, early for summer weather in Paris, and it was just beginning to rain. L'Ermitage was located at 13 rue des Deux Moulins in a blue-collar neighborhood of Paris on the banks of the Marne, a feeder river into the Seine and in many ways its poorer, scruffier cousin.[1]

The woman wore a smart white hat with matching purse and gloves, a fur stole hugged her shoulders, and she carried a pretty parasol. Even though she had been widowed for over two years, she still wore her engagement ring engraved "J. T. à L. N. II.9.29." At this moment, she was in a hurry and may have even glanced at her watch; it was 6:00 P.M. on the dot. Descending the steps, she quickly walked along a sidewalk next to a gray stone garden wall. The wall was low and an iron fence stood atop it. Enormous chestnut trees, doubtless planted hundreds of years ago, grew just inside the wall. Yellow light bulbs that buzzed and glowed from their strings clumsily festooned the branches of the trees, as close to a romantic atmosphere as the soldiers, factory workers and laborers who comprised the bals' usual clientele were likely to get. L'Ermitage catered to young people who loved to dance and socialize, and while most of the regulars were respectable working-class immigrant types, prostitutes and pimps were known to work the dance hall as well, especially its second-floor balcony.[2]

Laetitia Toureaux, for that was her real name although her friends knew her as Yolande, had danced away this particular Sunday afternoon with her younger brother, Riton, and his friend Maurice Kagan. They had sipped on Pernods and listened to Jean Salimbeni play his accordion with the band. Salimbeni had been a friend for many years, a fellow Italian immigrant whom Toureaux had engaged to teach Riton the accordion. Salimbeni was known to the Paris police as well. He was a talented musician, but he could not keep a job and was frequently picked up for vagrancy. On this day he had kept Toureaux's purse so she did not have to pay the coat check fee. Laetitia had also waltzed with twenty-one-year-old Marceau Marnef and his younger sister, Pierrette, whom she knew as bals musette regulars. For the most part Toureaux seemed content, although Marceau did report later that she had indicated she expected the evening to take a turn for the worse. "I'm laughing now," she supposedly said to him, "but I won't be laughing tonight because I don't expect things to go well."[3] She tried to get Pierrette to leave with her, but when the girl refused, Toureaux left L'Ermitage alone.[4] The owner, Monsieur Henri Begni, noted her departure.[5]

At 6:10 P.M. Toureaux arrived at a bus stop called Chateau, after the Chateau Gaillard, in whose former grounds the revelers at L'Ermitage now danced. The bus driver later claimed that he had made his rounds exactly on schedule and picked her up just beyond the garden at 6:19 P.M. He remembered her because of her striking green suit and the pin she wore, the medal of the Ligue Républicaine du Bien Publique (League for the Public Good), a public service organization. He'd seen her before as she flashed her radiant smile at him on her way to or from L'Ermitage. Often she stopped to chat with him or the other passengers, but not this afternoon. On May 16, she sat by herself and spoke to no one. She seemed rushed and maybe a little nervous, according to the bus driver when the police later questioned him. Perhaps she was just annoyed at getting her costly new hat, suit, and high-heeled shoes wet. Laetitia Toureaux was always one of the best-dressed passengers on his bus, especially on Sundays. By the time she reached her stop, the storm had broken and it was pouring rain. At 6:22 P.M. the driver dropped her off in front of the Métro station, Porte de Charenton.

Toureaux was not alone at the Porte de Charenton. It was Pentecost, a Catholic holy day and a long holiday weekend for even the most overburdened of the Parisian working class. The unexpected thunderstorm had driven many of the picnickers and strollers who had been enjoying the unusually warm afternoon in the Parc de Vincennes to take cover in the Métro.

The damp underground air reeked of stale perspiration and the nauseating odor of soot from the trains. At 6:25 P.M. the subway train pulled into the station. Toureaux got into the first-class car, its only passenger, according to the scores of fellow travelers who had seen her on the platform. Most everyone else crammed into the three gritty second-class cars. Witnesses would later recall her solitary figure framed in the window on the left-hand side of the car as the train pulled out of the station. That was at 6:27 P.M.

At 6:28, train number A.B. 356 arrived at the Porte Dorée. At this point witnesses' recollections of what happened next begin to conflict. Raymond Bruel and André Lejeune, two passengers traveling in a second-class car, told police that they heard a cry from elsewhere on the train just before it screeched to a stop. When the doors opened, they leapt out and ran to the source of the sound, the first-class car. On its floor lay the young women in green, her lips moving, forming words only she could hear. The handle of a knife protruded from her neck.[6]

According to the Parisian press, however, the first witnesses to discover Toureaux were passengers waiting on the platform at the Porte Dorée station, who intended to take the first-class car. A military dentist with the rank of major named Raymond Dubreuil, his fiancée, and their friend Jean Vigneau entered the first-class car through the door closest to Toureaux. On their way to a play, the trio wore their Sunday best and thought the dirty and crowded second-class cars would soil their clothes. Meanwhile, three young prostitutes, or *filles de joie*—Elisabeth Guy and Mary Catin, who were English, and Yvette Bailly, who was French—entered the first-class car through the door at the opposite end. Dubreuil and his party said they saw a young woman sitting on one of the single-person benches, facing away from them and in the direction of the front of the train. The car was stifling hot, and one of the English girls asked whether they might open a window. Suddenly the seated woman slumped over and slid slowly to the floor. Major Dubreuil later testified that he approached her and saw immediately that her jugular vein had been severed and that she was doomed. The three girls moved forward and seeing the knife protruding from the right side of the woman's neck, they began to scream. "There's nothing we can do here," Dubreuil said, and he and Vigneau briskly shepherded their female companion out of the car, hoping, so Dubreuil claimed, to avoid involving themselves in a scandal. They promptly disappeared into the crowd. Dubreuil volunteered their story only after the press tracked them down, and then only if the police and press promised to keep his name out of the papers. The three women left the car and waited on the platform until the police had taken their statements. It is possible that the cry Bruel and Lejeune heard was actually the screaming of the three women.[7] In the meantime, the Métro car's conductor, Joseph Fabre, tried to defuse the situation by keeping the curious from entering the ill-fated car. The sight was grisly. Blood was spattered across the bench where Toureaux had been seated, and large quantities of blood ran down the bench onto the floor, where it pooled in various spots. Later, someone remembered seeing a green and gold earring lying in a puddle of blood.[8]

On the street above, another Métro employee flagged down a passing policeman from the 12th arrondissement, Agent Isambert, and in a certain sense this act sealed the poor woman's fate. Moments later Isambert arrived at the crime scene, panting from exertion and soaked from the rain outside. He bent down over the injured woman and asked, "Who did this to you, Madame?" Her lips moved, but again she made no sound. Then Isambert yanked the knife out of her neck, and blood gushed from the wound in torrents. Almost immediately she lost consciousness. Bruel and Lejeune helped carry her to a bench on the platform while they waited for help. The situation appeared dire, and everyone feared she would die before the ambulance arrived.[9]

Shortly thereafter Monsieur André Baillet, a chief inspector of the police in the Picpus quarter of the city, where the Porte Dorée station was located, arrived on the scene with two investigators, Inspectors Lavaille and Chaillet. The moment the inspectors arrived, they realized that the knife that had been embedded in the dying woman's neck was a clue of enormous significance. Italian and Alsatian professional assassins typically executed their victims with a stiletto and left the murder weapon in the body as a sign that this was no random killing.

Even before the unfortunate woman was laid on a stretcher to be transported to a hospital, the police had begun to sift through the contents of her purse. There they found papers identifying her as Laetitia-Marie-Joséphine Toureaux, maiden name Nourrissat, born September 11, 1907, in Oyache in Italy. By the time she arrived at the Hôpital Saint-Antoine half an hour later, she was already dead, and the police investigation to discover the identity of her murderer geared up for the task that lay ahead. Dr. Paul, the physician at Saint-Antoine who performed the autopsy, confirmed the police's initial conclusion: that the woman's murder was a professional assassination or a "hit." He also definitively ruled out suicide. The killer had to have delivered the blow with enormous speed, accuracy, and force. This is the primary reason why the police from the start assumed that the perpetrator had to be male. Female professional assassins were rarer than male ones, and few women would have had the necessary upper body strength to have carried out the crime on a moving subway car. The knife had entered the victim's neck just behind her right ear, severed her jugular vein, and perforated her carotid artery. There were no other marks on her body. Only a practiced professional could have succeeded, and would have been brazen enough to attempt such a feat, in a crowded public Métro no less. Thus, from the beginning of their investigation, the police directed their search more toward the professional crime world of Paris rather than hunting for amateurs with a grudge. Laetitia Toureaux was not the victim of a random act. She had been executed.[10]

The Parisian police quickly found that they had a perfect crime on their hands, one which would be difficult if not impossible to solve based solely on evidence from the crime scene. The crux of the mystery was this: not a single witness among the dozens of people waiting at the platform at the Porte de Charenton station saw anyone but Toureaux board the first-class car, where she sat in the last bench seat, her back to the door. Neither did anyone remaining on the platform as the train pulled out of the station see anyone except Toureaux silhouetted against the large windows of the first-class car. During the ride from Porte de Charenton to Porte Dorée, no one in the adjoining second-class car who glanced through the glass door separating the cars saw anyone except the victim in the first-class car. By the same token, when the train arrived at the Porte Dorée station, none of the witnesses on the platform admitted to observing anyone leave the car in question.

Time adds a serious complication to the scenario. The killer had only about forty-five to ninety seconds, depending on the exact speed of the train, to complete his task if he killed his victim while the train was in motion between stations. If, as the police theorized, he leapt aboard the train while it was still at the Porte de Charenton station, grabbed the metal bar behind Toureaux's seat for balance and force, drove his knife up to its hilt into her neck with his right hand, and then dashed off the train before it ever left the station, he would have had to have accomplished the crime in even less time than he would have had during the brief train ride from Porte de Charenton to Porte Dorée. Moreover, why did none of the people milling about on the platform see him enter or exit the first-class car at the Porte de Charenton station?

The fingerprints on the metal bar behind Toureaux's seat were never identified, which is unsurprising, as the police would have had a record of them only if the killer was a known criminal. None of the fingerprints of the habitual criminals the police suspected at first in the murder matched those at the crime scene. Nor did they match those of the witnesses who discovered the dying woman. Equally frustrating for the police was the sheer number of people who used the Métro every day. Even if they had identified a match for the suspect prints, they would have had to have found prints on the murder weapon itself to prove that the owner of the matching prints had anything to do with the murder. And as the weapon was clean, it is likely that the murderer wore gloves and that the prints belonged to a passenger uninvolved with the crime.

The only other potential clue, a bloody shoe print near the exit behind where Toureaux sat, was also next to useless. At least eight people had entered and left the car before the police even arrived on the scene. There was no way of telling whether the killer had left the blood when exiting, which at least would have established how the killer got off the train, or whether one of the witnesses had accidentally stepped in the copious blood pooled around her body and left the smudge on the floor. And again, there remained the question of why no one noticed a bloodied person leaving the first-class car at either station.

The first-class car, it is important to note, was not widely used, because it cost more than most people could afford in Depression-era France. While it was reserved for wealthier travelers, it was also used by high-class prostitutes in search of well-paying clients. People tended to notice who came and went from first-class cars because they were few in number and usually well-dressed and prosperous or—like the three women who first entered the crime scene in the Toureaux murder, Guy, Catin, and Bailly—looking for a good time. All Parisians knew that only holders of first-class tickets were authorized to ride in first class. Tickets were checked often on the Métro, and scofflaws who were caught could expect to pay a steep fine. As such, the first-class car, and the area of the platform in front of it, would not have been packed with a crowd into which a killer could easily have melted without being observed.

So how did the killer commit his crime and flee the scene unobserved? Several hypotheses emerged among the police and in various French newspapers, which covered closely the sensational murder and its aftermath. One, mentioned above, was that the killer did the deed in the Porte de Charenton station. Another was that he killed Toureaux during the ride and then slipped through the doors separating the first- from the second-class car. The problem with this hypothesis, however, is that the doors between the cars were kept secured; and in fact an anonymous letter to the police from one of the second-class passengers on the train when Laetitia Toureaux was killed affirmed that the doors between his car and first class had indeed been locked. Even had the killer managed to pick the lock (which showed no signs of tampering), get between the cars, and enter the second-class car, why did no one in second class mention seeing a bloodied person—or anyone, for that matter—slipping illegally into their car from first class during the trip? A related possibility was that the killer stabbed Toureaux at the Porte de Charenton station, jumped out of the first- class car onto the platform, and dashed into second class before the doors closed and the train left the station, and then rode to Porte Dorée in second class and made his getaway there. Again, this sequence of events is problematic, not only because of the absence of witnesses noticing anyone entering the second-class car from first class, but also because of the time factor. The trains simply didn't wait that long in each station, and the killer would have had to have been waiting in first class for Toureaux to get on, hoping that she arrived at the platform sooner rather than later. If she had lingered even a few moments at the bal musette, the train would have left the station without her, forcing him to disembark and wait for her to arrive or to leave with the train. Either way, the murder would have been foiled.

Much less risky, from the killer's point of view, would have been to wait in the station for Toureaux to arrive and board with her, but wait until the train was in motion before committing the murder. While the train was in the station, there was always the possibility that Toureaux would get on too late to allow time for the murder and the getaway, or that some other person would follow the killer aboard and either witness the crime or prevent its accomplishment. While the train was en route, no one could get aboard and, better yet, no one could stand outside the train and see the assassin at work through the windows or the open door. Toureaux would have had nowhere to run if the first blow failed to immobilize her. As it was, the killer needed only to stab her once, wait until the train arrived at the Porte Dorée station, and leap off the train, hoping, reasonably, that he would be able to vanish into the crowd and perhaps even flee the station before anyone found the victim and sounded the alarm.

The only hitch in this theory is that the killer would have had to have been seen leaving the train at Porte Dorée. The Métro cars had two doors that opened onto the platforms, one at each end of the car. When the car carrying Toureaux arrived at Porte Dorée, two groups of passengers entered, one through each of the doors, and neither reported seeing anyone get off the train. The three young women entered through the door farthest from Toureaux; Dubreuil and his party got on through the door behind her. It would seem, therefore, that this scenario should be excluded.[11]

Doubts linger, however. Major Dubreuil's story was odd, to say the least; and equally odd, or suggestive, was the inability, or unwillingness, of the police to clear up the discrepancies in it. According to Dubreuil, he and his party were on their way to the theater on the evening Toureaux was killed. They entered the train, saw her slump to the ground, and approached her. Dubreuil had medical training and, so he claimed, bent over her, bloodying his clothes in the process, to ascertain the nature of the wound. He quickly realized that she was beyond help. But then Dubreuil and his companions left the scene and returned home without either sounding the alarm or giving a statement to the police.

When the police tracked him down, Dubreuil offered two explanations for why he had taken off so quickly. First, he stated that he had still hoped to get to the play before it started. Perceiving that his clothes were stained with the victim's blood, he needed to rush home and change before he could proceed to the theater. Obviously this explanation for fleeing the scene of a crime was inadequate. When the police pressed him, Dubreuil admitted that his primary concern was for his fiancé, whom he hoped to spare the scandal of being a witness, even after the fact, to a murder. Despite the obvious weakness of this chivalrous explanation, not only did the police refrain from reproaching him for his callousness toward the victim, but they also dropped the matter and never questioned him again. And they had their reasons for doing so. Neither Dubreuil nor any of the other witnesses were suspects in the case, primarily due to the nature of the crime itself. Toureaux's murder was no spontaneous act of violence or a murder that an amateur could have carried out, the police quickly concluded. Rather, it seemed most likely to have been the work of a professional or at least of an experienced killer who knew what he was doing. Dubreuil and the other witnesses on the scene all turned out to be who they said they were when the police investigated their backgrounds, and none of them appeared to possess either the nerve or the skill to have accomplished such a brazen hit. Dubreuil was only twenty-five years old, and this did not seem to fit the profile of the murderer the police had established of a seasoned professional assassin. Nor is it likely that Dubreuil, were he the killer, would have taken the immense risk of bringing with him two witnesses whose stories the police might later have been able to break under questioning. Thus unless one assumes a rather massive police conspiracy to manufacture a false identity and alibi for Dubreuil—a highly unlikely prospect that would have been extremely difficult to pull off—one must assume that the reasons for which the police ruled him out as the killer were valid. It is possible, however, that Dubreuil and/or the other witnesses either simply missed the assassin when he slipped off the train or lied when they claimed not to have seen him. Dubreuil's reluctance to involve himself and his companions in the investigation in any way, even to raise an alarm when he found the mortally wounded Toureaux, suggests that he may have been equally unwilling to admit that he might be able to identify the killer.

One constant runs through all these possible scenarios for Toureaux's murder: the probability of success for any one of them rose enormously if, as the evidence suggests, Toureaux was on her way to meet someone, and her assassin knew this. In fact, it is quite possible that the murderer knew what train she would be likely to take, as the Porte de Charenton station was the terminus of the line, and lay in wait for her. On weekends and holidays, French trains ran on a special schedule. There were fewer of them, and one could calculate fairly closely when a Métro train would arrive in and depart from the station. Because Toureaux's choice of trains would have been restricted, her killer could have had a reasonably good idea what train she would have to have taken to make her rendezvous on time if he knew her starting point (the bal musette), the bus she was taking to get to the Métro, and the line she had to take to get to her destination. It is possible that she planned to meet her killer on the train, in which case both would have known exactly when she would be there.

Again, however, there are difficulties with this scenario, the most serious being that before Toureaux left L'Ermitage, she told her friend Pierrette that she was "already late" for an appointment.[12] Although the killer could have been waiting for her in the station, it is unlikely that she planned to meet him on the train, since her tardiness would have caused her to miss the train chosen for the meeting. It is even possible that the prearranged meeting, if there was one, was merely a ruse on the part of her killer to lure her to the station.[13]

Laetitia Toureaux was clearly dressed for a special meeting that afternoon. She had dyed her brown hair blond, donned a new dress, and chosen to wear an unusual and striking pin signifying membership in the Ligue du Bien Publique. All seemed calculated to alter her appearance and to make her stand out. This may suggest that she was meeting someone whom she had never before met and not only wanted to make a good impression, but also needed some identifying mark, probably the pin. It worked well; many of the witnesses recalled the pin, which is not surprising as membership in the Ligue was very prestigious. Even if her assassin had never seen her before, it would have been quite easy for him to lie in wait for her and be sure he had the right victim.

Thus from the beginning, the murder of Laetitia Nourrissat Toureaux, alias "Yolande," had all the characteristics of a carefully planned, cold-blooded execution. Little did the police detectives first assigned to the case realize, however, how deep into the recesses of fanaticism and political intrigue, and how high into the preserves of wealth and power, their investigation would take them. One petite woman with a ravishing smile and a new green suit was the key that opened the hidden world of the Comité Secret d'Action Révolutionnaire, or the Cagoule. For us, she is the key to understanding the political climate and culture of France in 1937.

2

POLICE AND PRESS ON THE TRAIL OF AN ASSASSIN

In the sensational "murder in the Métro" case, the Parisian police found themselves saddled with a perplexing mystery, one that promised to entail a long and complicated investigation, and one that seemed extremely difficult, if not impossible, to solve. There was also an overwhelming sense of the tragic in this particular case. The woman involved, Laetitia Toureaux, was only twenty-nine years old. The police soon learned that by all accounts she was a very generous and compassionate person. A young life so quickly extinguished defied logic, yet the police knew that this was no ordinary crime. The execution-style death had obviously happened for a reason, and solving Toureaux's murder necessitated learning more about the young woman and her lifestyle.

The organization of the police investigation of the Métro murder was based on the legacy of the Napoleonic system of justice. For Paris, the Paris Préfecture de Police exercised authority, through the Police Municipale (the patrolmen who maintained order and worked to prevent crime) and the Police Judiciaire, often referred to by their original name, the Sûreté (the detectives who investigated crimes). Cities and towns throughout France had a similar, though much smaller, apparatus. Operating under the Ministry of the Interior was the Sûreté Nationale (Sûreté Générale until 1934), which was a detective force assigned, like the American Federal Bureau of Investigation, to important crimes. All local police forces resented the imposition of the Sûreté Nationale and especially so the Paris Police. Competition between the Préfecture and the Sûreté Nationale was intense and unfriendly. During the interwar period, allegations of blackmail, drug trafficking, and extortion were frequently made against detectives, who relied heavily upon paid informants and so had to tolerate some of their conduct. The Sûreté Nationale had the worst reputation, and its corruption was notorious. When a crime was committed, the detectives, whether from the Paris Sûreté or the Sûreté Nationale, had to work closely with the court system because according to French law a *juge d'instruction*—examining magistrate—had to conduct a judicial investigation before a felony could be tried in court. It was the job of the police to perform the leg work—to do the forensic analyses, track down witnesses and suspects, collect evidence, and produce their best assessments of the crime, which they synthesized in reports for their superiors. The juge d'instruction analyzed these reports and conducted his own investigation, and then made the decision whether to indict a suspect, close the case, or table it still unsolved.[1]

On the evening of Toureaux's murder, it was Chief Inspector André Baillet from the Picpus station, which was nearest to Porte Dorée, who took charge of the crime scene. He accompanied the victim to the Saint-Antoine hospital, where he ascertained her identity and place of residence; then, in the company of two subordinates, M. Chaillet and M. Levaille, he made a rapid inspection of her apartment. From evidence found in the victim's purse, Baillet suspected he would find some information about her at a banquet that the Union Valdôtaine et Mont Cervin Réunies was holding that very evening. Benjamin Arnold, the vice-president of the organization, who turned out to be related to Toureaux by marriage, met Baillet when he arrived at the banquet hall. Arnold led the inspector to a table where the murdered woman's family sat and there Baillet broke the terrible news to them. On May 17, Baillet interviewed the witnesses who had discovered Toureaux's body, eight people in all. There was Dubreuil, his fiancée, and their friend (the fiancée's brother), the three young women who entered the first-class car at about the same time as Dubreuil's party at the Porte Dorée station, and Bruel and Lejeune, who had been riding in second class on the same train as Toureaux.[2] The police again searched the Métro car where Toureaux had been killed, which by this time had been moved from the platform to the garage area of the Porte de Charenton station. In it, they found only a blood smear near the door and a single set of fingerprints on the bar behind the seat. Given the commotion that occurred at the crime scene, they could not be sure that the killer had left either clue. After accomplishing these vital preliminary tasks, Baillet reported his meager findings to the juge d'instruction who had been appointed to the case, a M. Normand. By May 18, however, Baillet had passed the file to Police Commissioner Charles Badin of the Police Judiciare, who assigned Principal Inspector Moreux, Corporal Lavail, and Inspectors Charlier, Bernard, Petit, and Coquibus to the case. A new juge d'instruction, M. Bru, took over for M. Normand, and over the next year the team conducting the investigation interviewed hundreds of people.[3] Meanwhile, the Parisian press had picked up the scent. Laetitia Toureaux's murder was a gold mine, which journalists and their editors intended to exploit to the fullest. The story excited the imagination of Parisians for weeks, months, and even years after the crime, and it sold truckloads of copy. The fact that the case seemed to be unsolvable only added to its mystique.

Toureaux had died on the way to the Saint-Antoine hospital without voicing a word and was pronounced dead on arrival. The autopsy revealed little. The criminal pathologist, Dr. Charles Paul, found only one wound, the fatal one, which had been delivered with such violence that the tip of the knife was embedded in the marrow of Toureaux's spinal column. Nor was there any sign on her body or at the scene of a struggle; her attacker seemed to have taken her entirely by surprise.[4] Only the fact that her head had been gently angled to the left when she was attacked gave the slightest hint that she might have been aware of his presence just before he struck. None of the handful of witnesses who had stumbled upon her as she lay dying in the Métro car could tell the police anything about the events prior to the arrival of the train at the Porte Dorée station, by which time, the police theorized, the crime probably had already been committed.

The knife that had taken Toureaux's life turned out to be a common model of the popular Laguiole brand. It was approximately eight inches long, with a blade a little over three and a half inches long, and had a bone handle decorated with three embedded copper threads. Manufactured in a factory in Auvergne sometime between September and December 1936, it was sold in Paris in only one of two shops, the first on the rue Pastourelle in the 3rd arrondissement, not far from where Toureaux worked, and the second in the suburb of Saint-Martin. To the disappointment of the police, both of these establishments were quite large discount stores for the era, rather than the much smaller and more personal boutiques common in 1930s France. To make matters worse, the two retailers served a high number of customers because they supplied owners of restaurants and cafes in bulk and at a reduced rate. Neither store kept records that allowed police to identify who had purchased the knife. By the same token, Toureaux's purse also contained little in the way of solid leads. The police found in it only some cash, an identity card, a *carte de visite* bearing her married name, along with a first-class Métro ticket taken from a book of tickets and, perhaps of some interest, a letter confirming a rendezvous with a man named Jean at 10:00 P.M. the evening of her murder.[5] It was a meager start to the investigation.

A search of Toureaux's apartment was more fruitful. Here the police were able to get a better sense of her style of life and her personal relationships. Toureaux lived in an upstairs flat at 3 rue Pierre Bayle in the 20th arrondissement. The tiny, curved street led directly to the famous cemetery Père Lachaise. Ironically, in life Toureaux had lived near the graves of the famous, while it was her death that rescued her from obscurity. The area around the cemetery was, and until recently remained, a mainly working-class neighborhood of fairly drab buildings housing many immigrants. It was by no means a slum, but it was far from chic enclaves such as the Île-Saint-Louis or the rue St. Honoré at the city's center. When Baillet searched Toureaux's apartment, he found it to be quite modest, with only an entry-way, a small kitchen, and one bedroom, and without running hot water. It was very well decorated, however, and journalists described it as "quite cute," with several attractive pieces of Empire-style furniture. In many ways it reflected the tastes of a typical single young woman of the 1930s with aspirations to respectability and dreams of adventure and romance. A sizable collection of popular novels and magazines indicated that Toureaux had been an avid reader, and in her desk the police discovered an impressive pile of letters from several smitten young men. One man, René Schramm, had sent her nearly seventy letters in the past year of her life. But neither the apartment nor interviews with the neighbors yielded any clues as to the identity of the murderer. The concierge said that Toureaux always paid her rent on time and received regular visits from her mother, who lived in the area, and, more rarely, from her brothers. Also, according to the concierge, every evening Toureaux "frequented the establishments of the night at Montmartre and had, outside of her home, a sentimental life that was . . . quite lively."[6]

The search of her apartment revealed two other significant facts about Toureaux's life. First, she was a widow. In 1926, when she was only nineteen, Toureaux went to work in a pottery factory on the rue des Muriers, in Paris. There she met Sylvain Jules Toureaux, the shy, awkward thirty-five-year-old son of her employer. Despite his bashful demeanor, Jules was handsome and well-bred, with dark eyes and hair. He also was a good dresser, sure to appeal to Toureaux's love of apparel, and sported a pince-nez that gave him a sophisticated and romantic air. Toureaux introduced her new companion to the world of the bals musette, where Jules must have enjoyed the carefree atmosphere, so far removed from bourgeois pretension. And he fell in love with the woman who led him into a world very different from his own. Officially the couple was "Sylvain et Laetitia," but to friends in the bals musette they were simply "Jules et Yolande." They began a romance and, after a three-year courtship, the two secretly married on December 21, 1929. Such déclassé romances were a common rite of passage among bourgeois men in French society, permissible as long as they did not result in marriage. Fearing his parents' disapproval, Jules kept his marriage a secret until 1934 when, dying of tuberculosis or throat cancer (the sources vary), he finally revealed the true nature of his relationship with Toureaux to his parents. During their marriage, the couple shared Jules's apartment or *garçonnet*, although Jules also spent many nights at home in his parents' apartment. When the journalists interviewed Jules's father after the murder, the elder Toureaux began to weep and had this to say: "This crime is a mystery as obscure to me as it is to everyone else. Besides, since the death of Jules, I have never seen Yolande again. How did she live? With whom did she spend her time? I have no idea. Despite our legal ties, my son's wife was nothing but a mystery to me."[7]

Despite Toureaux's close relationship with her own family, they found her marriage to Jules equally mystifying. In a letter dated July 14, 1929, her father upbraided Toureaux for agreeing to the marriage without first seeking his advice and permission. He also forcefully expressed both his confusion regarding the secrecy upon which Jules insisted and his fear that Jules was merely using her and would soon abandon her. "I am told that he is respectful, honest, good, fine, well raised, educated," Henri Nourrissat wrote. Yet Jules was "afraid to put his signature" on a marriage contract or openly to declare his love, "in order to be able to leave you on a whim, my poor daughter." Nourrissat added, "But the way you have acted is from nothing but pride, this is a trap and one day you will tell me that I was right."[8] Toureaux's older brother Vergilio, known in France as Virgile, although grateful for the money she sent him (obtained from Jules) while he was performing his military service, was also surprised by the marriage and full of questions about her new husband. In a letter dated May 5, 1930, after thanking Toureaux for a gift of money, he wrote, "My dear, I have a question to ask you. It is purely to satisfy my curiosity. You have told me your husband is an industrialist. Understood, but in what sort of industry? Does he work? What does he do?"[9]

In the class-bound society of 1930s Paris, even a secret marriage represented an amazing victory for Laetitia Toureaux; it was also a tribute to her seductive beauty, driving ambition, and formidable personality. How she felt about its clandestine nature is not known, but certainly in her world, the world of the bal musette, Jules and Yolande were known as man and wife. Only in his world was the union kept secret. The young woman's success was not to last, however. When Jules died, Toureaux found herself disinherited, since in order to maintain the deception Jules had continued to live with his parents and thus had few possessions and little money of his own. Her in-laws wanted nothing to do with her, or she with them, and she ended up with little more than her furniture, a modest sum of money, and her precious French citizenship, won through marriage to a Frenchman. Toureaux remained steadfastly faithful to Jules's memory, however, and her family testified that she visited his grave every Sunday, although evidently not on the day of her murder.[10] Perhaps in order to cling to her memories of marital bliss—as well as the veneer of upward mobility and status the marriage had brought her—Toureaux wore widow's black much of the time for two years after Jules's death.[11]

The second thing the police quickly discovered from their search of Toureaux's apartment was that she had spent her days toiling in the Maxi factory located at 5 rue Lécuyer, in the industrial suburb of Saint-Ouen. Obliged to find a new job after her husband's death, Toureaux had held the Maxi factory position since November 1936. The Maxi factory manufactured shoe and wax polish and other household products. Toureaux's first job there consisted of gluing labels on the jars of polish, although she quickly advanced to more interesting work. It seemed that she was a model employee. M. Gaston Dalit, the director of the factory and Toureaux's boss, offered this statement to the press:

> I owe it to the memory of such a perfectly dignified and respectable person as Mme. Toureaux to declare all the good everyone here thought of her. I hired her last November 1st as a probationary employee whose duties consisted of gluing the labels on glass jars. She worked in a shop with about twenty workers, under the orders of a forewoman. We quickly noticed her intelligence and diligence. Also, considering her a particularly talented colleague, we chose her to represent us as a demonstrator of Maxi products in our booth at the last Salon of Homemaking Arts. She carried out her duties with great spirit and success.[12]

The police also discerned that none of the employees of the Maxi factory whom they interviewed, including the forewoman, had anything but good to say about Toureaux. Although some did see her as reserved, all declared that they regretted her death enormously. Delegations from the Ligue Républicaine du Bien Publique (St. Denis Section) and from the Maxi factory attended Toureaux's funeral on May 23. Paul Orsini, a noted politician who led the group from the Ligue, described Toureaux as "devoted to everyone."[13]

Meanwhile, the police managed to establish a reasonably accurate timeline of Toureaux's activities in the hours leading up to her death.[14] Since
the murder took place on Pentecost Sunday of a holiday weekend, she had
the day off and did not need to worry about rising early on Monday for
work. At 10:00 A.M. Toureaux's youngest brother, Henri, called Oswald by
his mother but otherwise known as Riton, came by her apartment on the
rue Pierre Bayle. Riton was a bit of a handsome ne'er-do-well who earned
his living painting houses, still lived with his mother, and was devoted to the
bals musette, where he spent much of his time. To help him out, Toureaux
had paid for him to take accordion lessons so that he would be able to earn
extra income playing at the cafés and dance halls, an indication that the two
were quite close. Toureaux clearly had a maternal instinct and doted on her
baby brother. According to Riton, who knew his sister's moods well, Toureaux gave no hint that she was tense or afraid. Rather, she seemed happy
and carefree during the entire day of her murder, most of which she and
Riton spent together.

Riton made his visit to the rue Pierre Bayle on the morning of May 16 in
order to deliver the new, bright-green matching skirt and jacket that their
mother had just finished making for Laetitia. It was one of the first times
since Jules's death, according to Riton, that Toureaux had worn anything
other than black. Riton said that he gave his sister matching green earrings,
a necklace, and shoes to complete the ensemble. In an excellent mood,
and delighted with her new outfit, she laughed and joked with her brother,
prancing around in front of her mirror before sending him on his way so
that she could get dressed. They arranged to meet in a bistro, Chez Mme.
Giroldo, an hour later, where the two siblings drank an aperitif and then
headed off together to Toureaux's hairdresser, Mme. Alexandrine, where
Toureaux smoked a cigarette while waiting to have a wave put in and Riton
got a haircut. It was most likely at Mme. Alexandrine's, although Riton did
not mention it, that Toureaux had her hair dyed blond.

At noon Toureaux had lunch with her family at her mother's apartment on the rue d'Avron, where Mme. Nourrissat lived (even though she
worked as a concierge at 5 rue de Tlemcen), at most a mile from Toureaux's
apartment. Her mother asked Laetitia to try on a coat that she was making
for Toureaux. Virgile, Toureaux's older brother, who lived on the rue des
Pyrenées in the same general neighborhood as his mother and sister, came
by for lunch as well. Like Riton, Virgile earned his living as a house painter.
Virgile was married to the daughter of Benjamin Arnold, who owned a café

and hotel on the rue des Vertus, the same street where Toureaux had a job in a bal musette tending the cloakroom. Toureaux also had a sister, Simone, married to a taxi driver named Albert Barlod, who lived in the same building as their mother; the two did not join the rest of the family that day.

After their meal, Riton, Laetitia (whom he always called Yolande), and their friend and neighbor, a young tailor named Maurice Kagan, took a taxi to L'Ermitage. According to some reports Toureaux went first to another bal musette called L'As-de-Coeur (roughly, The Heartbreak), although Riton made no mention of this in his account of her last day, which he insisted they spent entirely together. L'Ermitage sat on the shore of the Marne River, almost directly across from the Île-de-Charentonneau. Today the site borders on a busy road and is surrounded by high-rise apartment buildings. The area was known as Maisons Alfort; it was, and still is, primarily a working-class neighborhood, although it has undergone gentrification recently. The owner of L'Ermitage was a woman, Madame Begni, whose husband Henri, when not helping her run the bal, worked with his brothers making furniture. Like Toureaux and the accordionist Jean Salimbéni, who played on the afternoon of the murder, many of the bals' customers or employees were Italian immigrants.[15] L'Ermitage was a particularly nice bal because it featured an enclosed oak-lined garden strung with electric lights, which were a novelty at the time. Customers of the bal could thus dance and drink outdoors when the weather was nice.

From about 3:00 until 5:00 P.M. on May 16, Toureaux waltzed and tangoed with Riton and Maurice Kagan, as well as with a close friend named Marceau Marnef. She also danced with several women, including Marnef's sister, Pierrette, as women dancing with other women was customary in the 1930s. At five, Toureaux told Riton that she intended to return home soon because she needed to change her clothes before she met with Virgile and Virgile's father-in-law, Benjamin Arnold, for dinner at eight-thirty at the Bonvalet restaurant. She and Virgile were to be Arnold's guests at a banquet for a public service organization for Italian immigrants. Toureaux danced for another hour, until 6:00 P.M., when she asked Jean Salimbéni, the leader of the orchestra, to tell Riton that she was leaving. Riton was chatting with friends, and she didn't want to bother him. She stopped and spoke with three women on her way out of the bal musette, who commented on her lovely outfit. Then she left alone and on foot for the bus stop nearest the dance hall, unknowingly on the way to her doom.

Who was Laetitia "Yolande" Toureaux?

The seemingly impossible mechanics of the audacious murder comprised only part of the police's dilemma. Motive, too, was extremely problematic at first, because there seemed not to be any. On its surface, Laetitia Toureaux's life resembled closely that of many other young women in 1930s Paris. She was born September 11, 1907. Her parents separated in 1920, when her mother moved to France with Toureaux, her sister, and her two brothers, while her father, a construction worker and farmer as well as a World War I veteran, remained behind in the Valle d'Aosta in Italy. The family, minus the father, spent some time in Lyon before they migrated to Paris, joining the burgeoning Italian immigrant community drawn to the French capital in search of work.

The police naturally found it odd that Toureaux's entire family had relocated to France, leaving the head of the family behind in Aosta. Toureaux's mother explained that she and Laetitia had migrated to Lyon in 1920. When they were quickly able to find factory work, Laetitia's siblings joined them in Lyon. Laetitia's father remained in Italy, her mother claimed, because he loved the simple life and had a horror of big cities. Subsequent police investigation suggested, however, that the Nourrissat couple was estranged, as Madame Nourrissat evidently took a lover in France, a M. Guiseppe Chatillard, with whom she lived for eight months. Only after she had broken with Chatillard in 1925 did mother and children relocate to Paris.[16]

Of all the children, only Laetitia remained close to her father, Henri Jean-Baptiste Nourrissat, despite his objections to her marriage. Like his daughter, Nourrissat père cobbled together a living, in his case primarily from farming and construction work.[17] When interviewed after her death, Toureaux's father praised her to the skies. "She was my darling daughter, whom I loved more than all the world, my only joy in life anymore. The others [Toureaux's brothers and sister] have abandoned me, for seventeen years now. Only she came to visit me every year. She was happy, sincere, intelligent."[18] Her mother, Marie Dauphine Nourrissat, also professed to adore Toureaux, declaring that "she was for me a spirit of joy."[19] Toureaux was also close to her sister and two brothers. Riton told *Détective* magazine that he was her "true friend" and spoke of how radiant and happy she was on the day of her death.[20] Toureaux was widely known for her kindness; she doted on her young niece (her sister's daughter), looked after poor children who lived on her street, and flashed a smile even at passing acquaintances in the neighborhood. She was a member of two respectable public service organizations, the Union Valdôtaine et Mont Cervin Réunies and the Ligue Républicaine du Bien Public, both of which required sponsors to attest to the good character of prospective new members. In fact, during the first days after Toureaux's murder, the police could hardly find anyone in her circle of family and friends with a bad word to say about her, let alone a motive to kill her.[21]

The police quickly followed up on Toureaux's note arranging a meeting with the unknown Jean, which they had found in her purse, and the amorous letters stored in her desk. Perhaps a disappointed lover had killed her? They discovered that the correspondence came from two young military men, one of whom had clearly been romantically involved with the victim. René Schramm was a soldier stationed at Longwy, a fortification on the Maginot Line. He had met Toureaux at a bal musette called Le Tango in June 1936, and the two quickly became lovers. Schramm, a plumber in civilian life, enjoyed waltzing and doing the java with Toureaux, and the two even talked of marriage before Schramm was called up for military service, joining the 149th Infantry. The other suitor, Jean Martin, was a sailor stationed in Toulon. An apprentice mechanic, he too met Toureaux as a civilian and in a bal musette, L'As-de-Coeur. Like Schramm, Martin was drafted, ending up in the navy. It was this Jean that Toureaux had arranged to meet the night of her murder, after the dinner party for the Union Valdôtaine. Hoping to be able to steal a night away in Paris during the long holiday weekend, Martin had arranged for his brother to give Toureaux his note confirming their appointment. Schramm's and Martin's commanding officers affirmed, however, that neither man had managed to obtain passes to leave their posts on May 16, and thus neither could be suspected in the murder. Nor did the police learn anything from their interrogations of the two men, other than the fact that Toureaux had an active love life. Martin insisted that he had just met Toureaux and that nothing physical had transpired between them, but Schramm freely admitted that they were sexually involved and had met regularly for sexual encounters, either at her apartment or at a hotel in the suburb of St. Antoine.[22]

Since both Martin and Schramm had an alibi, they proved to be another dead end in the investigation. Still, it was becoming clear that, at the very least, Toureaux was a flirtatious woman who enjoyed manipulating her many admirers, most of whom she met at various bals musette. While it is possible that Toureaux supplemented her income with occasional prostitution, like many working-class women who danced with men for money and were reputed to be *entraîneuses* (seductresses), the police never turned up any evidence that Toureaux had actually charged for sex. Rather, they discovered that she had been deeply in love with her husband and by all accounts was faithful to him during their marriage. After he died, however, friends and colleagues indicated that she had been driven by sheer loneliness to a string of lovers with whom she had enjoyed an active and exciting sex life. In late 1935, a year after Jules's death, she met a young man named Pierre Émile Le Boulanger at the bal musette Le Lotus, located in the Latin Quarter. Le Boulanger went by the sobriquet Petit-Pain. Within weeks they were lovers, and she went often to his room at 75 rue Pigalle to engage in lovemaking. Once Petit-Pain left Paris for active military duty, she took up with a buyer for Renault who often had business in Paris. This affair with Maurice Lamoureuse in March 1936 was brief, and while Lamoureuse later testified that he had found her elegant, he considered their sexual affair nothing but a "petit flirt." By the summer of 1936, she had met Schramm; she also had a brief affair with a fellow Italian named Giovanni Gasperini, a married barman whom she met at the bal musette Chez les Vikings, on the rue Vavin. Gasperini was known to the police because he belonged to the Italian fascist party that operated in Paris. He and Toureaux met on several occasions and had sex "en plein air" at the Bois de Boulogne and the Bois de St. Cloud. As Toureaux's relationship with Schramm intensified, her affair with Gasperini ended, although he claimed they remained friends. Nevertheless, Toureaux considered Schramm too immature for her, and by 1937 the couple was known to have had loud public disagreements. Letters found in Toureaux's apartment indicated that at one point they fought over Leonie Devouillon, who Schramm had apparently flirted with at a bal musette. Devouillon was known to police as an occasional prostitute. By 1937, it seems that Toureaux had set her sights on men of higher station, or at least the police had reason to suspect that sometime in 1936 she took a wealthy lover. Le Boulanger, Lamoureuse, and Gasperini, moreover, all had solid alibis on the day of Toureaux's murder, as did most of her friends and acquaintances from the world of the bals.[23]

One reason why Toureaux went so often to L'As-de-Coeur was that she had a second job there tending the cloakroom several evenings a week. Her dancing also turned out to be a source of income. Toureaux was paid to circulate among the male guests without partners and dance with them for money. This was a common practice in pre–World War II European dance halls, which often employed both men and women who were attractive and cut a good figure on the dance floor to make sure any guests who wanted to dance had a partner. The tie to L'As-de-Coeur seemed suggestive for another reason. One of the two stores where Toureaux's killer could have bought the murder weapon was located on the rue Pastourelle, less than two hundred meters from the rue des Vertus.[24]

But police interviews with M. Fageon, the owner of L'As-de-Coeur, and patrons of the bal led nowhere. While the police doubted that Toureaux's murderer hailed from the milieu of the dance halls or that, despite her reputation as a flirt, her killer was a jealous lover, official procedure required them to follow up all possible leads. Accordingly, they set about hunting down known violent criminals with whom she might have crossed paths. In an example of such a trail, Georges Albayez, a police inspector, interviewed Gustave-Jules Milhomme, a thirty-four-year-old "mechanical" dentist who lived in Paris on the rue de la Réunion. Milhomme declared that while he was living at 166 boulevard de Charonne, a friend of his named Henri Sicres came by from time to time, accompanied by a man with the descriptive nickname "Gros Louis." Gros Louis supposedly worked as a handyman and bouncer at L'As-de-Coeur. According to Milhomme, one day Gros Louis boasted that a criminal acquaintance of his named Jo L'Algerois had killed Toureaux for one thousand francs. Albayez tracked down Sicres, who was a forty-year-old waiter at a café, although he was in prison when Albayez found him. All Sicres was able or willing to tell the police was that the real name of Gros Louis was Louis Le Louarn and that in May 1937 Le Louarn seemed to have had more money than usual, despite the fact that (like much of the French workforce) he had been unemployed for some time. The police never caught up with Jo L'Algerois, but they couldn't find any motive or evidence linking either him or Gros Louis to Toureaux anyway.[25] As is typical in police work across the ages, the detectives had to follow up on scores of similar dry leads as they struggled to solve Toureaux's murder.

Meanwhile, rumors flew in the press about Toureaux's secret life. Her work at L'As-de-Coeur did not seem to be wholly innocent; a guest of the establishment claimed to have caught her rifling through the coat pockets of at least one of the guests. The police busily combed the newspapers for leads, where journalists asserted that Toureaux's expenses exceeded her salary. At 1,500 to 1,800 francs per month, she earned more than average for a factory worker, but not enough to pay for her lifestyle. Nor could the little she earned in tips at L'As-de-Coeur have supplied the difference. Had she found a sugar daddy among her lovers, or was she supplementing her income in more nefarious ways? Furthermore, although Toureaux had joined the Ligue Républicaine du Bien Public on November 20, 1936, her novice membership did not yet entitle her to wear the Ligue's signature red pin with black trim that she sported the night of the murder, and upon which the bus driver and ticket-taker had remarked. How did she obtain it, and why had she chosen to wear it? Did she want to be picked out of a crowd, and if so, by whom? The people she was supposed to be meeting that evening—her brother and, later, Jean Martin—already knew what she looked like. Did she have another appointment, perhaps with her assassin? Was she murdered to prevent her from keeping this secret rendezvous? It seemed that the deeper the police dug, the more mysterious a figure she became.[26]

On May 22, the newspapers and weeklies revealed the most sensational information of all about Toureaux: the police had discovered that she was a private investigator whose undercover name was Yolande. "We are raising the veil on the strange life of Laetitia Toureaux" ran the subtitle to the cover story of *Détective* on May 27, 1937.[27] Exposing Toureaux as "a sleuth in skirts" (*"un limier en jupons"*) who worked for the private detective agency known as the Agence Rouff, the politically neutral *Paris-Soir* concluded, "The life of Laetitia appears each day to be more and more adventurous."[28] For journalists, "Le Crime du Métro" had now become "L'Énigme du Métro," with the focus fixed squarely on Toureaux and her secret escapades.[29] The papers disclosed that Georges Gustave Rouffignac, head of Agence Rouff, had recommended her for a job opening at the Maxi factory. In the wake of the strikes in the summer of 1936, M. Dalit, the factory's director, needed an employee to replace a female union activist whom he had fired for stirring up trouble in his factory. He wanted someone who was not sympathetic to the communists, someone who not only would be a dependable worker but would also keep an eye on potential union activists. He thus had requested that the police recommend a capable candidate for an informer. The police in turn contacted Rouffignac, who offered them Toureaux.[30] Rouffignac and a police inspector, M. Cettour, had also sponsored Toureaux for membership in the Ligue Républicaine du Bien Public. Rouffignac seems to have had a much closer relationship with Toureaux than he had been willing to admit to the police or the press. The police offered no explanation as to how Toureaux and Inspector Cettour had become acquainted. Could Toureaux have been hired to infiltrate the Ligue, an organization on the political left, as well as the Maxi factory?[31]

As Michael B. Miller points out, "Spy fiction between the wars was never as good as fact."[32] French cities, especially Paris, swarmed with undercover agents and adventurers in the 1930s, and nowhere were the spies thicker than in the Italian immigrant circles, where pro-Mussolini and antifascist agitators carried their covert battles into France. The political tensions of the era, the conviction that the interwar period was a breathing space but not a permanent peace, and the strides professional espionage had made during World War I all meant that European governments placed a high premium on intelligence. The Italians had begun infiltrating their emigrant communities in France even before World War I, and they stepped up their activities in the interwar period. The French police, fearful as they were of both communists and fascists, also habitually used Italian immigrants to spy on their compatriots. By the same token, the French police relied heavily on paid informants, many of them women, to help them solve crimes, especially crimes committed in the underworld society to which the police had little access. And both the public police and private companies hired workers to infiltrate factories and other workplaces.

The French government, even under the socialist Popular Front, lived in terror of violent popular riots, such as those of 1934, and of mass general strikes, like those that paralyzed France in 1936. With the world economy mired in the doldrums, the political cleavage between left and right growing ever wider, and the threat of another world war on the horizon, the government wanted to prevent further street fighting and strikes at all costs.[33] Moreover, paranoia and subterfuge seemed to have a grip on the popular psyche. The police archives are replete with letters, many of them unsolicited and only rarely useful, from informants ratting on employers, friends, and family members. The police received quite a few anonymous letters in the Toureaux case, most of them spurious. Interestingly, Toureaux seems to have come by her penchant for spying honestly; evidence in the police files reveals that either Toureaux's mother worked as an informant in 1929 or that Toureaux had already begun acting as an informant while still in her teens.[34]

But how seriously should Toureaux's sleuthing have been taken? Was she really an experienced professional, liable to embroil herself in the kind of cases where her employers, their clients, or her quarry might have been willing and able to murder her? The dilemma of French journalists was that the men most likely to know—her boss at the detective agency, Georges Rouffignac, and the police commissioner in charge of the case, Charles Badin—seemed unable to make up their own minds on this issue. On May 22, Rouffignac stated, "I had the impression that she [Toureaux] was well acquainted with the detective profession well before she began to practice it in my service."[35] He elaborated, "When this young woman presented herself at my establishment, I immediately perceived that I was not dealing with any debutante in the profession. I had the impression that she had learned somewhere other than my place how to follow a trail."[36] In an interview with *Détective*, Rouffignac continued to praise her sleuthing prowess. "She was a model employee," he explained, "a real expert in all of her duties. I gave her delicate surveillance work and difficult investigations and she always did a great job."[37] *Paris-Soir* also quoted Rouffignac as saying, "Effectively, as I looked back on this affair, one of my collaborators confided to me that Mme. Toureaux boasted to him about two months ago that she had been at the Alcázar [probably meaning the Alcázar of Toledo, an important stronghold of the Spanish Nationalists during the Spanish Civil War] with a card [a calling card affording her entry to the building] signed by a political figure."[38]

Yet Rouffignac contradicted himself repeatedly and at times drew a less flattering image of Toureaux. On May 25, describing her demeanor when she first went to work for him, Rouffignac told the conservative newspaper *Le Matin* that when he offered her his best counsel and advice, assuming that he was dealing with a novice, Toureaux had smiled and replied, "I'll figure it out."[39] On May 22 in *Paris-Soir*, Rouffignac characterized Toureaux as being even more confident about her abilities as a spy. He claimed that she declared, "Don't take the trouble, I know how to do it [detective work]," when he had offered to instruct her on the ins and outs of sleuthing. He also said that when he asked her if she wasn't afraid to work at L'As-de-Coeur, she replied, "No, I'm used to that."[40] Yet Rouffignac averred that her work was mostly to tail other women and was not dangerous at all. And when a journalist asked, "Didn't you have the impression that this [kind of] work was nothing new for her?" Rouffignac changed course completely, replying, "Not in the least. Look at this, for example. In filling out her surveillance reports, she floundered lamentably. On this account, I was obliged to teach her the ABCs of the profession."[41] For that reason, he insinuated, he didn't employ her all that often and she spent much of her time idle, collecting unemployment. Rouffignac was not alone in his willingness to disparage Toureaux's work. The police seemed to have concluded that she was inept at her profession. "An examination of her notes and papers," stated a police communiqué, "shows conclusively that Laetitia had little aptitude for this type of vocation and that her reports had a childish character."[42] The same day Commissioner Badin himself expressed in an interview with the press his conviction that "Laetitia Toureaux, an inexperienced detective, could not have inspired hatred sufficiently powerful to legitimize the hypothesis [that her murder was a crime] of vengeance."[43]

Rouffignac and Badin both appear to have been disingenuous with the press on this issue. Despite the sloppy, thin reports that she supposedly prepared for Rouffignac, and the rarity with which he claimed that he called on her (only six cases, he told the press), Rouffignac admitted elsewhere that he had hired Toureaux for no less than sixteen assignments over several months, thus at a rate of about one a week. Five of these jobs involved surveillance of adulterous spouses, while the rest entailed the less challenging task of verifying addresses. For all this work, Rouffignac claimed to have paid her a total of 1,035 francs, 35 sous, less than a month's salary at the Maxi factory. Why did he continue to give her jobs if her performance was so unsatisfactory? Moreover, he recommended her to M. Dalit, the director of the Maxi factory, not only as a good worker, but also as a subtle sleuth well able to keep an eye on her coworkers without any of them suspecting anything. Dalit certainly had no complaints about her work. Nor did most of the people who worked with Toureaux at the Maxi factory suggest that she was anything other than a well-liked colleague, although a couple later confessed that they had had their suspicions.

That Rouffignac was less than forthcoming despite his vaunted cooperation with the authorities is not surprising, as he was rather a shady character himself. A rotund man with a small mustache, and a dapper dresser who sported straw hats at the beach and bowlers in town, he strongly resembled Agatha Christie's fictional character Hercule Poirot. Although he was a Frenchman, it was rumored—probably because of his thick southern French accent and dark hair—that he was actually Italian, perhaps even a spy. Born in 1895 in Marsac, in the Charente region of France, Rouffignac married in 1919 and was the father of a teenage boy in 1937. Although he claimed that his detective agency mostly performed routine surveillance, he clearly also provided spies for the police and for private industry.

Rouffignac never seemed to know quite how to play his relationship with Toureaux to the press. On the one hand, he denied any culpability in her death, insinuating that she was a seasoned detective with many espionage irons in the fire, of which her job with the Agence Rouff was only one. On the other hand, he disparaged her sleuthing abilities and minimized her work for him, exculpating himself by claiming that it was her rank amateurism that got her killed. It seems that he may have been trying deliberately to blacken Toureaux's reputation. He insinuated in his May 22 interview with *Paris-Soir* that she was a welfare cheat who took government handouts while working both for him and L'As-de-Coeur. Moreover, it emerged that the "guest" of L'As-de-Coeur who claimed to have seen Toureaux searching customers' coat pockets was none other than Mme. Paulette Vicarini (née Léonard), Rouffignac's secretary. According to Rouffignac, as soon as Vicarini informed him of Toureaux's unseemly behavior, he passed the information along to police, and he declared that neither he nor his secretary had the slightest idea why Toureaux would have done such a thing. It certainly wasn't in the course of a job for the Agence Rouff, and must have been related to her own private affairs.[44]

Eventually the police learned that Rouffignac had arranged for Toureaux to work in the cloakroom of L'As-de-Coeur as part of her sleuthing work for him. The cloakrooms of bals musette were often used in the 1930s as depositories for mail too sensitive to send through the regular system, and it appears that Toureaux facilitated such transfers. In this vein, an interrogation of one of Toureaux's friends revealed that she tried to arrange for other women to work in the bals for Rouffignac as part of his private surveillance force. In October 1936, Toureaux brought her eighteen-year-old friend, Yvonne Cavret, to meet Rouffignac in anticipation of securing a job in the cloakroom of a bal near the Place Pigalle. The young woman's fiancé, Victor Riou, later explained to Badin that Rouffignac had made it quite clear that Cavret would be part of his private investigative staff. Ultimately, Rouffignac found Riou too young and did not engage her. Riou later insisted that once she understood she would be spying for Rouffignac, she lost all interest in the position.[45]

The police also concluded that Rouffignac was correct that Toureaux had performed detective work for another employer in 1936 and 1937. According to Riton, Toureaux, in her campaign to improve his fortunes, had tried to induct him into the espionage business by giving him a few simple tasks to perform for her. In particular, she sent him to three addresses, all in the 18th arrondissement. Unfortunately, Riton proved to be an inept sleuth and was unable to fulfill his missions to Toureaux's satisfaction—an indication that she did have experience and professional standards in this line of work. She paid him the cost of his transportation to the addresses, but informed him that in the future she would do the jobs herself. Rouffignac denied giving Toureaux any assignments that involved the 18th arrondissement, however, which led the police to conclude that she "consistently worked as a private detective for a third party, other than Rouffignac."[46] They proved unable to ascertain who that person or persons might have been; nor did they admit the possibility that it was one of the branches of the police.

The mystery surrounding Toureaux's death deepened still further when witnesses came forward claiming that the seemingly confident, carefree adventuress was in fact well aware that she was in over her head in the days and weeks preceding her murder. Not all of their stories were credible; there were numerous inconsistencies in the statements that Toureaux's acquaintances, friends, and family offered to the police and to the press. There was, for example, the so-called "mystery of the green outfit." According to the newspapers, people accustomed to seeing Toureaux on a daily basis—such as Mme. Marie Quiniou, who sold tickets at the Métro Philippe-Auguste, the station nearest the rue Pierre Bayle where Toureaux lived—were astonished to see her sporting a new green suit and freshly tinted blond hair on the day of her murder. They claimed that they had never seen her wear anything other than widow's weeds since she moved into the neighborhood after Jules's death. Riton, in contrast, saw nothing surprising in her decision to wear the green outfit; he claimed that Toureaux's mother had just made it for her, and as Toureaux was lunching with her mother that very day, it stood to reason that her mother would have expected her daughter to be wearing the new outfit. By the same token, the testimony of Rouffignac's secretary Mme. Vicarini that Toureaux showed up on her first day of work at the Agence Rouff in a stylish gray suit and hat trimmed with mauve indicates that Toureaux did indeed wear colors other than black in the two years between Jules's death and her own. Still, journalists made much of her seemingly suspicious decision suddenly to change her wardrobe and hair color on the day she was killed.

The witnesses from the Métro marveled that Toureaux had traveled in first class on May 16, as they swore that in all the time they had known her, she had purchased only second-class tickets. Yet Toureaux's mother said at one point that because Toureaux was often dressed in her finest on Sundays, she sometimes treated herself to first-class seating. This did not stop the press from speculating about her decision to upgrade her fare on May 16, placing herself alone and vulnerable in one of the usually deserted first-class cars and thus providing her killer the opportunity he needed to strike. Were her changes in habits merely coincidence, or were they signs that she sought to disguise her identity because she sensed the net closing in around her?[47] Had someone unknown to the police instructed her to take the fateful first-class car as a rendezvous point?

Another odd piece of the puzzle surfaced. According to her friends Suzy Fiancette and Joseph Chatrian, Toureaux had feared for her life at the hands of a powerful and obsessed lover whom she could not shake, and even went so far as to consult a psychic for guidance. The psychic, a Mme. de Romanellas, claimed that Toureaux asked her to use black magic to rid her of this unwanted lover.[48]

Even more suggestive, was the testimony of M. Émile Martin, the station chief of Philippe Auguste. He and the other regular workers at the Métro station had good reason to be familiar with Toureaux, as she ordinarily took the Métro three to four times a day; around 7:15 A.M. on her way to work at the Maxi factory, around 6:00 P.M. when she returned home, at about 9:00 P.M. when she went to work at L'As-de-Coeur, and again on her way home if she returned before the Métro closed around 12:30 A.M. M. Martin, Mme. Quiniou, Mme. Louise Leclercq (the night clerk), and Mme. Alice Jhoupin (the newspaper vendor in the station) were all used to seeing Toureaux pass, flashing them her radiant smile. Sometimes she stopped to make small talk if she wasn't in too much of a hurry. According to Martin and Leclercq, on the evening of Thursday, May 13, only three days before her murder, Toureaux told them that she had been attacked by a man who had tried to knife her as she left the Métro station. She was able to drive him away by slapping him in the face. "In that case, aren't you frightened?" asked Martin. "No," she replied. "But now I take my umbrella to defend myself." Martin offered to walk her to the Métro exit, but she refused. "If someone attacks you again," he said, "cry out loudly this time." "Will do," she replied, with a laugh. Then she shook his hand and went on her way.[49]

Mme. Marie Chartrian offered a different version of the story. Toureaux and the Chartrians were good friends, as she and Joseph Chartrian came from the same region of Italy. Joseph worked in a café near the Agence Rouff, and he and Rouffignac both testified that it was Joseph who recommended Toureaux to Rouffignac when the latter was in need of a female sleuth for certain cases. His wife testified that Toureaux told her that the attack on May 13 took place not at the Métro station, but in front of the door of her building on the rue Pierre Bayle. According to Mme. Chartrian, Toureaux said, "I was returning home very late one night in a car with a [male] friend. I had gotten out at the angle of the boulevard Charonne and the rue Pierre Bayle. I was just about to ring the doorbell so that [the concierge] could let me in when a man got out of a car who evidently had been following us, and approached me in a menacing manner. I was about to attempt to defend myself when the door opened. I was able to go in and shut it behind me. But I was terrified."[50] The police gave the impression that they did not take the incident too seriously. Badin doubted that the attack on May 13 was related to the murder and suggested that Toureaux's assailant that night probably was "an enterprising stalker or a criminal who was after her pocketbook."[51]

By mid-June, in the absence of any obvious progress in the case on the part of the police, the Parisian newspapers were grasping at any straws, no matter how far-fetched, to keep the story alive. Much of what they wrote was a combination of rehashed information from stories that had broken in the first week after the crime, new and questionable testimony from people ever further from Toureaux's circle of close family and friends, and outright speculation. Every now and then, the police would get a false confession, such as that from Jean-Émile Goderoy, who claimed that he had shared a prison cell with Raymond Leblanc, whose sister dated the assassin. It turned out, however, that Goderoy's friends considered him a "bit crazy" and that Leblanc had no sisters.[52] But the police investigation was making little progress, and journalists suspected that the turgid pace was deliberate. As the communist daily *L'Humanité* asserted on May 27, "Quietly they are smothering the Laetitia affair."[53]

In one sense, *L'Humanité* had it right. On May 25, the newspaper stated in its daily story on the Toureaux case that the police had possession of "considerable correspondence" between Toureaux and her "protector," who the paper asserted was "a well-known politician of the right."[54] Why, complained *L'Humanité*, was no one discussing this? Further revelations appeared on May 28 in *Paris-Soir.* "My daughter was charged with delicate missions and she feared vengeance," Toureaux's father supposedly proclaimed.[55] These "missions" were for the police, and she continued with them despite her fears because she "loved this work," as it kept her from dwelling on her "unhappiness," and in particular the loss of her husband.[56] She had accepted the job in the cloakroom of L'As-de-Coeur precisely because it helped her with her detecting, and, when she realized that she was quite skilled at detection, she began to work for several different agencies. She knew that her life could be threatened, but the rewards made the risk worthwhile. This testimony was very similar to what Toureaux allegedly told her friend Mme. Chartrian, who stated that Toureaux declared that she loved her detective work because it afforded her the opportunity to forge relationships with people in "high places" and to "make something of herself."[57]

The judicial police remained mostly silent in the face of accusations that they were deliberately dragging their feet, in part probably because they were used to such complaints from the press and public. In the recent Stavisky and Prince affairs, the press had kept up an insistent drumbeat of reports that the victims in fact had been assassinated and had harshly criticized the police for their inability or lack of will to solve these "political crimes."[58]

On May 26 the judicial police did issue a statement that attempted to quell the wilder journalistic rumor-mongering. The inquiry so far had established, the police declared:

1. That Laetitia Toureaux was employed from June to November 1936 exclusively by M. Rouffignac, a private detective, to shadow people suspected of infidelity in six different cases involving individuals of no great importance. She was never charged with any other mission. The examination of the notes and papers furnished [by Rouffignac] on this subject demonstrated peremptorily that Laetitia had little aptitude for this type of mission and that her reports had a childish character. She never worked in a detective agency other than the Agence Rouff.

2. No one knows of any protector as such of the victim. She did have several flirtations. Her style of life was modest, her lodging, which was composed merely of one room and a small kitchen, was appropriately and nicely furnished with furniture derived from her marriage. Her means of existence were the fruits of her labor at the House of Maxi and the sums she earned as tips working in the cloakroom of L'As-de-Coeur, which in winter could be as much as thirty francs an evening, and in the summer up to twenty francs. Having fairly elegant taste, she often made the clothes which she wore herself. She had absolutely no other source of revenue and her lifestyle corresponded with her income.

3. The judicial police have established no relationship between the affair of the Porte de Charenton [Toureaux] and those of Fontainebleau or Morangis [other unsolved murders]. By the same token, Inspector Cettour continues to work in the section [of the police] relating to public theft and has never changed his branch of service.[59]

The last sentence of the statement is particularly curious, because it implies that the press suspected, correctly, that there was something odd in Cettour's sponsorship of Toureaux for the Ligue Républicaine du Bien Public. This suspicion lay behind the false rumor that Cettour had been transferred to a job outside of Paris, perhaps to put him out of reach of the press. Overall, the communiqué should be taken with a grain of salt because there is ample evidence that Toureaux was a much better detective than either the police or Rouffignac wanted to suggest. And the police themselves concluded privately that Toureaux had in fact worked for another detective agency besides the Agence Rouff, although they were not able to track down which one.[60] Possibly the police wanted to avoid tipping off the murderer, if he was connected to a job she had done for another employer, before they got the opportunity to follow up on that angle of the investigation.

Another reason for the police reticence to discuss their progress with the press may have been that L'Humanité was getting uncomfortably near the truth. Toureaux had, it seemed, formed some decidedly odd political alliances for a lowly factory worker and part-time cloakroom attendant. On the one hand, the Ligue Républicaine du Bien Public, for which Rouffignac and Inspector Cettour had sponsored her membership, was a fairly high-profile organization on the French political left. Founded by two prominent socialists in 1935 as the heir to an older antiroyalist organization, its mission was to oppose the spread of fascism in France. On the other hand, the police found in Toureaux's apartment a postcard from someone attending a conference called the "Rassemblement Universel pour la Paix" (Universal Assembly for Peace), held in Brussels in July 1936. This person, who signed the card only "I. CH," expressed fervent rightist opinions, which, the police deduced on the basis of other correspondence found in her apartment, Toureaux shared. I. CH informed Toureaux that he would be returning to France in September 1936.[61] The police were unable to identify who had sent her the card. This evidence suggested that there might well have been a political dimension to Toureaux's murder. But what sort of politics, right or left? Without more evidence, the police had no way of knowing which of the plethora of political groups sprouting like mushrooms in the increasingly tense political climate of 1937 France might have been involved in the crime.

Thus, despite the dogged police investigation and the journalistic frenzy, Toureaux's case remained unsolved as the summer and autumn of 1937 wore on. There was now an ample list of suspects who might have wanted her out of the way, but no concrete evidence linking the crime to any of them. Although the police seemed to have run into a dead end or were at least unwilling to tell all that they knew, journalists continued to report on the case. The closest they came to the truth in the days immediately following Toureaux's murder was in an article published on May 23 in Paris-Soir, which asserted, "But Laetitia Toureaux, who knew well the Italian milieus and who made many voyages (although less frequently than some have asserted) between France and Italy, could have been employed as an informant either by the national police, or by private organizations or groups."[62]

Might her work as a private detective or a police informant have led to her death? "It could well have been a drug trafficker from the circle of Toureaux's closest associates, a friend of the unfortunate woman, who decided to take it upon himself to put an end to her unpleasant police activities," speculated an evening paper, *L'Intransigeant,* in June.[63] But could journalists ever confirm this hypothesis? Not if the police had anything to say about the matter. They seemed determined to keep a lid on the whole affair. Other newspapers, especially *La Liberté* and *Paris-Soir,* were more au courant regarding the progress of the case, perhaps because they had cultivated better contacts within the police. Police reports indicate that some of the inspectors assigned to her case were aware of Toureaux's work as a paid informer at the time of her death. They eventually concluded that an extreme rightwing terrorist organization called the Cagoule may have had a hand in the murder.[64] As yet the judicial police knew very little about the Cagoule, beyond rumors from their informants that the group was highly secret with a penchant for violence. They were not eager to publicize what little they had learned, since doing so might have compromised their ongoing probe of the Cagoule. Moreover, competition and mistrust within various divisions of the police force, as well as political pressure from the government, made the inspectors at the Sûreté reluctant to divulge any information on Toureaux and the Cagoule, even to their colleagues in the Paris prefecture.[65] As a result, the judicial police got no further breaks in the Toureaux case until near the end of 1937.

3

GENTLE LAMB OR WICKED SHEEP?

EMBODYING LAETITIA TOUREAUX

Like many women living in interwar Europe, Laetitia Toureaux was a woman struggling with questions of identity in a fluid, rapidly changing society. Upward social mobility was difficult but possible in 1930s France, where class-consciousness remained a powerful force but old cultural markers of class and status had begun rapidly to erode during World War I. Immigrants flooded Paris before and after World War I, changing the ethnic composition of the working classes in particular, and nowhere more so than in Paris, which was a mecca for young people seeking to take advantage of new economic opportunities while shedding old identities. Gender roles were in flux as well. Again, Paris was the place where women flocked from all over France, and the world, to live fully the ideal of the "new woman."[1] All these forces influenced Toureaux as she sought to mold her own identity in the decade before her death. After her death, the Parisian press and others sought to subsume her identity into their models of "good" versus "bad" women, and to enlist her posthumously in their struggles to indict the police and the government alike for incompetency and corruption. In this chapter, we begin with the imagined Toureaux and then examine the identity, or identities, that Toureaux crafted for herself—both her public face and, to the extent the sources permit, her private, hidden self.

The issue of class in modern French social and cultural history has become more complicated in recent decades as scholars, most notably Sarah Maza, have raised legitimate questions regarding historians' use of the terms "bourgeois" and "middle class" when discussing the middle and upper reaches of French society. Maza argues, in essence, that France never developed a true bourgeoisie, by which she means a unified middle or upper class that self-consciously identified itself as bourgeois in Marxian economic and sociological terms, as owners of capital with interests in opposition to the working classes.[2] Despite the legitimate issues Maza raises regarding both "bourgeois" and "middle class" when applied to France, historians still need terminology with which to describe the wealthier but non-noble and not necessarily aristocratic levels in French society. And, as Maza herself points out, French people did and still do use the term themselves. As she writes, "To this day, when the French talk about *la bourgeoisie* in a certain context, what they have in mind is clearly an upper class."[3] In this book, therefore, the terms "bourgeois" and "upper-class" will refer to non-noble, affluent families such as that of Jules Toureaux—wealthier and of higher status than the Nourrissat family and their working-class neighbors, but neither noble nor self-identified aristocrats. We contend that Toureaux and others of her social class perceived very real differences in wealth, social status, cultural attitudes, access to political influence, and political interests between themselves and the bourgeoisie, whether or not the latter used that term to define their own identity. We also argue that Toureaux ardently dreamed of joining their ranks, even if her imagination of what that might mean was hazy and based as much on popular myths as on any concrete understanding of the French bourgeoisie. Hence we use the terms "bourgeois, "middle class" and "upper-middle class" to describe Toureaux's lived experience of the reality of social differentiation in her society and, in default of better terms, to describe the goal of her aspiration to upward social mobility and the more affluent people in French society who read about her life and tragic death, and passed judgment on them.

Journalists Imagine the Enigmatic Laetitia Toureaux

Much of the press coverage of the Toureaux case was not really about the unsolved murder. Rather, the focus was on Toureaux herself, and it derived from male journalistic anxieties about the newly assertive young women of the interwar period. Lack of knowledge about the case was by no means a hindrance to the flood of reporting about it. On the contrary, the less reporters actually knew, the freer they felt to speculate; and their speculations increasingly reflected their fears of modern sexual mores, their erotic fantasies, and their fixation on the at least partly imaginary underworld of the bal musette. Laetitia Toureaux's murder was a godsend to French journalists, because much of the Parisian reading public shared their obsession with jazz, gangsters, prostitutes, and bals musette.

The press initially portrayed Toureaux as an innocent, a "gentle lamb," a little naive, perhaps, maybe even a flirt, but essentially as a victim of cruel fate.[4] Yet within days after her murder, public opinion, led by the popular press, began to turn against Toureaux as the police investigation began to expose hints of a darker side to her life. It turned out, reporters asserted, that Toureaux was an ambitious social climber who lived beyond her means. Troubling hints of a double life, of nights spent at bals musette and in even more nefarious activity, began to surface. "LAETITIA TOUREAUX SPENT MORE THAN SHE EARNED: DID SHE HAVE A LOVER?" ran the sensational headlines in *Paris-Soir* on May 21.[5] The story went on to recount that the victim's apartment had been decorated with a taste and elegance that seemed beyond the means of an Italian-born factory worker, no matter how economical and Francophile she might have been. The papers all made much out of the fact that on the night of her murder, Toureaux's purse contained a book of first-class Métro tickets. Since most Parisians knew that high-class prostitutes frequently traveled in first-class cars, journalists hoped to raise doubts about just what Toureaux had been up to in the days before her death. How could a simple factory worker afford such a luxury, people wondered? The newspapers further alleged that the letters the police had found in her apartment, hundreds of them tied in neat bundles, were from many different men.[6] Journalists frequently contradicted both each other and the police, exaggerated, and just plain got the facts wrong. Still, it was becoming clear that this woman named Laetitia who called herself Yolande had constructed multiple careers and identities for herself in the very different worlds of the Parisian bourgeoisie and working class. This, of course, only made her story more compelling.

As more details of Toureaux's life emerged, the press, which saw itself as a champion of middle-class morality, was quick to condemn the young widow's lifestyle. Her clandestine marriage, far from having been an innocent love affair, actually constituted a scandalous threat to bourgeois propriety.[7] Worse, Toureaux's night life began to appear more and more risqué. Journalists had a field day dropping jargon about the milieu she frequented, the bals musette and cafés around the Bastille and Montmartre, in the Latin Quarter, and along the Marne. These were the haunts of unsavory characters, the addicts of "coco" (cocaine) and opium, the "tueurs" (hit men) and wise guys who "loved to give themselves over to the various pleasures of the dance in an atmosphere of popular jubilation."[8] In the basements and back rooms of these establishments, insinuated the newspapers, French, Neapolitan, and Algerian gangsters regularly plotted to "supprimer" (suppress) their enemies. The working-class men and women who in fact comprised most of the clientele of these businesses were suspect, tainted through association and innuendo. After all, bals musette were where "young girls go for misadventures!" cried the papers.[9] By May 27, journalists had begun to label Toureaux a "loose woman."[10] They also found her habits unusual and reported that she kept odd hours. Worse, she moved about the city alone, day and night, with what her contemporaries perceived as a masculine freedom from fear.[11] For her, the Métro was more than just a means of transport. It was also a liminal space, a place of transition from whence she could emerge at any time, day or night, ready to assume the identity of Yolande, to play a new role, to present a new face to the world.[12]

The idea of Laetitia Toureaux as a female private detective or "cachottière" (as her brothers Riton and Virgile called her) fascinated the press and the reading public.[13] Popular culture in the 1920s and 1930s was steeped in real and fictional detective literature. Détective magazine, which chronicled real-life murder mysteries and spy cases as well as fictional sleuthing and reported on notorious criminals, gangsters, pimps, and prostitutes, enjoyed fabulous success in the 1930s.[14] Its escapist stories, many of them featuring intrepid young women, allowed ordinary people to live out their fantasies. Newspapers followed closely murders and scandals, and Parisian journalists explicitly connected Toureaux's death to other unsolved murders upon which they reported, charging that an incompetent police and corrupt judiciary were permitting to run amuck a nefarious cabal with ties to French or foreign government officials. No one committed suicide anymore; they were all "suicided" by hit men or the police. Newspapers suggested that notorious murderers on the lam—such as René "le Balafré" (Scarface) and Max "le Roquin" (Shark), or Pierrot-le-Bancal (Sabre) and his girlfriend in London, Joséphine Martin, also known as "Fifi-la-Françoise"— might have committed Laetitia's murder, and that these canny denizens of the Parisian underworld hopelessly outmatched the police.[15] Toureaux, journalists suggested, would have been fair game for any one of these criminals, because she inhabited their dark milieu of indigence and crime. Moreover, she may even have been informing on them for the police in Paris and London, which, if true, meant that she was even more duplicitous and licentious than the criminals upon whom she spied—and more interesting.[16]

In the absence of hard facts about the murder, or at least of any facts that the police would permit to be published, the press made Toureaux into a lightning rod for much of the cultural angst of interwar French society. As cultural interpreters and powerful forces shaping popular attitudes, journalists used Toureaux's story to titillate its mostly middle-class readers while simultaneously reinforcing middle-class values. They led the public into a mostly imagined netherworld of seamy Parisian streets, bars, and dance halls. Through narratives laced with slang attesting to the "inside knowledge" of the reporters, readers experienced vicariously the thrill of exploring a world forbidden to respectable citizens. Yet by constructing each story as a morality tale in which transgressors of middle-class norms invariably came to bad ends, newspapers and magazines ended their readers' journey safely in the harbor of respectable values. Like children of the wealthy who delighted in slumming in the bals musette of Paris (or the speakeasies of Chicago), readers of sensational magazines and newspapers such as the weekly *Détective* and the dailies *Le Petit Parisien* and *Paris-Soir* could share Toureaux's adventures without the danger and discomfort inherent in actually living in her world. Thus the Parisian press was able to mold Toureaux's mysterious demise into a story that made sense to its readers, re-enforced a law-and-order mentality, and supported the established social order of the late 1930s.[17]

Embedded in each salacious adventure published in *Détective* and its more respectable competitors were two narratives with competing cultural meanings. Yet, through the descriptive format, these meanings were eventually reconciled at the conclusion of the story. One narrative lured the reader into the violent, sexually arousing world of the street, which was inhabited by lower-class characters with *Parigot* names like "Jo the Boxer," "Gina the Gypsy," "Kiki the Bouncer," and "Lili the Prostitute," whose lives seemed infinitely more exciting than those of the average reader. These unlikely heroes demonstrated courage, humor, and an ability to accept the vagaries of fortune—qualities embodied by the nonchalant shrug and matter-of-fact, *c'est la vie* lifestyle that reporters loved to attribute to them. Middle-class readers, especially women, could vicariously experience the adventure and sexual danger denied to them in real life. Working-class readers also found a release in the perspective of the popular press, which transformed their familiar and mundane public spaces into stimulating arenas of seduction, heroism, and villainy. Their part of the city exuded an attraction for their social betters that seemed to enhance their own status.

The second narrative reassured both the upper and lower strata of the reading public that this stimulating world of the streets was doomed to tragedy. Denizens of the bals musette, especially if they were women, never came to good ends. Journalists implied that happy endings were reserved only for those who adhered to traditional values that were grounded in respectability, Christian virtues, and patriarchal authority. Adventurous women like Toureaux were never truly victims, for their own intrepid determination to venture alone into the city streets brought about their downfall. One might safely visit the rue de Lappe, but one had to flee before the police raided it. To stay was to court sexual danger and almost certain disaster. Too much familiarity with working-class entertainments led to a loss of innocence that barred a fallen woman from returning to the parlors of the respectable upper classes. Men could enjoy greater exposure to the wine and easy women of the bals, but they too risked a fall from grace if they assimilated too well to the temptations of the milieu. A working-class woman could aspire to enter the ranks of the middle class only by eschewing the slightest taint of the bal musette. Unlike her more affluent sisters, she could not afford to flirt with the amusements of her peers if she hoped to rise in the world. Toureaux could not leave the bals musette behind, however, and even introduced her bourgeois husband to them. But Jules's presence at the bals and in Laetitia's life were part of his own deception. He was in essence a voyeur, sampling working-class pleasures without ever really leaving the safe confines of his own class. Laetitia attempted to straddle both worlds, but her entry into bourgeois society failed since Jules refused to acknowledge her publicly as his wife.

Even so, Toureaux acted out the textual complexity of these competing narratives, attempting to realize both fantasies in her own life. The police combed her apartment meticulously and found touches of bourgeois material culture—such as lace curtains and stylish furniture—that were not typical of immigrant homes.[18] The evidence from her life also suggests that she aspired to upward social mobility and respectability. Yet ironically, once Jules, her ticket to the middle class, died, she could fulfill this dream only by utilizing her familiarity with the working-class environment she sought to flee. In life and death alike, Laetitia/Yolande fed the Parisian police and press information from the streets of Paris that helped to make the "otherness" of that world intelligible to them, a service she could perform only by incurring the taint of membership in it. In another layer of irony, Toureaux's own perception of both the bourgeois and the working-class milieus was deeply influenced by the very publications that in turn incorporated her life and death into their fantasy of the Parisian streets. There was, in effect, a dialogue between Toureaux and the police detectives and journalists who investigated and reported on her murder, a conversation built as much on fiction as that found in the often highly embellished, even fantastic, articles in the Parisian papers and weeklies. Toureaux's life embodied this struggle between competing narratives, as she attempted to reconcile two different interpretations of the working-class world she inhabited and enjoyed, yet sought to escape.[19]

The press's spin on the story of Toureaux's murder and the fictional construct it created of her life must also be understood as a product of the ways in which gender was perceived in 1930s France. Journalists could only see Toureaux through the discursive prism of gender. They portrayed her as someone who purposefully rejected the role of respectable housewife and mother in order to invent a far more decadent and exciting life for herself in the Paris underworld. According to the press, Toureaux chose to be a woman of the night rather than the day, although in reality she was never a prostitute, and the evidence suggests that Toureaux was both: she literally worked night and day, from 7:00 A. M., when she took the Métro to the Maxi factory, until one or two in the morning, when she returned from her job at L'As-de-Coeur. In the press, gender was the aspect of Toureaux's identity that really mattered. It was not just how she had lived or died that sold copy; it was the fact that she was a woman who had lived a double life and died in a pool of her own blood. As recounted in the press, her story reflected a pronounced hostility toward women that permeated interwar French society and grew more intense as the 1930s progressed. Contemporary journalists embraced the ideals expounded by the employers and state officials of the day, who were conservative in outlook and articulated a gendered discourse that attempted to limit women's choices during the interwar period.[20]

Much has been written on the tendency of late nineteenth- and early twentieth-century writers, both in educated circles and in the popular press, to project upon the city their discontent with moral decay, working-class culture, and female sexuality. Magazines and newspapers in particular were caught between their need to titillate and their desire to uplift morally the reading public.[21] Journalism was just becoming a viable profession in France; in the 1920s and 1930s, the first schools of journalism were founded and the first national journalists' union was organized. There were roughly three thousand journalists in Paris in the 1930s, 97.5 percent of them men who were struggling to achieve their own bourgeois respectability as their profession gained serious social standing.[22] Even so, there were no restrictions placed on the press in the 1930s to keep journalists from writing anything they wanted to invent about a particular story or criminal investigation. Police chiefs often held press conferences to keep the reporters' imaginations from running wild on sensational stories and to impress on them the necessity of not publishing information that might compromise a case. But that did not keep journalists and policemen from socializing in order to pump each other for information, nor did it prevent unscrupulous journalists from posing as police officers in an effort to obtain confidential information from unsuspecting informants. These journalists helped to define the cultural logic of the 1930s as contemporaries understood it. Their sensational stories, embedded with multiple cultural meanings, involved them and those who bought their papers in an ongoing dialogue based on a kind of fantasy that sustained their collective imaginations. Journalists served the police by disseminating stories and photographs, often ones the police had deliberately leaked in order to jar the memories of witnesses and motivate them to come forward. They also created public opinion by educating their readers. Yet they were not above participating in a long French journalistic tradition of distorting their accounts and purposely misinforming the public for the sake of a good story.[23]

Nowhere was the penchant for sensationalism with moral overtones more evident than in the simultaneous fascination and revulsion of the French press with the bals musette. Journalists exploited the venue of the bals for story ideas and found leads to crimes, informants, and the colorful characters that populated their articles. Like slumming *flaneurs,* they observed with a jaundiced eye the pleasures of the bals without belonging to or truly understanding the culture that generated them.[24] But despite the discomfort of the press with Laetitia Toureaux's love of dance and dance halls, none of her family and friends found anything unusual or immoral about her nightlife. The disparity between mundane reality and journalistic fantasy derived from the projection of middle-class anxieties about Paris in general and its working class in particular onto the bals musette. The opportunity the bals provided women to interact informally with men aroused the fears of journalists and confirmed their belief that the bals were exciting but dangerous, the source of good copy but hardly venues of propriety.[25]

Détective was one of the first weekly magazines in Paris to take advantage of the new field of photojournalism, stimulating the public with suggestive photographs that emphasized the thrust of their headlines.[26] The cover story headline from one 1937 issue blared, "Under the fires of electric lamps, couples dance cheek to cheek. Love stories debut, which sometimes end in blood."[27] In the accompanying photograph, a seductive woman gazes triumphantly at the reader, her arms draped possessively around the neck of her male conquest. He looks away, whether out of modesty or guilt. Is she a fallen women of whom he is ashamed? That certainly was the picture's implication. Jean Chiappe, Préfet de Police in the 1930s, found *Détective* so distasteful that he banned the public display of posters of its covers throughout France.[28] The journalists at *Détective* were ambiguous, however, in their portrayal of the bals. On the one hand, they warned readers about the perversions of the dance halls; on the other hand, they glorified the dangerous and exciting life to be found there.

The journalistic accounts of Laetitia Toureaux's life and death reveal that for the press she embodied a fundamental contradiction in the image of women in 1930s France. The experience of World War I created a conscious sense—among the young of Europe especially—that the values and mores of the old order were moribund. People sought modernity, which for them meant youth, action, and adventure. Nowhere was this attitudinal change more significant than in the perceptions of gender relations and the role of women. Mary Louise Roberts has argued that during the interwar period, "gender was central to how change was understood."[29] This was the era of the flapper, of the female adventuresses who littered novels and the popular press. Women had more independence to work, more money, and more opportunities to spend their earnings freely, although the depression of the 1930s severely limited their spending power. Some women stretched the boundaries of the permissible in their sexual and social lives, and here too they found inspiration and encouragement, as well as cautionary tales, in new magazines such as *Marie-Claire* that catered to the female reading public. A tension thus existed between traditional Catholic values, which emphasized motherhood and domesticity, and the newer values, which stressed feminism and the need to affirm female sexual and economic independence from male control. The "new" woman always seemed to have more fun, but she also came to a predictably tragic end unless she bridled her ambitions and spending habits and cut short her flirtation with independence, reentering the domestic world of submission to male authority. Miranda Pollard has argued that the mid-1930s was a crucial period in the pronatalism movement in France, in which statistics reflecting the country's low birth rate were transformed into a dialogue of danger that threatened the country.[30] As the 1930s drew to a close, nearly all leaders across the political spectrum—and especially leaders of extreme right-wing organizations—began to insist more and more frequently that only the domestic and maternal roles of women really mattered. Yet Toureaux appeared to be the living embodiment of Victor Margueritte's heroine in his popular postwar novel *La Garçonne*, a "bachelor girl" who pursued financial independence and sexual pleasure wherever she could find them in the new age of the emancipated woman.[31] In many ways, Toureaux's portrayal in the papers prefigured cultural fears about the liberated woman, which became stereotypical propaganda during the Vichy regime.[32]

Journalists therefore found themselves with plenty of suggestive evidence that Toureaux's murder stemmed from her detective work either for the police or for Rouffignac. Frustrated by their inability to uncover any conclusive proof, they began to accuse the police of stonewalling. The communist newspapers were especially aggressive in their recriminations. "THEY DON'T WANT TO KNOW WHO ASSASSINATED LAETITIA," shouted the headlines of *L'Humanité* on May 29. "Everything is being put in place so that the assassin will never be discovered."[33] "What is M. Badin waiting for?" asked *L'Oeuvre* the same day. "There is no longer any great reason for hope; little by little they are moving toward classifying and forgetting [the case]."[34] And, concluded the socialist daily *Le Populaire*, "the inquiry into the Laetitia Toureaux affair is at the point of death."[35] The police response was that they in fact had not given up, and that such accusations from the press not only were unjustified and scurrilous but impeded them from doing their job.[36]

Only the Valdôtaine press seemed to know for sure who had killed Laetitia Toureaux. *L'Écho de la Vallée d'Aoste*, a paper founded in Paris by the Abbé Petigat for the Valdôtaine community, decried the portrayal of Toureaux by the other Parisian papers. They were certain that the newspaper industry itself had murdered the poor woman. Calling her murder a "double assassination," the Abbé Petigat went on to condemn the negative articles written about Laetitia as extravagant fantasies. "The poor victim has already been mortally wounded," he wrote, "and has now become the object of even worse outrages even after her death."[37]

Yet the Valdôtaine call for greater objectivity towards Toureaux's life went unheard outside the Italian immigrant community. As journalists found themselves increasingly frustrated in their efforts either to extract from the police or to confirm on their own the exact nature of Toureaux's work as a police informant, they resorted to speculations about her life and death that degenerated into the absurd, but which served to keep the story alive, sell copy, and turn Toureaux into a woman of low morals. Her sexuality in particular was fair game. She had been more than a flirt, it seemed, a real vamp, a dangerous seductress whose lovers supplied her with the money to support her parvenu lifestyle. Reporters thought that perhaps a *voyante* (seer) could uncover the truth about Toureaux's unknown lovers and even pinpoint the one who had killed her. One of these hired soothsayers, a Madame D., suggested that her killer was from the southeast of France and that she was "very close" to him.[38]

Immediately after Toureaux's death, it became apparent that she had male admirers in the military, including Jean Martin and René Schramm. "I was never her boyfriend," Martin insisted. "She was a friend, nothing more. . . . I thought she was on the level. She told me she worked days in a laboratory" (presumably he meant the Maxi factory).[39] This did not stop the press from reading more into her penchant for military men. "One mustn't forget that Laetitia, a foreigner by birth, loved to frequent both the sailors of Toulon and the soldiers of the garrison on the Maginot line," asserted *Paris-Soir.*[40] Was she a spy, using her wiles to infiltrate the French military, or simply a promiscuous camp follower in search of sex? Was "Yolande" merely a pretty new name she had chosen for herself, as her family and friends asserted, or was it the sinister sobriquet of a woman determined to mask her true identity with a criminal alias, as the press insinuated? For the press, there was no innocent facet of her life.

Toureaux also had a taste for foreign men, asserted the journalists. A South American, or a North African, or a Jewish Algerian had loved her and killed her in a fit of jealous rage. Jealousy? No, it was sexual frustration; she was a tease whose habits were *irrégulier* (irregular, meaning homosexual). The press insinuated that her assassin might have been a woman, maybe someone she had tailed but maybe a more intimate associate, even a female lover.[41] At every step of the investigation, both for the police and the press, Toureaux's sex played a central role informing how she was viewed.

Toureaux offered a perfect tableau for the press to explore and expound upon the issues of gender and, to a lesser extent, class, with both of which interwar France struggled. World War I had offered opportunities for women to enter the workforce for the first time. This accelerated their entrance into mass consumer culture, while also offering them an economic independence that at least some women sought to translate into greater sexual freedom. In reality, most women, even if they worked in factories and department stores in their youth, eventually abandoned paid employment for the traditional role of wife and mother. But women continued to be drawn to the allure of the narrative of the modern woman, with its sexual titillation and thrill of adventures shared vicariously from a safe distance in the popular literature.

For the average reader, Yolande was a dangerous *donneuse*, a woman who "puts out," made even more threatening in her immigrant guise.

Toureaux was the quintessential modern female consumer, and part of journalists' discomfort with her lifestyle lay in the fact that she not only consumed, but that she seemed to consume beyond her means.[42] Female working-class culture changed significantly in the 1920s and 1930s. First, after an era in which almost all large factories were located far from the city center, and factory housing tended to isolate workers and their families in the suburbs, there was a growing tendency for factories and workers alike to move out of these locales and closer to the city. Second, working women were increasingly cultivated as consumers, which resulted in significant cultural changes. Rising numbers of factory women were unwilling to wear clothing such as the ubiquitous apron that distinguished them from other, higher-class women. They began to adopt the stylish clothing and haircuts of middle-class women, or else they fashioned homemade garments to be as stylish as possible and wore those clothes to work, even though that meant changing into and out of work clothes at the factory. They cut their hair and abandoned the turn-of-the-century women's boots in favor of more fashionable shoes. Italians were noted for the lavish amounts of money they spent on their wardrobes, which they tended to wear especially during their leisure time on weekends and holidays, when immaculately dressed families would take walks in Parisian parks. And even though the Italians came in for particular criticism from the French for spending too much on clothes rather than saving their wages or spending them on better housing or other commodities, working-class French men and women behaved in much the same way and came in for similar criticism from higher-class moralists as a result.[43]

All the Paris newspapers remarked on the new, expensive-looking suit Toureaux wore the day she died. Only one saw fit to mention that her mother had made it for her, along with a new coat, and that Mme. Nourrissat was a skilled seamstress who often made her daughter's clothes.[44] News reports made much of her "adorable apartment and elegant furnishings," yet a single story told readers that she had only cold running water. None of the papers bothered to mention that her furniture derived from her marriage to the late Jules Toureaux, her sole inheritance from him.[45] Her clandestine marriage, with its overtones of social climbing, made good copy; but none of the reports criticized Jules for his snobbery or alluded to the fact that Laetitia's portion of her husband's estate amounted to very little.[46]

Yet the newspapers scrupulously added up every *centime* of her income, and, rather than lauding her for working hard to keep up a respectable appearance on a meager income, implied that she must have made ends meet with the help of a lover, despite the fact that the police stated that they had found no indication that she needed or had any source of income beyond her earnings. At the same time, journalists were only too happy to treat as fact Rouffignac's insinuation that Toureaux was a welfare cheat who collected unemployment while working for the Agence Rouff. Thus, Toureaux's drive to achieve a better lifestyle, or at least the veneer of middle-class respectability, became a reason to condemn her. Journalists faulted Toureaux both for her low-class origins and for her evident desire for upward social mobility. They never let the evidence about Toureaux's lifestyle get in the way of the image they created of her, blurring the parameters between what had been her real life and the fiction they created of that life.

Like most working women in industrial France, Toureaux had few opportunities to rise in her job, no matter how hard or well she worked. Even as technology evolved, job skills were continually defined and redefined in ways that ensured that better-paying jobs went to men, and the Popular Front did nothing to improve women's access to skilled jobs. Women's share of skilled work declined in the early twentieth century, even as the demand for unskilled female and child laborers in the factories rose.[47] And familialist legislation—such as the law passed in 1932 that gave family allowances to workers with children—disadvantaged all single workers but particularly women, who typically received lower wages.[48] This may well help explain Toureaux's restless efforts to better herself in other ways, through an upwardly mobile marriage, detective work, and intrigue. Toureaux also took French language lessons from a Mlle. Jeanne Désirée Landry between April and August 1936 to try to perfect her writing and elocution.[49] She held many jobs, but except for her work at the Agence Rouff, they were all of the same genre: factory work or checking coats and dancing with customers at bals musette. Paid employment was not, therefore, a promising means for the upward mobility she seems to have desired. Opportunities were very few for ambitious women from the French working class, especially if they were also immigrants. While Toureaux was always able to scrape together a modest living, she would not have been able to do much more than that, given the sorts of jobs she was able to obtain. Only another upwardly mobile marriage would have offered Toureaux an avenue of escape from her tiny apartment on the rue Pierre Bayle.

Even with the odds against her, Toureaux was a woman who seemed determined to remake herself, and in the process to push the accepted social boundaries into which she had been born. She seemed to embrace duality. She avidly sought out the adventurous life of a detective and she pursued male companionship in the bals musette, while refusing to reject the bourgeois respectability she desired. By day she was a conscientious, sober, hardworking woman whose coworkers in the Maxi factory liked and respected her. By night, she roamed the streets and corridors of the dance halls, sleuthing for pay and adventure alike. She fearlessly walked alone at night, attested numerous witnesses. She also satisfied her sexual appetite and engaged in somewhat risky sexual encounters in public venues. Thus while Toureaux appeared both radiant and chaste, she had a darker side that craved adventure.

In this Toureaux was not alone. The period spanning the late nineteenth and early twentieth centuries was a time in which women sought to appropriate the freedom to roam the city and immerse themselves in its delights. Parisians found in the nocturnal city "a theatre in which men *and*, if in a very restricted measure, women could experiment with themselves and the possibilities open to them."[50] Many women joined the ranks of spies, criminals, and adventurers living on the edge in big international cities, and many other women read about and admired them for their daring. This was an era that could not make up its mind about women, an era that worshipped simultaneously a wanton waif in the person of Édith Piaf, who got her start in the bals musette, the beautiful and seductive actress Simone Simon, who gave every new lover a key to her boudoir, and a fearless new woman, Amelia Earhart.[51] By following a lifestyle that fell outside the traditional roles for women, these heroines were both admired and feared, yet none were portrayed as truly happy. The same was assumed of Toureaux.

Clearly Parisian journalists and their reading public were uncomfortable with the "other" life Yolande chose. Instead of portraying her as a dignified widow, they focused on her as an independent and arrogant woman who embodied the *femme moderne* as opposed to the culturally preferred *femme au foyer.* All the papers ran pictures of Toureaux and remarked on her handsome appearance. Yet this was just a way of emphasizing that she was not round, robust, and maternal, but rather slim and sensual. The gendered discourses of the news reports reveal apprehension over an ambitious, attractive woman who held three jobs and tried to take charge of her own life. The contradictions within postwar society are made explicit in these stories. Opportunities existed for women like Toureaux to live full lives as independent women, but such women were also condemned in the popular press for exercising their options, and journalists and their public doubted that these women could ever really be fulfilled or content outside the settled domesticity of marriage and children. This made it easy to place Toureaux in the simplistic good woman/bad woman paradigm, subsuming her in a traditional narrative that criticized female emancipation and associated it with promiscuity. For many readers, it was easy enough to dismiss Toureaux as nothing more than a "childless coquette."[52]

Worse still, the press's patriarchal emphasis on the conventional female roles of wife and mother meant that Toureaux and women like her were the reason for France's declining birth rate. Toureaux lived in an era that targeted birth control and abortion as national evils that threatened the very existence of France; and, on a more personal level, her sexual history and childless existence made her into an imagined purveyor of banned contraceptive knowledge.[53] On the one hand, Toureaux's freedom made her interesting and alluring to the reading public. On the other, it unmasked her as dangerous and threatening. Such conflicting messages about gender roles, Mary Louise Roberts has written, "demonstrated the erratic movement back and forth in postwar discourse between optimism and anxiety concerning change, between proclaiming the new world and clinging to the old."[54]

Toureaux used her sexuality to get what she wanted. Her good looks made her popular at the various bals musette where she worked, danced, and sleuthed. They certainly facilitated her detective work. As one paper noted, "A pretty and clever woman is always appreciated in the secret services."[55] As a private detective she may have taken lovers in order to procure information related to her investigations. The Sûreté eventually concurred with the speculation in L'Humanité that Toureaux had a protector in high political circles. The police connected her to a brilliant opportunist named Gabriel Jeantet who had a good education and bourgeois upbringing and who was kin by marriage to one of the wealthiest families in France. Jeantet, a handsome and sophisticated young man with boundless enthusiasm for right-wing causes, appears also to have been yet another of her lovers.[56] Whatever the truth about Laetitia/Yolande, she was willing to take risks, and the Parisian reading public was told that her steamy sexuality, mixed with her independence and adventure, was the ultimate cause of her murder.

Nowhere was the press's dislike of the ambiguities of Toureaux's life more evident than in an article published in L'Oeuvre on May 25, 1937. The author used the image of Toureaux as a wolf in sheep's clothing, a shady woman of questionable morals interloping on the terrain of the honest, working-class woman, as a metaphor for the supposed duplicity of the government and its police.

> This Laetitia story, despite the overactive imagination of all of the apprentices of Simenon, is ending up by not amusing anyone. . . . First they pictured for us a pure young woman, a regular churchgoer and close associate of the Ligue du Bien Public, practically decorated with the red ribbon and sympathetic in every way: a woman of regular habits, well regarded by her landlady, her archbishop and her father confessor. A gentle lamb . . . then, by the end of one week of reflection, we learn that the price of virtue, after having been in charge of the back room of a Chinese establishment, was to oversee the restrooms of a bal musette: in the wings, she presided over regular transactions, special marriages and diverse traffics. . . . Better, in her spare time, in a factory, she was appointed to spy on her co-workers. . . . It matters little to us that the gentle lamb was, in reality, a wicked sheep. . . . It's the method by which we have been misinformed that we don't like.[57]

In this passage we see how the press twisted the facts of Toureaux's life into a commentary on the informants, frequently women, who the police recruited to spy on union organizers, socialists, and Italian immigrants. Toureaux is seen to be flirting with racial transgressions. Rather than plying her real job, checking the coats of customers in L'As-de-Coeur, here she is presiding first over the "back room" of a Chinese dance hall (an obvious reference to her work in 1935 in the bal musette Le Lotus), and then the "toilets" of L'As-de-Coeur. Moreover, she is in charge of all sorts of shady deals, sexual and otherwise, that were imputed to take place regularly in nightclubs. By day, she interrupted her work in the Maxi factory to spy on her coworkers, an activity that the leftist L'Oeuvre naturally viewed as "the lowest of professions."[58] As a police informant, Toureaux was an enemy of the working class into which she had been born. As a loose woman, she was an enemy of her sex. As a usurper of bourgeois status through her morganatic marriage to Jules Toureaux, she was an enemy of the social order.

Rather than viewing Toureaux's complicated, perplexing life in the context of the struggle for survival of an immigrant women in Depression-era Paris, the press saw her in simple black and white terms. Yet Toureaux's life, or the parts of it that can be reconstructed over seventy years after her death, refuses to fit neatly into the context of a morality tale. For L'Oeuvre and many other papers, Yolande was a Jezebel, pure and simple. Time and again, she was judged in the press by the standards of a class and a gender that were not her own. If Toureaux had been a man, would her tale have been different? Quite probably. Her sexual transgressions committed "in the line of duty" would more likely have been overlooked, and her daring lauded. The journalistic accounts of Toureaux's life and death, however, imprisoned her in her "otherness," clearly revealing a darkening climate of hostility toward women in the 1930s—a climate that became commonplace throughout Europe, especially in countries where the extreme right emerged victorious.[59]

Even so, Laetitia Toureaux should not be perceived simply as a victim. Although her life certainly was fodder for journalistic imagination, Toureaux also was an avid consumer of the French press's competing narratives of women. Even *Détective* magazine noted that Toureaux was not easy to decipher and possessed at least three personalities: the elegant and refined bourgeois widow, the secretive and seductive private investigator of the bals musette, and the good-natured and friendly factory worker.[60] With hindsight we can see that the many faces of Toureaux embodied the range of roles for women commonly found in the popular press. Above all, she was a skilled actress; in every facet of her life, she wore a mask corresponding to her conception of the stereotype of the widow, the spy, the factory worker. She was a woman who tried to live all the gender possibilities of her age except that of mother. Even today it remains difficult to ascertain with certainty the identity of the real Laetitia Toureaux. Nevertheless, perhaps Toureaux's greatest crime was not that she had loose morals and lurked in undesirable places, but rather that she read the narrative of the powerful women and acted on that narrative. In the end, the cultural logic of the "crime du Métro" stories tell us that Laetitia Toureaux was ultimately an interloper into a domain where women were allowed in 1930s Paris more often in fiction than in fact.

The Identities of Laetitia Toureaux

The interpretation of Toureaux's identity found in the press was in many ways a caricature, not least because it neglected the other important axes of the matrix of her life, class and, especially, ethnicity. In 1957, twenty years after her death, the newspaper *France-Soir* ran a retrospective on Toureaux entitled "The Perfect Assassination of Laetitia Toureaux," which was serialized in several editions and presented in comic-strip format. Toureaux was presented dancing in her beloved bals musette, reduced to a sexy pen-and-ink caricature of her former glamorous self.[61] It was not that journalists did not bring up class and ethnicity in their reporting, but that these facets of her identity increasingly were subsumed into what journalists perceived as the more important story, that of gender. Yet class and ethnicity, at least as much as gender, were at the heart of Toureaux's determined, even obsessive, battle to refashion her identity during the final decade of her life, even though gender was a tool she used to achieve her ambitions. As Robert Maier reminds us, "Identity should not be conceived as static, but as dynamic . . . no form of identity is ever complete nor is it totally stable."[62] Toureaux's identity was a conscious work-in-progress. So was Yolande's.

Nowhere is Toureaux's struggle at least to balance the very differing facets of her identity better exemplified than in the organizations that in some ways formed the two poles of her life in the year before she died: the Union Valdôtaine and the Ligue du Bien Publique. She joined the latter under the sponsorship of Rouffignac to spy on left-wing liberals. Both organizations had in common a membership that was held to comprise the most respectable representatives of their social group. The evening of her death, Toureaux was on her way to a banquet sponsored by the Union Valdôtaine. On the lapel of her stylishly tailored jacket, she had pinned the medal of the Ligue. In the 1930s, membership in the socialist Ligue was associated with humanitarian causes and was a sign of acceptance in more respectable, if left-leaning, social circles.[63]

Toureaux thus seemed on the cusp of the social ascension she so ardently desired, even while maintaining her fidelity to her Valdôtain friends and family. But even this seeming triumph proved to be an illusion, one of the many layers of calculated deception and conniving that marked Toureaux's life, for her entry into the Ligue was merely a ruse by Rouffignac concocted to afford her better access to the social circles of prominent people whom she had been hired to seduce and pump for information.

Despite her aspirations to circulate among the Parisian upper classes, Toureaux's personal history was most useful to her police employers because of the access she afforded to the streets of Paris, and the Italian communities, right-wing street thugs, petty criminals, and prostitutes that helped to make the otherness of that world intelligible to them. For representatives of the press and the police alike, Toureaux was a cultural broker between them and people who would be more inclined to confide in her than in reporters or policemen. Evidence from her life shows that even as she aspired and worked tirelessly to achieve a respectable bourgeois French identity, she could fulfill this dream only by utilizing her experience and contacts acquired in the ethnically Italian and working-class environment she sought to flee. The very aspects of her life that she most desired to shed actually made her of greatest interest to the people who she hoped would assist in her quest for a new identity.

Sociologists, anthropologists, literary theorists, and historians who wrestle with the question of identity have in recent years begun to move away from the postmodern disparagement of the concept of identity as anything more than a linguistic construction. These scholars accept the idea that social constraints play a fundamental role in setting the parameters of identity, that identity is always dynamic, contingent, and negotiated, and that identity is as a result often much weaker than the strong, autonomous identity advocated by social theorists prior to 1950. Still, they have also come to reject the idea that individuals possess no fixed identity and little or no agency in constructing or negotiating that identity.[64] As linguist Miguel A. Cabrera, among others, has pointed out, "Identities are not states but positions . . . differential and relational entities" that "do not make up a homogenous whole, but a plural and fractured one."[65] Toureaux exercised agency during her life in many ways—she was a woman constantly on the make, working multiple jobs and attempting to craft multiple identities for herself. But nowhere was her strong will to exercise agency in her own life more apparent than in her internal struggle to find a way, any way, to become French and to enter the middle class, and thus to mold a new interior identity for herself, exemplified in her preferred name, Yolande.

Toureaux achieved remarkable success in creating multiple social identities for herself, but she never really extricated herself from the web of categorizations in which she was enmeshed. This was due in part to her ambivalence. Her social-climbing ambitions clashed with the roots she clearly cherished in her ethnic community in Paris, both because her circle of family and friends was also embedded in that social milieu and because upward mobility for someone of her background and gender was difficult to achieve. It is questionable whether she would have been able to have created a completely new social identity for herself, given the centrality of class and ethnicity in constructing identity in 1930s Paris, but it is likely that the price of success—abandonment of family and friends, perhaps even of her beloved bals musette—would have been too high for her. As it was, she seemed most content to operate in the interstices of multiple social structures and networks. It may well have been that role-playing and the ability to adopt different personas depending on her audience and situation became a goal unto itself for Toureaux.

Robert Charles, who employed Toureaux at the bal musette Le Viking in 1934, summed up her life, "This woman gave me the impression of being a scheming intriguer determined to climb out of her condition by any means possible."[66] The "condition" to which Charles referred had to do with Toureaux's status as a working-class Italian immigrant. But Toureaux could never really succeed in her quest to negotiate a new identity for herself that separated her from her past because identities subsist within communities that also have identities, which are continually shored up in part through exercising control over membership. Sociologist Riva Kastoryano has argued, "Identities are not commodities and are therefore difficult to negotiate. Abstract, fluid, and changeable, they reflect and reveal the profound emotions of individuals, peoples and nations. They are redefined and affirmed in action and interaction and change with the cultural, social, and political environment."[67] While the "evolving and multifaceted" personal identity and the "alternative self" that results from negotiating identities "is sensitive to its own situatedness," Linda Maria Brooks contends, "it is still chiefly characterized by a personal responsibility . . . that stands accountable for its actions."[68] But that agency is limited because, as Robert Maier states, "The individual as social actor can redefine him/herself, but this identification will always take place within categorisations imposed by various more or less powerful other actors and the group and the community to which the individual belongs. Sometimes, categorisations will be dominant but there will also be cases in which individuals are able to extricate themselves almost completely from the web of categorisations they are caught in."[69]

One irony of Laetitia Toureaux's life was that the aspect of it that became the focus of the police and press investigations after her death, her gender, was for Toureaux not the greatest challenge in her own quest for a new identity and lifestyle. If anything, this resourceful woman found ways to turn her gender and sexuality into positive advantages. Gender did not hinder her from leading an extremely independent life very much on her own terms, even if society at large disapproved of her lifestyle. Rather, Toureaux's ethnicity and class were the barriers she perceived to achieving the upward social mobility that seems to have been her ultimate goal. But she also had a yen for intrigue and adventure that drove her in more dangerous directions, including straight into the arms of a group of men also struggling over questions of identity. For these men, however, it was the identity of France that was at stake. It is to their exploits that we now turn.

PART II

THE CAGOULE

4

PROVOCATIONS AND
ASSASSINATIONS IN 1937

By July 16, 1937, the Parisian police had been investigating Laetitia Toureaux's murder for exactly two months. So far, they had made little headway.
The murder weapon, a generic Laguiole knife, still could not be traced to its
owner. No witnesses had come forward who could identify the murderer
and, despite the efforts to tie the crime to Toureaux's unorthodox lifestyle,
so far none of the usual underworld characters who haunted the same bals
musette and cafés as she had emerged as a likely suspect. Rouffignac continued to maintain that her death was unrelated to her work for him, and
the police were making no headway in tracking down either the mysterious
"I. CH." from the postcard found in her apartment or whoever had employed
her to perform surveillance in the 18th arrondissement. Her friends, family,
and coworkers professed nothing but love and admiration for the attractive,
charming widow, while the family of her deceased husband claimed to have
had no contact with her after his funeral. In sum, the hunt seemed rapidly
to be coming to a dead end.[1]

That day, however, the Parisian left-wing newspaper *La Liberté* suggested a new angle, linking Toureaux's death to other assassinations that
also took place during the first six months of 1937. It was not the first time
that the popular press had tried to forge links between her murder and
other sensational unsolved crimes, but so far the authorities had ignored
them. The Parisian police were well aware that journalists often ferreted out
sources unavailable to representatives of the law, and thus they were assidu-
ous readers of the press. The police also were quite skeptical, with good reason, of the more far-fetched theories about and reconstructions of crimes,
based as often on gossip as on reliable information, that found their way
onto the pages of popular newspapers. Still, sometimes the bottom-feeding
journalists sucked up some gold along with the dross. On July 16, the inspector general of the criminal police evidently had read *La Liberté* over his
morning coffee. Thinking there might be some truth in its story on the murders, he asked his subordinate, Police Commissioner Jean Belin, chief of the

première section responsible for investigating ordinary crimes, to comment on it. Belin produced a report the next day in which he assessed the pros and cons of the newspaper's theory. He doubted that there was much to it. But whether through good luck, good intuition, or good sources, *La Liberté* was eventually proved to have been correct.[2]

The year 1937 was a busy one for the French police. The Clichy riots that took place on March 16 resulted from the clash of right and left and seriously undermined Léon Blum's government in the process, but an analysis of the crowd dynamic led police to believe that unidentified *agents provocateurs* had worked the demonstration and incited the riot. A series of strange, unsolved murders took place, including separate assassinations of well-known émigrés living in France, Dmitri Navachine and Carlo and Nello Rosselli. There were a number of bombings and attempted bombings, one causing two deaths. In addition, incendiary bombs and sabotage were used to destroy two American planes and disable two others, which the French government had secretly commissioned to donate to the Republican cause in Spain. There were many attacks that particularly affected southern France, including multiple attempts to disable rail lines around Perpignan in order to interrupt the secret government campaign to transport volunteer fighters and military supplies to the Spanish Republicans. On September 18, an attempt was even made to hijack and disable two Spanish Republican submarines that had taken refuge in Brest. Both the Spanish Nationalists and the Italians maintained dense networks of agents in France, and Spanish and Italian undercover agents were likely responsible for many of these attacks. But members of the French extreme right took part in them as well and were active in channeling vital intelligence to the foreign operatives to facilitate their task.[3] The year began, however, with a brutal murder in a Parisian park.

Around 10:30 in the morning on January 25, Russian economist and financier Dimitri Navachine was stabbed to death in an empty avenue of the Bois de Boulogne. Six months later, on June 9, two Italian émigré brothers, Carlo and Nello Rosselli, were murdered in the late afternoon on the side of a lonely country road outside of the Normandy spa town of Bagnolles-de-l'Orne. In both cases, there was only one witness, and neither witness was able to shed much light on the crime. Because Navachine and Carlo Rosselli were both expatriates of countries with turbulent politics, the French police initially focused their search for the responsible parties among the Russian and Italian communities in France, a method that profascist publications in France and Italy alike loudly advanced. Although few people among the general public or the antifascists were fooled, since everyone knew who the Rosselli and Navachine were and that their political activities had created enemies both in Italy and France, the police at first adopted the line that the victims had died as a result of political disagreements with their fellow émigrés or with their home governments.

Despite the immense resources that France was pouring into the Maginot line and rearmament during the 1930s in response to the obvious and growing threat of war in Europe, French leaders and ordinary citizens alike perceived France to be politically and militarily incapable of taking on Germany unaided. This perception reflected the lingering wounds that the depredations of World War I had caused the French psyche, as well as real flaws in French military and political structures. Still, the resulting French weakness in the face of German aggression strongly affected the course of French diplomacy during this decade. In particular, it helps to explain the French willingness to go along with Britain's insistence on nonintervention in Spain. This sense of vulnerability also suggests why France was extremely reluctant in 1936 and 1937 to antagonize Mussolini, in whom the French hoped they could find an ally against Hitler.[4] No one wanted to risk offending the Italian authorities by prying too deeply into the activities of Italian agents in France, although the reluctance of the authorities to implicate Mussolini's government in the Rosselli slayings persuaded few in Paris who followed the case. In contrast to the more cautious stance of the French police, some publications, such as the previously mentioned *La Liberté*, promoted the theory that the same group was responsible for both sets of murders, and that these murders were related to Toureaux's homicide as well.[5] Commissioner Belin was not ready to admit such a possibility, for which there seemed precious little evidence outside of the fact that each victim had been stabbed, and each also had clearly been caught in a meticulously planned ambush. In the absence of other evidence, these similarities in modus operandi could easily be ascribed to coincidence, especially as nothing else seemed to link them—yet.[6]

The Navachine and Rosselli murders shocked French public opinion at least as much as that of Laetitia Toureaux, because unlike Toureaux, Dimitri Navachine and Carlo and Nello Rosselli were no ordinary, working-class immigrants. Rather, they were high-profile émigrés, who, for different reasons, were familiar not only to the French Foreign Ministry at the Quai d'Orsay but also to French intelligence agencies. They were in different ways well-known opponents of fascism, and it was in fact because of their prominence, their outspoken and controversial political opinions, and their willingness to act upon those opinions, that they were targeted for assassination. The Rosselli brothers were in the vanguard of Italian antifascists in exile in France, and they were highly popular among France's Italian immigrant population. Between one and two hundred thousand people attended their funeral in Paris. Moreover, the attacks were carried out brazenly in broad daylight in a public place. In these murders, like that of Laetitia Toureaux, the killer was willing to incur significant risk in order to bring down a victim whom he had carefully stalked beforehand.

Navachine

Dimitri Navachine (also spelled Navatchine and Navashine) was born in Moscow on August 30, 1889, of a Jewish mother whose family was from Kiev and a Russian father who was a professor of botany.[7] Navachine was a trained economist, and under Russia's 1917 provisional government of Alexander Kerensky he agreed to accept the vice-presidency of the Russian Red Cross, which was overseeing the Russian prisoners of the Germans during World War I. Despite being an active Freemason and a supporter of the moderate socialist Kerensky, Navachine managed to stay in good standing with the new Bolshevik government under Lenin when it came to power in the fall of 1917, perhaps because the Bolsheviks valued his brilliance as an economist and the contacts in the West he had nurtured during his tenure with the Red Cross. The Soviet government employed Navachine on at least two important missions in the 1920s. In 1921 it sent him as its envoy to Spain, where he succeeded in persuading the Spanish government to turn over its petroleum monopoly to Russia rather than to the Royal Dutch or Standard Oil companies. In 1927, Navachine was sent to Paris to assume the directorship of the Banque Commerciale pour l'Europe du Nord (Commercial Bank of Northern Europe), which was officially in charge of the Soviet Union's financial affairs in France. Navachine left the Banque Commerciale in 1929 and thereafter worked either for or with a group of right-wing bankers connected to the Banque Worms.[8]

Navachine remained in Paris after Stalin's rise to power in 1928. Well respected in France as an economist, he published a two-volume study of the economic crisis in 1932. Another leftist economist in France, Anatole de Monzie, wrote the preface.[9] Navachine became an important advisor to the

French Popular Front in 1936. He was especially close to Charles Spinasse, Léon Blum's economic minister, to whom he offered advice on how to fight the effects of the worldwide depression in France. Given that he counseled Spinasse, among other things, to break the power of the industrial cartels that controlled the provisioning of Paris, it was obvious to the police that his consultant work for the government had won him few friends in French corporate circles.[10]

There was also an extensive ring of Soviet spies and their French supporters in France to consider. The French police kept track of Russian émigrés in France and as a rule welcomed them, or at least those (the majority) they labeled as White Russians and viewed as higher class, better able to assimilate in French culture and, as opponents of communism, likely to be a force for law and order.[11] Nonetheless, some émigrés were kept under close surveillance. This included Navachine, who the police were convinced was a Soviet agent, since in 1922 he had enrolled in the Tcheka (the predecessor to the KGB). Ostensibly, Navachine's situation in France in the 1930s resembled that of many other moderate Russian expatriates. By no means a White Russian—although he did have some contacts in that milieu—Navachine had been able to accommodate himself to Lenin but fell out of favor with Stalin.

Navachine claimed to have broken with the Soviet government by 1929, when he ceased to direct the Banque Commerciale pour l'Europe du Nord. Thus it seemed plausible to the police that Stalin had dispatched an assassin abroad to eliminate him. Yet right-wing journalists—and some historians, following their lead—insisted that Navachine had never really fallen out with Moscow and was actually a Soviet spy. Navachine was in Moscow in 1934, at the beginning of Stalin's purge of Trotskyites, and at the time vowed that he was still loyal to Stalin's government, despite his earlier assertions to the contrary. This may have been merely an effort to stave off an unwelcome visit from Stalin's agents in Paris, however, as by 1936 Navachine's mentor, Iouri Piatokov, who had been a close friend of Trotsky, was under arrest. Navachine received a summons to return to Moscow, which he refused. His friends warned him to beware of ending up like Alexander Koutiepov, another prominent Russian in Paris, who, upon his refusal to return to Moscow, was kidnapped by Soviet agents and brought home by force.[12] Although some of Navachine's fellow Russians refused to believe that he had really burned his bridges to Moscow, French police could find no evidence that he continued to engage in espionage in the 1930s.[13] Moreover, the police noted that by 1937 he had attracted the open hostility of a known Russian agent in France named Bogovoud. The police interrogated Bogovoud, who had a solid alibi for Navachine's murder. It was clear to the police that both communist and anticommunist Russians had motives to want Navachine dead. But they could find no evidence from either the crime scene or their informants leading them to a Russian perpetrator.

Meanwhile, Navachine also had generated enemies in France. In the 1930s, he accepted a great deal of consulting work with powerful multinational firms, such as the American Matford automobile company. He attended conferences and wrote books on the Depression, in the process becoming an increasingly prominent figure in French political circles, especially among the socialists. Considered a mathematical genius by many, he offered advice on credit manipulation, state financial planning, and the recycling of old debts. His brand of socialism, however, was closer to that of the Popular Front than that of Stalin. In France, Navachine helped to organize a circle of like-minded moderate industrialists, intellectuals, and politicians who were dedicated to exploring ways in which France could escape from the worldwide economic crisis. The group, known as "X-Crise," became the bête-noire of left-wing conspiracy theorists in the 1930s and 1940s, such as Marcel Déat, editor of the newspaper *L'Oeuvre*.[14] Déat and his followers insisted that X-Crise was merely a front for the much more sinister Synarchie or Mouvement Synarchique d'Empire, a sort of clandestine organization they were convinced sought to dominate France through a secret corporate technocracy that would eventually overthrow the republic. This conspiracy theory, like those associated with Jews and *The Protocols of the Elders of Zion*, derived from forged documents and overwrought imaginations. Those who fought the Synarchie in France evinced a profound fear of rapid and morally disruptive modernization and the all-encompassing, dehumanizing capitalist society they believed resulted from it.[15] Collaborating with X-Crise brought Navachine into contact with the group's founder, Jean Coutrot, and other controversial figures associated with right-wing politics and the Banque Worms, such as future Vichy collaborators Gabriel Leroy-Ladurie, Pierre Pucheu, and Hippolyte Worms.[16] Navachine moved in multiple but often opposing political circles, and thus there were probably many people from a variety of hostile camps with cause to want him eliminated.

Navachine's activities as a Freemason aroused as much suspicion in French rightist and anti-Semitic circles as his Soviet nationality, Jewish heritage, and socialist politics. *The Protocols of the Elders of Zion*, the infamous forgery distributed in many editions throughout Europe during the first four decades of the twentieth century, purported to contain the proceedings of a session of Jewish elders, who were plotting, in league with Masonic lodges, to seize control of the world.[17] This scurrilous work, whose author has never been conclusively identified, was so popular in France that *Franc-maçon juive* became a popular epithet for one's enemies not long after the period of the infamous Dreyfus affair, which had deeply divided turn-of-the-century France.[18] For many Frenchmen in the 1930s, the unholy alliance between Jews and Freemasons for world domination remained an article of faith, as it was for the Nazis as well.[19] The police thoroughly investigated this angle, and although they concluded that Navachine's economic activities in Spain and France, combined with his opposition to the capitalist "trusts" and his participation in Freemasonry, probably generated the motive for his murder, they could find no solid evidence which could shed light on his death.[20]

Thus in January 1937, Navachine was an influential man with enemies from his homeland, but no more or fewer than many other Russian exiles in France. Seemingly unconcerned about a possible attempt on his life, he kept a busy schedule of seminars, consultations, and publishing. A middle-aged, professorial fellow of regular habits who lived a respectable upper-class lifestyle in a fashionable neighborhood near the Bois de Boulogne, his high public profile meant that he was a difficult target for assassination despite the many political enemies he had accrued. Given that in the 1930s Paris was home to at least twenty thousand Russian exiles, many of them actively plotting to overthrow the Soviet government, the city seemed to be crawling with easier prey.[21]

Yet around 10:30 on the morning of January 25, 1937, the police found Navachine sprawled on a path in the Bois de Boulogne, his fox terrier lying beside him, both of them dead. Navachine had gone to the park that morning, as was his habit every day, to walk the dog. Evidently he had been followed this time, and the police surmised correctly that his killer was familiar with his routine. According to the sole witness, a M. Théophile Leveuf, a blond man had approached Navachine, seemingly engaged him in conversation for a moment, and then attacked him. Leveuf, who was passing through the park on a shortcut to catch his bus, was a good hundred meters (about three hundred feet) away from the fracas, and at that distance it appeared that the two men were merely fist fighting. Leveuf therefore did not rush to intervene. In fact, Navachine's attacker had hidden a weapon up his sleeve, probably strapped to his arm, and what seemed to Leveuf to be punches were in fact stabs with that weapon, which later proved to have been a sawed-off French army bayonet. As Navachine fell to the ground, gravely wounded, his small dog loyally attacked his master's assailant. Although neither Leveuf nor any of the residents in the vicinity of the park heard shots, the assassin yanked a revolver out of his coat and killed the dog. Meanwhile, Navachine struggled to pull himself to his feet. Before he could do so, his attacker leapt upon him and stabbed him again, this time fatally. According to the witness, the entire crime took only a few moments.[22]

When the police got to the crime scene, they found empty cartridges around Navachine's body, which at first confused them. The investigating officers assumed that Navachine had been carrying a gun when he was attacked, which he had discharged defending himself, and that the killer had taken it when he fled. Once the absence of corroborating physical evidence (such as powder burns on Navachine's hands or clothing) had disproved that theory, it became evident that the killer had been armed with both some sort of dagger and a gun fitted with a silencer. This only deepened the mystery, however. It seemed quite odd that, rather than simply shooting Navachine as he did the dog, the murderer went to the considerably greater effort and risk of stabbing his victim to death. Only later did the police learn that the method of the murder, and the special weapon used in it—the sawed-off bayonet, which left a distinctive triangular wound—were employed deliberately as the assassin's unique calling card.[23] Both the stab wounds and the empty cartridges, which the police identified as hailing from a lot of Imperial Chemical I bullets, subsequently played a central role in linking Navachine's murder with those of the Rosselli brothers.[24]

Navachine's death was carefully plotted and executed. Witnesses stated that an attractive young woman later identified as Jacqueline Derville tailed him for weeks before the murder to study the intended victim's habits and choose the best time to find him alone and in the open. Jacqueline and her brothers—Joseph, a journalist at the French newspaper *Paris-Soir*, Ignace, a soldier, and Jean-Baptiste—as well as their friend Jean Bouvyer, a callow young man given to exaggerating his rather meager record of violent crimes, were followers of the more ruthless Jean Filliol. Filliol was an experienced political agitator, familiar to the police for his physical strength and agility, which had helped him to slip the noose of more than one police dragnet. Too much of a wild card for any of the more mainstream right-wing organizations, Filliol was in 1937 a former section leader of the Camelots du Roi, the youth wing of the Action Française. It was Filliol who planned and executed Navachine's assassination, with the assistance of the Dervilles and Bouvyer, who provided reconnaissance and drove the getaway car.[25] The police soon learned that Filliol was also behind another political assassination, the murder of the Rosselli brothers, although a mostly different cast of characters took the supporting roles.

The Rosselli

From the beginning the police knew that Nello Rosselli died on June 9, 1937, simply because he had the misfortune to be visiting his more famous and volatile older brother Carlo that day. Carlo Rosselli's death, in contrast, came as a surprise to the police only in its manner and timing; they, and he, had long known that his antifascist activities were likely to end in his martyrdom.[26] The French police and Italian agents both kept a close watch on Italian refugees from fascism in France, and Carlo Rosselli was among the most active and high-profile of Mussolini's opponents operating in France.[27] Carlo was born in Rome on November 6, 1899, to a wealthy and prominent family of Italian Jews. He and Nello were raised in an atmosphere of bourgeois comfort, intellectual ferment, and Italian patriotism. Their mother, Amelia Pincherle, was a well-known author and ardent Italian nationalist who separated from their musicologist father, Guiseppe Rosselli, when Carlo was two years old. Amelia raised Carlo, Nello, and Aldo, their older brother who died during World War I, mostly on her own. The influence of her courage and love for Italy, as well as her rather secular Jewish identity, were dominant in the boys' lives. Like his older brother, Carlo fought in World War I. Although he obtained degrees in political economy and jurisprudence, authored numerous books and articles, and taught at Bocconi University in Milan, Carlo was first and foremost a man of action, in spite of his poor constitution and lifelong battle with phlebitis. He was drawn to socialism, although he preferred the moderate, reformist variety, and sought throughout his life to reconcile it with liberal republicanism—a stance that frequently put him at odds with mainstream socialist and communist followers of Marx, who eschewed any truce with bourgeois values. What truly forced Carlo out of the halls of academe and into political activism, however, was the rise of fascism in the early 1920s. Nello was more scholarly than Carlo; he studied history and taught at the University of Florence. Even so, he found the courage to take part in his brother's antifascist activities and, like Carlo, ultimately died as a result.[28]

By November 1926, Mussolini had cemented his grip on power in Italy. The Exceptional Decrees forbade all antifascist activities and organizations, declared all political parties except for the Partito Nationale Fascista (National Fascist Party) dissolved, nullified the seats in the Chamber of Deputies of the 120 antifascist deputies, and created a special Tribunal for the Defense of the State, which promptly sentenced to extended prison terms dangerous antifascists, such as the communist economist Antonio Gramsci. At the same time, Mussolini's Blackshirts began a veritable reign of terror throughout Italy. In December, Carlo helped smuggle his elderly friend Filippo Turati, a founder of Italian socialism, to safety in France. Rather than remain out of harm's way in exile with Turati, however, Rosselli insisted on returning to Italy to continue the fight against fascism there. He was promptly arrested as soon as he set foot on Italian soil and was sent into internal exile, first on the island of Ustica and then on the penal island of Lipari, which was populated almost entirely with political prisoners. Escape from Lipari was extremely difficult, but Carlo succeeded in July 1929. With the help of a fellow prisoner who had been released and had fled to France, Rosselli managed to purchase a motorboat from an Egyptian prince in Tunisia and to engage a pilot, a former World War I war hero. Because it was too dangerous for the boat to approach the shore, Rosselli and his fellow escapees, Emilio Lussu and Francesco Nitti, had to swim several hundred yards in the dark to complete their escape. After two failed attempts, in which the prisoners first almost drowned and then were nearly caught out after curfew by guards patrolling the beach, they at last succeeded on July 27. The ship captain who piloted them to safety was the same man they had engaged to rescue Turati. They fled first to Cape Bon in Tunisia, where their antifascist associates awaited them, on to Corsica, and finally to Marseilles. Once in France, they made their way to Paris.[29]

By November of that same year, 1929, Carlo had founded the "largest and most influential non-Marxist movement" in opposition to fascism, Giustizia e Libertà.[30] In the organization's newspaper, also called *Giustizia e Libertà*, he continued the struggle against fascism by publishing not only theoretical articles and propaganda, but also actual classified state documents quite damaging to Mussolini that antifascist agents managed to smuggle out of Italy. Much of the funds for both the movement and the newspaper came from Carlo's private inheritance. Whenever possible, he found ways secretly to distribute the journal in Italy, often with Nello's help, so as to carry on the fight there as well by giving ordinary Italians an alternative to the fascist-controlled Italian newspapers. He regularly recruited and funded flights over Italy to drop antifascist leaflets. The Italian regime viewed him as particularly dangerous, precisely because he was extremely articulate in his ability to communicate his ideas and daring in the lengths he was willing to go to get them aired throughout Europe, including in Italy. In Barcelona, on November 7, 1936, Carlo Rosselli gave a incendiary speech on Radio Barcelona that was beamed into Italy. This especially significant speech came after a defeat of Mussolini's forces, who were fighting in the Spanish Civil War on the side of Franco's Nationalists, at the hands of a pro-Republican force in which the Italian Ascaso column Rosselli had organized fought. In the speech, Rosselli sought to capitalize on the victory to show that Italian antifascists could be effective on the battlefield, thus encouraging Italians openly to oppose Mussolini. He declared that the victories of the Italian antifascists in Spain were the first stage of an uprising that ultimately would also liberate Italy from the fascist grip. The speech was broadcast in Italy as well as in France, and no doubt spurred Mussolini's government to take action to eliminate him.[31]

Despite his fragile health, Carlo did not limit his antifascist activities in exile to writing. His speech was aired in Barcelona in 1936 because he was there fighting the fascists. His passionate support for the Republican cause in Spain stemmed from his belief that victory there would galvanize antifascists of all stripes across Europe to unite to overthrow both Mussolini and Hitler. He recognized the grave danger the latter posed to European socialism well before most other European intellectuals. Rosselli backed up with action his exhortations to his fellow Italians to support the Spanish Republic while opposing fascism in Italy.

In July 1936, the Spanish Civil War was launched with an attempted coup. The Nationalists—composed of the army, which was based in Morocco, and the conservative factions in Spain who supported it—under the leadership of Generals José Sanjurjo and Francisco Franco attempted to overthrow the democratically elected Republican government, which was comprised of a coalition of socialists and democratic liberals. The Republicans were able to hold their own at first, mainly because the bulk of the Nationalist army was trapped in Morocco and the navy and air force remained loyal to the Republic and refused to transport the Nationalist soldiers to Spain. It did not take long, however, for the war to be internationalized into a struggle between right and left in Europe that was fought on Spanish soil.

In the international arena, Republican Spain found itself at a distinct disadvantage compared to the Nationalists. The Depression and the lingering cultural shock of World War I fostered a strong public sentiment in favor of appeasement among the Spanish Republicans' natural allies, France and Great Britain. Public opinion thus tied the hands of those nations' leaders. The conservative Tories who controlled the British government, mistrustful of the Republicans' socialist politics, secretly hoped the Nationalists would win. Léon Blum, while personally favorable to the Republican cause, dared not act alone without British support, especially given the open aid that the Germans and Italians were giving to the Nationalists. French timidity and British diffidence resulted in farce, as neutrality became the official policy of the League of Nations. Ironically, neutrality was only binding on those states which still professed loyalty to the League—that is, nearly every nation who might be inclined to assist the Republicans. Thus neutrality became the death knell of Republican Spain. Hitler and Mussolini, neither of whom was inclined to respect either the League or neutrality, were quick to grasp the advantages of intervention on the Nationalist side. Soon both dictators were sending their ships to ferry the Nationalist army from Africa to Spain. They also sent planes and pilots, including those which bombed the Basque town of Guernica, as well as weapons and ground troops. Some historians have even argued that Hitler used the Spanish battlefield to test the military techniques that he later employed so successfully in Poland, Czechoslovakia, and France. Eventually, the Soviet Union stepped in on the side of the Republicans, which lost them the meaningless passive support of the Western governments but gained them effective military assistance from the Soviet army. Thus the struggle became in many ways a proxy war between the international forces of the extreme right and left, with moderate liberals in Spain forced into exile.[32]

Carlo Rosselli, like many other antifascists from Europe and the United States, was appalled at the inaction of the democratic governments which was allowing the tide of the war to turn in the Nationalists' favor. In keeping with his character, fulminating against the situation in the pages of *Giustizia e Libertà* was not enough. So in 1934 he formally chastised Pierre Laval, Minister of Foreign Affairs, and the French for collaborating with Mussolini, even while he worked with André Malraux to create an air squadron to help defend the Spanish Republic. Rosselli took the lead in recruiting Italians and other antifascists in France, encouraging them to turn their sentiments into action by following him to Spain to fight for the Republic. His task was difficult because many of the communists, in thrall to Moscow's leadership, were unwilling to take action until they received permission from Moscow. Hence the planes that he and Malraux managed to scare up kept the Nationalists from completely dominating the skies over Spain until the Soviets finally sent in airplanes in support of the Republicans. In August 1936, Rosselli went to Spain and joined the Ascaso column that he had helped create, comprised of Italians fighting on the Republican side. He even drove his own car so that he could put it to service in the war. Members of Giustizia et Libertà joined the column along with Rosselli. When Mario Angeloni, Rosselli's co-leader of the column, was killed, Rosselli assumed command until, slightly wounded in action, he was forced to return to Paris to recuperate, as well as to raise more recruits and funds for Spain. For Rosselli, the war in Spain was crucial to the struggle against fascism because it allowed antifascists a true battlefield upon which they could fight fascism in its own element and demonstrate that they were as capable of martial prowess and shedding blood for their beliefs as the fascists. He returned to Barcelona in November, where he remained until the end of the year, when further problems with his still unhealed wound and an attack of phlebitis obliged him to head back to Paris. Six months later, he went to the resort town Bagnoles-de-l'Orne in Normandy with his wife and brother to receive treatment at the spa there for his phlebitis.[33]

This proved to be his undoing, for Mussolini had taken out a contract on his life. The trap was carefully set. Carlo and his English wife Marion Cave arrived at Tessé-la-Madeleine, the village next to Bagnoles-de-l'Orne, on May 27, where they registered at the Hotel Cordier. They stayed for over a week before Nello joined them on June 6. The unusual speed and efficiency with which Nello, a known and barely tolerated antifascist, received his passport from Mussolini's officials—only three days—aroused the suspicion of his Italian friends, who urged him not to make the trip. But Nello dismissed his friends' misgivings and visited his brother and sister-in-law in France even though he regretted leaving his wife and children behind in Italy. For several days after Nello's arrival the brothers enjoyed the spa and the tranquil town before leaving the hotel on June 9 to take Carlo's wife to the train station. After waiting to see the departure of her train for Paris, where Marion was headed to help celebrate her and Carlo's son John's tenth birthday, the Rosselli brothers proceeded by car to the larger town of Alençon to do some shopping and sightseeing. They bought some gifts and enjoyed afternoon tea before heading back toward Bagnoles-de-l'Orne around 6:30 in the evening. When they got to the town of Couterne, as was his habit, Carlo turned his old black Ford off of the main route and onto a side road with less traffic.[34]

The assassins chose their moment and location well. Many rural French roads were built on former footpaths dating back to the Middle Ages. They were (and are) so worn down that these country byways disappear between high hedgerows and possess little or no shoulder. Around 7:00 P.M., Carlo Rosselli drove into such a narrow and confined stretch of road—although only a few hundred meters from a local chateau, the patch of road was relatively isolated. Suddenly, as if out of nowhere, a newer and larger car, a 402 Peugeot, carrying a driver and three passengers, rushed upon them from behind very fast, squeezed by them, and came to a halt in the middle of the road. Two men, the driver and a passenger, stepped out of the car and began to behave as if they were looking at a flat tire or a mechanical problem. Unable to advance or go around the other car because of the high hedgerows, Carlo and Nello stopped as well. Carlo remained behind the wheel, while Nello got out and approached the other car. Meanwhile, a third vehicle with two men and a woman inside drove up behind the Rossellis' Ford, blocking their escape. When Nello got close to the men from the other car, a man later identified as Jean Filliol yanked out a revolver and fired several shots. Nello fell face down in a shallow ditch on the side of the road, gravely wounded. Another man, later identified as Fernand Jakubiez, leapt upon him and finished him off with seventeen stabs from a knife, which the police later found at the scene. At that moment Filliol sprinted up to the Rossellis' car and shot Carlo, who died instantly. The assassins threw the bodies in the trunk of the Ford and drove both their own and the Rossellis' car a couple of kilometers further, to a place where the hedgerows gave way to a small forest. Here there was a deeper ditch just off the shoulder of the road, and woods on each side of it. They dumped the bodies in the trees, one on top of another like so many sacks of garbage, well out of sight of any passing motorists. Filliol searched their pockets and removed some papers he later sent on to Italy, but left their money and personal possessions. Although Filliol kept the dagger he had used, Jakubiez abandoned his, evidently in an effort to give the appearance that inept communist amateurs had committed the murders. After driving a few more kilometers, the killers abandoned the Rossellis' Ford, in which they planted a primitive time bomb (a Molotov cocktail with a long fuse) and escaped in their own vehicle. Fortunately for the police, it began to rain, and the fuse was extinguished before the bomb could explode, thus preserving the forensic evidence in the Ford. Meanwhile, the third car was on its way back to Paris.[35]

Two local farmers found the Rossellis' car. The evening of the murder, at about 8:00 P.M., they passed by just as the killers were leaving the Ford by the side of the road. At the time, they did not remark much on the abandonment of the older car. Given the frequency with which mechanical problems could plague cars in that era, it probably wasn't unusual to see parties leave their cars to go find a mechanic or a tow. But when the farmers passed by the same spot the next day and saw that the car was still there, with its headlights still on, they decided to investigate. They warily approached the vehicle and spotted an empty bullet casing and a bloody glove in the car. Alarmed, they noted the license plate number and alerted the police. The same day, a man from Couterne named Henri Jarry, out for a lonely walk in the woods near the Chateau de Couterne, stumbled across the bodies and a bloody knife.[36]

Because the bomb had failed to destroy the car, the police found plenty of clues with which to work, enabling them to reconstruct the basic elements of the crime. It was obvious immediately that robbery was not the motive, because when the police examined the corpses, they found expensive rings still on the men's fingers and twenty thousand francs in cash untouched in Carlo's coat pocket.[37] Moreover, witnesses interrogated in Bagnoles-de-l'Orne, especially at the Hotel Cordier and the restaurant where the Rosselli brothers had eaten lunch on the day of the murder, quickly volunteered that suspicious strangers in town had been covertly observing the brothers' habits for at least a week. One of these spies turned out to be a small-time criminal well-known to the police, Louis Huguet, also known as "Le Boxeur" because he was a former boxer. The Boxer was a big man with a face that bore the marks of the beatings he had taken in the ring, and witnesses immediately picked him out as suspicious. When the police later went to arrest him, however, he had already fled the country.[38] As yet, they had no evidence linking him to any political groups or to a larger conspiracy, although that would change as time went on. Subsequent investigation also revealed that the assassins had been keeping Carlo Rosselli under observation for some months while they planned the murders. In 1938, Marion Cave Rosselli recognized Jakubiez as a "traveling carpet salesman" who in the fall of 1936 had shown up at the Rosselli home in Paris, "asking suspicious questions about Carlo." And there had been at least one other assassination attempt on Carlo in the spring of 1936, although it failed when the would-be assassin, who claimed that an agent of the Italian consulate in Paris had recruited him, lost his nerve.[39]

There was only one other witness, a seventeen-year-old hairdresser from Bagnoles-de-l'Orne named Hélène Besneux, who in her official deposition of June 22, 1937, testified that she had seen the assassins' cars, one of them with blood on the dashboard, from about ten feet away as she passed by them on her bicycle on the way home from work. She was able to get a good look at the cars' occupants, although all she could tell the police was that they definitely were not locals. Although Besneux was not yet able to identify the killers, they were sufficiently spooked when they read the sensational reports quoting her in the newspapers that they sent her a threatening letter, postmarked at Casablanca on June 18:

> Mademoiselle,
>
> This farce has gone on long enough. If you were actually acting out of a sense of honor, everything would at least be better for you. But it is your vanity as a common woman that incites you to thrust yourself into the limelight, by one means or another. Appearing in the newspaper, maybe in the *Police-Magasine*, it's enviable, isn't it? But we beg you, and need to give you the order to end this comedy. You have already said too much and made a mess. By good luck, you have made yourself the auxiliary of the most miserable and inept police force in the world. But given time, you may very well do and say some stupid things. People are going to show you photos. Perhaps they will confront you [the writer seems to be referring to the possibility of a police line-up]. Once and for all: silence and forgetfulness, you understand, Mademoiselle, don't you? You will receive other letters from our friends. Their postmark will have nothing to do with their true location; of them, your sorry police will without doubt intercept a few, everything which is easy and lazy is their forte. Obey the orders which reach you. It is your tranquility, your happiness, and your life that are on the line. Life for us counts for nothing, especially the life of as vile a creature as you. You have been warned.[40]

The signature on the hastily written note was illegible.

When Mlle. Besneux received the threatening message, Police Commissioner Belin was still skeptical of the news report that the execution of the Rosselli, for execution it clearly was, had anything to do with the murders of Dimitri Navachine and Laetitia Toureaux. His subordinate, however, Superintendent Chenevier, who was already famous for his crime-solving instincts, was convinced that the same person or organization had committed all of the mysterious murders. The forensic evidence supported his theory. The police soon found that the triangular wounds that the dagger left in Nello Rosselli were identical to those found on Dimitri Navachine, and very similar in shape to those on Laetitia Toureaux. The bullet shells found at both the Rosselli and Navachine crime scenes were also identical. But in the absence of any obvious connections among the lives of the victims, or common enemies they might have shared, the police had no means of establishing a motive that could encompass all three murders. It was the literally explosive events of the autumn of 1937 that allowed the police to identify the culprits in all four murders as Jean Filliol, Robert Puireux, Jean-Marie Bouvyer, François Baillet, Fernand Jakubiez, Jacques Fauran, and Alice Lamy.

Toussus-le-Noble

The story of the Spanish Civil War (1936–1939), the policy of nonintervention that, with the exception of the Soviet Union, almost all of the allies of the Republicans observed, and the resulting paralysis of France and Britain in the face of Nazi and Fascist aggression has been told many times. While the Nazis and the Fascists bombarded Spain from the air and offered extensive support to Franco's Nationalists, taking a terrible toll on Spanish civilians in the process, Léon Blum's Popular Front government officially observed the nonintervention policy developed by Britain in August 1936. Many in the Popular Front government—including Blum personally, Pierre Cot, a former Radical deputy and Minister of the Air Force, and Yvon Delbos, Foreign Minister—deeply sympathized with the cause of the beleaguered Spanish Republicans. When the Nationalists initially rebelled against the Republican government, then in the hands of the Frente Popular or Spanish Popular Front, the first instinct of Blum and his cabinet was solidarity with the Republicans, who had modeled their movement after the French Popular Front. Thus on July 23 the French government agreed openly to honor the request of the Spanish government for aircraft. That decision raised such a storm of protest in the rightist press and among the Radicals in Blum's government that by July 25 the government had changed course, deciding not to deliver the planes after all. With Blum's approval, Pierre Cot, Minister of the Air Force, then spearheaded a clandestine effort to funnel arms, including the planes the Republicans desperately needed, into Spain via third countries. The Popular Front was feeble even in 1936. Half of the ministers were in fact members of the Radical Party and were often at odds with their Socialist partners, the French Right orchestrated a steady drumbeat of opposition, and the labor unions engaged in a series of massive strikes in 1936 that undermined the Popular Front and fed conservative hysteria about the Socialists. This political weakness hobbled the Socialists' ability to offer substantial aid to the Republicans. The fall of Blum's government in June 1937 effectively sealed the Republicans' fate. Even though the Socialists participated in the new government under Radical Camille Chautemps, Chautemps was less inclined to support violating the Non-Intervention Pact, even clandestinely, for fear losing British support.[41] Thus in August 1937, ten of the aircraft that Cot had scrounged for the Republicans still sat in a hangar in Toussus-le-Noble near Paris, awaiting transshipment to a third country from which they could quietly be sent on to Republican Spain.[42]

The planes themselves were of American make and belonged to the Société Française de Transports Aériens. They were housed in two hangars, one of which contained six aircraft that were refurbished and ready for shipment. The other hangar contained four planes that were still under repair and partially taken apart. It was these latter planes that were targeted for attack because they were less well guarded than those ready to fly. The members of the Garde Mobile, in charge of security for the planes, were more concerned with theft than sabotage and assumed that the dismantled planes would be safe. Surveillance of the hangars revealed that most of the time only the mechanics working on the disabled planes were present in the hangar, which apparently was left open night and day, unlike the other one.

Around August 22, officers at Toussus began to notice an unusually high level of interest in the unassuming aerodrome. This extra attention was particularly unwelcome given that France was in the process of trying to persuade Italy, Germany, and the Soviet Union to join the Non-Intervention Pact it had proposed to the League of Nations, and itself had already renounced any intervention in the Spanish Civil War. Given that Cot, with Blum's tacit approval, was secretly planning to circumvent the Non-Intervention policy that Blum was publicly championing, the officers running Toussus wanted to attract as little attention as possible. Instead, by night and day curious visitors trickled into the aerodrome, attempting to visit the hangars where the planes were stored.

Finally, on the afternoon of August 28 a young couple showed up at the office of the camp's senior officer. Dressed in a uniform and claiming to be a military captain, the man was visibly angry, and the woman on his arm was slightly disheveled. Claiming that she had been sexually assaulted, he demanded to search the camps, including the interior of the hangars, to ascertain whether any of the military personnel or mechanics was the man who committed the alleged assault. Not wanting to risk further angering a captain—apparently of a higher rank than he—the camp officer permitted the search. Naturally the search yielded no assailant, but only after the man and his wife had thoroughly inspected every inch of the camp and its contents. That night the hangar containing the four aircraft still under repair burst into flames. Despite the best efforts of the Garde Mobile, two planes were entirely destroyed and two others damaged beyond repair. The detectives working on the case could find no evidence except for the weapons themselves, two of which survived because they failed to explode. They consisted of cleverly fashioned home-made incendiary devices with timers, which closely resembled those that Italian secret service agents had used in an earlier bombing of a mountain tunnel.

Police informer and undercover agent Thomas Bourlier told the police that a secret society called the CSAR was responsible for the attack. He claimed to have attended a meeting in which a prominent CSAR leader named Jacques Corrèze had argued with another member about whether the attack at Toussus had been a success, given that the six refurbished planes had already left for Toulouse and arrived safely in Republican Spain by the night of the attack. Corrèze had boasted that the attack had indeed been a success because another CSAR sympathizer had succeeded in introducing grit into the engines of the two planes salvaged from the fire that would have rendered them useless to their recipients. When the detectives showed photos of several known members of the CSAR to the camp's chief officer and his men, he and they recognized several of them. Jakubiez, Corrèze, and André Hallumié had been among the camp's curious visitors prior to August 28, and Jean Filliol was the irascible captain who had arrived at the camp on August 27 with his offended wife (no doubt Filliol's longtime girlfriend Alice Lamy) on his arm. Further investigation after World War II revealed that in February 1937, Colonel Ungría de Jiménez, chief of Franco's Special Services, had signaled to CSAR leaders the arrival of the planes in France and requested that they destroy the aircraft in return for assistance from the Nationalists.

The leadership of the CSAR or Cagoule, like much of the French right, shared as deep an antipathy toward Spain's Popular Front as they did toward that of France. They were quite willing to use any means necessary to aid Franco's cause and inhibit their own government from using French resources to support the Spanish Republicans.[43] It did not hurt that attacks such as that at Toussus-le-Noble furthered the Cagoule's domestic aims, not only by weakening the center-left governing coalition but also by sowing fear and discord in France. Indeed, part of the Cagoule's aim in committing their provocations in 1937, it was later determined, was to incite an increased sense of insecurity about future civil war. Certainly by August 1937, many police investigators were beginning to put the pieces together about a suspected right-wing terrorist organization. Some even hypothesized a connection between the other sensational murders of that year and the murder of Laetitia Toureaux. But what their investigations revealed about the Cagoule turned out to be more shocking and chilling than they could have imagined.

The beautiful, enigmatic Laetitia "Yolande" Toureaux
Photograph by Dazy. RA/Lebrecht Music & Arts

Georges Rouffignac, head of the detective agency that employed
Toureaux, and Police Commissioner Badin. Rouffignac is pictured
without his usual moustache.

Reproduced from *Paris-Soir,* May 24, 1937

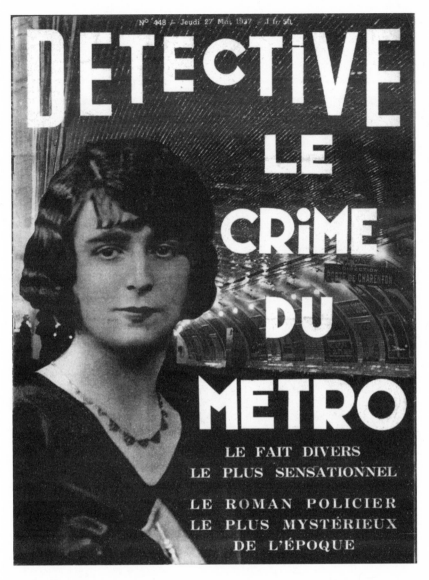

Cover of *Détective* magazine after Toureaux's murder

A typical evening at a bal musette, 1925
Copyright Albert Harlingue/Roger-Viollet/The Image Works

Bombing of building on the rue de Presbourg in Paris, headquarters of the
Confédération Général du Patronat Français, September 11, 1937

Copyright LAPI/Roger-Viollet/The Image Works

Commissaire Badin investigating Cagoule bombing of the home
of Marx Dormoy, 1941

Cover of *Détective* magazine showing Pierre-René Locuty,
the bomber in the L'Étoile attacks

Courtesy Bibliothèque Nationale de France/ACRPP

Eugène Deloncle, head of the Cagoule

Jean Filliol, chief assassin for the Cagoule

François Méténier, one of the Cagoule's
top liaisons with Mussolini

Laetitia Toureaux's Cagoulard lover, Gabriel Jeantet
Courtesy Pierre Jeantet

5

ENTER THE CAGOULE

TERRORISTS OF THE EXTREME RIGHT

On September 10, 1937, a chemical engineer at the Michelin Company in Clermont-Ferrand received a phone call that prompted him to take a night train to Paris. The young man, Pierre-René Locuty, headed to the French capital to participate in a grand conspiracy designed to weaken the Third Republic and convince the French nation of an imminent communist threat. Locuty, who espoused an extreme hatred of communism and belonged to a provincial right-wing political organization, later claimed that he had had little idea of what awaited him in Paris but assumed he would be reporting to right-wing leaders about communist activity in his home region. On his arrival at the Gare de Lyon station on the morning of September 11, agents of the Cagoule met Locuty and immediately took him into their charge.[1]

Locuty spent the day with two of the Cagoule's most notorious members, François Méténier, one of the organization's top liaisons with Mussolini in Italy, and Jean Filliol, the group's chief assassin. After meeting Méténier at the Café de la Paix, Locuty dined with him and his mistress at a nearby restaurant. Next, he was taken to a secret arms depot on the rue Ampère, where another Cagoule chief, Jean Moreau de la Meuse, ordered him to assemble two bombs, each containing six kilos of explosives. At six o'clock that evening, Locuty took a taxi to the 16th arrondissement in Paris and left a bomb-filled suitcase at 4 rue de Presbourg, while another man named Léon Macon deposited a similar valise nearby at 45 rue Boissière. Locuty was safely back on a train headed for Clermont-Ferrand when the bombs exploded at 10 o'clock that evening. The bombs destroyed the headquarters of two major business associations, La Confédération Général du Patronat Français and Le Groupe des Industries Métallurgiques et Mécaniques, and killed two police officers in the process.[2] Cagoule chiefs promptly gathered at the home of Méténier on the rue Georges-Ville to monitor the ensuing police and rescue-worker activity.[3]

The explosions sent France into a panic, exactly as the Cagoule had planned. Left-wing papers pointed their fingers at external powers, such as

Germany, Italy, or Spain, who they accused of trying to destabilize France; right-wing papers pointed to the communists, who, they claimed, were planning an insurrection at the behest of the Comintern, the international Communist organization based in Moscow. On September 13, *Le Temps* trumpeted, "The truth is that the origin of the affair lies with the Marxists and Syndicalists, who are against the established order of society."[4] A right-wing paper, *La Liberté*, echoed this theme a day later, saying, "With certainty, we can affirm that the bombings are the consequence of the violent climate created by the communists."[5] In the press, the bombs that Locuty and Macon detonated came to be known as "the Étoile attacks" ("les attentats de l'Étoile") and "the affair of the terrorist attacks" ("l'affaire des attentats terroriste"). The immediate result of these attacks was an increased sense of insecurity and fears about an imminent communist putsch and a civil war to come.[6] Indeed, the bombs at l'Étoile were apparently set because the head of the Cagoule, Eugène Deloncle, grew tired of waiting for what he believed was the inevitable communist uprising that would bring his pro-right organization into the limelight. He therefore decided to create the impression that a communist takeover was in the offing by placing bombs in locations that would cause much of the public logically to connect the explosions with left-wing violence. Deloncle later called the bombings a "warning shot across the bow" ("un coup de semonce").[7] This was not mindless violence, but rather purposeful action meant to focus public discourse on the fate of the Third Republic.

Immediately after the L'Étoile attacks, various branches of the French police, including the Sûreté, set about investigating the crime. The police already had a good idea of the culprits behind the bombings. On December 1, 1936, the Action Française had given the police a document alerting them to a secret organization that was in the process of being formed to combat communism. Although written in the conditional tense, as if the new group was a not-yet-actualized possibility, the document nonetheless connected the organization to various right-wing leagues and even named three men—Eugène Deloncle, Jacques Corrèze, and Gabriel Jeantet—as its presumptive founders.[8] Motivated by the seriousness of the bombings at Étoile and determined now to act, on the afternoon of September 16, 1937, a police inspector named Morin was sent to the spacious apartment that a man named Aristide Corre shared with his mother at 9 rue Raynouard. Morin expected to find illegal arms, but he turned up only one unregistered pistol.

A more thorough search of the apartment, however, revealed something far more important than weapons. Corre's apartment included a study where he evidently did a great deal of work and claimed to be writing a novel. Papers of all sorts littered his desk. Drawers revealed even more notations. Here, Morin made a significant discovery. In a red box he found a file marked "Paris-Banlieu," which contained numerous lists written in a strange code. In the mother's bedroom, Morin subsequently unearthed Corre's fatal mistake: a similar list, but this one decoded, recording the names, addresses, and registration numbers of over 1,260 affiliates of a group to which Corre obviously belonged. The police immediately recognized many of the names on the list and put those people under surveillance. Some of them were brought in for interrogation, even as the police continued to try to infiltrate what was clearly a potentially dangerous subversive organization.[9] By September, the police were well aware of the existence of the CSAR, the right-wing political organization that, as historian Joel Blatt has noted, was "monarchist, authoritarian—even totalitarian, nationalist, anticommunist, antisocialist, antidemocratic, antiliberal, anti-Semitic, and anti-Masonic."[10] The press soon picked up on the mocking label Maurice Pujo slapped on the group, "the Cagoule."[11] The nickname stuck in part due to what many in the rightist press claimed was the wildly inflated estimation on the part of Léon Blum and his government regarding the threat the Cagoule posed to the Third Republic. To reporters, the newly revealed organization seemed more amateurish than menacing, an assessment that has tended to endure in both scholarship and popular culture ever since. What, then, was the real nature of the Cagoule?[12]

Enter the Cagoule

The CSAR, or the Cagoule, sprang from a split that appeared in 1934 in the shock troops of the Action Française, a pro-royalist, highly conservative political party founded in 1898. On February 6, 1934, the members of roughly twenty right-wing leagues—such as the Croix de Feu, the Francistes, and the Jeunesse Patriotes—protested government corruption in the Stavisky affair by participating in a demonstration that turned into a bloody riot around the Place de la Concorde. The riot brought down the radical government of Édouard Daladier and laid the groundwork on the left for the rise of the Popular Front government of Léon Blum in 1936. By 1934, men like Eugène Deloncle, a successful naval engineer who had served in World War I and was made a knight of the Légion d'Honneur in 1920, and

Jean Filliol, a young salesman at the Hachette publication firm, had grown tired of the lack of action from more mainstream rightist political leaders, such as Charles Maurras. Deloncle belonged to the 17th équipe (team) of the Action Française, and Filliol was the head of the Camelots du Roi (the militant youth wing of the Action Française) for the 16th arrondissement. Filliol, always the advocate for violent action, accused the Action Française of passivity and especially for failing to take advantage of the immense opportunity the February 6 riots had offered. Ninety-five of the more radical members of the Action Française, including Deloncle and Filliol, were expelled from the organization in late 1935, although they probably would have argued that they had seceded. In February 1936, Deloncle formed a legitimate political organization, the Parti Nationale Révolutionnaire et Social. Léon Blum's ban on right-wing leagues ended the group's short life that June, but not before police raided its offices at 31 rue Caumartin.[13]

By June 1936, Deloncle had created the CSAR, and other men who shared his and Filliol's political views and urgent desire for action—including Deloncle's brother, Henri, a former army officer turned jeweler, Jean Moreau de la Meuse, an engineering consultant, and François Méténier, an army reservist and industrialist—joined the terrorist group, becoming its inner circle. Their core beliefs, common among most right-wing conservatives at the time, included a hatred of communists, Jews, and Freemasons, as well as distrust for the liberal, democratic institutions that were the legacy of the French Revolution. They saw liberal democracy as overly secular, immoral, and weak, and they had nothing but disdain for governments that attempted to embody democratic values; they also had a positive horror of socialism. But the Cagoule leadership, like that of many other fascist groups in Europe at that time, added to these conservative political views a yearning for immediate action and a willingness to use violence to achieve their ends. Ultimately, the Cagoulard leaders planned a paramilitary coup in 1936–37, hoping to oust the new Popular Front government and to install a military dictatorship based on the Italian model. Some founders of the Cagoule may have originally envisaged an eventual return of the French monarchy, and they maintained close ties with Jean d'Orléans, comte de Paris, the exiled heir-apparent to the defunct French throne. But by 1937, the clever and ambitious Deloncle had clearly developed a quite different vision of the future, one with himself as a future dictator allied with Mussolini.[14]

The Cagoule received significant funding from major French industrial leaders who appreciated its antisocialist agenda, especially from the group associated with Banque Worms. It never achieved the full support of the army that Deloncle craved; nonetheless, it did recruit a number of retired military officers into its leadership ranks and received the quiet approval of many active military leaders, probably even Marshal Philippe Pétain. Pétain seems to have known about the existence of the Cagoule and used it as a means of maintaining unofficial contacts with members of the extreme right and keeping himself apprised of their activities, as did Marshal Louis Franchet d'Ésperey, who also provided the organization with significant funding. Between May and November 1936 Franchet d'Ésperey sent one of his staff, Colonel Georges Groussard, to investigate the CSAR; this led to at least fifteen meetings with the group's leading members, including Deloncle.[15] Then, in December 1936, a member of Pétain's staff, Commandant Georges Loustaunau-Lacau, founded a network known as the Corvignolles, which sought information on communist activity in the army. In March 1937, Franchet d'Ésperey facilitated several meetings between Loustaunau-Lacau and Deloncle and probably Groussard as well. These contacts ultimately allowed the Cagoule to feed information to the army intelligence service inside the Deuxième Bureau of the General Staff, one of two branches of the French army in charge of gathering intelligence, about real or imagined communist conspiracies. Deloncle seems to have left these meetings with the idea that in the event of an uprising, his Cagoulard street fighters would wage war alongside the regular French military.

The Cagoule veiled its activities under the cover of a legal organization whose statutes it obediently registered at the prefecture as was required under French law. Known as the Union des Comités d'Action Défensive (UCAD), this body came into existence in June 1936 through the auspices of two men. One was a retired air force general, World War I hero, and reservist named Édouard Duseigneur, and the other was the wealthy duke Joseph Pozzo di Borgo, who first became the organization's president and later held its vice presidency. Duseigneur's old friend Deloncle was also involved in creating UCAD, and the two men worked together to create a cover for the subversive and illegal Cagoule, which Deloncle founded sometime between June and November 1936. Ostensibly the mission of the UCAD was to assemble right-wing organizations, especially those formerly allied with the Croix de Feu, to fight politically against the perceived communist threat, whereas the Cagoule was formed to take the sort of violent action that would lead to the banning of legal organizations such as the UCAD. The Cagoule was, in other words, the underground, clandestine wing of the UCAD, as well as a major source of weapons for Duseigneur and his followers. Deloncle said in a 1938 interrogation that, after the dissolution of the leagues, many young men on the right came to him for advice. "I opened their eyes to the communist peril," he explained, "and demanded that they forget their differences in order to form a united defense against the communists."[16] The UCAD used the French daily *Choc* as the vehicle for its right-wing agenda and ran an article on September 17, 1936, entitled "The house is on fire! Assemble!" It thus gathered a variety of organizations under its purview, including but not limited to the Cercle d'Études Nationalistes, the Association des Milices Secrètes d'Action Révolutionnaire, the Centre d'Information et de Coopération, and the Comité de Rassemblement Antisoviétique (CRAS).[17]

The Cagoule was organized much like the French army, with four bureaus. Eugène Deloncle headed the premier bureau, which oversaw recruitment and discipline. The deuxième bureau gathered information and carried out surveillance. Aristide Corre supervised this bureau, in conjunction with medical doctor and proud royalist Félix Martin. Retired lieutenant-colonel Georges Cachier ran the troisième bureau, which managed operations and trained recruits. Jean Moreau de la Meuse was in charge of the quatrième bureau, which was devoted to logistics and gunrunning. It was Cachier's division that strategically secured architectural plans and keys to the buildings housing the various ministries in Blum's government, as well as access to the major utilities in Paris.[18] An État-Major (General Staff) of the Cagoule also existed, which included Deloncle and his most trusted allies. Deloncle was known as the chief and closely consulted with his brother, Henri. They in turn received advice and support from Jean Filliol, Jacques Corrèze, and gunrunning expert Gabriel Jeantet. Corrèze actually lived in Eugène Deloncle's house. The État-Major met every day, sometimes in conjunction with the bureau chiefs but often without them. Retired army officer François Méténier also seems to have been a part of the État-Major, although he traveled extensively for the Cagoule and thus was often away from Paris; he worked most closely with Gabriel Jeantet and another gunrunner named Armand Crespin. Of all these men, Filliol seems to have had the greatest influence on Deloncle. Corre bemoaned how, in his view, Filliol led Deloncle around by the nose. Jeantet was probably the most intelligent member of the group, at least according to Corre, who noted that he was "smarter than Jupiter."[19] Although Jeantet completed numerous dangerous missions for the Cagoule as an arms broker, he tended to advise caution regarding more rash or violent activities, most of which sprang from the febrile imagination of the hot-headed Filliol, with whom Jeantet had a tense relationship. Jeantet did what he could to thwart Filliol's wilder schemes, including the proposed assassination of Léon Blum. Jeantet later self-servingly insisted in his postwar accounts of this period that he disavowed all terrorist actions such as the bombings at L'Étoile and took no part in them.[20]

The rank-and-file of the Cagoule was divided into cells, units, battalions, regiments, brigades, and divisions. Paris was split into two divisions, each division was made up of three brigades, and each brigade comprised one to three regiments. Since the Cagoule was a clandestine operation, it is impossible to know exactly how many members were in its ranks. Deloncle boasted that by 1937, 12,000 men in Paris and over 120,000 from the provinces had joined the Cagoule, but this was clearly an exaggeration. Historian Frédéric Monier has speculated that the Cagoule had only about 3,000 members in Paris. At most, the Cagoule probably consisted of less than two hundred known affiliates who had some sense of the organization's structure and mission, another 1,200 sworn adherents, and several thousand foot soldiers who were loosely tied to the CSAR through some other association. Its alliance with UCAD tied the Cagoule to numerous right-wing groups throughout France, such as the Union des Enfants d'Auvergne as well as Les Chevaliers du Glaive in Nice. Filliol created a link between the Cagoule and Amouni Amari's Algérie Française. Affiliate groups also existed in Nancy, Nice, Marseille, Toulouse, Bordeaux, Lille, Laon, Evreux, Clermont-Ferrand, Domfront, and Meaux. Even so, the police exposure of the Cagoule in 1937 and 1938 turned up only 102 suspected members.[21]

What lay behind the Cagoule's strategic success was that few of the rank and file really understood what kind of organization they had joined. This was due to the leaders' careful control of the information that flowed to the rest of the membership regarding the organizational structure and personnel of the Cagoule. Combat cells consisted of either seven or twelve men, and they were recruited from the most trusted friends of individuals who had already proven themselves as members of such right-wing groups as the Croix de Feu or the Jeunesses Patriotes. The cells were led by cell chiefs, who instructed subordinates in the correct operation of rifles, grenades, and machine guns. Each cell member was responsible for a particular duty that ensured the survival of the cell in combat. These duties mostly revolved around loading and operating the munitions. New recruits participated in an elaborate initiation ceremony held in a secret meeting place, where they were asked to swear on the French flag an oath of fidelity to the Cagoule.

Each initiate swore "fidelity, discipline, and absolute secrecy to the Comité Secret d'Action Révolutionnaire.[22] The initiation had great psychological meaning, not only because the leadership of the Cagoule used passwords and pseudonyms to communicate with each other, but also because the initiates were made to understand that any exposure of the existence of the Cagoule or any other treason would be punishable by death.[23]

Most importantly, the initiate was made to believe that he (and sometimes she) was joining an organization that, in conjunction with the French military, would defend "Marianne" from the imminent communist threat. This was the most important deception on the part of the Cagoule's leaders. Deloncle and others made it clear that low-level recruits were never to be told that the high-ranking Cagoulards were planning a coup d'état, nor that they intended to head the government that would be formed after such an event. Recruits believed that they were joining an autodefense group to protect their country, not a terrorist organization intent on staging a violent coup. One such recruit, Raymond Lainey, later testified that he believed that in the event of a communist uprising, he and his fellow Cagoulard street fighters would be waging war at the side of the police and the army rather than against them.[24] Finally, as with most secret societies, there were no horizontal ties in the organizational structure of the Cagoule. The head of each cell reported to his unit commander, but no relationship existed between cells. Consequently, the Cagoule leadership could more easily control the kinds of information that was offered to recruits and more quickly manipulate them into action. The État-Major only interacted with recruits during initiations as a way to boost morale and add drama to the oath-taking.[25]

The Cagoule's byzantine structure helps to explain how the leadership communicated with recruits and ultimately prompted them to action without exposing itself or revealing its plans or identity. By deceiving the rank and file in the Cagoule, Deloncle and others could easily enough order recruits to rent buildings and construct arsenals for the arms they were smuggling from Belgium, Switzerland, Italy, and Spain without arousing undue suspicions regarding the true goal of these efforts. The patriotic recruits believed that the prisons they constructed inside the Cagoule's underground arsenals were meant for communist prisoners who would be captured during the upcoming putsch. Many of the stonemasons brought in to build the underground prisons and ammunition depots, moreover, did not formally belong to the Cagoule but were bound to its leaders through ties of family relations and friendship. Most high-ranking Cagoulards enjoyed an upper-class lifestyle, and they maintained a class division between their elite leadership cadre, their shock troops, and the laborers they brought in for manual work.[26] The linkages inside the Cagoule resembled the patron-client networks found in early modern cities, in which overlapping layers of kinship, neighborhood, and fraternal associations bound people of various social stations into interlocking relationships that were characterized by mutual expectations of reward.

Cagoulard Profiles

There seem to have been several types of Cagoulards. Those like the Deloncle brothers were the senior thinkers and leaders of the organization. Men such as Filliol represented a younger cadre of leaders, who organized and participated in the violent crimes the Cagoule plotted and carried out, some of which met their objectives while others did not. Parallel to or just below these men in the leadership ranks were those who operated the Cagoule's gunrunning operations. Gabriel Jeantet played a central role in this aspect of the Cagoule's activities, traveling to Belgium, Spain, Germany, Italy, and Switzerland to negotiate arms deals on a regular basis. He also relied upon subordinates who facilitated his role in the arms trade. Gaston Jeanniot, for example, owned a garage on the boulevard Picpus, from which gunrunning operations often began, and Fernand Jakubiez physically transported weapons into Paris or across the border to Spain, where the Cagoule stockpiled weapons. Jeantet's personal secretary, Michel Harispe, and two other close associates, Pierre Parent and Pierre Proust, stored and maintained the illegal arms in the underground depots they had constructed. Another group of men, including André Tenaille, were responsible for the Cagoule's cache of explosives. Finally, there were a number of women inside the Cagoule, such as Aristide Corre's mistress, Hélène d'Alton, who participated in Cagoulard activities in a variety of ways, most importantly as liaisons with both the Paris police and the army's deuxième bureau.[27]

In general, the Cagoule's men of action tended to be younger and more volatile than their bureaux leaders, Deloncle, Martin, Cachier, and Moreau de la Meuse.[28] They may well be one of the reasons that the history of the Cagoule is usually presented as a tale of hooligans who could neither shoot straight nor properly execute their missions. An often-recounted example is that of Henri Philippe Roidot. Roidot headed an execution team with two other members, Léopold Sauvage and Paul Billecocq. Thirty-five in 1937, Roidot was around the same age as his good friend Jacques Corrèze, a confidante of Eugène Deloncle, which may be why the Cagoule awarded Roidot the relatively prestigious job of assassinating one of their enemies. Interested in the best way to accomplish this task, Roidot enrolled in a course at the famous Institut Pasteur, hoping to learn how to wage germ warfare. Specifically, he wanted to ascertain how to cultivate typhus and botulism bacilli in test tubes without infecting himself. He decided to try out this newly acquired knowledge when his superiors ordered him to eliminate a member of his own cell, a man named Jules Sallé, who was passing along information about illegal Cagoulard activities to a rival right-wing group.[29]

Roidot gave an operative named Louis Boucher a test tube Roidot thought contained an active typhoid culture, as well as a gun for backup, both to be used against Sallé. Much discussion ensued about how best to slip the typhoid into Sallé's drink. Boucher was insecure about his ability to pull off the execution using the bacilli, however—and perhaps not unreasonably worried that the method would backfire and he would end up infected instead—so rather than carrying out the scheme, he turned the test tube over to the Parisian police and fled. Afterwards, scientists at the Institute Pasteur examined the bacilli in the tube and determined that it was not strong enough to have done any damage, especially in a hot drink such as coffee, in which the typhoid could not have survived. Moreover, Roidot had already elicited much attention at the Institut Pasteur by posing too many unusual questions and requesting too many samples. His professor, Iwo Lominsky, later concluded that Roidot had learned very little about bacterial cultures during his short time at the institute and was really not a threat to anyone, not even to himself.

If Roidot was no bacteriologist, he was not much of an executioner either. Since the attempt to poison Sallé had failed, he ordered Sauvage and Billecocq to shoot the marked man instead. The two were supposed to take Sallé to the Fontainebleau forest and kill him, but evidently the assignment was too much for them; instead, they got drunk and stole a car. After a night of joy riding, the pair proceeded to wreck the car the next day, after which escapade they ended up safely in police custody. Luckily for Sallé, Roidot and his underlings—like many young men of the Cagoule—proved to be inexperienced, untrained, and inept. Sauvage and Billecocq may even have been fortunate, because they both received prison terms of nearly a year and thus were not in danger of Cagoule reprisals for bungling their assignment.[30] Despite these mishaps, Roidot remained in the Cagoule, eventually putting his experience and talents to work for Vichy and the Germans during the war.

Amateurs like Roidot may well have embodied the rank and file of the Cagoule, but they have also tended to overshadow the talents and abilities of the Cagoule leadership. Many men inside the Cagoule were highly intelligent and well educated. A significant number of them had been born in the 1890s or before and thus had served in World War I. As decorated war veterans, they shared a common memory of service to France during the worst of times, which shaped how they felt about their obligations to their country in the interwar period. They envisaged themselves as extremely patriotic and dedicated to the hearths and homes of France. Cagoulard preparations for communist insurrection included the designation of units responsible for protecting and removing from Paris the city's women and children, showing that Cagoule leaders imagined themselves as the protectors of France. They also mentored a much younger group of provocateurs, gunrunners, street fighters, and assassins within the Cagoule, who in most instances had been born just prior to World War I and accordingly had much less military experience and little recollection or understanding of the horrors of war.[31]

The brothers Eugène and Henri Deloncle were the primary force behind the Cagoule. Born in Brest, they were the sons of a sea captain who died heroically at sea in 1898 when Eugène was only eight and Henri was twelve. Because the boys were orphaned, their uncle, Paul Grossetti, a retired army general and distinguished World War I hero, played a formative role in their upbringing. Eugène, a brilliant student who won many academic awards, graduated from both the École Polytechnique and the École du Génie Maritime, after which he pursued a career in the navy before transferring to the army during World War I. During the war he served on the western front under the direction of Marshal Franchet d'Ésperey. He was wounded and decorated several times.

After the war Eugène grew wealthy as a consultant and naval engineer to a variety of companies tied to the engineering, banking, and maritime industry, including La Société Anonyme des Chantiers et Ateliers Penhoët de Saint-Nazaire, Le Groupe des Constructeurs Français de Réservoirs, La Caisse Hypothécaire Maritime et Fluviale, and La Société de la Pêche au Large. A consultant and expert witness for all maritime matters for the Parisian court of appeals, he was also well known in the banking world and was rumored to be part of the so-called Synarchie, perhaps even one of its founders.[32] By all accounts, Eugène had achieved great success by the 1930s. He had an attractive and elegant wife, Mercédès, a posh townhouse in the chic 16th arrondissement in Paris, and a castle in the Yonne region of France, not far from Auxerre. Forty-seven years old in 1937, he cut a striking figure and flattered his vanity by cultivating his slight resemblance to his hero, Mussolini. Considered charming and brilliant by his contemporaries, he was also noted for being excessively proud and obsessed with intrigue.[33]

Henri Deloncle, born in 1886, had a less visible presence in the Cagoule than his brother, but this should not diminish his importance in the organization. He was a part of the group's inner circle, but his business was in Cannes, so he divided his time between his two homes in Cannes and Paris. Like Eugène, Henri also received accolades for bravery during World War I, and he pursued a career as an officer until 1923, when he retired as a captain. He then worked for a number of businesses before establishing himself as a jeweler in Cannes. Henri was responsible for the 4th brigade in the Cagoule. More importantly, he was the organization's treasurer and accountant. Large sums of money came into Cagoulard coffers, and Henri managed these funds at La Caisse Hypothécaire Maritime et Fluviale, where Eugène sat on the board of directors. Henri distributed this money as necessary to the network of Cagoulard agents who put into action the organization's agenda. His expertise in finance was thus critical to the organization. He also had connections inside the army's deuxième bureau, and he collected information on communist activities that he passed on to his army liaisons.

The Deloncle brothers built the Cagoule as a quasi-military organization. But Édmond Duseigneur and Georges Cachier more strongly reflected its military culture and provided the most important liaisons between the Cagoule and active military men. Duseigneur and Cachier were born in the same year, 1882, in Lyon and Reims respectively. Both received numerous citations and honors for their participation in World War I. Cachier, as chief of the Cagoule's troisième bureau, was also a lieutenant-colonel in the army reserves. He had strong ties in the business and banking worlds as well, especially with the Banque Nationale de Crédit. He was connected by marriage to the Deloncle family; his daughter Mercédès married Eugène Deloncle. Duseigneur pursued a career as an aviator in the army, retiring as a general in 1936. He was part of Eugène Deloncle's inner circle and headed the UCAD, the legitimate arm of the Cagoule. Duseigneur does not seem to have taken part in any of the Cagoule's illegal activities; however, the general did offer Deloncle access to his contacts in the army, and he accompanied Deloncle on trips to Italy and Spain. As an outspoken leader in right-wing organizations, Duseigneur encouraged men belonging to the UCAD to join the Cagoule and proved an effective recruiter for the organization due to his prominent military credentials.

François Méténier, Jean Moreau de la Meuse, and Henri (Félix) Martin represented the type of talented professionals—what we would call today "technocrats"—whose pro-capitalist ardor, aversion to socialism, and extreme nationalism drew them to the Cagoule. Méténier and Moreau de la Meuse both had engineering backgrounds, and Moreau de la Meuse became an industrialist. Martin was a doctor. The three were born in 1896, 1880, and 1895 respectively, and they all participated in World War I. Méténier made the army his career and retired in 1930 as a captain in the reserves. Of the three, the least is known about Martin, who deliberately cultivated a personal aura of mystery and secrecy. Head of the Cagoule's deuxième bureau, he gathered information and organized surveillance operations on suspected communists and Cagoule traitors. Moreau de la Meuse was head of the quatrième bureau for the Cagoule, and in this capacity he was tied to the creation of the arms depots that the Cagoule constructed in and around Paris. A consultant to La Société Commerciale des Pétroles and well known in the engineering industry, not just in Paris but throughout France, Moreau de la Meuse was recruited into the Cagoule by Eugène Deloncle himself.

Despite strong evidence of his ties to Deloncle and the Cagoule, including testimony linking him to its more violent actions, Méténier always swore during interrogations both before and after World War II that he had never belonged to the Cagoule. He appeared to enjoy access to large amounts of Cagoulard funds, however, that he used for traveling in style and eating in fine restaurants. A self-indulgent man, Méténier cultivated two personas, a refined artistic type who was passionate about music and a bold extremist willing to do anything to promote his ideas. He always maintained that he worked officially for the army's police force, the deuxième bureau, and claimed he had connections within the Sûreté as well. Given his status as a reservist in the army, this was probably true, although he steadfastly refused to disclose his contacts. Thomas Bourlier, an informant who infiltrated the Cagoule at the behest of the deuxième bureau, verified parts of Méténier's story. Méténier made numerous voyages to Italy for the Cagoule and was in contact with Mussolini's government. He seems to have brokered the deal between the Italians and the Cagoule for the murder of the Rosselli brothers.

Méténier was also something of a loose cannon, who bragged too often and too loudly to family and friends about his Cagoulard exploits. He and Deloncle were close friends, and the wives of the two men often socialized together. A car wreck in 1937 in which both women were seriously injured seems to have cemented the friendship of their husbands even further.

Aristide Corre and Jacques Corrèze made unlikely Cagoulards. Despite their sincere right-wing convictions, they were drawn into the leadership ranks of the organization primarily because of the personal ties they cultivated with Eugène Deloncle rather than any particular talents, connections, or skills they could contribute to the cause. Born in Brest in 1895, Aristide Corre was a childhood friend of Eugène Deloncle. Despite the five years' difference in their ages, Deloncle had a special affection for the younger man, at least until the police discovered the decoded list of Cagoule adherents in Corre's apartment in 1937. Corre had a delicate nature and saw little action during World War I. An intellectual who held a diploma in literature from the Collège de France, he worked in the banking industry in both the United States and.France from about 1919 to 1932. After that he lived off his investments in the apartment in Paris he shared with his mother, a domineering woman who had a very controlling influence over her son and often treated him like a child. In the Cagoule, Corre achieved, at least from Deloncle, the respect he craved in his role as the group's theoretician. Passionate about writing, Corre kept a unique diary that chronicled the history of the CSAR movement.

Born in 1912, Corrèze was an interior decorator by trade. Deloncle met him in 1928 when he summoned the younger man to his castle to discuss window dressings. The friendship they struck up must have been quite profound, for not long thereafter Corrèze moved into the Deloncle home in Paris. As Deloncle's right-hand man and putative son, Corrèze was intimately involved in every aspect of the Cagoule. The close association with Deloncle quickly went to Corrèze's head, and other Cagoulards found him unnecessarily arrogant and hard to tolerate.

Close ties of friendship also bound Corrèze to the Cagoule's chief assassin, Jean Filliol; Corrèze served under Filliol in the turbulent Camelots du Roi in the early 1930s. Born in 1909 in Bergerac, the son of a postal employee, Filliol was a poor student. Too young for active duty during World War I, he served briefly in the infantry in 1929 before joining the Hachette newspaper and publishing firm, where he worked in a variety of capacities, most notably as a paper buyer. He established his own bookstore, Filpa, on the rue Félicien-David in 1935. A profoundly devout Catholic who attended mass every Sunday, Filliol was extremely violent by nature. Co-founder with Eugène Deloncle of the Cagoule, Filliol frequently circulated throughout Paris with members of his own assassination team, which included twenty-seven-year-old Fernand Jakubiez and twenty-eight-year-old André Tenaille, both of whom shared Filliol's penchant for action but lacked his intelligence. Weapons and violence obsessed Filliol, who was a risk-taker by nature and always inclined toward overkill. He seems to have been a true terrorist in outlook, who sought to use violence to make a terrifying statement to those who witnessed the crime scenes he left behind. Filliol was bloodthirsty and ruthless. He headed the Section Terroriste of the Cagoule, along with Eugène Deloncle and Méténier.

Filliol was linked to a man in Nice who was the head of the Cagoule for the southwest region of France, Joseph Darnand. Darnand was born in 1897 in Coligny, the son of the stationmaster at the Gare de Bourg. A poor student, he nevertheless served heroically in World War I, but his inability to obtain a commission after the war embittered him greatly. He eventually opened a transport business in Nice and did quite well until the economic downturn of the mid-1930s. A member of the Action Française until 1930 and head of the Camelots du Roi in Provence, he joined Doriot's right-wing Parti Populaire Français in 1936 before becoming involved in the Cagoule that same year. Devoutly Catholic, Darnand was absolutely frank in discourse and convinced of the righteousness of his beliefs. Violent and stubborn by nature, he was also unhappily married and utterly promiscuous. To these characteristics must be added a complete devotion to anti-republican, anti-democratic, and anti-Semitic ideas, as well as to the music of Beethoven. Involved in gunrunning operations, he frequently met with key Cagoulards in San Remo. He felt no remorse over killing anyone he viewed as a traitor to his right-wing cause.

The suave, educated and always calculating Gabriel Jeantet could not have offered a better contrast to Filliol and Darnand, who were scions of France's *petite bourgeoisie*. Jeantet was born in 1906 to a wealthy *haute bourgeois* family with strong ties in the publishing world. His father, a doctor and poet, boasted of friendship with Victor Hugo. Originally from the area around Pomponne, his family owned a small castle in St. Lupicin and properties in Switzerland. An excellent student, Jeantet took courses in literature at the Sorbonne and in political science at L'École de Science Politique, but he never received his diploma from either school. Early on he and his very

Catholic family were drawn to right-wing politics. As a young man, he held the position of secretary-general in the organization Les Étudiants d'Action Française. He worked briefly in copy editing and publicity for a number of companies before securing a job with an oil company, La Société Huiles Antar. With Huiles Antar he traveled throughout France under instructions to court the clients of an aperitif company known as Byrrh. Perhaps not coincidentally, given that Jeantet was a part of the Cagoule's inner circle and had family ties to the company, Apéritif Byrrh became one of the major financiers of the Cagoule. Despite his cautious nature, Jeantet was not afraid to take significant risks for his cause, including using the money he helped raise to broker arms deals for the Cagoule. Behind his round, wire-rimmed glasses was a handsome man known as a lady-killer ("un tombeur"). Sometime in 1936 or 1937 he and Toureaux became lovers. The police report is exact in asserting that Toureaux was without doubt Jeantet's mistress.[34]

The Culture of the Cagoule

Aristide Corre wrote in his diary that 1937 was the best year of his life, a year that brought him many "wonderful moments."[35] A close reading of his diary reveals the intensity and excitement of that time for those who belonged to the inner circle of the Cagoule. For young men seeking adventure and for older men thirsting after power, the Cagoule offered a tantalizing means of realizing their dreams while destroying the hated socialist government. The world of the Cagoule revolved around life in the most fashionable and upscale parts of Paris. The group's organizational structure overlapped pre-existing networks of friendship and political allegiance, cementing an even stronger fictive kinship. The secrecy members of the Cagoule adopted gave them a sense of importance as harbingers of revolution possessed of special knowledge and arbitrators of future rewards under a new government they controlled. Cagoulards lived in the exhilaration of the moment in what surely felt like heady times. They lurked in the shadows as gun-toting secret agents who based their identities on a magnification of their own self-worth, which was tied to warped fantasies of themselves as the self-proclaimed saviors of France. The men of the Cagoule had access to piles of cash that ushered them into the finest restaurants and gave them access to easy, even dangerous, women. Little surprise that in hindsight Corre would remember 1937 as a wonder year—although many others in France would have disagreed.[36]

The leaders of the Cagoule, for the most part, lived in the exclusive 16th arrondissement of Paris, the section Parisians called *le seizième*. They felt most at home in this wealthy, conservative neighborhood, which was known for its opulence, privilege, and upper-class values; as Victor Hugo remarked, this section of the city was "the capital of Paris."[37] Many Cagoulards had attended school together in this privileged enclave. Such was the case, for example, with two of the men associated with the Rosselli murders, Jean Bouvyer and Jacques Fauran, who both attended L'École Privée Chauvot on the rue Louis-David and were known as childhood chums.[38] Many others in the CSAR got much of their early right-wing political experience as members of the Camelots du Roi, representing the 16th arrondissement. So much of the history of the Cagoule revolved around life inside the 16th that the neighborhood must have felt in some ways like a small village or province to its members. Le seizième was the largest arrondissement in Paris and included some four thousand acres of land. It had been annexed to the city in the mid-nineteenth century but was extremely rural before Baron Georges Haussmann began its urbanization in 1860. Cagoulards lived in the 16th during a very interesting period of its history, when architects Rob Mallet-Stevens and Le Corbusier were at work on the geometric style of Art Deco in the 1920s and 1930s. This new style of modern art may have stood out to the Cagoulards at the 1937 World's Fair, when the now-famous Palais de Chaillot was erected in the 16th arrondissement as a companion piece to the Eiffel Tower.[39]

Eugène Deloncle lived at 2 avenue Rodin, Jean Filliol resided at 21 rue Felicien David, and Aristide Corre dwelt at 9 avenue Raynouard, in what was once the village of Passy—all within easy walking distance of each other. Cagoulard meetings often took place at the home of the Puireux family at 2 rue Nicolo, also in the Passy section of the 16th. The Puireux residence served as the location where Filliol inducted new recruits into the organization. There, in a solemn ceremony beneath portraits of the count and countess of Paris, new members took their oaths of allegiance before Eugène Deloncle. Jean Bouvyer was likely in attendance at these initiations, since he lived off and on with the Puireux family as a personal friend of Cagoulard Robert Puireux. Sometimes meetings were held at the apartment of Gabriel Jeantet's sister at 20 rue de la Source, a smaller street that crossed the avenue Mozart in the Auteuil district of the 16th, known for its many buildings erected around 1900 in the Art Nouveau style. Jeantet's sister lived a few blocks from Eugène Deloncle's chauffeur and part-time Cagoule assassin Jakubiez at 12 rue l'Yvette.[40]

More festive events occurred in the northern part of the 16th, just off the place Victor Hugo, at 28 rue Copernic in the home of an aging countess. Many Cagoulards gave the impression that the Cercle de Grand Pavois, at 52 avenue Champs Elysées, was the chic center for Cagoule meetings. In fact, Count Robert Jurquet de la Salle, a Cagoulard member as well as the founder of Le Comité de Rassemblement Antibolchevique, was ejected from the Cercle for engaging in political discussions in what was primarily a literary group.

Nonetheless, political discourse and frivolity were staples at the lunch and dinner meetings that members of the Cagoule held at favorite restaurants in the 16th. Filliol and his henchmen often ate at the Doucet d'Auteuil, near the Porte d'Auteuil, or at Au Vrai Saumur, at 67 rue de Boulainvilliers; Corre frequently took his meals with other Cagoulard comrades and their lovers at a restaurant on the avenue Kléber, not far from Méténier's apartment near the Arc de Triomphe. Other rendezvous points included the Tabac de la Muette, which was next to the metro station La Muette near the center of the 16th, the café Le Fetiche on the rue d'Auteuil, or at numerous bars around the Trocadéro. Cagoulards were also known to eat from time to time at the gastronomically renowned restaurant Le Doyen, on the Champs Elysées. Thus the 16th arrondissement of Paris formed the backdrop to the Cagoule. It was the political center of adherents' former membership in the Camelots du Roi and became the focal point for the Cagoule as well. Aristide Corre bemoaned the loss of this home base while in exile in Spain in 1937, noting in his diary that "I dream of my long-lost Passy."[41] This is not surprising, given that he lived in one of the most picturesque parts of Passy on a street known for its outside markets and beautiful eighteenth-century oil lamps, or *quinquets*, that still lined the rue Raynouard in Corre's lifetime.[42] Cagoulard identity was very much synonymous with the upper-class culture associated with life in the 16th. The plotting, planning, and excitement that accompanied belonging to a secret underground organization largely took place in the streets, restaurants, apartments, and townhouses of this elite section of Paris.

Because of their longstanding friendships, members of the Cagoule shared a certain intimacy with each other. To disguise themselves and their intrigues, they used special code names to mask their identities in correspondence, but these sobriquets soon became common in friendly conversation as well, a reflection of the fictive kinship the men created within the organization. Many of these names mirrored the person's place in the hierarchy of the Cagoule. Eugène Deloncle was "Marie," presumably in reference to "Mary, mother of Jesus" since as the creator and founder of the Cagoule, he was in some sense the mother of everyone. The name was not unusual in an age in which many men in France had "Marie" as a middle name, a direct connection to their Catholic heritage. Eugène's brother Henri was known as "Grosset" in honor of General Grossetti, the uncle who helped to raise him and whom he may have physically resembled. Jacques Corrèze was "La Buche," while Aristide Corre was "Dagore." Félix Martin was "Toubib," a play on the word "bibliothèque," in reference to his position as information officer for the Cagoule. Jean Filliol and Gabriel Jeantet had code names closer to their real names, "Fifi" and "Gabès." Méténier and Duseigneur were referred to as "Mété" and "Dudu." These nicknames underscore the intimately familiar society of the Cagoule.

The members of the inner circle of the Cagoule were in constant contact with each other. They saw each other nearly every day or night. Jeantet's concierge, Madame Élise La Vergne, reported to police that in the summer of 1937, Jeantet held meetings almost every night around eight o'clock in his apartment. She later identified Méténier, Filliol, and Jakubiez as frequent visitors. Police officers traced an automobile license plate number that Madame La Vergne copied down to a car owned by Eugène Deloncle.[43] Members of the Cagoule developed a distinct way of communicating with each other. They not only had code names, but they also used passwords and special signs. A napkin tied in a knot lying on the edge of a table indicated to new recruits entering a designated restaurant how to identify their handlers. While Cagoulards did not sport particular clothing, they certainly prepared for the eventuality of needing such dress. Police uncovered black leather riding pants and leather jackets adorned with white crisscrossed leather bands in the possession of several Cagoulards, and stored in their arms depots as well. All of this indicates the purposeful development of a unique Cagoulard identity, manifested in signs and objects that were reflective of both the organization's camaraderie and its sense of its mission.

The leaders of the Cagoule strove to create a culture of terror in their society. Deloncle well understood the various types of personalities that existed inside his organization and knew how to stratify his adherents into a hierarchy that took advantage of individual predispositions.[44] There was a spectrum of character traits inside the Cagoule; some, like Filliol, were emotionally detached from the consequences of their actions while others, like Jeantet, appeared not only more intelligent but also more psychologically engaged. While the CSAR's low-level recruits cannot be classified as terrorists and were far removed from the plotting and planning of a political coup, the leadership certainly contained a number of men who exhibited psychopathic and/or sociopathic behaviors.[45] Filliol and Darnand both killed indiscriminately and displayed a remorseless disregard for human life. During their years in the Cagoule they were violent brawlers always looking for a fight, eagerly waiting to do the organization's dirty work. Later, under Vichy and the Occupation, they graduated to even more violent and heinous crimes. Even so, all the bureau chiefs and men within Deloncle's inner circle, while not necessarily sociopaths, can be classified as terrorists because they used violence to sow fear and havoc among the French public in order to destabilize the Third Republic. They were also self-consciously aware of themselves as terrorists. As Aristide Corre reflected analytically in his diary, "There is no solution other than terrorism. But a terrorism that is wise, transcendent, that strikes only the leaders of regimes but that strikes them without hesitation and without respite, always at any hour, in every circumstance, in order through terror to render all government impossible and to oblige them to hand over power."[46] The Cagoule leadership, furthermore, employed a modern form of terrorism that was not associated with any direction from the French state but one that operated instead through secrecy and in association with at least one foreign power (Italy).[47] "We are malicious," Deloncle boasted to an army officer in 1937 when trying to scare him into cooperation with the CSAR.[48] He and his co-conspirators were time bombs, ready to explode in the hands of not only their enemies but also of anyone affiliated with those enemies, which explains why so many of them met violent ends.[49]

Women of the Cagoule

Along with many violent young men, the leaders of the Cagoule won many young women to their cause as well. While usually less violent than the men, these women were no less integral to the success of the organization's operations. Many of them were the sexual partners of the Cagoule elite, while others functioned as more serious operatives; in most instances they were both. Cagoulards lived by their own code of honor, and perhaps in emulation of the general culture of the powerful in their day, this code did not include marital fidelity. Almost all the Cagoule's leaders kept mistresses and enjoyed easy access to sex. Money flowed copiously, and men like Méténier frequented nightclubs until the early hours of the morning, most often in the company of prostitutes, mistresses, and would-be sexual conquests. Cagoulards also shared women among themselves. Deloncle and Filliol reportedly once fought a duel—although not a fatal one—over Deloncle's wife Mercédès. Alice Lamy broke up with Filliol in the summer of 1937, supposedly because Filliol was cheating on her with Hélène d'Alton, and to make him jealous moved in briefly with Filliol's fellow Cagoulard, François Baillet. At that point, Hélène was the steady girlfriend, or at least the regular sexual partner, of Aristide Corre.[50]

Corre referred to these tales of sexual conquest and drama as "stories within the margins" of the larger collective narrative of the Cagoule.[51] His mother put it less elegantly, complaining that her son had "nothing but women on the brain."[52] One of the sexual narratives in Corre's diary focused on Michel Harispe, who was married to a woman named Thérèse. According to Corre, Thérèse slept with a number of men in the Cagoule, among them Corrèze and Jeantet, the latter Harispe's childhood friend. One night Harispe became so upset over his wife's infidelities that he went looking for her at Jeantet's apartment, armed with a gun. He found Jeantet at home but evidently not with Thérèse. Jeantet mollified him with the assurance that there was nothing but history between them. Improbably, this explanation sufficed to soothe Harispe's wounded feelings and Jeantet escaped unscathed.[53]

Corre's diary reveals that women formally joined the Cagoule and acted in a variety of ways that made them invaluable to the clandestine society's operation. He cited numerous examples of women who took oaths of loyalty to the Cagoule. On July 23, 1937, new recruit Marie de Massolles swore allegiance to the Cagoule at the home of Pierre Proust, one of the men in Corre's circle of Cagoulard friends and Massolles' son-in-law. Corre believed that her connections in a variety of milieus would be "an excellent source of information" for the organization.[54] The Cagoule specifically used women to conduct surveillance work for them, since women were less likely to draw attention to themselves than men. In this way, Jacqueline Derville had followed Dimitri Navachine in the days before his murder to help lay the groundwork for his assassination.[55] Women also accompanied Cagoulards on their assignments. For example, Alice Lamy went with Filliol and Baillet to Normandy to murder the Rosselli brothers, and in August 1937, Corre and Marie de Massolles went on a mission together to St. Malo. In his diary, Corre recorded how he eagerly anticipated the trip because it would give him the opportunity to share a hotel room with Massolles, whom he intended to seduce. "After a day's work, we will have the right to a little physical relaxation," Corre mused before the trip.[56] The Cagoulards exploited women even while employing them in serious tasks.

Hélène Marie Anne d'Alton was probably the Cagoule's most important female operative. The daughter of deceased vicomte Charles Prosper d'Alton and his widow, Anne Orban de La Rocque, a relative of the Colonel François de La Rocque, Hélène d'Alton was fiercely passionate about her right-wing ideas. She held Croix de Feu reunions in her home on the rue Copernic and was arrested in 1936 for throwing rocks at communists. A somewhat eccentric woman of loose morality, the police noted that she lived off her "galanterie."[57] In 1937, she was engaged in a relationship of sorts with Aristide Corre. He described her as a nymphomaniac who made no secret of her enjoyment of sex and who shunned ever wearing underclothes. The most erotic passages in his diary are descriptions of her and of their sexual encounters.[58] Indeed, Corre compared his many other sexual conquests to d'Alton and few, if any, measured up. D'Alton was also one of the Cagoule's key liaisons with the police. On August 7, 1937, for example, she had a rendezvous in the place St. Michel with "our man" in the police prefecture.[59]

From Corre's diary, it is clear that women like Hélène d'Alton delivered messages, followed suspects, acted as go-betweens, and recruited members into the Cagoule, often through their personal connections with members of other groups, such as those of d'Alton with the Croix de Feu. Corre credits the promiscuous Thérèse Harispe with the success of their movement in Toulon and the adhesion of so many naval officers and engineers to the Cagoule.[60] He referred to her with the formal title of Cagoulard *agent de liaison*. Marie de Massolles, Hélène d'Alton, and another recruit, Countess Nicole de Monteynard, offered the Cagoule access to the army's elite officer core by developing relationships with those men. These three women made contact for the Cagoule with such central figures in the French military as Colonel de Bellefond, Colonel de La Rocque, General La Laurencie, and General d'Humières, the latter d'Alton's uncle and de Monteynard's cousin.[61] Corre stated that he put Deloncle in contact with Colonel de Bellefond through Monteynard.[62]

In many ways, women were indispensable to the mission of the Cagoule. The reliance on women as special agents continued during the period of the reincarnation of the Cagoule during World War II. Eugène Deloncle, for example, used operative Anne Mouraille to place a bomb under the bed of his hated enemy, the former minister of the interior in the government of Léon Blum, Marx Dormoy, while Dormoy was under house arrest in Montélimar. The bomb exploded and decapitated Dormoy in bed on July 26, 1941. Pétain, who had ordered the house arrest and guaranteed Dormoy's safety as long as he stayed out of sight, was reportedly appalled.[63] By relying on women who were often their own relatives to act as liaison agents, army leaders could subsequently deny any involvement with the more extreme right-wing groups, even while they manipulated women to feed them information. Women had not yet been enfranchised in the 1930s, and their use as go-betweens continued an age-old practice in which men relied on female agents to travel in dangerous areas, pass information, or perform acts that might be less noticed because of their sex.[64] Indeed, the Cagoule may well have been the training ground for many female Resistance heroes in World War II. For example, it was often rumored that Marie-Madeleine Méric (later Fourcade), a notable Resistance figure, began her clandestine work with the Cagoule.[65] This cannot be proven, however, although she worked closely with Loustaunau-Lacau and the Corvignolles before World War II and formed a Resistance network with Loustaunau-Lacau under Vichy. The point is that clandestine groups needed female operatives and exploited gender stereotypes to their advantage as part of their operational strategies.

Corre's diary makes clear that members of the Cagoule's État-Major surrounded themselves with a coterie of men and women to do their bidding. He jokingly referred to Marie de Massolles and Nicole de Monteynard as "his wives."[66] When they were in the company of his lover, d'Alton, he referred to all three women as his "secret feminine team."[67] Each member of the inner circle seems to have had his own secretary, chauffeur, team of supporters, and mistress, who all worked together to gather information and carry out the Cagoule's operations. The group's leaders particularly needed women who were fearless and unafraid to travel at night. Laetitia Toureaux, who was well-known for her intrepid behavior and frequent late-night stints in Parisian bals musette, would have possessed many of the qualities Cagoulards sought in their female operatives.

How the Cagoule first recruited Toureaux is difficult to determine, but Cagoulards frequented many of the same establishments as Toureaux, where her wit, beauty, and feisty personality likely brought her to their attention. In the spring of 1937, Gabriel Jeantet was known to visit the bals musette in Paris, along with Méténier and Filliol. Jakubiez was a regular client at L'As-de-Coeur, where Toureaux worked. Cagoulard chiefs liked to

eat in Le Doyen, where Toureaux filled in from time to time in the cloakroom, and at Le Petit-Riche on the rue Le Pelletier, not far from the Agence
Rouff where Toureaux was a private detective. Toureaux and the Cagoulards could easily have crossed paths in the streets of Paris. The Messageries
Hachette, where Filliol once worked and where his subordinate and fellow
Cagoule operative Michel Bernollin was employed in 1937, was located at 3
rue Réamur. The rue des Vertus, where Toureaux worked at L'As-de-Coeur,
led directly off the rue Réamur. Toureaux's ex-lover Gasperini also worked
for Hachette in 1937 and may have even known Jean Filliol. By the same token, Toureaux may well have come into contact with some members of the
Cagoule through her activity as a private detective for the Agence Rouff.
She began work at the L'As-de-Coeur and at the Maxi factory in November
1936. The next month she joined the Ligue du Bien Public. If she was spying
on communists for the police or for others, so too was the Cagoule—they
shared mutual aims.

Toureaux was linked to the Cagoule in three ways. She appeared to be
spying on them and perhaps for them, and she was involved with Cagoulard Gabriel Jeantet. She was the kind of woman that the Cagoule leadership appreciated. She knew how to travel alone and maneuver through the
streets of Paris late at night. She was a sexual free spirit, able to strike up
conversations with strangers and charm them into her bed. She was willing
to recruit friends for her detective work and intelligent enough to hold—
or at least to articulate and claim to hold—strong political opinions. All of
these attributes were greatly appreciated by many Cagoulards. The Cagoule
needed women inside their operation, and sometime in 1936–37 Toureaux
very probably became one of their many undercover female agents. As a result, her life took a dramatic turn.

6

PLANNING THE APOCALYPSE

ARMS TRAFFICKING IN 1930S FRANCE

The Spanish Civil War and the Flow of Arms
into and out of France

It should come as no surprise that private individuals and leagues of all sorts were immersed in arms smuggling in France during the 1930s, given the political situation in France. Even the prime minister himself, Léon Blum, resorted to clandestine and technically illegal shipments of arms to the Spanish Republicans when he failed to muster sufficient domestic or international support to assist them openly. It was his passionate conviction that failure to come to the Republicans' aid would only further nurture fascism in Europe. Thus Blum felt obliged to set aside his pacifist convictions and divert huge sums from the state budget to pay for the costly rearmament of France. Not only did this money have to come from social programs near and dear to his heart, but gearing up the munitions factories also meant sacrificing many of the hard-won gains for workers in the Matignon Accords, in order to give employers more leeway to raise worker productivity. Time was running out, Blum believed, and in the face of growing German and Italian aggression, rearming France had to take priority even over cherished Socialist Party goals.[1]

Prior to the interwar period, the European arms trade had been primarily in the hands of private enterprises that negotiated profitable deals for themselves largely free of government interference. After World War I, however, the character of the arms trade changed. Weapons manufacturers ceded control over arms sales to governments and "business interests usually came second to diplomatic interests," although arms manufacturers were quite willing to negotiate deals with private parties under the table as well.[2] This process culminated in the nationalization of the French arms industry under the Popular Front in August 1936. The result was a "public-private partnership," in which dealing in arms "had become state-to-state arrangements viewed as extensions of political alliances."[3] These alliances could often involve strange bedfellows, such as Germany and Ethiopia in 1935, or Italy and the Soviet Union.[4] Because of these shifting alliances—which were at times at odds with official policies and declarations, not to mention public opinion—governments sought to keep their dealings as secret as possible. Often they relied on informal civilian emissaries and, increasingly, undercover agents of all kinds to negotiate deals. These kinds of arrangements provided a cover of sorts for other, less salubrious arms deals, such as those the Cagoule concluded. Arms manufacturers could not always be sure whether they were negotiating with a private individual or group interested in acquiring weapons for their own purposes or with an undercover agent of an official, authorized government agency.

The Spanish Civil War greatly complicated this situation, and nowhere as much as in France. Within a week of the Nationalist revolt, Spanish premier José Giral requested military aid from France, aid that Blum believed was perfectly within the rights of the French government to grant. The Spanish Republicans were the duly elected government of Spain, and Spain and France had a commercial agreement dating from 1935 that authorized extensive arms sales to Spain. Blum knew the decision to aid the Republicans would be unpopular, however, and not just with the right wing, but also among centrist and left-wing pacifists. Although he tried to keep his decision to intervene quiet, the news quickly leaked to the press, raising strenuous protests from opponents of his government. The British, moreover, intensely pressured France and the other European democracies to hew to the Non-Intervention Pact. Blum and those in his government who supported intervention on the side of the Republicans pointed in vain to the rapid mobilization of Italian and, later, German support for the Nationalists, despite the fact that both Italy and Germany had signed the pact. With the exception of the USSR, supporters of the Republicans in France and elsewhere in Europe were unable openly to assist the Republicans, and they felt obliged to channel whatever clandestine, unofficial support they could. This smuggled aid could not begin to match the arms and logistical support received by the Nationalists, and the resulting military imbalance played an enormous role in Franco's ultimate victory.[5]

Officially, the French government felt it had no choice but to accept nonintervention, largely because France itself seemed close to civil war between supporters of the left and the right. Extremists on both sides believed that such a war in France was inevitable, and indeed seemed determined to provoke it. In the meantime, they armed themselves in anticipation of it. French policy was thus aimed at stemming the tide of arms flowing into France, and preventing French supporters of either side from exporting arms to Spain. The Belgian government was in a similar predicament, which was exacerbated by the fact that Belgium was a leading arms producer, as well as a conduit for arms (with Switzerland) from Germany into France. As Louis Boucher pointed out in his letter to the police regarding Cagoule weapons purchases, "Everything took place in Belgium."[6] Moreover, Belgian unity, dependent on a fragile understanding between the Flemish and Walloon halves of the population, could not withstand the further polarization that Belgian leaders believed would result from siding openly with the Spanish Republicans.

The result was a vast but clandestine effort to smuggle arms into Spain that, perhaps predictably, embroiled the leaders of France and Belgium alike in scandal. Opposition leaders expressed outrage when it became clear that even as the French and Belgian governments were publicly proclaiming their neutrality, members of these same governments were privately sponsoring arms shipments to Spain.[7] The outcry from the French right was enormous, despite the fact that the right too was deeply involved in smuggling arms to Spain on the Nationalist side. In fact, the propaganda battles waged in the French press over Spain were part of the deep struggles in France between the left and the right, and "the left-wing press was no less diligent than the right in unearthing plots and exposing spy networks."[8] The Spanish Civil War greatly exacerbated the political divisions within France. It also hardened the determination of extremists on both sides to prepare for a civil war that they were convinced soon would erupt, and one they thought they might even be able to provoke. Finally, it increased the smuggling and stockpiling of arms in France.[9]

The Cagoule and Arms Smuggling

Arms smuggling was a primary activity of the Cagoule, both in order to stockpile weapons for themselves and their followers in France and to raise funds by exporting weapons to Spain. Thus it is unsurprising that one of the charges the police leveled against the members of the Cagoule they indicted and/or arrested was arms trafficking.[10] The police also uncovered numerous direct connections between the Cagoule and the Spanish Nationalists. The leaders of the Cagoule, when not purchasing arms from Belgium and Germany for their own use, were active in smuggling them to the Nationalists in Spain. Most of the money to acquire these weapons came from industrialists in France, who fervently hoped that the largely civilian Cagoule would be able to rally French defenses against the socialist and communist threat within France's own borders. Mussolini's government was also a source of funds for Cagoule arms purchases. The weapons themselves were often transported via Switzerland. In this respect, the Cagoule was tapping into an extensive network of overland arms smuggling via Switzerland that already existed, in which weapons were funneled into France and through France to Spain. Many German weapons reached Franco's Nationalists by this itinerary, or by a sea route that originated in Belgium, went from there to England, and then on to Spanish or Portuguese seaports.[11] By the same token, the Cagoule was able to import weapons from Spain, including ammunition for Mauser guns that had been manufactured in Toledo and other munitions, including machine guns, from San Sebastian. The Parisian police found some of these Spanish weapons stored in a hidden depot on the boulevard de Picpus.[12]

Extensive evidence ties members of the Cagoule to both fascist Italy and Nationalist Spain. In January 1938, the Bordeaux police commissioner, a man named Penavayre, addressed a letter to the Sûreté in which he detailed information he had obtained regarding connections between Duseigneur and Deloncle and an arms dealer named Robert Orain, with whom the two chiefs of the Cagoule had arranged a meeting in Saint Sebastian in January 1937. Orain, who had a false Spanish passport issued by Franco himself, had lived for some time in Bordeaux, although at the time Penavayre's letter reached the Sûreté, he was residing in Paris. Orain was well-known to the police in Bordeaux; he had been the subject of police reports in August, October, and November 1937. Penavayre described Orain as the "right-hand man" of the regional leader of the Front National (FN) and also a suspected leader of the Cagoule in Bordeaux, before whom, according to a police informer, new recruits swore their oaths of loyalty upon joining the group. According to Penavayre, Orain and his personal secretary, a man named Gaden, purchased arms in Belgium, Switzerland, Portugal, and "even in Nationalist Spain" for the Cagoule. On his return from one of these missions to buy weapons in Switzerland, Orain came to the attention of the police when he drove his car into a tree. Using his passport from Franco and passing himself off as a Spaniard, Orain traveled frequently in Spain with his wife. Moreover, the police informant told them, correctly, that Orain knew in advance of the movements and activities the Spanish Nationalists were planning, and that he was never bothered by the authorities in Spain. Penavayre also asserted that Orain was currently helping the Bordeaux FN leader, Ponteau, as well as Charles Trochu, leader of the FN in Paris, to obtain and stockpile weapons, even while performing the same services for the Cagoule. This belies the arguments of historians who have contended, following the later testimony of the leaders of various right-wing groups, that these organizations were all strictly separate from and at odds with the Cagoule. In a suburb of Bordeaux, the police found some of the weapons Orain helped the Bordeaux Cagoulards acquire. As he did with the Cagoule, Orain acted as an intermediary between the FN and Franco. FN leaders at the time were receiving large sums of money to finance propaganda campaigns against the Popular Front government, as well as to pay to train and equip French volunteers of the "Bandera Juana de Arco" to fight for the Nationalists in Spain.[13]

The intrigues in the region of Bordeaux related to the war in Spain were even more tortuous. Penavayre related that in 1937 two French officers of the army reserve and an English doctor arrived in Saint-Jean-de-Luz, on their way into Spain. They were carrying typhoid cultures that, evidently with the concurrence of at least some members of the French government, they intended to use to infect the Nationalist troops. Spies in the region warned members of the FN, who in turn arranged for the trio to cross the frontier and land safely in the arms of the Nationalists, who arrested them and condemned them to death in a military tribunal held in Pamplona. Penavayre concluded his report with this chilling statement: "One thinks that there is a unity of views and action between the CSAR and the Front National directed by Trochu. One finds the same men in the two organizations, all receiving instructions and funds from Germany, Italy, and Nationalist Spain. Their goal is: overthrow the government of the Left in order to impose on France a fascist dictatorship."[14] For Penavayre and his colleagues, the Cagoule posed a real threat. Its members were not acting in isolation but, at least in southwest France, were merely the most violent and secretive of a number of right-wing organizations that shared members and goals, and that received money and support from fascist governments abroad. Moreover, it is unlikely that the powerful and pragmatic men in France and elsewhere funding the Cagoule would have sunk so much money into it if they had not believed that it, in concert with other rightist groups seeking the overthrow of France's government, had some chance of success.[15] Orain was not the only member of the Cagoule with strong ties to Nationalist

Spain. Filliol, who was from Bergerac, reputedly had a Spanish lover. Jean-tet, Corre, and other Cagoulards on the run in 1937 and 1938 took refuge in San Sebastian when the French police dismantled the Cagoule and arrested most of its leadership in November 1937.[16]

The Cagoule was at a nexus linking Italy, Spain, and France. On several occasions in the autumn of 1936, Cagoule arms smugglers Maurice Juif and Léon Jean-Baptiste made trips to Italy to acquire weapons, renting a villa in San Remo to use as a way station in transporting arms. They made overtures to the Italian military high command and to Mussolini himself for assistance in their cause, overtures that met with a favorable, albeit wary, response. Most of the Cagoulards, as extreme nationalists, shared a profound distaste for Germany, which they saw as a threat to French independence. They were great admirers of Italy, however, and Deloncle claimed even to have had a private meeting with Il Duce himself. Deloncle likely believed that any implication that these activities might smack of anti-patriotism would be assuaged by the fact that many powerful Frenchmen shared his fervent desire for French rapprochement with Mussolini, including General Henri Parisot, the French military attaché in Rome, and Pierre Laval, French foreign minister under the Radical government of Camille Chautemps and broker of the 1935 Laval-Mussolini Accords.[17]

For their part, the Italians were only too happy to cultivate Deloncle and his organization, as long as it didn't cost them too much; but they seem to have had doubts about the ability of the Cagoule to effect regime change in France. Filippo Anfuso, a midlevel official in Mussolini's government, was charged with the task of maintaining the relationship between the Cagoule and the Organizzazione per la Vigilanza e la Repressione dell'Antifascismo or Organisation for Vigilance and Repression of Anti-Fascism (OVRA), Mussolini's secret service, whose representatives in France most likely had Laetitia Toureaux on their payroll as an informant. In late 1936, Anfuso received a visit from Lieutenant Colonel Santo Emanuele, the head of the Italian counter-espionage service. Emanuele informed Anfuso that he was in contact with an officer in the French deuxième bureau who in turn was a liaison with a French political group comprised of wealthy individuals. These men were pro-Mussolini and anti-Popular Front in their political sentiments. Anfuso informed his superior, Count Gian Galeazzo Ciano, of these developments. Ciano, after participating in the Italian invasion of Ethiopia, became Mussolini's foreign minister in 1936. He was also Mussolini's son-in-law.[18] Ciano, after consultation with Mussolini, instructed

Anfuso to get as much further information about this French group as possible, which Anfuso proceeded to do, meeting an emissary of the Cagoule in Turin in the spring of 1937. The meeting was held in the office of the head of counter-espionage in Turin, Commandant Roberto Navale, a military intelligence officer. Emanuele, who was present at the meetings, later stated that the French representative was François Méténier.[19] In his testimony to the juge d'instruction overseeing the case against the Cagoule, Méténier claimed that he had been working secretly for the deuxième bureau at that time, both carrying out missions in Spain, where he made contact with officers loyal to Franco, and working along the Spanish and Italian frontiers with France. He denied that his work was in any way related to the Cagoule. Anfuso subsequently reported verbally to Ciano and in writing to Mussolini about these discussions.[20]

A few months later, Anfuso had a second meeting with a member of the Cagoule, this time at San Remo. The intermediary again was Emanuele, but the Cagoulard was none other than Joseph Darnand, former colleague in Nice of Cagoule arms broker Juif and now head of the Cagoule there. Darnand turned over to Anfuso a letter of credit signed by Franchet d'Ésperey. Anfuso had some doubts about the authenticity of the letter, although unnecessarily, as Franchet d'Ésperey was a major supporter and financier of the Cagoule. Anfuso informed Mussolini about the results of this second meeting, and Mussolini showed a lively interest in the possibility of an alliance. Anfuso later claimed that his involvement in the affair ended at this point, although he subsequently learned that the Italian military did respond favorably to the Cagoule's request for weapons.[21] The high-level support for the Cagoule among prominent French conservatives, along with the ample funds they were willing to supply the Cagoule for weapons purchases, helped smooth the way for this rapprochement between Mussolini and the French fascists, an accord that reached its high point with Deloncle's trip to Rome in October 1936, when he met Il Duce himself and subsequently speculated on a Rome-Paris-Madrid alliance.

The murder of Carlo and Nello Rosselli is the key to understanding the true activities and goals of the Cagoule, illuminating the ties between the Cagoule's leaders and Italian fascist operatives in France. Historian Clifford Rosenberg has argued that "Italians scared the Paris police more than any other community in the mid-1920s," excepting the North Africans.[22] Not only was Paris home to many thousands of Italian immigrants—the Paris police estimated their number at over 53,000 in 1926—but among them were both pro- and antifascists who brought their political disagreements with them to France, engaging in espionage and violence against each other on the streets and in the cafes of Paris.[23] Although most of the bloodiest clashes between Italian supporters and opponents of fascism living in France took place in the 1920s, including a dozen deaths in Paris between 1923 and 1929, murders continued into the 1930s, including the 1937 assassination of the Rosselli brothers.

There is little doubt that even though the assassins themselves were French, they carried out the Rosselli killings at the behest of, and in the pay of, OVRA, not only in order to reap short-term rewards but also because Eugène Deloncle nourished dreams of a much closer collaboration with Mussolini's government.[24] Cagoulard Jean-Marie Bouvyer openly vaunted his part in the murders, while in his diary Aristide Corre stated that two central figures in Italian espionage, Navale and Emanuele, had induced the Cagoule to carry out the assassinations in return for a hundred machine guns and the promise of further weapons and support.[25]

During 1937 and 1938, the French government was in no hurry to pursue the Italian angle in investigating the Rosselli murders, due in part to the prospect, albeit increasingly remote, that France could pry Italy away from its alliance with Germany.[26] Up to and even after the Anschluss, the British and French alike continued to nurture the forlorn hope that the Rome-Berlin alliance could be fractured with the right combination of incentives and pressures. Their optimism may in part have been due to Mussolini's obviously wary attitude toward Hitler and reluctance to be subsumed under Hitler's shadow, although Mussolini was clearly happy to string the French and British along if that kept them reluctant to challenge him too energetically. Throughout the mid-1930s, Mussolini preferred to keep his options open. In 1934, he thwarted Hitler's initial attempt to annex Austria, which Mussolini wanted to maintain as an independent state and thus a buffer against any designs Germany might have on Italian territory. Hitler eventually brought Mussolini around, however, in part by backing Mussolini's 1936 invasion of Ethiopia. The French could only look on as their influence over Mussolini faded, which forced them ever more firmly into the arms of the British. Still, as late as January 24, 1938, less than two months before the successful Anschluss in which Germany devoured Austria, Robert Coulondre, the French ambassador to Moscow, wrote to French foreign minister Yvon Delbos that "it is on the Italian side that the Rome-Berlin 'axis' could most easily be broken."[27] Even during and after the Anschluss, when Italian support for, if not complicity in, the invasion of Austria was evident, French diplomats preferred to believe that Mussolini and Ciano were reluctant onlookers to the German aggression.[28] Thus, although the police and the juge d'instruction investigating the Rosselli case stated unequivocally in their reports that they suspected a connection between the murders and OVRA, neither they nor the French government pushed the matter further.[29] The postwar trials in Italy of members of Mussolini's government linked to the Rosselli murders, as well as papers the police eventually discovered in France (including Deloncle's files), uncovered substantial evidence that OVRA commissioned the murders and that the Cagoule was charged to accomplish them. Emanuele's testimony also bears out this conclusion. The lack of an official verdict to this effect, however, left the Rosselli case officially unsolved.

The Cagoule for their part agreed to perform certain errands for Mussolini's OVRA in France in return for shipments of arms purchased in Germany and Belgium with Italian funds and shipped via Belgium and Switzerland by arms smugglers Jean-Baptiste and Juif. The request that the Cagoule eliminate the Rosselli brothers came during a meeting held in Monte Carlo on March 22, 1937, between Emanuele and Navale and an emissary of the Cagoule (probably Darnand, but possibly Jeantet). The Cagoule requested as a down payment for this service help in purchasing a hundred semi-automatic Beretta rifles, with further orders for weapons to follow. The deal was struck, and soon after, Cagoulards carried out the brutal murders.[30] OVRA also used members of the Cagoule, such as Orain and Filliol, who had contacts in Spain, to facilitate communications with and arms deliveries to the Nationalists in Spain.[31] The Cagoule seems to have benefited from the willingness of OVRA to divert some of these arms to France in hopes that the Cagoule would be able to use them to weaken the Popular Front government.

In short, the Cagoule was well-supplied in late 1937 with weapons derived from a variety of sources. Some of these weapons were imported from Belgium, Switzerland, and Italy. Others seem to have derived from the Nationalist forces in Spain, now so well-equipped that they had arms to spare for their French sympathizers.[32] Cagoule arms smuggling and stockpiling was efficient and well organized. So central was it to the mission of the organization that Deloncle devoted a separate bureau entirely to it.[33] The French police were well aware that the Cagoule had numerous agents in Italy, Spain, Switzerland, and Belgium who were charged with the task of purchasing weapons, and another cadre of agents whose job it was to smuggle them into France.

The French industrialists who paid for these arms got their money's worth. The weapons the Cagoule purchased were, for the most part, of the highest quality, acquired from Europe's most respected arms manufacturers. Once in French territory, a third group of Cagoulards took over the responsibility of storing them in depots. A smaller, inner group that included Henri Deloncle was in charge of grenades and explosive devises. Members of the Cagoule also stole weapons from the military and other legitimate stockpiles of weapons in France, even acquiring them from enterprising dealers who scavenged World War I battlefields.[34] The remarkable quantities and types of weapons amassed by the Cagoule bespeak an organization preparing for far more significant military action than isolated attacks on individuals and relatively minor explosions and other provocations.[35] More significantly, the arms were by and large of German make, while the ammunition was mostly of Italian origin. The explosives were a kind manufactured in Italy and sold to the Germans under a special agreement.[36]

The Assassination of Arms Smugglers Jean-Baptiste and Juif

The Cagoule assassination of Léon Jean-Baptiste and Maurice Juif, the former in October 1936 and the latter in February 1937, is quite informative of the nature and extent of Cagoule arms smuggling. In mid-1936, Léon Jean-Baptiste was a small-time artisan living in Paris. An ex-member of the Camelôts du Roi and a dedicated adherent of Action Française, in May 1936 he joined a new militant right-wing organization, the Parti Républicain, Nationale, et Social (PNRS). He thus circulated among the people who during that same summer banded together to create the Cagoule. Because the Cagoule was soon able to tap into a veritable flood of money intended for the purchase of weapons, Eugène Deloncle needed to find people he could entrust with this vital mission. One of his first picks was Jean-Baptiste, who in turn immediately recruited his own trusted friend Maurice Juif. Juif, like Jean-Baptiste, originally was a royalist and a member of Action Française who had come to the conclusion that royalism was a lost cause. Both Jean-Baptiste and Juif were committed fascists—the latter even attended the Nazi Congress at Nuremberg in 1936—and both believed that the ultimate goal of the Cagoule was to establish a fascist dictatorship in France. Juif was the more independent of the two. With Joseph Darnand, he had founded his own rightist group in his home town of Nice called the Chevaliers du Glaive, a fervently anti-Semitic group modeled on the Freemasons that held its meetings in the basement of Juif's shoe store.[37]

By June 1936 Jean-Baptiste and Juif were in the arms-buying business, along with two other associates of lesser importance named Barbier and Duchamp, whose job it was to transport and guard the weapons that Jean-Baptiste and Juif bought. Acting directly under Deloncle's orders, the four men rented a villa in Oudenbourg, Belgium, and entered into contact with Belgian arms manufacturers. Deloncle visited them in Oudenbourg on at least one occasion. Oudenbourg became one of the Cagoule's transit points for the weapons they were purchasing before sending them on to France. The Belgian and French police quickly became aware of the Cagoulards' activity, which they tracked closely. In June and July, Jean-Baptiste and Juif purchased weapons from the Grimard Company in Liège. In August, they began to buy from the firm Armes et Matériel Militaire, which was based in Antwerp and whose director, a M. Froment, they met via an intermediary. Most of the weapons they acquired from Froment were made in Berlin by the Weyland Company. Deloncle sent a weapons specialist to Oudenbourg expressly to verify their quality and authenticity. Among the orders for weapons Jean-Baptiste and Juif placed in Belgium were two million francs' worth of Schmeisser machine guns and Bayard and Lepage pistols as well as three hundred small machine guns from another weapons maker, Pieper, for 152,750 francs. A military officer in the French army reserve named Pierrot was to pick up this shipment and smuggle it into France. In addition, Deloncle ordered five hundred automatic pistols from the Lepage firm, although this deal was never concluded.

The beginning of the end for Juif and Jean-Baptiste came quickly. In September 1936, the Belgian police seized the three hundred Schmeisser machine guns before they could be sent on to France. Jean-Baptiste's financial dealings had already begun to arouse Deloncle's suspicion. The temptation of all the money Jean-Baptiste found passing through his hands was too much for him, and he began to live high with the Cagoule's funds. Alarmed, Juif and Barbier sought to rein him in. They succeeded in smoothing things over temporarily by demoting Jean-Baptiste to second-in-command under Juif, who up to that point had been acting under Jean-Baptiste's orders. But the seizure of the machine guns convinced Deloncle that his arms brokers were getting dangerously sloppy and greedy, and that he needed to take action before the Cagoule's entire operation was either compromised or fleeced. Deloncle, Crespin, and Jeantet met with the representatives of arms manufacturers in Antwerp, where they discovered that Jean-Baptiste had skimmed a small fortune by doubling in his accounts rendered to the Cagoule the actual cost of the weapons he was buying.

Not surprisingly, it wasn't long before Jean-Baptiste received a telegram from Paris commanding him to meet with the leadership of the Cagoule there. Terrified, he begged Juif to go to Paris in his place, which Juif gamely agreed to do, while Jean-Baptiste headed to Italy to rebuild their operations, now compromised in Belgium. Juif duly met with Deloncle and offered his and his colleagues' explanations for the padded weapons bills, excuses the Cagoule leader viewed with skepticism. Deloncle seems to have placed most of the blame on Jean-Baptiste at this point, however. He allowed Juif to join Jean-Baptiste in Italy and ordered Jean-Baptiste to return to Paris immediately, which Jean-Baptiste finally did on October 26. After a brief private visit with his godson, Lucien Weyland, also a member of the Cagoule, Jean-Baptiste dined at a restaurant on the Champs-Elysées with Weyland and Jacques Corrèze. After dinner, Jean-Baptiste wanted Weyland to accompany him to his meeting with Deloncle, but Corrèze refused to allow it. The last Weyland ever saw of his godfather was that night, as he left in Corrèze's car. When Jean-Baptiste failed to reappear the next day, Weyland met with Deloncle to try to find out what had happened to him, but Deloncle threatened to convoke Weyland before the Cagoule discipline board if Weyland refused to drop the matter.

During this meeting between Weyland and Deloncle, Deloncle told a man named Friess (who had accompanied Weyland) that Jean-Baptiste had swindled the Cagoule while undertaking an assignment in the Midi. Corrèze then produced a false obituary for Jean-Baptiste, published in a little-known and possibly equally counterfeit magazine called the *Gaceta Regional*, which supposedly originated in Salamanca. After writing the obituary, Corrèze had sent copies of it to, among others, Jean-Baptiste's wife. It claimed that Jean-Baptiste was a hero of the right who had died in Spain while fighting in Franco's army. In fact, Jean-Baptiste was stabbed to death, most likely by the man who wrote his counterfeit, laudatory obituary, and his body was disposed of in an unknown location.

At first it seemed that Juif would escape Jean-Baptiste's fate. After notifying his Cagoule comrades in Nice of his change in headquarters, Juif and his new associate Hallumie rented a villa in San Remo, Italy, and for about two more months he continued to purchase arms for the Cagoule. He also entered into business relations with a Commander Bocalaro in Genoa and, using Hallumie and Bocalaro as intermediaries, began to purchase arms from the Beretta company branch in Brescia. Both Hallumie and Bocalaro later attested that by the middle of December, Juif in his turn was becoming anxious that his lavish lifestyle was eliciting Deloncle's suspicion. Unsurprisingly, on February 8, 1937, a local inhabitant found Juif's body near the Italian Riviera. He likely had been killed at least a month earlier. He was strangled with a wire by his former Cagoulard compatriots from Nice, shot twice in the head for good measure, and, in keeping with the Cagoule trademark, stabbed several times as well. Thus the Cagoule's leaders rid themselves of Juif, although they decided to keep the conveniently located villa he had rented in San Remo, where they continued to do business and where some of them took refuge when the police later began to dismantle their organization in France.

In this case, however, the Cagoule's cure turned out to be worse than the disease. Juif, realizing soon after Jean-Baptiste's arrival in Paris that his friend was dead and that his end too was nearing, decided to arrange matters so that he would be able to avenge himself and Jean-Baptiste from beyond the grave. He filled a trunk with compromising papers that detailed their activities for the Cagoule. Knowing that the French police were likely already searching for the missing Jean-Baptiste and that they were alert for arms smuggling activity across the Belgian frontier, Juif addressed the trunk to Jean-Baptiste, giving a return address in Brussels. He then sent it to Lille by way of Milan.

Juif possibly hoped to use the trunk as a form of insurance or blackmail to keep the Cagoule from acting against him. If so, his ruse failed. Still, customs officials did ultimately find the trunk, which had been languishing, unclaimed, in the Lille train station since October 19, although they only discovered it on February 19, 1937, about a week after Juif's body turned up in Italy. The papers it contained furnished the authorities with a great deal of evidence that helped them to unmask the Cagoule later that year.

Ultimately, it was the Cagoule's arms smuggling, more than their terrorist activities, that alarmed the police. Methodical and persistent police investigation, as well as some amazing blunders on the part of the Cagoule's members, provided the authorities with the information they needed to unmask and dismantle the organization. The arrest of Jakubiez in October 1937 was an enormous break for the police. On October 16, Swiss customs officers discovered on the road from Geneva to Paris a trail of ammunition sprinkled in the road like a trail of breadcrumbs. They alerted their French colleagues, who discovered more bullets on the French side of the border. Realizing that the ammunition must have come from a weapons smuggler on his way to Paris, they were able to track down all the vehicles that had crossed the Swiss border that day, which led them to Jakubiez and doomed Jeantet. The police were already aware that Jakubiez and Jeantet had made several trips to Switzerland for the purpose of purchasing weapons in 1937. Because Jakubiez almost immediately proceeded to inform on his colleagues once he was in the hands of the authorities, even going so far as giving them Deloncle's name, he played a central role in the police investigation that ultimately led to the apprehension of Deloncle and the rest of the leaders of the Cagoule, although at the time Deloncle avoided immediate arrest thanks to his spies in the Sûreté, who alerted him to the danger in time for him to flee to Spain.[38]

Arming for the Apocalypse

The ability of Eugène Deloncle and his underlings to amass and dissimulate a huge stockpile of weapons of war, ammunition, and other equipment—such as uniforms, bandannas, radios, medical supplies, and chains for prisoners—was the Cagoule's most significant accomplishment. Two aspects of the process of stockpiling arms are of interest here. The first is the funding of the whole operation. Conservative businessmen, such as the founders and executives of the Taittinger, Michelin, Renault, and Byrrh companies, provided much of the Cagoule's money through their personal and corporate funds. They also put engineering and explosives expertise at Deloncle's command, in the latter case especially the engineers of the Michelin company. The second aspect is the contest between fascists and socialists, and their sympathizers, to arm the opposing factions in the Spanish Civil War. The Cagoule was able to tap into a nexus of European arms smuggling that was already extensive before the Spanish Civil War began, but which expanded even more with the outbreak of hostilities in Spain in 1936. Not coincidentally, this was the year in which the Cagoule's activities in France also accelerated, and in which most of the organization's arms depots were established.

The Cagoule amassed one of the more spectacular weapons collections in France—or anywhere else in Europe—outside of national armies, and they stockpiled even more weapons across the border in Spain. The evidence on arms smuggling in the 1930s preserved in the Archives Nationales and the Archives de Paris suggests a country, and a continent, awash in weapons of war. The Archives Nationales contains at least a half dozen cartons of documents related to arms smuggling in the 1930s. In them, scattered among official reports and newspaper clippings, one can find scores of letters from ordinary French men and women from every corner of the country. Many of them are anonymous, although some are signed. Both accusers and accused in these letters came from across the French political spectrum, but the discovery of the Cagoule's arms stockpiles in November 1937 seems to have swelled the numbers of loyal French men and women who felt compelled to report to the police about the unorthodox activities of their neighbors. One such anonymous letter from "St. Quentin Compagne," dated December 16, 1937, declared, "All the good citizens adhering to the Popular Front rejoice at the energy with which your service and you, their Chief, work to discover the weapons of those miserable people who have no fear of spilling the blood of their compatriots with the help of foreigners. But the Comrades of the region of St. Quentin would be delighted if a search was made of our villages, among the peasants who were so violent at the time of the agricultural strikes. They alert you that arms depots must exist. . . . Every night cars drive around—is this to move arms or to get rid of them . . . Don't forget that the thieves of weapons of war at Laon had as accomplices the people of the Aisne."[39]

These letters mirrored the anxieties of the French people who wrote their government to denounce their neighbors, friends, and sometimes even their kin as spies, Cagoulards, and owners of weapons caches. Many of the denunciations, perhaps a majority, were levied against socialists rather than against members of conservative political parties. There seems to have been a general atmosphere of paranoia. For example, a maid working for a farmer at Oulchy-le-Château declared that she was sure that her employer "owned numerous hunting rifles and one military rifle that she thinks is a German rifle."[40]

Some gems emerged from among the plethora of letters and anonymous information sent to the police from every corner of France, such as the tip regarding an unauthorized radio transmitter in Laon that turned out to be the work of the Cagoule.[41] This was of special concern to the police because they had received word from "an informant from a reliable source" that "the secret group known as the C.S.A.R. or O.S.A.R. has organized in our territory a clandestine network" of radio receivers and transmitters, three of which were located in Paris and one in Toulouse.[42] A number of these radio posts were mobile and could be set up in private automobiles. The source proved to be remarkably well-informed, even detailing exactly who constructed and installed the radio transmitters. By the same token, the members of the Cagoule had their own informers among the police, and the police themselves admitted in a memo that at least one Cagoulard, a Dr. Matry in Laon, had received a tip that the police were on their way to search his home, allowing Matry to dispose of any weapons before the police arrived. Matry also possessed an unlicensed radio transmitter.[43]

Although the Cagoulards were a bloody-minded group, their aspirations alone were not what made them so alarming to the French police and judiciary. Rather, it was how surprisingly well-armed and equipped they were to carry out their plots, as well as the extensive political and financial support they seemed to enjoy. For the most part, however, the leadership of the active military forces in France appears to have kept its distance from the Cagoule. The extent of the support for the Cagoule among active military officers is difficult to gauge, among other things because the judicial investigation of those who were implicated in its activities was squelched. Even so, Cagoulards found sufficient sympathizers in the police and military to be able to infiltrate both organizations.[44]

Financing the Cagoule

The Cagoule was extremely well financed, probably excessively so in light of its limited membership. Their military-style organization makes it very difficult to determine the true size of the Cagoule. Prominent industrialists and conservative politicians clearly expected great things from the Cagoule, judging by the money they supplied to finance its operations. The Cagoule also enjoyed significant political support from these industrialists. In 1939 and again in 1940, long after the Cagoule had been exposed and many of its members were in prison, Pierre Taittinger, the champagne mogul, even wrote two letters to the minister of justice, demanding that the leaders of the Cagoule be released from custody. Since many of them were officers of the reserve or even active soldiers, Taittinger contended, they were needed to protect France. By 1940, with the outbreak of war, the ministry succumbed to the pressure and released the remaining Cagoulards still in custody.

In the Cagoule's heyday, Deloncle may have been short on recruits, but he certainly was awash in funds, money he used to finance the purchase of enormous numbers of weapons, far more than the official members of his organization could have used. Still, since Deloncle boasted in court that he could call upon 120,000 followers throughout France, he seems to have believed that enough people would rally to his cause once the putsch was launched to guarantee that the weapons he was stockpiling would eventually be put to good use. Quite a few shrewd industrialists with extensive political experience sufficiently shared Deloncle's optimism to put substantial sums of money at his disposal. Moreover, the secretary of an organization of arms manufacturers who also joined the high council of the combined CSAR-UCAD and military-based Corvignolles was willing to help Deloncle spend these funds.[45]

Even though we know the identity of some of the largest contributors to the cause, information about the Cagoule's finances remains sketchy.[46] In addition to purchasing arms and other supplies, including cars and trucks, Cagoulards rented villas and basements and paid for outfitting them as arsenals and prisons. In 1937, for example, they spent 7459.25 francs building an arms depot and prison at the villa La Futaie in Reuil. Another indication of the Cagoule's wealth is the extravagant lifestyle for which the leadership in particular was noted. They lived lavishly, with much conspicuous consumption that seemed to surpass even the considerable private means many of them possessed. Corre recounted one occasion in which he, Jeantet, and three others feasted on caviar at a chic restaurant called Komiloff and ran up a bill of nearly 500 francs.[47] Eugène Deloncle boasted that he had a budget of over 40 million francs for the Cagoule, and he seems to have had personal accounts in Spain totaling 50 million francs. Documents seized from Deloncle's offices revealed that in 1936 and 1937 he paid out 89,782 francs to Cagoulard operatives. At one point, Corre advanced Filliol about 5,000 francs from his personal account at the National City Bank in New York. A gun dealer named M. G. Fromont indicated that Jean-Baptiste and Juif paid him 1 million francs in an arms deal conducted inside an automobile in Liège.[48] Another arms company, C. G. Haenel Suhl, acknowledged receiving 1,877,077.50 francs in four separate transactions from Jeantet during 1936 and 1937.[49]

Both during and after World War II, the police declared themselves unable to track down the source of all this money flowing to the Cagoule, but they speculated that the Cagoule had an operating budget of about 40 to 80 million francs. Through their connections in the army, Deloncle and Duseigneur obviously raised a great deal of funding from right-wing supporters fearful of a communist insurrection. The UCAD probably raised money for the CSAR, and UCAD vice-president Pozzo di Borgo was known to be a very wealthy man who may have contributed some of his personal resources toward the cause. Franchet d' Ésperey donated 1.5 million francs of his own money to Deloncle; French industrialist Jacques Lemaigre-Dubreuil, owner of Lesieur Huile, donated another 1 million francs himself after apparently having raised funds for the Cagoule from a variety of industrial firms. Lemaigre-Dubreuil, like Deloncle, was also a part of the so-called Synarchie. Jacques Violet, owner of Aperitif Byrrh and Jeantet's brother-in-law, was also a Cagoule supporter. Félix Martin claimed he collected 3.5 million francs from Michelin, although other documents indicate that Édouard and André Michelin may have given as much as 8 million francs to the Cagoule. Corre wrote that an automobile manufacturer had given the CSAR 2 million francs, implying that he referred to Renault. Another contributor to the Cagoule was the future Vichy minister Pierre Pucheu. Indeed, Pucheu's ties to Deloncle and other fascists in the 1930s were strong enough that he is frequently referenced as a Cagoulard.[50] Pucheu, through the Banque Worms, more probably acted in the role of paymaster for the Cagoule. A story often told but never proven was that Navachine was identified by rightest bankers in the so-called Synarchie as too anti-German, and this is why Lemaigre-Dubreuil or Jean Coutrot ordered Deloncle and the Cagoule to kill him. The police archives indicate that Navachine may have been assassinated because he uncovered fraud in association with the French stock market and L'Association Générale des Producteurs de Blé, to which prominent Cagoulard Pierre Proust belonged. Proust, in this telling, was involved in the decision to assassinate Navachine but did not take part in the actual event. A less radical narrative contends that the Cagoule killed Navachine for pure provocation, to heighten fears among the French public of Communist agitation.[51]

The money trail was difficult to follow, however.[52] Police inquiries into the books of Lesieur Huile, for example, revealed no definitive evidence that funds had been diverted to the Cagoule, even though the company's owners supported the organization.[53] In 1937, Méténier received a check for 3,050,000 francs written off an account at La Banque Italo-Belge in what was undoubtedly an arms transaction.[54] In addition, L'Oréal founder Eugène Schueller funded Deloncle's Mouvement Social Révolutionnaire (MSR)—Deloncle's wartime incarnation of the CSAR—and employed Corrèze, Henri Deloncle, and Filliol after the war as high-level executives in L'Oréal's international operations. All these men shared similar passionately right-wing and anti-Semitic beliefs. The ties between Schueller and the Cagoule leaders were so strong that he more than likely supported the Cagoule financially as well.[55]

Conclusion

The Cagoule's acquisition of arms—rather than assassinations, other violent attacks, and street riots, or even its members' lofty aims of a revolution— should be the real scholarly focus when assessing the danger posed by the organization. The French police seem to have realized as much, judging by the emphasis they put on this aspect of the Cagoule's activities in their reports. Whereas the Cagoule might have been a fringe organization in a sea of other, less extreme leagues and militias in 1930s France, many of its members —including Orain, the Deloncle brothers, Méténier, and even Filliol—came from, and retained contacts with, other groups that were more legitimate and less extreme, but no less hostile to the Popular Front government and equally sympathetic to fascism.[56] There was no reason for French authorities to believe that the Cagoule's vast weapons stockpiles would be, or were even intended to be, reserved solely for the use of the limited membership of the Cagoule itself. What guarantee was there that these weapons would not fall into the hands of sympathetic nonmembers, especially if far-right leaders attempted an actual uprising? This was not necessarily a fantastic idea, given the overthrow of republican governments in Germany and Italy only a few years earlier and the uprising against the Republican government in Spain then underway. The Cagoule could perhaps have been doing the dirty work for legitimate right-wing groups that maintained tenuous ties with the radicals through expendable agents. Was this what Deloncle meant when he boasted that he would be able to rally 120,000 men overnight in France were he to begin an uprising? And if so, was he exaggerating as wildly as historians have contended?

Deloncle's goals aside, it nevertheless seems unlikely that Mussolini seriously believed that the Cagoule would be able to overthrow the French government, but such a view was not necessary to make the organization a good investment from Il Duce's point of view. What the Cagoulards were able to do effectively was to sow fear and thus help destabilize the Popular Front government in France. If the Cagoule could force the French authorities to divert valuable time and resources from projects such as supporting the Spanish Republicans and the Italian antifascist refugees in France, Mussolini's government would benefit immediately. If the Cagoule managed to usher into power a new French regime less willing than that of Blum to aid the Republicans in Spain and Mussolini's opponents in Italy, and to thwart Italian imperial aims in Africa, so much the better. It was not necessary for the Cagoule actually to achieve their much more ambitious goal of bringing to power in France a pro-Italian dictator to make Mussolini's support for the Cagoule worthwhile.

The focus of the press and the public tended to be less on the success of the police in finally bringing the Cagoule down than on the concrete reality of the extent to which its members had been able to amass enormous arsenals under the very noses of the authorities and hide them in ordinary homes, apartment buildings, shops and villas. Who could be sure whether or not one's neighbor had a basement bunker stocked with explosives? No one knew then and, as historian Steven Zdatny has pointed out, no one really knows today how many people adhered to, or at least sympathized with, the aims of the Cagoule. Still, the Cagoule's seeming ability to effect what we would call today terrorist actions, combined with its massive arsenals and widespread doubts about how many similar organizations with communist or fascist sympathies and the means and inclination to use violence were still in operation, deeply worried the French public.[57] This is the true legacy of the Cagoule.

The Cagoulards ultimately were thwarted in their plans to enact regime change in France, as we will see in the following chapter. Luck and treachery, as well as informers such as Laetitia Toureaux, played a significant role in the chain of events that led to the disintegration of the Cagoule. But the Cagoule's potential to create havoc in an unstable France on the brink of war should not be gauged by the outcome of the failed coup alone, and they came far closer to achieving their goals than many people, then and since, have realized.

7

EXPOSURE AND DISPERSION OF THE CAGOULE

NOVEMBER 1937–1948

The Night of November 15–16

In Paris, the night of November 15–16, 1937, was unusually calm for what had been a year filled with an unremitting succession of mysterious crimes, unsolved murders, bombings, arsons, and street violence, as well as massive strikes. The weather was good for Paris in November, and the streets were quiet. Not everyone was at home in bed, however. Jean Wiart, a small-scale commercial broker of German origin residing at 8 avenue Adrien Héberard in the 16th arrondissement, had received a summons from the commander of his brigade in the Cagoule, Jacques de Bernonville, to report during the night of November 15 to the Cercle de Jacques Bainville in Paris. Wiart was thirty-two years old. Like many members of the Action Française who had become disillusioned with the organization's leaders, Wiart and some of his comrades from the Cercle Bainville had joined the Cagoule at the end of 1936. Bernonville had taken him to an apartment on the rue de Rennes, where Wiart had sworn fealty to what he believed to be a "self-defense association." He was appointed a liaison agent, or messenger. He later also joined the UCAD, the Cagoule's political wing, and attended its meetings, including one at the home of Maurice Duclos during which Duclos himself instructed Wiart and twenty other men in the operation of a Schmeisser machine gun. Wiart thus had every reason to take seriously the warning he received upon joining the Cagoule that any disloyalty would lead to his death. So when Bernonville ordered him to prepare for action on the night of November 15, Wiart was ready and willing to obey.[1]

At the Cercle Bainville, Wiart found another member of the Cagoule named Michel Bernollin waiting for him. The two men then went to a building on the boulevard Victor-Emmanuel, near the Champs Elysées, where Filliol joined them. They proceeded to the home of Robert Gautier, where Bernonville ordered the men assembled there to prepare themselves. Filliol left with Wiart, whom he ordered to accompany him while Filliol made the rounds of the city in Wiart's Citroën. They proceeded to the Carrefour

Auteuil-La Fontaine, where Filliol entered a café. By then it was well after midnight. Fifteen minutes later Filliol emerged from the café. He exchanged a sign with two men waiting outside on the sidewalk whom Wiart did not recognize. Filliol gave the men their orders and rejoined Wiart in the car. Wiart drove to the Roland Garros stadium on the boulevard Sarrail, where Filliol went to look for another Cagoule foot soldier named Roger Illarthein, who was also supposed to mobilize. The two men went from meeting place to meeting place, and at each hideout Filliol ordered the waiting men to prepare for action. Finally, Filliol ordered Wiart to drive him around the Bois de Boulogne so he could see "whether anything was going on."[2]

Unfortunately for the Cagoule, nothing was going on. Wiart, no doubt by now cold, tired, and irritated, made the mistake of remarking, "But this is all a joke!" upon observing the quiet streets.[3] Filliol's response was not reassuring: "Old boy, we have to stay the course. It's all up to us now and we can't screw up."[4] In light of the menacing tone in which Filliol delivered this response, Wiart meekly drove Filliol back to the traffic circle on the Champs Elysées and parked the car. Filliol ordered Wiart to wait for him for a quarter of an hour and to proceed to Gautier's place if he did not come back, which Wiart did at the allotted time. By then it was three in the morning. At Gautier's apartment, Wiart found the men he'd seen earlier. They all hung around until about 5:00 A.M., at which point Gautier ordered them to return to their homes. The night had passed uneventfully in Paris. Despite the dire warnings of the Cagoule to the French military as well as to its own members, no communist uprising had taken place. Neither had the Cagoule succeeded in provoking an uprising of the right.[5]

Prelude to an Uprising

On November, 1, 1937, safe in his refuge in San Sebastian, Aristide Corre noted in his diary the recent arrest of Jakubiez. Although Corre did not as yet have any details about the event, he was certain that Deloncle was furious about yet another disaster striking his organization—a fury with which Corre was doubtless quite familiar, given that he was responsible for the catastrophic raid on his apartment that September. Indeed, he was fortunate that Deloncle had not ordered him executed when the police discovered decoded Cagoule documents and a membership list in his home the preceding September.

Corre also remarked in his diary that "the presence of Filliol around Eugène can only bring disaster."[6] He later opined that it was Filliol who had persuaded Deloncle to launch preparations for a counterattack against the communist uprising that the Cagoule's intelligence service had learned was to take place on the night of November 15–16. Dr. Félix Martin, the voluble head of Cagoule intelligence, brought the news to Deloncle himself, insisting that his sources were reliable informants in the communist headquarters. Cagoulard Henri Charbonneau later blamed the debacle of November 15–16 on Martin, whose excessive and unwavering enthusiasm persuaded an overly credible Deloncle to act despite the very unfavorable moment.[7] A series of arrests and police raids on Cagoule safe houses resulting from the discoveries at Corre's apartment had forced some of its most talented leaders, such as Jeantet, into exile and had weakened the Cagoule significantly. Corre was convinced that Filliol had pressured "Marie" (Eugène Deloncle) to embrace the disastrous November mobilization in the hope of provoking a right-wing uprising that would provide Filliol, ever eager for violent combat, with an opportunity to engage in the long-awaited battle with members of the French left.

Corre seems prudently to have kept his doubts to himself, busying himself with preparations to ready Cagoule weapons stockpiles in Spain for immediate shipment to France. In early November, when he first heard the news about the expected communist uprising, he wrote, "In effect, our information service has been alerted that the communists have decided on a coup and that it will take place the night of the 16th to the 17th, at two-thirty in the morning. I admit that such precision given this far in advance leaves me extremely skeptical."[8] The night that the Cagoulards ultimately decided that the coup was supposed to take place, November 15, Corre talked late into the evening with Jeantet, Corrèze, and the other fugitive Cagoulards in the San Sebastian villa about the Cagoule's situation. Jeantet was pessimistic, given the number of arrests and the flight of Méténier to Clermont, Lainey to Papeete in the French Pacific, and many other members of the organization to Spain or Italy; he argued that the entire operation now hinged on Eugène Deloncle. The Cagoule could only hope to succeed if its members in San Sebastian could get the arms they had stockpiled in Spain across the frontier, and so far the Spanish officials along the border had raised a series of obstacles to prevent that from happening. The weapons were ready and waiting at the border crossing at Pasajes, but they remained in Spain. Meanwhile, Corre avowed that, as far as the communist coup was concerned, "I cannot manage to believe in it."[9]

Corre's skepticism was well-founded; all remained calm in Paris that night. How, then, was the much more intelligent and canny Deloncle persuaded that the coup was imminent? Or was he? In a newspaper article he wrote in August 1941, after the German invasion and defeat of France, Deloncle insisted that the threat of a communist coup was quite real and that the Cagoule's intelligence had been accurate. Why had he not alerted the police or the government? In Deloncle's estimation, the French government and its police forces, led by Socialists as important ministers and rife with corruption, lacked the motivation to prevent the coup, and were too weak and disorganized to succeed anyway. As he declared, "I sincerely believe that during that night we spared the country from falling under the Soviet yoke or, at least, from enduring a long and murderous civil war."[10] Yet if it was apparent even to Corre, who lacked Deloncle's military expertise and political savvy, that the coup—if even attempted—was unlikely to succeed, why was Deloncle persuaded? Corre suspected a ruse on the part of the communists. It was more likely that the ruse was on the part of none other than Deloncle himself.

By November 1937, Deloncle knew better than anyone the precarious state of the Cagoule. The September 16 raid on Corre's apartment had put into the hands of the police a list of over twelve hundred sworn adherents of the organization, as well as other compromising documents, and they promptly moved to arrest several important Cagoulards. Jakubiez had been apprehended crossing the Swiss border in June. He cracked under police interrogation and provided the authorities with information about arms caches, although it is likely that they already knew about at least some of the Cagoule weapons stockpiling thanks to their informants inside the organization. Even Deloncle was hauled in for questioning, although the police still lacked sufficient evidence to arrest him. Deloncle knew that it was only a matter of time, however, which is probably why he uncharacteristically overlooked Corre's breach of security in decoding precious data and leaving it poorly hidden in his apartment. Deloncle eschewed his usual solution to this type of blunder and spared Corre's life. Instead, he sent Corre packing for San Sebastian with his ever faithful mother, who accompanied him to Spain, unlike his less faithful mistress Hélène d'Alton, to whom Corre nevertheless addressed long, passionate, and pornographic letters from his exile.

No matter how badly Filliol was itching for a showdown with the Parisian police, it is unlikely that Deloncle would have allowed himself to be persuaded to launch the risky maneuvers of the night of November 15 on the basis of questionable intelligence about a far-fetched plot on the part of the communists to attempt a putsch. As Corre pointed out, it was difficult to believe that the communists would have been so foolish or imprudent as to let slip so far in advance the exact date and time for which such a drastic move was planned. Moreover, given the number of communist operatives that had infiltrated the organizations of their rightist enemies in Paris, just as the rightists had infiltrated them, it was equally implausible that they would not simply have changed the date once they realized the proverbial cat was out of the bag. So what was Deloncle's plan?

That plan appears to have been to persuade the army that a nonexistent putsch was about to take place, and then to take to the streets and provoke one, forcing the army to respond to support the right against the communists. The result, Deloncle hoped, would be the long-desired fall of the Third Republic and its replacement by a military government that was aligned with Franco and Mussolini in a "Latin Front" that would stand firm against both the "Anglo-Saxons" and the Germans.[11] It was an enormous gamble, which demonstrates not only Deloncle's willingness to take risks, but also his realization of the danger facing his organization. He understood far better than any of his followers except Jeantet how little he had left to lose. Deloncle had worked hard to cultivate the army, with the assistance of retired general Édmond Duseigneur and active marshal Franchet d'Ésperey, under whom Deloncle had served during World War I. As we have seen, Franchet d'Ésperey funded the Cagoule and introduced Deloncle to Commander Georges Loustaunau-Lacau, a highly respected officer and head of the Corvignolles. Loustaunau-Lacau recounted in his memoirs that he became disillusioned with Deloncle and had ordered members of his organization who had joined the Cagoule to abandon it because its "dark designs" were a greater menace to the security of France and the urgent preparations for war with Germany than even the threat of an imminent communist putsch.[12] Loustaunau-Lacau, like most of the other military commanders whom Deloncle tried to persuade that an attempted communist coup was imminent, were highly skeptical of Deloncle's intelligence for much the same reasons as Corre. The communists had to have known better than anyone how unlikely they would have been to succeed.[13]

Thus Deloncle's campaign to convince the army to mobilize against the communist putsch—and, he hoped, to provoke one if one were not already in the works—ultimately came to naught. And even Deloncle recognized that if the Cagoule launched its own violent actions that night in order to provoke the reluctant police and army into the streets, as Filliol urged him to do, the forces of order would only turn against the Cagoule. Deloncle knew that his organization, weaker even than the communists, lacked the weapons and manpower to win in such a confrontation. Filliol may have been willing to go out in a blaze of glory. He had stated on more than one occasion to comrades such as Corre that he would never be taken alive. But Deloncle had no intention of destroying what was left of the Cagoule's resources, including its sympathizers among the military and conservative bourgeoisie, in a hopeless battle.

According to Roger Illarthein, a thirty-year-old artist and Cagoule recruit who was present the night of November 15–16, Filliol was furious at Deloncle for refusing to order his men into the streets. When Filliol demanded that Deloncle unleash the Cagoulards, Deloncle replied "We are organized for defense; we don't have the right to descend into the streets without provocation."[14] This statement was rather disingenuous on Deloncle's part. Even though he consistently took this line when explaining the Cagoule to the authorities, he showed himself on more than one occasion to be quite willing to act without provocation when the risks seemed more manageable and the chances of success higher. By the same token, Deloncle stated to the police on April 7, 1938, that "this feeble and incompetent government that would allow a communist putsch to be unleashed did not merit the confidence of the country then any more than it merits it today. No, we would not have returned to our hearths to take up our ordinary lives without having first put in place a government composed of honest and competent Frenchmen who would envisage and enact needed reforms."[15]

When it was clear to Deloncle in the early hours of November 16 that the army would not support him, he preferred caution to bravado. According to Illarthein, Filliol retorted, "You are always the same! You will wait to act until someone comes to cut your throat in your own home!"[16] Deloncle and Corre both subsequently accused Loustaunau-Lacau of treason for having abandoned the Cagoule on that critical night; they believed that he had played a significant role in the resulting failure. In fact, they had greater problems with disobedience—"treason," in their view—within their own organization.[17]

Around November 10, 1937, Wiart's commander, Bernonville, summoned Wiart to accompany him by car to Versailles to meet with a man named Schmedlin on the rue de Chantiers. Bernonville informed Schmedlin about the impeding communist putsch and ordered him to plan on mo-

bilizing the Versailles contingent of the Cagoule on short notice and prepare them for combat in the streets of Paris. Schmedlin replied that his men
uniformly refused to help defend Paris and that only a few of them had any
weapons. According to Wiart, who witnessed the exchange, Bernonville retorted to Schmedlin, "Don't worry yourself about this question of weapons.
Everything will be furnished to you at the right time." But Schmedlin ada-
mantly refused to agree. In an uncanny echo of the narrow perspective of
a medieval militia leader, Schmedlin stubbornly insisted that the Versailles
contingent had been created to defend Versailles and not Paris, and finally
Bernonville gave up.[18] This anecdote suggests strongly that Deloncle would
have had little success in mobilizing even his own troops in the Parisian
suburbs, who were likely just as skeptical about the supposed impending
communist putsch as high-ranking army officers and even Cagoule stal-
warts such as Corre. Schmedlin's statement about a lack of weapons was
likely a mere pretext. As the police raids on Cagoule weapons depots that
began on the morning of November 16 revealed, Bernonville's response to
Schmedlin was quite accurate. The Cagoule had concealed enormous stockpiles of arms throughout Paris and the provinces.

The Cagoule Exposed

The police had been on the trail of the Cagoule since February 1937, when
they opened Jean-Baptiste's trunks at the Lille train station, and probably
even earlier, given the number of right-wing infiltrators who were informing the police about this extremist group. The authorities had managed to
obtain information from men such as Thomas Bourlier and Louis Boucher.
Boucher was a thirty-nine-year-old army veteran who had joined the Cagoule. He probably began informing after having been arrested, although
his testimony would suggest that prior to his arrest he was already suffer-
ing from doubts arising from the nature of the assignments his Cagoule superior was giving him. In a letter dated November 23, 1938, and later transmitted to Monsieur Buissiere, the directeur générale de la Sûreté Nationale,
Boucher reminded the authorities that it was because of his testimony that
the police had been able to arrest at least two members of the Cagoule. He
also asserted that he had offered precise information on the location of
many of the Cagoule's weapons deals. Despite this assistance, Boucher complained, and the fact that he was not ideological himself and wanted only to
help defend the Republic, he had been arrested along with other members

of the Cagoule. Boucher was therefore soliciting Buissiere's advice, to guide him in the upcoming trial. He likely deserved the help he was requesting, given that he had tipped off the police regarding the Cagoule's experimentation with germ warfare.[19]

The police also received a variety of anonymous tips in the form of letters regarding the Cagoule, some of which turned out to be accurate, providing valuable intelligence that assisted the authorities in infiltrating the Cagoule and tracking down its hidden arsenals. "JV.16" was especially helpful and regaled the police with surprisingly accurate information about Cagoulard activity, which he was able to do because, like many of the police informers, he was a disgruntled member of the organization. On October 28, 1937, JV.16 wrote to the head of the Sûreté to inform him that a "coup d'état" was rapidly approaching, and that he would help the police find arms depots and unauthorized radio transmitters, stop arms trafficking, and arrest the leaders of the coup, in return for a payment for "each arms depot" found and "each arms deal stopped," as well as police protection and immunity from all charges. He also cautioned that the police needed to "beware of their own entourage, since there had been leaks." If the police accepted the deal, they were to notify him by publishing "JV.16" in the journal *Paris Soir*, after which a meeting could be arranged, but only on a Saturday, because, JV.16 wrote, "I have to look after wealthy people who forget those who work for them." He added in a postscript, "This meeting must be held in absolute secrecy, for you if you want to succeed, for me if I don't want to be murdered. We must beware of the numerous spies whom I have warned you are among you and who inform."[20] Evidently JV.16 was satisfied with the police response; in a letter of April 1938, he named names. JV.16 noted that he had offered his assistance to Marx Dormoy, the government minister behind the investigation of the Cagoule, but Dormoy had not accepted.[21]

Until November 16, 1937, however, the police seemed to be in no hurry to take aggressive action. For much of the year, they allowed the investigation slowly to accumulate data without making many arrests. Even though they questioned Filliol shortly after the murder of the Rosselli brothers, he was released, and this pattern continued until September. In fact, the police seem to have been willing to leave the Cagoule alone until the organization itself escalated its activities. The raid on Corre's apartment took place on September 16, exactly four days after the bombings at L'Étoile. This was very unlikely to have been a coincidence. The authorities knew the Cagoule was planning and committing provocations and even murders, but they were content to watch and wait as long as the Cagoule's victims were inconvenient émigrés (such as Navachine or the Rosselli brothers), low-level operatives with dodgy reputations (such as Laetitia Toureaux), or suspected traitors to the organization (such as Jean-Baptiste or Juif). But once the Cagoule began attacking respectable establishments, such as the targets of the L'Étoile bombings, or threatening public order as they did on the night of November 15–16, it was time to roll up its operation, as the police very efficiently did in the weeks after November 16.

Deloncle and the other leaders of the Cagoule seem to have placed their faith in their supporters in the army to back them in their intended putsch and to protect them should the police move against them. Once the Cagoule was exposed in 1937–38, however, that illusion was shattered. The army's chief of staff denied any involvement with the group on the part of anyone in the armed forces. Even Colonel Georges Groussard, Pétain's liaison with the Cagoule, later claimed that he had advised against any collaboration with the CSAR.[22] It would seem Pétain was not formally a Cagoulard, but feared a communist insurrection enough to tolerate the Cagoule's existence, using the secret organization to his advantage.[23]

By the beginning of 1938, many of the major operatives and quite a few smaller fry of the Cagoule were in police custody, including Henri and Eugène Deloncle, Méténier, Jakubiez, Jeanniot, Charles and André Tenaille, Duseigneur, Pozzo di Borgo, Grosset, and Moreau-de-la-Meuse. The rest were in hiding or were fugitives abroad either in the villa in San Remo or in one of the villas in San Sebastian. Members who fled to the latter location included Filliol, Jeantet, Corrèze, and Dr. Martin. The heaviest blow was the arrest of Deloncle himself by Inspector Porchier and his men in the early morning hours of November 26 and the ensuing police searches of the heart of the Cagoule's operations, Deloncle's office at the headquarters of the Caisse Hypothécaire Maritime et Fluviale at 78 rue de Provence. By now the Cagoulards knew that they had been betrayed, not only by informants but also by overly loquacious members of their own organization and sometimes even by their own mistresses, such as the famous *femme blonde*, Jacqueline Blondet, the mistress of Méténier. The police raided one arms cache after another, especially in and around the region of Paris, and seemed to be successfully dismantling the organization.[24]

The amount of weapons the police had to store and destroy was so large that the process resulted in tragedy. At 9:45 A.M. on January 27, 1938, a series of explosions began at the municipal laboratory of Villejuif, a suburb of

Paris. The blasts continued for a half an hour and resulted in fifteen deaths, at least ten of them soldiers and the rest scientists. The military had sequestered in the lab crates of Cagoulard grenades that began to explode as the chemists were trying to defuse them.[25] Meanwhile, each new raid resulted in further arrests, and each arrest led to further raids. The lower-level operatives whom these raids usually netted—often tenants or landlords who had allowed the Cagoule to use their basements or garages as hiding places for weapons in exchange for tidy sums of cash—tended to talk freely and amply during interrogations. Corre railed about Jeanniot, for example, who was in charge of the garage at Picpus that the police raided and in which they uncovered one of the most important Cagoule arms caches. During Jeanniot's interrogation, Corre noted, he told the police about other arms caches of which he was aware, such as the one at Reuil. This "miserable fellow" also named names, including those of Deloncle and Corrèze.[26]

Despite the discouraging news, the Cagoulards remained optimistic. For one thing, even with the disarray in their operations, many of their operatives were still at liberty, albeit in exile or in hiding. And even though the police raids yielded huge stores of arms, numerous other caches stayed undetected, including most of those concealed in the provinces.[27] By the same token, the Cagoule continued to enjoy the clandestine and in some cases overt support of many elements of the right in France. Officers of the deuxième bureau seem to have been sympathetic and willing to help out the Cagoule even while infiltrating the organization. The goal seems to have been to control and contain these "men of action" on the right, not to break them, but to use them as a source of manpower in the struggle against the communists while keeping them firmly under the thumb of the police. For example, the French deuxième bureaux kept an agent in San Sebastian named Paloc. Within days of Corre's arrival in that city, Paloc attempted to recruit him as an agent to keep the French government apprised of the Italian and German arms flowing to the Spanish Nationalist forces in the region. Corre refused because he despised the Third Republic so heartily that not even his patriotism could move him to lift a finger to aid it, but he and Paloc maintained a friendly relationship.[28] And Paloc became a quite useful ally of the Cagoule, evidently with the full knowledge of his superiors. Even as the Parisian and national police were scouring France for Cagoulards and setting up roadblocks on every highway, Paloc picked up Jacques Corrèze at Corrèze's hiding place in Paris after Eugène Deloncle had sent Corrèze several urgent letters from prison via his lawyer insisting that Corrèze, who was devoted to Deloncle and wanted to remain near him, flee the country. Paloc then drove Corrèze out of Paris and, when his brand-new Hotchkiss sedan broke down outside the city, escorted Corrèze safely to San Sebastian by train.[29]

Thomas Bourlier, who freely admitted to being a deuxième bureau operative who had infiltrated the Cagoule under orders from his superiors, rendered Cagoulards aid when the police were on their tail. As a liaison agent between Méténier and Deloncle, he doubtless had access to much information that he passed on to his superiors. But he also warned Méténier when arrest was imminent and tried at that moment to recruit Méténier to inform on his fellow Cagoulards in return for immunity from prosecution for his own crimes. Even Deloncle's arrest seems to have been the result of a prearranged meeting. Deloncle freely emerged from his hiding place and into the waiting arms of the police, who nevertheless insisted on handcuffing him, much to Corre's disgust. Finally, it is important to note that Corre and his fellow Cagoulards, even those in hiding in Spain, were far too well informed about events in France to have garnered all they knew through the newspapers. How, for example, did Corre know the details of what Jeanniot or Jakubiez had told the police if someone was not feeding him information from within the investigation as it unfolded? The deuxième bureau was quite probably familiar with the progress of the police and was potentially feeding information to the Cagoulards through their many female informants.[30]

Other authorities were also sympathetic to the cause of the Cagoule and willing to help keep Cagoulards and/or their weapons out of the hands of the police. According to Corre, a juge d'instruction in Bordeaux allowed a Cagoulard, a retired military man, to refrain from revealing in court the location of an arms cache. After the Cagoulard had railed against the communist threat and the need for France to defend itself, the judge supposedly said "General, you have the arms. Keep them and know that you can use them when it becomes necessary."[31] Even if the story was apocryphal, it no doubt reflected the reality of complicity between many judges, policemen, and army officers and the Cagoule. Those who could not be brought around for ideological reasons might instead be bribed. In the same journal entry where Corre related the preceding story, he alleged that police in Bordeaux agreed to leave an arms depot there alone in return for ten thousand francs. Thus the Cagoule used a variety of means to avoid confiscation of most of the arms caches it had stored in France. And Corre's diary offers copious information about the many weapons the Cagoule had stockpiled just across the border in Spain, out of reach of the French authorities but close enough to be delivered quickly to France should the need arise. One likely reason the deuxième bureau cast an indulgent eye on all these weapons stockpiles was because they could also be drawn upon in the event of war with Germany, and the authorities hoped to recruit the ultra-patriotic Cagoulards in the battle against the German threat.

The Cagoule also benefited from significant support from the French political right and its outlets in the press during the aftermath of November 16. At first the tide seemed to run strongly in favor of the left. On November 23, Interior Minister Marx Dormoy solemnly announced to the nation the downfall of the Cagoule and the extent of its plot against the government. "It is a true plot against the republican institutions that has been uncovered." Dormoy intoned. Worse, he asserted, "The documents we have seized establish that the suspects took upon themselves the task of substituting for the republican model our country freely adopted a dictatorial regime that would precede the restoration of the monarchy."[32] He went on to explain that the Cagoule had amassed substantial arms, drawn up lists of all known communists, secured copies of the keys to all the offices of the various ministries of the government, and devised detailed plans about how to seize the gas, electrical, and water works in Paris. All of this pointed towards civil war, and the left-wing papers immediately produced articles about the plot from which the government had narrowly escaped. *Le Populaire* went further, blaming the entire right for complicity in the conspiracy.[33] All the leftist press reacted with alarm and fury; they universally condemned the Cagoule as a treasonous organization in the pay of Mussolini and Hitler. Moreover, the left-wing press was implacably opposed to treating the Cagoulards as political prisoners, as they and their lawyers had requested. In the view of the left, their crimes were, as a writer for *l'Humanité* put it, "crimes of ordinary law committed upon individuals and goods for the purpose of fomenting civil war in France and without doubt along with it foreign intervention." For the left, the Cagoulards were traitors and thugs.[34]

But the French government was slow to move forward with the case against the Cagoule, probably because they did not want to alarm the public further with revelations about the Cagoule's foreign connections or stir up trouble in the army, where the CSAR found many of their recruits. As a result, the right-wing press, which had originally denounced the bombings at l'Étoile as communist conspiracies, now embraced the Cagoule.[35] *L'Action Française,* for example, declared that the government's imprisonment of Cagoulard leaders was nothing less than a plot staged by the Sûreté against the entire right. Baptizing their version of this anti-Cagoulard plot "Fantomarx," the right-wing papers accused Dormoy of deliberately using scare tactics to drum up support for socialist-communist politics.[36] In sum, the right dismissed the Cagoulard threat as little more than a left-wing conspiracy designed to damage the right.

Letters from right-wing adherents poured in to the press and the government demanding the Cagoulards' release. Pierre Taittinger wrote in defense of some of the most notorious Cagoulards, including Jakubiez, who was by then implicated in the murder of the Rosselli brothers.[37] Anonymous letters were published in the newspapers and also sent to the government. One individual interpreted the arrest of the Cagoulards as the left's attempt to take away French civil liberties, writing, "We understand that every French citizen who doesn't adhere to the Popular Front . . . will lose all their goods and liberties."[38] The Cagoulard leaders also defended themselves, engaging their adversaries in verbal skirmishes in the press. When the left-wing L'Oeuvre characterized Eugène Deloncle as a dangerous conspirator whose plan could have led to the massacre of French women and children, Deloncle wrote indignantly to the daily in 1938 from his prison cell, insisting that he would shed blood for French women and children just as he had in World War I.[39] Ultimately the right-wing campaign against the left was successful. Most of the Cagoulards who had been arrested in 1937 and 1938 were released in 1939 and not tried until 1948.[40]

The Cagoulards' ability to escape from the consequences of their crimes was due largely to the efficacious support they received from a large portion of the French right. Even lower-level Cagoule operatives seemed to have been able to engage lawyers almost immediately, and most of the more important Cagoulards found prominent, high-powered attorneys willing to defend them. In particular, Xavier Vallat, a leading representative of the anti-Semitic extreme right in France and the former founder of the Faisceau, represented a number of high-level Cagoulards, including Pozzo di Borgo. Vallat later became head of the Commissariat-Général aux Questions Juives (General Commissariat for Jewish Questions) under the Vichy government from 1940 to 1942. Corre asserted in December 1937 that already "the lawyers had taken on a primary role," acting as liaisons between the Cagoulards in prison and their supporters and sympathizers at large, as well as those members of the organization still in hiding. Every morning Deloncle gave written orders to his lawyers, who then passed them on to the intended recipients. In this way Deloncle was able to maintain control of the Cagoule even from prison, and it was in this manner that he ordered Corrèze to flee to San Sebastian in December despite the latter's reluctance to abandon his chief. "Everyone at the Palace (of Justice) wants to be a lawyer for the Cagoule," Corre declared.[41]

To counter the left's emphasis on the seriousness of the Cagoule plots, conservatives sought in their public statements and in the press to make a joke of the organization and downplay the danger it posed to the Third Republic. Conservatives who secretly supported the Cagoule—as well as competing groups on the right opposed to it, such as the Action Française—joined in the mockery. They were motivated primarily by their desire to protect the reputation of their own parties and organizations. Moreover, some were only too happy to see their competitors floundering in their quest for the allegiance of France's conservative citizens. In this campaign to draw the teeth of the Cagoule through ridicule, the conservatives were largely successful. An avalanche of articles and editorials from the pens of well-known figures such as Pozzo di Borgo, Maurice Pujo of the Action Française, and Léon Daudet ridiculed the "pseudo-plot" the government had uncovered. The Cagoule, according to Pujo, was "a useful instrument for provocation that up till now Marx Dormoy has employed as a diversion from the bombs at L'Étoile and as the centerpiece of his Socialist-Communist electoral campaign."[42]

Most right-wing writers echoed this view, and over time the skepticism of the moderate press grew as well, testament less to any paucity of evidence regarding Cagoule activities than to the generally low esteem in which most French people held their government. Eventually the press campaign to discredit the case against the Cagoule succeeded in swaying public opinion, especially after the excitement of the sensational revelations of late 1937 and early 1938 died down. The Cagoule became a topic of derision, and cartoons appeared in the papers poking fun at the hooded hoodlums. Underscoring the idea that the left had fabricated the Fantomarx plot, one right-wing paper showed hooded prisoners in the window of every jail cell and a caption that read "Six more, Monsieur le Directeur. If this continues we're going to have to lodge them in people's homes."[43] Around the same time, hooded costumes became all the rage at fancy dress balls in Paris. The investigation seemed to slow, and the government was less and less willing to pursue the primary figures involved, in particular Cagoulards and their sympathizers in the army.

By the middle of 1939, most French people seem to have come to believe that the Cagoulards, while misguided and perhaps even despicable in their intentions, were also few in number and hopelessly incompetent amateurs who posed little threat to the nation.[44] According to Corre, this misinformation campaign succeeded admirably:

> In truth, this is a curious situation. The government is persuaded, and in this it is correct, that it has gotten a grip on an organization whose goal it is to overthrow the regime. It discovers the weapons, announces that this organization is very highly developed, with its own first, second, third and fourth columns and its own medical service. It is paramilitary. Its troops are divided into brigades, regiments, battalions, etc. Yet there is no truth anymore and almost everywhere, on the right at least and in the center, people snicker at it (the government) and it is mocked and ridiculed. No one believes what it says, or everyone pretends not to believe and, in fact, this government so proud of its discovery can't prove a thing.[45]

Ironically, this deliberately misleading analysis seems to have stuck not only in popular memory but also among professional scholars who have studied the Cagoule down to the present day.

The Coming of War and the Aborted Trial, 1938–1940

The support of many in the French right for the Cagoule, and the ambivalence and the skepticism of the rest of the right and the moderate center in France toward it, only grew with the approach of war during 1938 and 1939. According to Frédéric Freigneux, a historian of the Cagoule, "Many people were scandalized by the arrests that seemed to them to be completely arbitrary. For them, the personality and high social standing of those indicted made it impossible to believe that they had participated in such a plot."[46] In a major victory for their cause, the Cagoulards and their lawyers managed to have the status of the prisoners awaiting trial at the Santé prison changed to that of political prisoners rather than that of common criminals, even though none of them had been indicted for political crimes. "Associating with criminals" was the most common charge levied against them.[47] Their success owed much to the strong outpouring of support they received from the public, which included letter-writing campaigns both from ordinary citizens and from such exalted personages as champagne mogul Pierre Taittinger.[48] The arrest of World War I war hero Joseph Darnand caused an especially great outcry, and a number of newspapers took up his cause. On October 19, 1938, the Union Nationales de Combattants, Groupe de la Région Parisienne, a Parisian veterans' group, addressed a letter to the minister of pensions in Paris requesting that he intervene to get Moreau de la Meuse, Deloncle, and Darnand out of prison.[49]

The coming of war and the need for national unity—and for the mobilization of experienced war veterans, which would include almost all the members of the Cagoule—only increased the outcry. In August 1939, shortly before the beginning of the so-called phony war that commenced with the invasion of Poland on September 3, the commander of a squadron of the cavalry wrote to the president of the Paris appeals court and asked him to release Jeanniot, whose services the commander claimed to need in his squadron. The day after the invasion of Poland, Chief Military Engineer Curières de Castelnau wrote to the appeals court with the request that Eugène Deloncle be released to be mobilized in the army engineers as soon as possible. On September 1, Pierre Taittinger addressed a letter to the minister of justice in favor of a number of Cagoulards who were in the military reserve, and of Jean-Marie Bouvyer, an active member of the military. Bouvyer was still in prison in early 1940 when Taittinger addressed a second letter to the minister, making the far-fetched assertion that the Rosselli brothers were Soviet spies and that therefore Bouvyer had committed no crime in participating in their murder and should be released immediately to rejoin his regiment.[50]

By September 7, the chief prosecutor in charge of the Cagoule dossier was forced to relent and free a number of Cagoulards. Others, such as Jeantet, returned to France from exile once the war broke out and were initially arrested. Corrèze by then was already under arrest, having returned to France in May 1938 to visit his mistress. Those whom the government was reluctant to release, such as Méténier, launched hunger strikes until they too were freed as a consequence of the mobilization at the beginning of the German invasion of France on May 10, 1940. On July 21, 1940, the Garde des Sceaux declared that everyone detained in the case should be released.[51] Dr. Martin was posted to the military hospital at Bicêtre. Many of the former Cagoulards served with distinction and won citations for bravery, including François Allo, Gabriel Jeantet, and Jacques Corrèze. Some, such as Joseph Darnand, were captured by the Germans but managed to escape and return to France. Prior to his capture, Darnand received the medal of the Legion of Honor; a photograph of him wearing his military uniform and performing a jaunty military salute appeared on the cover of *Paris Match.* Only Filliol categorically refused to serve. Having made himself unwelcome among his fellow exiles in San Remo, in April 1938 he followed Jeantet to San Sebastian with Alice Lamy and their two children, where he remained, much to Corre's dismay, until the French capitulation in June 1940.

The case against the Cagoule, while not officially closed, was indefinitely suspended at the onset of the war. Like that of Laetitia Toureaux, it seemed to be getting nowhere despite the confessions of a number of Cagoulards to a series of assassinations and assassination attempts as well as other crimes. As Police Commissioner Charles Chenevier had remarked in his March 15, 1938, report, all the different roads in the Toureaux case really did lead to the Cagoule.[52] And as the prosecution of the Cagoulards petered out due to the need to preserve national unity in the face of the German threat, the Toureaux affair faded from view entirely. The police unearthed little evidence that formally linked Toureaux's murder to the Cagoule during the long investigation of the organization after November 16, 1937. In a report written in Paris on November 29, 1939, at the behest of the minister of the French navy, who was requesting information on Deloncle now that the latter had been released from prison and mobilized, Marx Dormoy informed the minister about what was known about the Cagoule and its activities. He stated that he would "only indicate proven facts, and leave aside suspicions regarding the CSAR touching on other affairs such as the assassination of Laetitia Toureau [*sic*], the murder of Navachine, and the bloody events at Clichy."[53] Even the man who was perhaps the greatest enemy of the Cagoule recognized that regardless of widespread suspicions about the organization, the official investigation lacked solid evidence to tie the Cagoule to Toureaux's murder.

Faustian Choices, 1940–1945

War broke out between France and its allies and Germany with the invasion of Poland in September 1939. The so-called phony war lasted until the German invasion of France and the Low Countries in May 1940. On June 10, the French government fled Paris for Bordeaux, and Italy formally entered the war on the side of Germany. On June 16, French president Albert Lebrun replaced Prime Minister Paul Reynaud, who had resigned in opposition to the decision to surrender, with World War I hero Philippe Pétain. When it became obvious that French capitulation was imminent,

Charles de Gaulle, undersecretary of national defense, who was already in London, refused to accept the surrender and began to organize the Free French forces. The French surrendered on June 25, 1940, and during the first two weeks of July, Pétain formed a new government at Vichy with Pierre Laval as his vice president and Fernand de Brinon as his representative to the German High Command in Paris. Pétain immediately appointed right-wing politician and alleged Cagoulard Raphaël Alibert as his minister of justice, an act that boded well for the employment possibilities that other Cagoulards would enjoy in the Vichy regime.[54]

Like all French men and women after the fall of France, the Cagoulards faced difficult choices. The decisions they made resulted from the individual balance of hatred of the Germans, patriotism and nationalism, and personal self-interest and ambition. The members of the Cagoule lacked neither courage nor the willingness to take risks, and almost all played significant parts in the French drama of the Resistance, Vichy, and collaboration, although they chose markedly different paths.[55] A minority of former Cagoulards—including François Allo, Loustaunau-Lacau, and Maurice Duclos—opted almost immediately for the Resistance or joined the Free French. Loustaunau-Lacau spent two years in the German prison camp at Mauthausen for his pains. The Germans executed Aristide Corre for passing information to the British intelligence services. De Gaulle awarded Duclos the Croix de Guerre for his work organizing resistance networks. Others, including most notably Deloncle and his lieutenant Corrèze, as well as Filliol, always accompanied by Alice Lamy, and Darnand and his nephew, Henri Charbonneau, opted for outright collaboration with the Germans. Some, such as Filliol, appear to have made that choice out of pure conviction, while the actions of others, such as Deloncle and Darnand, indicate that they were motivated out of a combination of conviction and self-interest. Jeantet later told friends and family that he could have gone either for the Resistance or for Vichy; however, sources indicate he represented Deloncle in Vichy.[56]

The majority of the Cagoulards initially chose Vichy, which seemed to embody both their dislike of Germany and their desire to reform French government on an authoritarian model. Darnand, for example, who had served the Cagoule as a key intermediary with the Italian fascists in 1936 and 1937, ultimately came to head the infamous Milice, a paramilitary force created under Vichy for the purpose of destroying the French Resistance. Others, such as Eugène Deloncle, flirted with Vichy but soon found their prospects better in the Occupied Zone. Most remained steadfast supporters of Pétain and his government until the end of the war. Jeantet appeared to be a particularly faithful ally of the elderly Maréchal Pétain until the bitter end, although he also secretly began to cultivate ties with the Resistance via his old friend and ally Duclos almost on his first day on the job as an advisor to Pétain and the Vichy government.[57]

From the inception of Vichy, Pétain surrounded himself with former Cagoulards and other members of the extreme right, and his cabinet was packed with them. Even before the Senate and National Assembly voted to appoint Pétain head of the French state on June 16, 1940, Pétain had already chosen Raphaël Alibert to run his civilian cabinet. Although the German military controlled the Occupied Zone, technically the Vichy government was supposed to oversee civil and domestic affairs throughout France. Within weeks the infamous Alibert laws were passed, subjecting all naturalizations since 1927 to revocation and outlawing Freemasonry, among other things. Xavier Vallat, put in charge of the "Jewish question" at Vichy, began to oversee the internment of Jews that the October 3 statute regarding Jews authorized.

Deloncle was evidently present for the momentous occasion on July 10, when the Third Republic essentially voted itself out of existence and addressed a letter to his wife Mercédès that day expressing his great joy to have witnessed the end of the hated government.[58] "The Republic is no more," he exulted. "Today I watched these puppets commit suicide. I have observed their agony, I who they persecuted. My dream has half come true, that for which you and I have so suffered. If you had seen their faces contorted with fear, that would have filled you with joy . . . I can't tell you my role in the affair, you must already know; it was not inconsiderable. The future will tell whether I was right."[59]

Deloncle soon found, however, that although a number of ex-Cagoulards and fellow-travelers found a welcome at Vichy and achieved considerable success in its regime, he was considered too much of a a wild card and was not offered a post, or at least not one commensurate with what he considered to be his abilities and services rendered to the cause. Jeantet was head of propaganda for Vichy from 1940 until a falling out with Admiral Darlan, also an ex-Cagoulard and the minister of the navy, led to his forced resignation in August 1941. From that time forward, he remained a close adviser to Pétain but held no cabinet post. Darlan, Laval, and Weygand—all members of Pétain's successive cabinets between 1940 and 1945—had been members of or sympathizers with the Cagoule during the late 1930s. Other ex-Cagoulards found less exalted positions within Vichy. Colonel Georges Groussard, not formally a Cagoulard, but a Cagoule supporter in the French military before the war, was appointed inspector general of the Sûreté during Vichy; he in turn appointed Méténier head of the Groupes de Protection (GP), the rump military force that the Germans permitted Vichy for maintaining order after the armistice. This ultra-right-wing police force also served as Pétain's personal guard and included a number of former Cagoulards. As head of the GP, Méténier participated in the December 13, 1940, arrest of Pierre Laval at the Hôtel du Parc, the first of many breaches that soon put ex-Cagoulards and their allies at odds with each other as their differences regarding collaboration grew. Pétain, urged on by Alibert, hoped to distance himself from Laval, who preferred a far more openly collaborationist stance toward Germany than either Pétain or Alibert desired. Laval's ally Marcel Déat was arrested in Paris on the same day, but German ambassador Otto Abetz forced Pétain to free both prisoners, although Pétain steadfastly refused to return Laval to his post as foreign minister.[60]

No one, however, neither the Germans nor the Vichy government, really trusted either Deloncle or Filliol, both of whom were considered to be too uncontrollable and given to indiscriminate plotting, although they could be useful if handled with care. In April 1941, the Vichy Sûreté disseminated a confidential dispatch throughout France warning of possible assassination attempts against government figures, and it singled out Filliol as especially dangerous.[61] Kept at arms' length by Vichy, Deloncle and Filliol joined forces and together chose the path of collaboration. On September 1, 1940, Deloncle officially launched his own political organization, the Mouvement Social Révolutionnaire (MSR). His technical director and chief source of funds was Eugène Schueller, owner of L'Oréal. Filliol was in charge of intelligence for the MSR, while Jacques Corrèze and Henri Charbonneau shared responsibility for the Paris region and Jacques Fauran took charge of organizing the MSR in the provinces. Jean Fontenoy was Deloncle's next-in-command. Even Gabriel Jeantet agreed to support his former comrade and joined the MSR's directorate. Hence the MSR reunited some of the most committed ex-Cagoulards in a new movement dedicated to old goals—nationalism, patriotism, anticommunism, anti-Semitism—but with a new, pro-German twist. Still, everyone, including the Germans, who agreed to tolerate the MSR but withheld their full support from it, were skeptical about the depth of Deloncle's conversion to the German cause.[62]

The years 1940–1942 must have been exhilarating ones for Eugène Deloncle despite his disappointment with Vichy. His collaboration with the Germans and the tacit support of members of Pétain's government, such as Jeantet and Darlan, allowed him to indulge in what he loved best, plotting and intrigue. In February 1941, Pierre Laval, now in opposition to Pétain and ever more closely tied to the Germans and the collaborationist cause, brought together Marcel Déat and Deloncle to create a new group to unify the pro-German political parties that had formed in France since the Armistice. The five-man directorate included Déat, Deloncle, Fontenoy, Jean Vanor, and Jean Goy. Unlike the MSR, which enjoyed only "tolerated" (*Geduldigte*) status with the German authorities in Paris, the Rassemblement National Populaire (RNP) almost immediately received the more coveted designation of a "favored" (*Genehmigte*) organization.[63] On June 22, Germany invaded the Soviet Union, introducing a new phase of the war and creating the opening for a new French collaborationist organization, the Légion des Volontaires Français contre le Bolchévisme (LVF). Deloncle was a cofounder of the LVF and Fontenoy commanded its troops.[64]

Tensions quickly began to rise, however, between Deloncle and Déat and Déat's ally, Laval, over leadership of the RNP. During a ceremony held at the Vélodrome d'hiver in Paris on August 27 to celebrate the deployment of the first LVF contingents to the Eastern Front, the three men shared the podium. Paul Collette, a self-proclaimed Resistance fighter who had infiltrated the LVF ranks, shot and wounded both Déat and Laval. Despite Collette's steadfast insistence that he was working for the Resistance, Déat and Laval were convinced that Deloncle was behind the assassination attempt and summoned him to their side-by-side hospital beds to explain. His adamant denials failed to sway them, and for good reason. Several weeks prior to the attack, Deloncle's former lover and his secretary at the MSR, Tonia (or Tania) Masse, began to suspect that Deloncle was embezzling funds from the MSR treasury. When her blackmail attempts failed with Deloncle, she turned to Déat and informed him that she knew Deloncle was planning to assassinate him and take over leadership of the RNP.

On September 23, Masse imprudently met with Deloncle one last time and then went to a brasserie where she was to have dinner with Deloncle's ally and her current lover, Fauran. Instead of Fauran, two men showed up, with whom she again unwisely left the brasserie, supposedly to meet her lover. She was never seen alive again. Her body was found floating in the Seine wrapped in coal or potato sacks and tied with wire on October 8. She had been beaten to death with a club. On the night of September 23, someone had broken into her apartment and stolen some of her possessions, evidently in an attempt to make her murder look like a robbery. Neither the police nor the Germans were fooled or particularly amused, especially given that a bomb planted under the bed of Marx Dormoy had blown the former Popular Front minister's head off on July 26. Dormoy had been under house arrest in Montélimar at the time, but he had received assurances from both Pétain and the Germans regarding his personal safety. It was clear that Deloncle himself was behind that event and another bomb that exploded in Nice near the Promenade des Anglais on August 14 as well.[65] Deloncle was getting out of hand.

As a result of the rift between himself and Déat and Laval, Deloncle removed his MSR from the RNP. This did not bother him excessively; he was more interested at this point in his own party, the MSR, and in expanding recruitment for the LVF. But he was concerned to rescue his failing credit with the Germans. As a result, he took a fateful decision that irrevocably tied his future to the Gestapo. At this time, the German military command and the SS were in a struggle for power in France. Deloncle approached SS Obersturmführer Hans Sommer and requested assistance in a plot to destroy several prominent synagogues in Paris, evidently a bid on Deloncle's part to demonstrate his loyalty to the Germans and his unyielding anti-Semitism. Without informing his counterpart in the German military, General Carl-Heinrich von Stülpnagel, commander of the Wehrmacht in Paris, Sommer provided Deloncle with the explosives with the understanding that Deloncle and his MSR would assume full responsibility for the bombings.

During the night of October 2–3, Deloncle's men blew up the synagogues. The results were not what he had hoped, however. He failed to raise his stature among the Germans, as Stülpnagel was furious and refused to have anything to do with him; it was doubtless with Stülpnagel's backing that Filliol and Charbonneau joined forces and literally ejected Deloncle and Deloncle's ever-loyal lieutenant Corrèze from the headquarters of the MSR. Bad blood had been building between Deloncle and Filliol at least since the failed putsch of November 16, 1937. Meanwhile, the Gestapo was also finding Deloncle too unpredictable. By the end of 1941, Deloncle was increasingly forced to focus his attention on the LVF, the one remaining organization where he retained standing and influence, thanks largely to the support of his former Cagoulard ally, Admiral François Darlan.[66]

It did not take Filliol long to wear out his welcome with Vichy and the

Germans either. Although in July 1942, he was made a member of the Comité Central d'Honneur of the new Légion Tricolore, created at Vichy to supplant the LVF, by that October, Laval had ordered him interned and arrested. Laval suspected that Filliol had helped Deloncle engineer the assassination attempt against Laval the preceding year. His pretext, however, was that Filliol had accused someone in the German embassy of being a Freemason. Filliol languished in internment at Saint-Paul-d'Eyjaux until 1944.

The year 1942 changed everything for the war, and for the ex-Cagoulards as well. On March 24, the Vichy government arrested Dr. Martin and incarcerated him at Castres. A week later, the Germans executed Corre. On April 18, Pierre Laval replaced Darlan as prime minister in the Vichy government. Pétain at this point became little more than a figurehead, and Laval was free to pursue aggressively his collaborationist and anti-Semitic policies. Although Darlan retained his post as head of the French navy, it was no accident that only weeks after the fall from power of Darlan, Deloncle's only remaining patron, Filliol succeeded in ousting Deloncle as head of the MSR. As long as Darlan remained alive and active in Laval's cabinet as head of the navy, however, Deloncle remained protected.

In 1942, Darlan and Deloncle both began to have serious doubts about a German victory in the war, doubts that the strong North American role in the Allied invasion of North Africa greatly reinforced. They began in tandem to put out feelers to the Allies and to German military commanders in France, most notably Admiral Wilhelm Canaris, chief of the Abwehr in France and two years later a principal plotter in the failed assassination attempt against Hitler. Corrèze evidently shared Deloncle's changing views and in January 1943 joined the Resistance, probably with Deloncle's blessing. The direct result of the American invasion of North Africa on November 8, 1942, however, was that Darlan, sent to combat U.S. forces in French Algeria, surrendered instead and joined the Allies. Darlan's defection meant that Deloncle lost both his contact with the Allies and his protector in France as well. On November 11, the Germans launched Operation Case Anton, in which they invaded Vichy, diminishing its independence but also cementing the power of the truncated Vichy government—and thus of Laval—over all of France. On December 24, the final blow struck; Darlan was assassinated. Deloncle's own end soon followed. The Gestapo had been well aware of the double game Deloncle and Darlan had been playing in 1942, and on January 7, 1943, four Gestapo agents burst into Deloncle's apartment in Paris, shot and killed him, and seriously wounded his son, Louis.[67]

Les Dûrs: **Filliol, Darnand, and the Milice**

By the end of 1943, most of the rest of the ex-Cagoulards had come to share the view of Darlan and Deloncle that the Germans were not likely to win the war. During 1944, if they had not already, most chose to cast their lot with the Resistance and/or the Free French forces, which was one reason so many of them benefited from amnesty after the war. The story of the former Cagoulards who remained loyal to the collaborationist cause is not edifying. By June 1943, Roidot, the Cagoule's germ warfare specialist before the war, had been appointed by the Germans Directeur départmentale de la main d'oeuvre (Departmental Director of Labor) at Pau, where he was in charge of all deportations to Germany for the Service du Travail Obligatoire, or Service of Forced Labor (STO). During the night of July 16–17, 1942, René Bousquet of the Vichy police and his lieutenant in Paris, Jean Leguay, launched the first mass arrests of French Jews, the infamous Vélodrome d'hiver raid, in which 12,384 Jews, including 4,051 Jewish children the Nazis had not requested, were arrested and sent to concentration camps. Bousquet rounded up another seven thousand Jews in the southern zone in August. But even he was evidently insufficiently extreme for the German command in France, which was increasingly under the control of the SS. By December 1942, Pétain, yielding to pressure from Laval and the Germans, had appointed Darnand as Secrétaire-général au maintien de l'ordre (General Secretary for Maintaining Order) in the place of Bousquet.

Worse was to come. On January 30, 1943, Pierre Laval created the terrible Milice, a sort of French Gestapo, to combat the Resistance, putting former Cagoulard Joseph Darnand in charge of it. In August 1943, Darnand took an oath of loyalty to the Waffen SS. In May 1944, under pressure from Darnand and others, Laval finally agreed to free or, perhaps better, unleash Filliol from internment. Asked to make himself scarce, Filliol promptly joined the Milice of Limoges using the pseudonym Deschamps (his nom de guerre in Spain had been Miguel Deschamps), probably with Darnand's connivance. Filliol quickly assumed command of the Limoges branch of the Milice and began a veritable reign of terror. On May 10, he interrogated a hundred prisoners at Périgueux in the cinema the Palace; his victims testified that he did not shrink from torture. Thirty of those interrogated at Périgueux were deported to Germany, and others were sent to labor on the submarine base in Bordeaux. On May 28, the Gestapo arrested the Bishop of Clermont; it was the devoutly Catholic Filliol, with Alice Lamy by his side and with the assistance of two Germans, who interrogated him. Filliol and his Milice supplied intelligence to the Germans and played a principal role in the Germans' decision to destroy the town of Oradour-sur-Glane in Limousin. Over six hundred people were killed in Oradour during the German attack that Filliol helped orchestrate, including two hundred children in town to receive vaccinations that day. This proved to be too much even for his fellow members of the Milice. By the end of June Filliol had been transferred to Clermont-Ferrand, where, under a new pseudonym, Chef Denis, he again joined the combat against the Resistance as a member of the Milice. On June 13, Pétain appointed Darnand as interior secretary, but the reign of the *dûrs*—the hard-core ones—was fast coming to an end.[68]

1944–1948: Trial and Amnesty

On July 29, 1944, the Vichy police arrested Gabriel Jeantet. Transferred into the hands of the Germans, Jeantet was deported to the Eisenberg fortress in Germany on August 15. One week later, a member of the Resistance assassinated Roidot near his office in Pau. It was the beginning of the end. On August 25, Allied forces liberated Paris, and almost exactly two months later the Allies recognized the Provisional Government of the French Republic with Charles de Gaulle as its head as the legitimate government of France. Filliol and his militia, meanwhile, retreated with the Germans from France. In Germany, he and Darnand joined a short-lived French government in exile; when that fell apart, determined to fight on against the Allies, they fought side by side with the Germans in a special regiment of French collaborators known as the "SS Charlemagne." While Santo Emanuele under interrogation was telling the Italian police all about the relationship between the Cagoule and Mussolini during the 1930s, Filliol, Fontenoy, and Darnand—the last surviving Cagoulards who had not come around to join the Allies—remained loyal to the cause in Germany. Fontenoy died in May 1945 in the final battle for Berlin. Filliol was luckier; with the unwilling assistance of two hostages, he was able to escape Germany and flee to Spain. Accused of collaborating with the enemy, Filliol was condemned to death by a court in Limoges on July 25, 1945. Franco's government refused all extradition requests from France after the war, however, and Filliol settled in Spain. By contrast, the Allies caught Darnand, whom they executed on October 10, 1945, five days before they executed Laval.[69] At his trial for collaboration in August 1945, the prosecution accused Pétain of having been a Cagoulard. During the proceedings, when former premier of the Third Republic

Édouard Daladier was asked if Pétain had in fact belonged to the CSAR, he famously shrugged. Who knew?[70]

This decision on the part of most of the former Cagoulards to rally to the Allied cause had a tremendous effect on the final disposition of the case against the Cagoule after the war. On May 19, 1945, Jeantet was freed from his German prison and returned to France. In October 1945, the court of assizes of the Seine was supposed to reopen the postponed but never officially closed case of the Cagoule, although its official start was delayed. Judge Pierre Béteille had survived the war and again took charge of investigating the case. Locating the now dispersed documents and evidence that had been assembled prior to the war required great persistence. Just when he was ready to give up hope, Béteille received a tip that in June 1940 men from the ministry of justice had hidden a number of the most important dossiers related to the case in a secret compartment in the lavatories of the courthouse at Lesparre, perhaps to keep them out of the hands of the Germans. The concierge who witnessed the deed was sworn to silence but was willing to guide Béteille to the location, where the documents were found, rather dusty and damp and smelly, but intact.[71]

The investigations continued until October 11, 1946, when the trial was officially restarted where it had left off in 1940 before the court of assizes of the Seine. There were sixty-five defendants named, of whom sixteen were dead. Forty-nine others were alive and present, including Maurice Duclos, who had returned to Paris from his safe haven in Argentina to join his former Cagoulard comrades in the dock. The remaining defendants were fugitives. The trial continued throughout 1947 and most of 1948. Finally, between November 26 and 28, the verdicts and sentences were handed down. Maurice Duclos, François Allo, Walter Blondin, Armand Hasenfuss, Gustave Vauclard, and Henri Vogel were acquitted. Only sixteen others present at the trial were actually found guilty; presumably the charges were dropped against many of the others. The sentences were mostly quite light, excepting Fernand Jakubiez, who was sentenced to life in prison with hard labor, and François Méténier, who got twenty years, also with hard labor. Jacques Corrèze was sentenced to ten years in prison, and the rest five years or less. The court was much harder on the fugitives. Jacques Fauran, Jean Filliol, and Jean-Marie Bouvyer were sentenced to death for the Rosselli murders, Yves Moynier and Anne Mouraille were likewise sentenced to death for the assassination of Marx Dormoy, and René Locuty received the same for the L'Étoile bombings, which had resulted in two deaths.

In October 1948, Jeantet was sentenced to four years of hard labor and twenty-five years of *indignité nationale*—the loss of civil and political rights. During the 1950s, however, most of the collaborators sentenced for their activities during the war years were pardoned or benefited from reductions in their sentences. Because Jeantet was tried for his prewar activities as a member of the Cagoule, we do not know whether he benefited from the amnesty of the 1950s. Jeantet himself asserted that the severity of his sentence relative to the treatment of other Cagoulards who were active during the war resulted from the desire of his judges to punish by proxy his brother Claude, who had been a much more active collaborator with the Germans during the war, but who after the war was safely in Switzerland, out of the reach of French justice. His role in the MSR certainly further tarnished his reputation. Jeantet, who envisioned himself as a *"homme politique"* best suited to a political career, suffered greatly from the repercussions of his sentence. Although upon emerging from prison he enjoyed a successful career in publishing and media, his political prospects were ruined. He was an *"homme fini,"* a finished man.[72]

And what of the case of Laetitia Toureaux? In February 1948, the public prosecutor reopened her case briefly, but not as part of the official trial of the Cagoulards. The February 26 report of the Procureur de la République to the Procureur Générale is worth reproducing in part:

> Object: Premeditated murder of NOURRISSAT (Loetitia) widow TOUREAUX— Reopening of the investigation on new charges. I have the honor to inform you that I have received from my colleague at Strasbourg a letter and a memo dated the 11th of this month from a gentleman named HELLEU (Lucien Robert) committed in the psychiatric hospital of Hoerdt (Bas-Rhin).
>
> This person confesses that he is the author of the assassination of the said NOURRISSAT (Loetitia Marie Joséphine) widow TOUREAUX, whose body was discovered—a knife planted in the throat—May 16, 1937 in a car of the Metropolitan at the Porte Dorée station.
>
> It is not necessary to note that the said HELLEU was suspected at the time of being the author of the crime because of the relationship the investigators established between this assassination and the arrest of the aforesaid person on August 21, 1937, while he was in the process of killing with two knife blows a Miss DIETA Jacqueline in the basement of a drinking establishment at 80 rue de Rivoli in Paris.
>
> HELLEU, indicted for the murder of the said Miss DIETA was recognized as mentally ill. His case was dismissed and he was committed at the Asile Ste.-Anne on September 2, 1937.

Subsequently, the investigation was unable to establish his participation in the assassination of Madam NOURRISSAT, widow TOUREAUX, and that case was equally dismissed on September 30, 1940, with the author [of the crime] still unknown.

In his memorandum of February 11, 1948, HELLEU explained that this assassination was a political crime that he committed under orders while he belonged to "a secret organization" attached to the C.S.A.R. (Comité Secret d'Action Révolutionnaire) directed by General Duseigneur.

He insists that the mental illness that was the motivation for his commitment is simulated and he accepts entire responsibility for his acts.[73]

Not surprisingly, the prosecutor does not seem to have taken Helleu seriously. But neither was he able to come up with any more viable leads in the case. With Locuty—the only solid witness who had tied the Cagoule to Toureaux's murder and willing, for a while at least, to testify to that effect—on the run and under a death sentence in France, the prosecutor had very little new information with which to work. Thus the murder of Laetitia Toureaux remained in 1948 what it had been in 1940: officially unsolved.

PART III

SPECULATION AND MEMORY

8

A SCENARIO FOR A MURDER

In 1938, after a year of investigation into the murder of Laetitia Toureaux, Inspector Charles Chenevier pointed out in his final report that every trail of evidence in her death led directly to the Cagoule. It was there that the police reached a dead end, however, both before and after the war, and despite periodic flare-ups of interest in the following decades, the case remained— and remains—officially unsolved. As a cold case that has continued to elicit as much fascination in France as the famous Black Dahlia murder in the United States, sensational new revelations—implausible confessions from self-professed murderers, bits and pieces of testimony from people who knew her or claimed to have done so—have led to periodic resurgences of interest in Toureaux. None of the new evidence or retrospectives of the decades since World War II has succeeded in closing the case or in contradicting Chenevier's conclusion that Toureaux's undeniable relationship with the Cagoule led to her death. Nor, however, has any researcher succeeded in establishing the precise nature of that relationship or in linking any particular Cagoulard to her murder. No hard evidence that could stand up in a court of law existed then, or has surfaced since. By the same token, various theories have emerged as to why Toureaux had to die, most recently in Liliane Riou's 2007 article, based on the testimony of Riou's mother Yvonne, who knew Toureaux and believed that an Italian connection was behind her murder. Again, little evidence exists to establish the validity of this or any other theory. Toureaux remains, in life and in death, an enigma.[1]

Still, enough evidence exists to make a very strong, plausible case for why and how Toureaux was killed, and that is what we will present in this chapter. Like Chenevier, we will argue that all roads lead to the Cagoule, and like Riou, we believe that an Italian connection existed as well, as a central factor behind her murder. We will also show that her killer most likely had to have been a professional, possessed of greater expertise and cunning than even the most seasoned of the Cagoule's hit men, Jean Filliol. Toureaux was enmeshed in a complex web of relationships that produced a surfeit of individuals and organizations with ample motivation to want her dead, and any scenario of her murder, including the one detailed in this chapter, will necessarily remain speculative in the absence of new evidence or until the release of the entire Toureaux file in 2038 (assuming that the most compromising evidence wasn't destroyed during World War II). We believe, however, that our scenario is the most plausible one, and the best fit with the evidence that does survive. It represents years of data collection and cross-referencing. We begin with a retrospective of the data our research uncovered.

Reviewing the Pieces of the Puzzle

It is likely that soon after the 1921 arrival in Paris of Madame Nourrissat and her children, including the teenaged Laetitia, the family was not only quickly absorbed into the extensive milieu of Italian immigrants in the city that provided a support network for new arrivals, but also into the equally extensive net of informers the Italian secret service recruited to keep an eye on Italians in France. As a concierge and a part-time seamstress, Madame Nourrissat was well placed to garner information on her fellow immigrants ensconced in the 12th arrondissement, a center of the Italian community in Paris. She may have informed for the French police from time to time as well. It was not long before the Toureaux clan established close ties with influential fellow immigrants from the Valle d'Aosta. Toureaux's brother married the daughter of the vice president of the Union Valdôtaine et Mont Cervin Réunies in Paris, and Toureaux and her family maintained a close relationship with a Valdôtaine priest and prominent antifascist in Paris, Auguste Petitgat. Despite these ties to a region and its immigrants known for strong antifascist sentiments, during the 1920s Toureaux fell in with a profascist crowd and developed, or at least espoused, strong profascist views by the 1930s. In 1929, she was listed as a member of an Italian network of spies and informers based in Saint-Denis in Paris that worked for the Italian embassy. In 1936, she became the mistress of Giovanni Gaspirini, a fascist party member in Paris, and in 1936 and 1937 her friend Yvonne heard her champion the fascist cause on more than one occasion. "She was a fascist. Absolutely a fascist," Yvonne Cavret Riou is quoted as saying.[2] Clearly, by the time of her death, Toureaux was deeply enmeshed, albeit as a low-level operative, in the network of fascist sympathizers and spies that the Italian secret service maintained to keep a close watch on Italians living in Paris. How Toureaux came by her support of fascism is unknown. Perhaps she learned her convictions from her mother or another family member caught up in the fascist cause, or perhaps she was lured by the opportunity to earn money that the Italian secret service dangled before her. It is also likely that her husband Jules, the son of a factory owner whose family leaned to the right, shared and/or nurtured her conservative views. The origins of her fascist views and the roots of her inclination to work for fascist groups in Paris remain a mystery, but there can be no doubt that by 1936, Toureaux moved in profascist circles among Paris's Italian and French communities alike.

Toureaux was at least as well-placed as her mother to work as an informer. As an Italian national with a close relative—her father—still living in the Valle d'Aosta, Toureaux possessed the perfect excuse for her frequent trips to Italy in the 1920s and 1930s. Thus she was able easily to work as a "mule," carrying information across the border on behalf of individuals and groups in Paris—such as the Cagoule—to and from their contacts in the Italian government; she could also serve as a go-between for the Cagoule's arms dealers based in Italy, Jean-Baptiste and Juif among others. We know that Jeantet and Méténier also made many such trips, but it is likely that as the liaisons between the Cagoule and the fascists, they focused their energies on meeting more important operatives in the Italian government and secret service. Many other messages and documents, less significant but still too sensitive to be committed even in code in a telegraph or letter, would need to be transmitted across the border. The Cagoule employed numerous liaison agents even within the Paris region—Wiart was one such agent—to carry messages and run errands for its leadership.[3]

During 1936 and 1937, the Cagoulards were assiduously cultivating ties with the Italian government, in particular via Count Gian Galeazzo Ciano and his secretary, Filippo Anfuso, soliciting money and arms in return for services carried out in France. These contacts became especially dense from mid-1936 through the first half of 1937, the period in which the Cagoule planned and carried out the murder of the Rosselli brothers at the behest of Mussolini. It is likely that Italian fascists, familiar with Toureaux because she had been performing errands for them since the late 1920s, recommended her to the Cagoule as an ideal liaison to carry messages for them between France and Italy. Some Cagoulards may already have known her as they frequented the same bals musette as she did. Cloakrooms of bals musette were often used as mail drop sites for correspondence too sensitive to send through the regular mail service, and in the bals Toureaux passed messages and gathered information on behalf of various clients, including, at this point, private detective agencies. Rumors circulated that she was the lover of a high-ranking Cagoulard, Gabriel Jeantet, and perhaps another, whom she described to friends as an older man, an *homme politique*. We believe that her relationship with Italian fascist groups preceded her relationship with the Cagoule, and that it is at the nexus of this mutual relationship linking her both to the Italians and to the Cagoule that the motive for her murder lies.

It may also have been through agents of OVRA that Toureaux first came into contact with Georges Rouffignac, head of the Agence Rouff, the private detective agency for which Toureaux was working at the time of her death. Rouffignac, a native of Bergerac like Jean Filliol, had familial and/or friendship ties with Italians in Paris and elsewhere in France. Perhaps it was through Rouffignac that Toureaux began to cultivate a relationship with the French police and to play the very dangerous game of being a police informant. It was Rouffignac who recommended her to the owner of the Maxi factory, where she was employed ostensibly on an assembly line but in reality to inform on communist and union infiltration of the factory's workforce. She may have done this sort of informing on communists and their sympathizers in other factory settings as well, although that cannot be verified. But there can be no doubt that, with Rouffignac's help, she became a *mouche* for the police and for the Maxi factory's owner. Rouffignac also employed her for at least sixteen cases, in which she followed people and verified addresses for Rouffignac's clients. It is impossible to know what other work she did for him off the books. It was likely Rouffignac who cultivated her as an informer for the police, because it was he and a police inspector, Cettour, who arranged her induction into the left-wing organization, the Ligue du Bien Publique. The goal was probably for her to infiltrate the Ligue and report to the police on pro-communist activities and activists within the organization. But Rouffignac was playing a potentially deadly double game here. Several of his agents, who attended Toureaux's induction ceremony into the Ligue and had themselves infiltrated it, were also members of the Cagoule. It is most likely that they had infiltrated both organizations, one on the right and the other on the left, as subcontractors for Rouffignac, and on behalf of the police.

It is equally probable that this was exactly the role that Toureaux was supposed to play. The police report reveals, for example, that as a private detective she was sent to 14 avenue Rachel in Paris and turned over her findings from this venture to the Paris police. The address was the home of Willy Mucha, the secretary to Robert Jurquet de la Salle, a Cagoulard, Franciste, and member of CRAS, an organization to which Jeantet also belonged. Jurquet de la Salle was also identified as a director of the UCAD.[4] But the Cagoule and the communists alike played for keeps and were wont to eliminate those whom they considered traitors. If, as seems certain, Toureaux was a police informant at the same time that she was working for the Italian secret service and for the Cagoule, even if she were only informing the police about the activities of communists and not on Cagoule itself, she was taking a terrible risk.

Those risks had begun to materialize by the beginning of April 1937, when Toureaux began to be visibly anxious, even fearful, in her demeanor and to tell family and friends that she feared for her safety. During the week prior to her death, there had been at least two failed attempts to kill her. Toureaux recounted to a friend from the Valle d'Aosta, Mme. Marie Chartrain, that on May 13 a car had approached her late one night on a Parisian street. In a maneuver similar to that used in the unsuccessful Cagoule attempt to assassinate traitor Jean Sallé and in the successful 1943 murder of Tonia Masse, the two men in the car tried to tempt her into the vehicle. When she refused to get in, they tried to abduct her by force. Fortunately for Toureaux, she was close to her apartment building at the time and was able to run to the entrance and rouse the concierge and the neighbors. In the same week, another assailant—also evidently unknown to her, according to her own testimony—attacked her with a knife just after she had left the Métro station closest to her home, but again she was able to escape. She reported neither assault to the police, but she did tell those closest to her and, in the case of the latter incident, also told the station manager at the Métro. When he asked her if she was afraid, she made light of the whole affair. To her close family and friends, however, it was clear that her anxiety was rising as April gave way to May. In the days before she died, she began to change her behavior and her appearance as though she anticipated that affairs would come to a head, and she even expressed a sense of foreboding to Marcel Marnef on the day of her death.

Had she decided at some point in the six weeks or so before her death to, as her lover René Schramm claimed, "change her course" and try to extract herself from the web of intrigue in which she had enmeshed herself?[5] It seems likely. Her brother Riton even claimed she planned to leave France and find work in Egypt.[6] Why had she come to this radical decision after almost a decade of work as an informer and a private detective, work that according to testimony from her relatives and friends she avowed to enjoy, and that after the death of her husband helped to distract her from her grief? The most plausible reason was that she had come into possession of potentially explosive information, perhaps from Jeantet, about the plot that the leaders of the Cagoule and the Italians had hatched to eliminate the Rosselli brothers. Meetings between the representatives of Mussolini, Anfuso, and the Cagoule began in the late summer of 1936. The timing fits. In the spring of 1937, Eugène Deloncle and his lieutenants, including Méténier, had made several or more trips to Italy, and it was during one of these voyages that the decision was made that the Cagoulards would eliminate Carlo Rosselli, who had by this time become a serious problem for the Italian government. Deloncle agreed that his men would kill Rosselli in return for a down payment of a hundred machine guns and promises of future aid. Deloncle was in Italy working out these negotiations in late April and early May 1937. On May 16, Toureaux was killed; three weeks later, the Rosselli brothers were murdered. It is thus likely that in some way Toureaux became privy to information relating to these negotiations and either passed it on to the police for whom she was also working or planned to do just that. But rather than becoming a source of profit, her acquisition of this information was the beginning of the end for her.

Her behavior on the day of her death offers clues that support this theory. In the morning she went to a hairdresser and dyed her dark hair blond. After having a quick drink with Riton, she went to her mother's house for lunch, where she picked up a new green outfit to wear. Why Toureaux decided to get so dressed up on this particular Sunday to go dancing with her brother and his friend at L'Ermitage is not clear. Before leaving the bal musette, moreover, and within an hour of her murder, Toureaux tried to convince Pierrette Marnef to accompany her as far as the Port de Charenton so that she did not have make the journey alone. In theory, Toureaux was headed to L'As-de-Coeur, the bal musette where she worked, in order to deliver a letter to her colleague, Kiki, to give to Toureaux's sailor friend, Jean Martin. The letter instructed him to meet her later that night at 11:00 P.M. at the banquet being held by her Valdotâin compatriots. She never made it to Kiki, however; the police found the letter to Martin unopened in her purse. Finally, there is the red and black ribbon of the Ligue du Bien Publique that she wore prominently on the lapel of her green suit the evening she was murdered. Was this a sign meant to indicate Toureaux's identity to someone she was scheduled to meet? It certainly would seem so. It was during that crucial gap of several hours between when she intended to drop off the letter and when she was due to show up at the reunion of the Union Valdôtaine, in other words between 7:00 and 11:00 P.M., that Toureaux had arranged another rendezvous, one that, she confided to friends, she did not expect to "go well." She never kept that fateful rendezvous, however, because Toureaux's assassin waylaid her on the Métro before she could get as far as L'As-de-Coeur.

Conflicting Confessions

By late 1937, the police investigation of Toureaux's murder had lost momentum for lack of new leads. None of the usual criminal elements of the Parisian underworld could be tied to her murder. The police knew that the manner of her death made it unlikely to have been either a random act on the part of a deranged killer or a crime of passion on the part of a scorned lover. The theory surfaced from time to time in the press that her murder had been a political crime and that it was tied to the murders of Navachine and the Rosselli brothers, but the police as yet had found no evidence to support the idea, or at least none to which they were willing to admit. Things also began to unravel for the Cagoule in the autumn of 1937, beginning with the raid on Corre's apartment in mid-September, followed by the arrest of Jakubiez in October while he was ferrying a load of weapons and ammunition in his truck from Switzerland into France—an act that also implicated Jeantet—and culminating with the wave of arrests of most of the leaders of the Cagoule, and the flight of the rest during November and December. Two of the arrested Cagoulards avowed to the police during their confessions that someone in the Cagoule had assassinated Laetitia Toureaux. Locuty asserted that Méténier offered him this information. Jakubiez claimed that the Cagoule's most experienced, successful, and vicious assassin, Jean Filliol, had told him that he [Filliol] had killed Toureaux.[7]

The closest the official police reports came to drawing a conclusion about Toureaux's death can be found in a report that the Inspection Générale des Services de Police Criminelle furnished to M. Bru, the juge d'instruction, on August, 1, 1938:

> Information relevant to the inquiry underway regarding the organization of the CSAR, informing the investigators that the author of the murder with which we are occupied was the man named FILLIOL, Jean Paul Robert, born May 12,

1909, in Bergerac (Dordogne), at present at large and implicated in the affair of the CSAR.

The following version has been offered to us regarding this crime:

Loetitia TOUREAUX, it would seem, was engaged in espionage for the "Intelligence Service." It has equally been indicated that this woman was at one time the mistress of someone affiliated with the CSAR (we do not know the name of this individual).

Concerning the execution, Loetitia TOUREAUX was kept under surveillance for several weeks by André TENAILLE, an affiliate of the CSAR, at present detained in the Santé prison. It was this last named person who supposedly pointed out Loetitia TOUREAUX to FILLIOL, Jean.

The assassination of Loetitia TOUREAUX was decided upon in a CSAR council, and the gentleman METENIER (also detained) one of the leaders of this organization was informed about the preceding events.

At the same time it should be noted that the engineer LOCUTY after his arrest at Clermont-Ferrand declared right away during his hearing in that city to M. CHAUVIN Police Commissioner, of the service, regarding the attack at L'Étoile, that Loetitia TOUREAUX had been executed on the order of the CSAR.

M. CHAUVIN proceeded to interrogate LOCUTY by order of letters rogatory of the Parquet de la Seine.

We have also been led to understand that the 17th of January having passed LOCUTY indicated to M. BARRUE, Juge d'Instruction au Parquet de la Seine, who interrogated him regarding the "Étoile" attack, that METENIER told him [Locuty] while discussing the CSAR that this organization was very powerful, that it extended throughout France, and that it had organized the assassination of Loetitia TOUREAUX.

We do not know whether this declaration was registered in legal form by the Magistrate of Instruction.

In any case, last January 20 M. ALBAYEZ revealed the preceding to M. BRU, Juge d'Instruction who is instructing the TOUREAUX affair.[8]

Most researchers—both popular authors and more serious scholars—who have concerned themselves with Toureaux's case have assumed that the information in the summary reproduced above was essentially correct, that Locuty and Jakubiez were telling the truth and that the information they offered was valid. Filliol murdered Toureaux in the Métro for the same reason that the Cagoule murdered, or attempted to murder, a number of other traitors to the organization: because she knew too much and was too willing to talk to whomever would pay the highest price. There is likely some truth in this analysis, but we prefer another scenario, based on the manner of the crime itself, the information we have garnered about Toureaux and her activities prior to her death, the existence of statements from two other, more highly placed members of the Cagoule, who suggest that different motives and a different assassin caused her death, and the weakness of the confessions of Locuty and Jakubiez.

The first and most fundamental problem with the theory that Locuty and Jakubiez were telling the truth, and that they knew what they were talking about, lies in what wasn't said and what didn't happen as a result of those interrogations. It is important to note that the language used in the above résumé the judicial police provided to the juge d'instruction strongly suggests skepticism about the validity of its contents. Almost every verb form is in the conditional (*aurait été*, would have been). The author of the report noted that the information "has been furnished" to his office, and that he and his colleagues do not know whether Locuty's supposed confession related to Méténier was ever even recorded in proper legal form or put in the official report. In short, the very language of the report implies that the judicial police did not view it as conclusive, or even as particularly reliable. They seem to have known other facts about Toureaux that they were unwilling to put into any official documentation. For example, not long after Toureaux's murder, the police interviewed Émile Domaine, president of an antifascist immigrant group known as the Ligue Italienne, to which Toureaux had belonged. The police report records Domaine as saying, "I never knew that Madame Toureaux had sought to immerse herself in our group because she was obeying instructions coming from the fascists."[9] We do not have the question the police inspector asked Domaine, but it can be inferred from the man's reply that Toureaux's fascist leanings were well known to the interrogator.[10]

From that point forward, the police subsequently noted the confessions of Locuty and Jakubiez in their reports, including the assertion that Filliol killed Toureaux. But the matter always more or less died there. Although the police asked leaders of the Cagoule in custody, including Deloncle, in both 1938 and 1948 about any involvement the Cagoule may have had in the Toureaux murder, they did not aggressively pursue the matter. This is telling for two reasons. First, except for Locuty and Jakubiez, none of the members of the Cagoule admitted any culpability of any member of their organization in Toureaux's death, not even Méténier, who Locuty claimed had boasted to him that the Cagoule had killed Toureaux. Yet the Cagoulards did eventually admit to involvement in all the other assassinations and terrorist acts about which the police questioned them, including Navachine, the Rosselli brothers, Toussus-le-Noble, and L'Étoile. Second, had the police given much credence to the testimony of Locuty and Jakubiez, why did they not add Toureaux's murder to the long list of crimes for which members of the Cagoule were indicted? Jean Filliol was condemned in absentia for a number of crimes before and after the war; he was condemned to death, again in absentia, in 1948. Why not add Toureaux to the list?

The answer most likely derives in part from the manner in which the confessions were elicited. Jakubiez was the Cagoulard whom the police and the courts treated most harshly. A member of the French working class, probably of immigrant background, whom Filliol had recruited into the organization, Jakubiez's superiors, including Deloncle, seem to have been content to leave him hanging out to dry once he was arrested. Jakubiez lacked the social standing and powerful connections that protected men such as Deloncle, or even Locuty, from mistreatment while in custody, and the police beat him on at least one occasion. Corre described Jakubiez appearing at his indictment in Paris dressed in a hospital robe and slippers, with his face and one arm swathed in bandages, information that Corre must have gotten second-hand, given that he was in San Sebastian at the time. Thus the police most likely beat a confession out of Jakubiez and may have suggested to him that Filliol killed Toureaux, a suggestion with which Jakubiez may have been willing to agree in order to end his mistreatment.[11]

This theory becomes even more plausible when one looks at Locuty's confession. Although Locuty purportedly was sufficiently guilt-stricken after the bombings at l'Étoile that he freely, if tearfully, confessed all to the authorities, including what he knew about Toureaux's murder, he changed his story dramatically after spending a few months in prison. In January 1938, he wrote the first in what was to be a series of letters to the judge in charge of the Cagoule case, in which he attempted to retract his earlier confessions. Locuty charged that "an odious abuse" had taken place, against which he protested vigorously.[12] Most notably, he claimed that after his arrest for his part in the L'Étoile bombings, an officer of the Sûreté named Le Comte met with him between the middle of September and the end of October. According to Locuty, Le Comte "offered him stupefying information," confiding to Locuty that Méténier, Moreau de La Meuse, and other individuals had been the real culprits behind the September 11 attacks and that the "OSARN had arranged the assassination of the Rosselli brothers, Loetitia TOUREAU [sic],

NAVACHINE."[13] Locuty now claimed that he had met with neither Méténier nor Moreau de la Meuse on the day of the L'Étoile attacks, but rather with the mysterious Le Comte. A man named Le Comte did exist. He was a Paris policeman in the 1930s who was later killed during the war as a member of the Resistance. Of even more interest, a certain Jean Le Comte was an accordionist at L'As-de-Coeur during the period that Toureaux worked there. He knew Toureaux well enough that he appeared in her address book. What is startling, moreover, is that in the police investigative report of Toureaux's murder, the Le Comte in her address book is identified as a Cagoulard. Was this Le Comte the same man Locuty identified as an undercover agent? If so, it would seem he was a police informer, possibly even working with Toureaux to infiltrate the Cagoule.[14]

More shocking information followed. According to Locuty, Le Comte revealed that Méténier was a double agent working for the intelligence service. Le Comte appealed to Locuty's patriotic sentiments and asked whether he would consent to aid the Sûreté, with which Le Comte was affiliated, in unmasking Méténier and the CSAR. Locuty agreed, but only on the condition that he receive immunity from prosecution, which he claimed the public prosecutor at Clermont-Ferrand had already promised him. He also expected to be imprisoned only for three months or less. Once the parties had come to terms, Locuty claimed, Le Comte proceeded to provide him with the necessary information to form his confession and documents to back it up. Among the things Locuty was supposed to confess was that Méténier was a Cagoulard and was complicit in a number of crimes. Later, when Locuty found himself still languishing in prison at the beginning of 1938, well after he had expected to be released, with no reduction in the charges against him in sight, he decided to retract his earlier confession.[15] Thus his confession would have been legally tainted, meaning that the police and prosecutor could not rely on it to convict members of the Cagoule for Toureaux's murder and, in the absence of corroborating evidence, probably could not even have used it to obtain an indictment. And no corroborating evidence, in the form of physical evidence, a witness, or another confession to support those of Locuty and Jakubiez, was forthcoming that could tie the Cagoule to Toureaux's murder. Just the opposite was the case. The only other members of the Cagoule who had anything to say about Toureaux beyond merely denying any culpability of their organization in her death were Corre and Jeantet, and both proffered a different and more plausible theory regarding the identity of her assassin.

On May 22, five days after Toureaux's murder exploded into the Parisian newspaper headlines Corre, who seemed always to be remarkably well informed, noted the murder. He commented, "In vain are they searching everywhere for the murderer. For our part, we at some point learned that it is a question of a political murder. The young woman was of Italian origin and that already explains quite a bit. Without doubt other details will be forthcoming."[16] Corre never mentioned Toureaux again in his diary, suggesting that he did not consider the murder particularly relevant to the affairs of the Cagoule. In 1970, Gabriel Jeantet—who remained somewhat sentimental towards Toureaux throughout his life—espoused a similar interpretation during an interview with Philippe Bourdrel, the author of a book on the Cagoule. Jeantet, who as Toureaux's lover must have known some intimacies about her, also claimed that her murder was a political assassination committed by the Italian secret service. Toureaux was an agent working for them, he told Bourdrel, and they had "accounts to settle with her."[17]

Finally, the newspapers reported that during the late summer of 1936, Toureaux made a trip to Italy. That summer she engaged her friend, Yvonne Cavret (later Yvonne Riou), to help her make an evening gown of burgundy satin. "While I was sewing she bragged to me that she was going to a reception in Italy where Count Ciano would be present," Riou remembered.[18] The timing of this trip seems entirely possible. From December 3, 1935, until October 12, 1936, Toureaux was registered with the unemployment office.[19] During this time she seems to have worked occasionally at bals musette and restaurants, as well as for Rouffignac, which gave her the flexibility to travel if necessary. Even more interesting, Jeantet's passport, which the police later confiscated, revealed that he entered Italy on August 20, 1936, at Mont-Cenis, the Alpine passage along the French-Italian border near Toureaux's homeland.[20] Perhaps the couple were traveling together en route to the reception that Toureaux mentioned to her friend. Jeantet returned to France nine days later. In November, Toureaux took up more regular employment at the Maxi factory.

Thus our best scenario for Toureaux's murder is as follows. Toureaux worked as an informant for the Italian secret service, which employed an extensive network of informers from all classes and social backgrounds who helped to facilitate their operation in France. She probably began this career for the Italians early, and certainly by 1929. In particular, she traveled back and forth between France and Italy on missions for the Italians, carrying information. Perhaps she attended a reception that Ciano gave in Italy, as she later boasted. She certainly held profascist sentiments, and she attempted to recruit other Italian immigrants in France to perform similar intelligence work. Probably sometime between 1929 and 1936, when Rouffignac admitted to having first hired Toureaux, she began to hire out her services to private detective agencies. It likely was also during this period that she began to work as an informer for the police, although we cannot definitively establish that she was engaged in either of these activities before 1936, even though Rouffignac and the police seemed to have had a substantial relationship with her. Meanwhile, the Cagoule came into being in mid-1936. By this time, Toureaux was already experienced in espionage, with at least a five-year history of work for the Italian secret service, for one or more private detective agencies, and for the police. Toureaux clearly traveled in the same milieu—bals musette and bars—where even the more bourgeois members of the Cagoule could be found drinking and dancing in their free time, and which were the sorts of establishments where they recruited their foot soldiers. She may even have helped recruit some of those young men herself. It is likely, however, that her main involvement with the Cagoule was the result of her experience with espionage and as an informer. She was skilled in exactly the sort of activities—carrying secret messages, following suspects, seducing and recruiting new members—of which the Cagoule had need at this time. And by all accounts she was level-headed and calculating. As a result, she succeeded in finding adventure and romance.

Even more important to the murderer may have been Toureaux's pre-existing ties to the Italian secret service, not only because that would have made her seem more trustworthy to the leaders of the Cagoule, but also because the fact that the Italians already trusted her and employed her would have made her the ideal go-between. By the same token, as the lover of Jeantet and someone who made numerous trips to Italy to discuss Cagoulard activities, she had even more opportunities to travel to Italy and circulate within upper-class circles in France and Italy alike. All therefore seemed to be shaping up well for Toureaux at the end of the 1936. She had developed new clients, including Rouffignac, she was earning more money than she ever had before, and she was enjoying the opportunities and status that her intrigues with powerful men—Italian agents, Cagoulards, and even the French police—brought her, about which she exulted in conversations with her close confidants in her immigrant neighborhood.

Between January and May, however, things began to take a more risky turn for Toureaux. The most likely scenario is that as the Cagoule began to plot and carry out more serious crimes, such as the murders of Navachine and the Rosselli brothers, and began to develop closer ties to the Italian government involving ever-larger sums of money and shipments of arms, the information that began to trickle down to Toureaux in her capacity as messenger became ever more dangerous and alarming. She may even have obtained advance knowledge of the plot to assassinate the Rosselli brothers or have been aware of the real intentions of the Cagoule's leadership to overthrow the French government. She likely informed the French police about CSAR arms smuggling as well.

At this juncture, sometime in the spring of 1937, Laetitia Toureaux decided that she wanted out of her entanglements with the Cagoule and the Italians alike. At least that was what her former boyfriend, René Schramm, came to believe. She began to feel overwhelmed.[21] At that point, Toureaux most likely began to increase the amount of information she was feeding to her handlers among the French police. Only they, after all, could offer her any hope of protection against the dangerous organizations in which she was involved. Given that a police officer had sponsored her membership in the Ligue du Bien Publique and that she was wearing the pin of that organization when she was killed, she may even have been on her way to meet with an undercover police officer that fateful evening of May 16, 1937. There can be little doubt that it was either the Cagoule or the Italian secret service that ordered and carried out her assassination, the execution of a too chatty and now inconvenient woman from a poor immigrant background with no real protectors beyond the men she bedded, who had no vested interest in her longevity. But which organization was responsible?

Although most writers have assumed that someone in the Cagoule, and in particular Filliol, carried out the murder, we disagree. The main problem with the theory that a Cagoulard did the deed lies in the modus operandi. It is clear that the Cagoule and the Italians both had motives to remove Toureaux from the scene before she could do any more damage, especially prior to the Rosselli assassinations. But the actual murder does not bear the hallmarks of a typical Cagoule killing, even though some authors have claimed otherwise. It is true that Filliol frequently did stab his victims, sometimes with a knife, although his signature was a sawed-off bayonet attached to his arm that left a characteristic triangular wound. In every successful assassination he personally carried out, and even in violent attacks he perpetrated that did not result in death, Filliol was known for employing a high level of violence and for leaving a messy crime scene. He not only stabbed Navachine, but shot him as well, and shot Navachine's dog for good measure. He and his men similarly stabbed and shot both Rosselli brothers numerous times before trying to blow up their car. Other Cagoule assassinations where Filliol was not directly implicated were equally violent. Tonia Masse was beaten about the head and shoulders with a club, tied with wire, and dumped in the Seine; Juif had also been beaten, tied with wire, and dumped in a river when the Italian police located his body. Marx Dormoy's head was blown off. Whoever killed Laetitia Toureaux clearly intended to remain anonymous. Whatever else one can say about Filliol, he was not a man who craved anonymity.

Toureaux, by contrast, was killed with a single, exquisitely accurate stroke that did not even knock her off her seat, let alone create much blood at the scene until inexperienced Agent Isambert removed the knife from her neck, at which point blood flooded the floor where she lay. Only a veteran and highly accomplished assassin, interested in speed, accuracy, and anonymity—qualities that did not seem to interest the Cagoulards in their assassinations—could have accomplished the murder, as both Dr. Paul, who examined Toureaux's body immediately after the crime, and the police noted. The Cagoule seemed to want their murders to create tension and fear, although they also sought to obscure the trail just enough to keep the police from tracking the homicide directly to their door. Shocking publicity was something they enjoyed. Toureaux's assassin, by contrast, was clearly a professional, probably brought in by OVRA precisely because the more amateurish Cagoulards had bungled the job on two previous attempts and the Italians wanted to be certain before the Rosselli brothers were killed that the person most likely to inform the police of their role in those murders was out of the way.

So Toureaux went to the police during the spring of 1937, hoping that her contacts among them would protect her from the menace she sensed was accumulating around her. Around the same time, Ciano or Anfuso or some underling working for either man decided that she was expendable. She knew too much about the planned Rosselli murders, and neither the Italians nor the Cagoule could risk a leak before or after the event. However, the French police were not to be trusted. During the 1930s, the police did not even trust each other. Each branch of the police regularly spied upon the other, and the deuxième bureau spied on them all. The police and especially the deuxième bureau were rife with sympathizers with the French right and even with the Cagoule; just as the police had planted agents within the Cagoule and cultivated informers from among the organization's members, so too did the Cagoule possess informers among the police who fed information to Deloncle and his men on a regular basis. It was one of these police sympathizers with the Cagoule, we believe, who tipped off the leaders of the Cagoule that Toureaux was feeding information to the police about their plots and activities. The Cagoule and the Italians took such betrayals seriously, and Deloncle would have been especially concerned, given the delicate stage at which he had arrived in negotiations with the Italians for support in the early months of 1937.

It is highly likely that the Cagoule did indeed sentence Toureaux to die during a council meeting, just as they did other traitors, because she leaked information about their gunrunning. But it is also most plausible that it was a professional assassin in the employ of the Italians who actually carried out the murder after the Cagoule proved unable to do it with the efficiency and professionalism the situation demanded. This also would explain why the French police were reluctant either to accept the scenario offered to them, in which Filliol performed the murder, or to pursue the more likely culprit, an Italian agent. They had enough information to know that Filliol most likely did not commit the murder, and that a professional probably did, in the service of Italian intelligence. Thus on May 16, 1937, Toureaux's Italian killer, perhaps tipped off by members of the Cagoule, boarded the first-class Métro car she took from the Porte de Charenton, murdered her en route, and slipped off into the crowd at the Porte Dorée before anyone ever noticed what had happened. But in 1937 and 1938, the French government was desperately trying to coax Mussolini's government away from the Germans and into an alliance with France. The police were therefore willing to overlook the activities of Italian intelligence agents in France and to keep Toureaux's fascist past a guarded secret. They were probably strongly discouraged by the government from pursuing any angle of Toureaux's murder that was likely to lead them straight to the Italians. Filliol and the Cagoule certainly were more convenient criminals upon whom to pin the crime, but, thanks especially to Locuty's retraction, that theory did not hold up well. Rumors circulated that Gabriel Jeantet dispatched Filliol and one of Deloncle's cousins, André Tenaille, to follow Toureaux during her final days, but no concrete evidence that any one of them murdered her was ever forthcoming.[22] Hence the only solution was the one for which the French police, then and now, opted in their official reports. The case was closed unsolved.

By 1948, interest in Toureaux's case had faded from public view. At the same time, the potential political and diplomatic repercussions from pursuing the case to the doorstep of the Italians, despite the confessions of Emanuele, Navale, and Anfuso about Italy's involvement in her murder as well as those of the Rosselli brothers, were similar to those that impeded the investigation before the war. France again wanted to cultivate Italian amity. Added to this political motive was the strong desire to forget the recent war and the deep divisions within French society it had engendered. The amnesty from which most of the Cagoulards had benefited by 1948, and which meant that only a handful served even part of their sentences, was really deliberate amnesia. This was why the conviction of the culprits, including Navale and Anfuso, in the Italian trials for the Rosselli murders was overturned. This is also why the Toureaux case was never reopened, and why it remains an unsolved mystery in France today.

CONCLUSION
WHO'S AFRAID OF LAETITIA TOUREAUX?

Why was the file on Laetitia Toureaux's murder sealed for 101 years? Why does one need to apply to the French Ministry of Culture for special permission to see these documents? Why did so many archivists we encountered in pursuing this research deny that documentation on Toureaux had survived the war, attempt to thwart our access to the archives, or tell us the file on Toureaux had been lost or purged? Why did friends in the 1990s try to steer us away from the history of the Cagoule? Why did it take five years of persistence to gain access to the police files on Toureaux's murder? The answers to these questions are connected to the history, and historical memory, of France in the post–World War II world.

The main problem with Toureaux's story is that it is entangled with the history of the Cagoule. After World War II, the French rushed to obscure or even obliterate all collaborationist history of the Vichy period, and many former Vichy supporters emerged postwar as Resistance fighters. A similar collective amnesia occurred with regard to all fascist leanings of the prewar period. As a case in point, many former Cagoulards followed Pétain in 1940 but ended the war as staunch Gaullists. Few people wanted to reopen old war wounds after 1945, and as a result few Cagoulards were ever held accountable for their prewar crimes. As such, the Cagoule conspiracy was discredited in popular discourse as the "gang who couldn't shoot straight," and scholars have been similarly dismissive of its real destructive potential in the prewar period.[1] The Cagoule's leaders were simply too important to punish for the death of an Italian immigrant of questionable reputation, and after the war most former affiliates successfully denied their Cagoulard ties. French scholars and political leaders alike preferred to dismiss the Cagoule and its designs for a coup d' état as a preposterous farce.

Another reason the history of the Cagoule was rewritten in the postwar period was that many of its members or affiliates came from some of the wealthiest and most important families in France. A case in point involves the late French president François Mitterrand, who never belonged to the Cagoule, but developed close ties in his youth to many men in its ranks. When a seventeen-year-old Mitterrand arrived in Paris in 1934 to attend university, he held very conservative, even right-wing beliefs. For a short time he belonged to La Rocque's Croix de Feu, and in this capacity he must have encountered many similar young men of the right drawn to political action. He lived in the same part of Passy that was home to many Cagoulards. He was close to Cagoulard assassin Jean Bouvyer, and in fact numerous ties linked the Mitterrand and Bouvyer families. François Mitterrand and Jean Bouvyer were childhood friends whose families came from the same elite milieu in the Charente region of France. Throughout his youth, Mitterrand had been a frequent guest in the Bouvyer home. In addition, during the most active period of the CSAR in 1936–37, Mitterrand's sister, Marie-Josèphe, and Bouvyer were lovers. Even after that romantic liaison ended, the future president remained a devoted friend to Bouvyer and visited him regularly during Bouvyer's imprisonment in 1938–39. During the war, Bouvyer worked for the Vichy commission, the Commissariat Général aux Questions Juives, that deported some 300,000 French Jews to Auschwitz, and rumors circulated subsequently that Mitterrand helped to facilitate Bouvyer's escape to Paraguay after the war. Bouvyer's mother, Antoinette, was known to have been a German collaborator. Even so, Mitterrand once told affiliates that during his tenure with the Resistance, she and her husband Louis-Paul Bouvyer hid him in their home.[2] Perhaps this is why Antoinette Bouvyer became the godmother of Mitterrand's oldest son, Jean-Christophe.

Other ties existed between Mitterrand and the Cagoule. Mitterrand's brother, Robert, married the sister of Eugène Deloncle's wife and both women were the daughters of fellow Cagoulard Georges Cachier. Président Mitterrand attended the funeral of the former Mercédès Deloncle, who remained a close Mitterrand family friend long after she became Madame Jacques Corrèze. François Mitterrand also knew Gabriel Jeantet, although how they met is unknown, perhaps at the École Libre des Sciences Politiques, where they were both students around 1934. In 1942, the future president published an infamous article in the right-wing journal Jeantet edited, *France: Revue de l'État Nouveau*. In this article Mitterrand characterized the history of France after the French Revolution as "one hundred and fifty years of errors."[3] During Vichy, Mitterrand received the prestigious Francisque medal in 1943 given by Marshal Pétain's council. Jeantet nominated Mitterrand for this honor and served as his patron. After the war, Mitterrand went to work as an editor for the magazine *Vôtre Beauté* through the auspices of Jeantet and Eugène Schueller, a wealthy industrialist who had bankrolled the Cagoule and who had strong ties with Eugène Deloncle before and during World War II.[4] Schueller's business partner André Bettencourt, who later entered politics, was linked to the same right-wing circles as Eugène Deloncle and became a life-long friend of Mitterrand's. Bettencourt was a pro-Nazi collaborator who during the war worked in the French division of the German propaganda ministry, the PropagandaStaffel. After the war, Mitterrand's brother, Robert, moved into an apartment Bettencourt had once owned in the 7th arrondissement of Paris that Bettencourt had used in the 1940s for his propaganda activities. Mitterrand and Jeantet remained friends until the latter's death in 1978. They were often seen together at the Brasserie Lipp.[5]

Mitterrand was also linked to François Méténier. This tie went back to the Bouvyer connection because Antoinette Bouvyer and Méténier's wife, Mimi, were close personal friends. Mitterrand's own wife, Danielle, also enjoyed the company of Mimi Méténier, who apparently had a jovial disposition and knew how to prepare a proper tea. For his part in the bombing at L'Étoile, Méténier received a sentence of twenty years of forced labor. He spent only a short time in prison however, because in 1951, when he began serving his sentence, Mitterrand had become minister of justice in the government of Guy Mollet. Through Mitterrand's influence, Méténier was released for reasons of poor health. The whole Mitterrand-Méténier clan celebrated the event at a dinner together in November 1951. Méténier ended up living another five years before dying of cancer in 1956.[6]

During his long political life, and well after his own political views had moved to the left, François Mitterrand steadfastly refused to discuss his Cagoulard ties, even though those ties continued to be apparent to anyone who looked for them. For example, during Vichy, Mitterrand met and grew close to Jean Védrine, a Cagoulard arrested in 1937 who later served as chief secretary to Pétain. In the 1990s, Védrine's son Hubert served as Mitterrand's chief secretary.[7] In 1994, Pierre Péan's biography of Mitterrand's youth stimulated a good deal of controversy and speculation about the president's connections to far right-wing organizations and his political beliefs up to 1947. Mitterrand apparently cooperated with Péan in the hopes of illuminating some of his youthful beliefs and actions, but the plan backfired, and the publication of the book actually stimulated both controversy and public discourse about the nature of France during Vichy. Mitterrand's personal history and family alliances thus help to explain why any discussion of the CSAR during his lifetime was officially taboo.

Other families were also vested in the collective amnesia that occurred after the end of World War II. As discussed in Chapter Seven, few former Cagoulards served significant prison time for their prewar crimes, and many of those who actually received serious punishments, such as Méténier, never served more than a small fraction of their sentences behind bars. Several of the top CSAR leaders were protected after the war by their connection to Eugène Schueller and André Bettencourt. Bettencourt is often cited in the literature on the CSAR as having belonged to the Cagoule; however, he did not appear on Corre's infamous list. Nonetheless, the L'Oréal business enterprises gave safe haven and lucrative careers after the war to Henri Deloncle, Jean Filliol, and Jacques Corrèze, and these sexist men who used women so effectively before the war helped sustain a fashion empire thereafter instructing women in how to look beautiful.

Henri Deloncle's good fortune began in 1945 when he was released—supposedly by mistake—from La Santé prison, where he had been awaiting trial as a former Cagoulard. He quickly moved his family to Madrid and thereafter became director of Cosmair, L'Oréal's Spanish affiliate. He was soon joined by his old ally, Jean Filliol, who also won a place at Cosmair and thanks to the protection of Franco escaped extradition to France, where he faced no less than three postwar death sentences. Similarly, Jacques Corrèze headed to Spain after the war and then to Latin America, where he shunned any contact with Jean Bouvyer but profited from his connection to Schueller. Schueller sent Corrèze to Latin America to establish an overseas market for L'Oréal. Corrèze ended up in New York City, where he directed L'Oréal's North American headquarters until scandal connected to his anti-Semitic past caught up with him and forced him to resign shortly before his death in 1991.[8] The careers of these men reflect one of the most insidious features of postwar France—the life of wealth and privilege many prewar and wartime criminals enjoyed after the war, thanks to their networks of influence and a general French hunger to forget the divisive struggles in France of the 1930s and 1940s. In this context, the life of one Italian immigrant of questionable reputation seemed of little significance to a French population who were working hard to rewrite their own histories and recraft their own identities in the postwar world. Official memory of Toureaux was thus consigned to the trash bin.

Another reason that the French have largely forgotten or dismissed the history of the Cagoule may have something to do with the fact that several of the descendants of the Cagoule leaders are important individuals in France today. Few want to rehash their father's or grandfather's dirty laundry, and even the administrators of the French archival system warn researchers not to use the names of important families in publications that might tarnish family respectability. Gabriel Jeantet, for example, after serving in Pétain's cabinet during Vichy, enjoyed a long postwar career as a successful editor at *Les Éditions de la Table Ronde*, a publishing house that Schueller's L'Oréal financed. Jeantet even wrote and published a laudatory version of Vichy France in 1966 under the title *Pétain contre Hitler*.[9] Jeantet's son Pierre maintained the family ties to journalism, carving out a career as a highly respected journalist before becoming director-general of the French newspaper *Le Monde* in May 2006. On July 2, 2007, Pierre Jeantet reached the pinnacle of France's journalism industry when he took the helm of *Le Monde* after being elected president of the newspaper's directory, although he tendered his resignation from that post by the end of the year. He is now president of the largest newspaper conglomerate in France, Groupe Sud-Ouest, and probably the most influential journalist in France today.[10] Similarly, a person linked to a prominent Cagoulard, whose name cannot be used here, is a major industry head in France today, with financing that came early in his career from L'Oréal sources.[11] Schueller's daughter, Liliane, was only a child in the 1930s and has no direct history with the Cagoule, but she went on to marry Schueller's business partner, Bettencourt, and is recognized as the wealthiest woman in France today. In other words, neither Eugène Schueller's prewar tie to the CSAR, nor his creation during the war of the MSR with the aid of the Gestapo, nor even his pro-Nazi and anti-Semitic beliefs ever stood in the way of his cosmetics industry. Moreover, his global business empire in the postwar world benefited from the savvy, experience, and ambition of former Cagoulards in its employ.[12]

Much has changed in France during the past two decades, however, and particularly since the death of François Mitterrand and the revelations prior to and after his passing of his strong and lingering ties to former comrades from the French right. Although people are still reluctant to go on record about the Cagoule, eyewitnesses to the events of the 1930s and those with knowledge of those turbulent times have become more willing to talk about the past. Indeed, while this book was in press, the son of a prominent Cagoulard very graciously accepted an invitation from us to discuss the Cagoule and Laetitia Toureaux, although he did not want to be cited. The

Cagoule is very much a hot topic in the realm of French popular culture to-day, as exemplified by the 2008 television movie *Mitterrand à Vichy*, based on Péan's book, and the 2008 television miniseries *À Droite Toute*, which includes a cast of characters representing key Cagoulards. Nevertheless, our research likely will discomfit some scholars from either side of the Atlantic who have been more comfortable with a historical memory in which 1930s France remains largely immune to fascism. Still, we believe that our research has revealed a more fraught and nuanced political and social atmosphere in France during the interwar period. In this era, people like Mitterrand gravitated between extremes of right and left, not necessarily out of ambition, malevolence, or hypocrisy—although there was certainly plenty of that to be found, especially in the Cagoule—but rather because they were struggling to find the meaning of patriotism, and the means to express that patriotism and defend France from what seemed to them and in fact were dire threats to the nation, during a particularly volatile, confused, and dangerous time. This is also why so many French men and women associated with the extreme right before the war ended up as heroes of the Resistance during and after the war, and why France came to the brink of civil war both before and after the Occupation. France in 2010 is not the France of the De Gaulle years or even the France of 1997, when we began this project. As researchers, we experienced a palpable lifting of the anxiety associated with the 1930s during the many long years it took to produce this book and especially as the twentieth century came to an end. Today, France and French historians are in the process of constructing a more complex historical memory of the 1930s, one in which the deep political divisions that threatened to tear the country apart in those years can emerge fully from the shadows to which they were consigned in the immediate postwar period. If our book can contribute to that process, it will have achieved one of our goals.

Remembering Laetitia Toureaux

The link between Toureaux and the Cagoule raises more questions than it answers, given the fact that one can never be certain about how or why Toureaux infiltrated the Cagoule or if she was murdered by Jean Filliol, as it is often assumed, or by an Italian assassin, as we strongly suspect. Many documents from the period have been destroyed, and this is likely the case with material pertaining to Toureaux and her murder. Works published in the early 1960s refer to the massive police archive related to the investigation of her murder. We were given two large boxes filled with vital information on Toureaux. While the documents contained in these boxes constituted an important find, the file on Toureaux is hardly a "massive" collection. In talking with the archivists at the Préfecture de Police, we learned that much of the information contained in the Toureaux file was destroyed, stolen, or even sold off piecemeal as ghoulish curiosities sometime between 1945 and 2002. Other documents may still exist in the liminal state known as "noncommunicable," in which they can linger indefinitely without any explanation of why researchers may not see them. In other words, we may well have been given access to only a small sampling of the documents connected to Toureaux's murder. In all probability, however, the postwar authorities who wanted to suppress Toureaux's story saw to it that all really damning evidence in her file was purged before we were born.

More than likely one reason among many that Toureaux's file was classified has to do with her connection to Gabriel Jeantet. She is identified as his mistress in most of the literature on the Cagoule and in the file on Jeantet housed in the police archives. *Maîtresse,* however, was used very broadly in 1930s France, and its meaning was different from what is implied by the use of the word today, especially in English. The investigators of Toureaux's murder noted that she was the mistress of several men during the period 1935–37, and under interrogation these men referred to her using the word "maîtresse." Yet it is clear from other testimony that few of these encounters led to long-term relationships. It would appear, in fact, that one act of sexual intercourse could give rise to the use of the word "mistress," even if there was no further contact. As such, it is hard to evaluate the kind of relationship Laetitia Toureaux may have had with Jeantet. His name does not appear in her address book, nor her name in his. What is certain is that during the most active period of the Cagoule's history, Jeantet frequented many of the bals musette where Toureaux was known to have worked and danced. In addition, during 1936 and 1937, both Jeantet and Toureaux took trips to Italy, perhaps together. What is known is that she was his mistress for a time in those years, and he was upset by her assassination. As the man identified as the most intelligent Cagoulard and the one least prone to violence, he particularly believed that one did not kill a woman. Still, Jeantet's later history, his position in Pétain's cabinet, his friendship with Mitterrand and their time together right after the war at *Les Éditions de La Table Ronde* all necessitated the suppression of Toureaux's history and her ties to him and to the Cagoule. Too many skeletons were hanging in her closet, and those skeletons had complex histories with friends in high places.

Why, then, is it important to remember Laetitia Toureaux now? For over thirty years, scholars have been revising the history of Vichy France, which was carefully crafted in the 1940s, 1950s, and 1960s into a myth of glorious resistance. After Robert Paxton's 1972 publication, *Vichy France: Old Guard and New Order, 1940–1944*, it was no longer possible to deny France's collaborationist history, and since then much scholarly attention has been focused on the complex and conflicted legacy of Vichy.[13] The same cannot be said, however, for France in the 1930s. General histories of the decade abound, but serious analyses of the far right in that period still grapple with the "immunity thesis"—the notion that France was "immune" to fascism—although the 1930s are drawing growing scholarly attention today, as more questions are being raised about the nature and extent of fascism in France in the prewar period.[14]

The history of Laetitia Toureaux, moreover, strongly underscores the fact that most scholars have never really taken the CSAR seriously. The French have always chosen to follow the lead of the right-wing press in the 1930s, which deliberately denigrated the Cagoule conspiracy by arguing that the imprisonment of exposed Cagoulards in 1937–39 was nothing less than a plot that the Popular Front supposedly staged against the entire right. Baptizing their version of this anti-Cagoulard plot "Fantomarx," the right-wing papers accused Marx Dormoy of deliberately using scare tactics to drum up support for socialist and communist politics.[15] Dormoy perceived the Cagoule as a real threat, and this insight led to his vendetta-style assassination in 1941 at the hands of Deloncle's and Schueller's MSR.[16]

Scholars of modern France have chosen to accept the history of the Cagoule as a group of incompetent bunglers who never posed a serious threat to the country as valid. In doing so, they have ignored much evidence to the contrary. Dismissing the Cagoule also means rejecting all its reincarnations during and after the war in the MSR, Pétain's cabinet, and the Milice. This is not to say that the Cagoule was ever strong enough to have pulled off a successful coup d'état, but relegating it to a mere footnote in the prewar period seriously misrepresents the strength of the extreme right at that time. In addition, it dismisses the terrorist tactics employed by the Cagoule and legitimizes the tired postwar narrative of the 1940s, 1950s, and 1960s, in which collaboration was the anomaly and fascism in France an impossibility. A complete understanding of Vichy must incorporate into the historical narrative a consideration of the forces that led to both the creation and the carefully guarded postwar rejection of the Cagoule. Analysis of Toureaux's life should thus serve as a guidepost to future historians calling for a thorough evaluation of the CSAR and its incorporation into the history of the Third Republic and its fall. This book contains a good deal of information on the Cagoule, but it is not meant to be a definitive study. It is an introduction in English that hopefully points the way for future research. We believe that a reassessment of the influence of the Cagoule on the political and social ruptures of the pre- and postwar periods is imperative, not because the Cagoule could have staged a successful coup-d'état, but because the Cagoule in all of its manifestations was far more adept at manipulating France's political environment than historians have wanted to admit. Indeed, historians have rarely challenged the misinformation the French right disseminated regarding the Cagoule, despite the evidence that many talented and capable engineers, soldiers, businessmen, and journalists joined and financed the organization. The desire on the part of right-wing competitors like Maurice Pujo to downplay the Cagoule's significance suited the Cagoulards perfectly. Like Corre, the Cagoulard leaders were content before and after the war to vaunt their escapades in private while mocking the inability of those who did take them seriously to persuade the French public of the gravity of the threat they posed during the 1930s.

What the Cagoule did brilliantly in the prewar environment was to master a kind of psychological warfare though the use of terrorism. The history of 9/11 in the United States has forced scholars to perceive more acutely than before the fact that terrorism is extremely effective in inducing fear, even when the damage to life and property may not be that great.[17] D. L. L. Parry has argued of the Cagoulards, "These rebels were not a handful of *exaltés,* but were numerous, well armed and well connected, and they took France to the brink of a bloody civil conflict."[18] We understand today that terrorism is a complex attempt to communicate messages to society at large. The Cagoule used violence as a means of promoting disorder in France in 1937 in its bid to destabilize the government of Léon Blum. Each message to the media that the Cagoule sent, whether through an act of violence or through the publicity surrounding the arrest of its members, contributed to the social and cultural anxiety that engulfed France before the war.

The Cagoule's leaders deftly employed the theatrical aspect of terrorism, which engages terrorists and the public in the exchange of ideas, an exchange enhanced by the emotionally charged atmosphere that political violence creates. As such, the media frenzy generated by the Cagoule's exploits helped to undermine Blum's government while serving to ensure that the leaders of the Cagoule would never be severely punished for their violent crimes, since the polarization of left and right in 1937 meant that any right-wing aggression would be dismissed in the right-wing papers as either left-wing conspiracies or government hoaxes. Once the Cagoule's employment of this clever political dialogue is acknowledged, its members emerge looking less like the inept bunglers of the traditional historical narrative and more like the savvy architects of the educated political milieu from which they came. By interpreting the Cagoule as successful terrorists who never really were called to account for their actions, we allow for a more sophisticated analysis of their role in the political climate of the 1930s.[19] Ultimately, the CSAR failed to bring about their goal of establishing an ultraconservative and authoritarian state. Even so, their use of violence as a means of promoting disorder needs further examination. At the very least, such a study would provide critical insight into how this French terrorist organization operated through secret cells, incited fear, and influenced the unstable dynamic of prewar France.

Today the remains of the intrepid Laetitia Toureaux lie in an isolated cemetery known as Thiais on the outskirts of Paris. Her tombstone reads "Yolande Toureaux." Yet for all her exploits and fleeting notoriety, Toureaux's grave is not listed on the cemetery website. But the memory of this fascinating woman has not been obliterated. Laetitia "Yolande" Nourrissat Toureaux was no flawless heroine, but she embodied the complexities of interwar French society. The five-hundred-page summary of the investigation that the police compiled after many months of searching for her murderer paints a fascinating picture of one woman's struggle to achieve respectability in a world that denied upward mobility to people of her sex, class, and ethnicity. In the end, what can be made of this woman killed in the Métro, this hardworking immigrant with fluid, even multiple identities? To breathe life back into her, we have allowed her to interpret the 1930s for us, and we have tried to see the Cagoule through her eyes. Allowing Toureaux to guide our interpretation, a new picture of the CSAR emerges, one that gives critical insight into France in the immediate pre–World War II period. In recounting Toureaux's story, our goal has been to show how one remarkable woman, even though of humble origins, can illuminate a critical moment in French history. We hope we have drawn Laetitia Toureaux out of the shadows that have obscured her life and untimely death. Or has the elusive Yolande donned her mask and slipped back into the interstices of historical memory and myth once again?

APPENDIX

THE CAGOULE IN HISTORIOGRAPHY

In 1948, former prime minister Léon Blum reflected on his days as leader of the Popular Front government in 1936–37 to the Socialist Party newspaper, *Le Populaire*. He stated, "During the period when I was head of the government, I believed that the threat of a fascist-style 'putsch,' in which the Cagoule was the most active element at the time, was real. And if the intervention in Spain had led us to civil war, we would have seen an analogous movement in France to that which Franco directed against the legitimate authorities in Spain and following the same course."[1] Blum's opinion aside, historians for the most part have never seen the CSAR as a genuine terrorist organization or as a threat to the prewar French state. Even after the escalation of terrorism worldwide in recent decades—including both home grown terrorists, such as the Basque Euskadi ta Askatasuna (ETA) in Spain and France or the Oklahoma City bombers in the United States, and external fundamentalist groups, such as Al Qaeda—most historians of France persist in viewing the Cagoule as a group of bumbling fringe armchair extremists. It was little more than a privately funded hobby of industrialists and politicians of the extreme right, which was never capable of seriously affecting French society. Although the Cagoulards may have scored a few hits and garnered a few victims, most notably the Rosselli brothers, the consensus remains that for the most part they posed no real threat to either the state or public order in France.

As a result of this lack of scholarly interest, the Cagoule merits little attention in works on the 1930s. Serge Berstein does not mention the organization in his *1936: Année Décisive en Europe* (1969), despite the fact that in February of that year the Cagoulard Jean Filliol attempted to assassinate Blum in the streets of Paris and succeeded in wounding him. The Cagoule is equally absent from Eugen Weber's synthesis of 1930s France, *The Hollow Years* (1994), although he did discuss it seriously in his earlier work, *Action Française: Royalism and Reaction in Twentieth-Century France* (1962). Benjamin F. Martin's well-written narrative *France in 1938* (2005) provides excellent background for the 1930s but says nothing about the Cagoule, even though the newspapers were still full of accounts about it in early 1938 after its exposure in late 1937. Jean-Baptiste Duroselle, in his *La Décadence, 1932– 1939* (1979), devotes a single page of his 500-odd page text to the CSAR. Finally, the Cagoule merits nary a mention in the recent volume of essays entitled *France in the Era of Fascism,* edited by Brian Jenkins, who views more debate on the contested terrain of French fascism and its nature as essentially sterile.[2]

Most other scholars of 1930s France—even those who specialize in the extreme right and grapple with the problem of whether or not fascism was a significant factor in interwar politics, such as William Irvine and Julian Jackson—devote little or no attention to the Cagoule. It gets a brief mention in Philippe Machefer's *Ligues et Fascisms en France (1919–1939)* (1974) and a bit more attention in Olivier Dard's *Les Années 30* (1999), which includes a small section on its activities. Robert Soucy, in his landmark study of the phenomenon of fascism in France, *French Fascism: The Second Wave, 1933– 1939,* devotes about seven pages to the CSAR in a chapter entitled "Minor and Declining Fascisms." Jacques Nobécourt, in his magisterial if perhaps overly sympathetic study of Colonel de La Rocque (1996), was obliged to come to terms with the Cagoule, if only to disavow La Rocque's role in creating or guiding the organization. In his monograph on the Croix de Feu and La Rocque, *Reconciling France against Democracy: The Croix de Feu and the Parti Social Français, 1927–1945* (2007), Sean Kennedy similarly dismisses the idea that the colonel had any dealings with the CSAR.[3]

Joel Blatt in the United States, D. L. L. Parry in Great Britain, and Frédéric Monier in France are probably the only scholars who have shown real interest in the Cagoule. Blatt produced an excellent chapter-long synthesis on the Cagoule in *Crisis and Renewal in France, 1918–1962,* edited by Kenneth Mouré and Martin S. Alexander (2002), presenting serious evidence to support his conclusion that the "Cagoule plot has been underestimated."[4] In *The Right in France, 1789–1997* (1997), edited by Nicholas Atkin and Frank Tallett, Parry wrote a chapter underscoring the strength of the extreme right in pre-war France and arguing that the CSAR took France to the brink of civil war.[5] Monier's *Le Complot dans la République: Stratégies du Secret, de Boulanger à la Cagoule* (1998) includes several chapters devoted to the CSAR in the context of other secret organizations and identifies members of the Cagoule as some of the first modern terrorists.[6] In 1975 Bertram Gordon authored an excellent but rarely cited article on the heir of the Cagoule during the Vichy years, the Mouvement Social Revolutionnaire (MSR), which Eugène Deloncle organized in 1940–41 to carry on the work of the CSAR. In this article Gordon recognizes, like Blatt and Monier after him, the "obvious importance of Deloncle and the CSAR in 1936–1937," and he laments that little has been published on the MSR.[7] The same could be said of the Cagoule. In 1991, Frédéric Freigneaux produced a well-researched thesis on the Cagoule at the University of Toulouse, but to date it has never been published as a book, although Freigneaux did summarize his work in the popular French magazine *L'Histoire* in 1992.[8] D. L. L. Parry wrote a piece that appeared in the *European History Quarterly* in 1998, which set the Cagoule within the context of the proliferation of conspiracy theories that marked the Third Republic.[9] In 2000, Jean-Claude Valla published a short work entitled *The Cagoule, 1936–1937,* which, while replete with good photographs and containing some useful research, offered little new in the way of analysis or interpretation. Indeed, perhaps the best recent work on the Cagoule in French is not a book at all, but William Karel's well-researched documentary that aired in 1997 on French television. Entitled *La Cagoule: Enquête sur Une Conspiration d'Extrême Droite,* Karel's film can be viewed at the Bibliothèque Nationale, François Mitterrand.[10]

Thus, few historians have really analyzed the Cagoule, and no scholarly monograph exists placing the CSAR in the political context of the 1930s. In recent years, a number of new works have been appearing on interwar France, but the debate about the extent and significance of fascism in interwar French politics that began with Robert Paxton's *Vichy France: Old Guard and New Order, 1940–1944* (1972) and heated up considerably in the 1990s seems to have subsided without an examination of the Cagoule. Perhaps because the Cagoule was more willing than most other organizations of the extreme right to translate its political rhetoric into violent action and to operate as an underground terrorist organization, historians have preferred to dwell on its failures rather than its successes or to acknowledge the danger it posed to the French government, especially during the Vichy era. This is not the case with historian Annie Lacroix-Riz, whose *Le Choix de la Défaite: Les Élites Françaises dans les Années 1930* (2006) contains a large amount of well-documented information on the Cagoule. Lacroix-Riz's work must be read carefully, however; while it contains interesting information, her thesis is highly controversial and the work is largely dismissed in France. Lacroix-Riz argues that the authors of Vichy were part of the "Synarchie" who plotted their rise to power and the fall of France during the years 1933–36. She sees the Cagoule as part of this Synarchie or, at the very least, agents of the Synarchie.[11]

Historians, and especially Italian scholars, researching the murder of the famous antifascist Rosselli brothers have been much more willing to give the Cagoule its due as a dangerous group of terrorists.[12] Some of the most recent scholars of Vichy France have begun to take it more seriously, perhaps because of the inescapable fact that so many former members of the Cagoule went on to play prominent roles in Vichy and/or the Occupation. Historians of the 1930s, ironically, downplay the Cagoule much more than their colleagues who study the war years. See, for example, Jean-Marc Berlière, *Policiers Français sous l'Occupation d'après les Archives de l'Épuration* (2001, 2009).[13]

For the most part, therefore, the Cagoule has remained the province of popular historians, often from a journalistic or literary background, who have happily and profitably mined the archives to tell the story of this fascinating group. Their narratives, while often well-researched and entertaining, lack the serious analysis the Cagoule merits regarding its role in the politics, society, and culture of 1930s France. The earliest of these more sensationalist narratives of the Cagoule, Fernand Fontenay's *La Cagoule contre la France: Ses Crimes, son Organization, ses Chefs, ses Inspirateurs* (1938), appeared shortly after the CSAR was unmasked.[14] Although clearly the work of a journalist with left-wing sympathies, this book contains data that its author could not have obtained without access to the police and judicial files on the Cagoule—some of which subsequently disappeared after World War II. Thus despite its polemical tone, it is an extremely useful work to historians. Most of Fontenay's basic conclusions—for example, about the connections linking the Cagoule to the assassination of the Rosselli brothers—were eventually proven correct and demonstrate his excellent access to the police and government officials involved in the investigation. Knowledge of the Cagoule quickly made it into the English-speaking world with Joseph Gollomb's 1939 book *Armies of Spies*, which contained a chapter entitled "The Hooded Ones in France." Gollomb must have relied on Fontenay or had good access to French journalists because his chapter is remarkably accurate about the CSAR's German and Italian connections with regard to the arms trade. He even predicts the end of the French colonial empire in Africa. Even so, this chapter had little influence on historians of the period and is never cited in scholarly works about the Cagoule. Another sensationalist book about the Cagoule, Joseph Désert's *Toute la Vérité sur l'Affaire de*

la Cagoule: Sa Trahison, ses Crimes, ses Hommes (1946) appeared soon after
the war and was based on Fontenay's work. Naturally neither Gollomb nor
Désert could incorporate the information that emerged in the postwar trials of the surviving members of the Cagoule, which did not take place until
November 1948.[15]

A handful of books on the Cagoule appeared in the 1960s and 1970s, including J. R. Tournoux's *L'Histoire Secrète: La Cagoule, le Front Populaire,
Vichy, Londres, Deuxième Bureaux, l'Algérie Française, l'O.A.S.* (1962). More
important is Aristide Corre's *Les Carnets Secrets de la Cagoule* (1977), edited
by Christian Bernadac, which contains extensive extracts from the personal
diary that Corre, a Cagoulard, kept between 1937 and 1940. Most of the diary had been overlooked during the police raid on Corre's apartment in 1937.
Before Corre was executed by the Germans in 1942, he somehow managed
to smuggle the diary to a fellow former Cagoulard turned Resistance fighter
and future inmate at Dachau, Father Joseph Fily. The priest kept it a closely
guarded secret until at the age of seventy-eight he passed it on to Bernadac,
who had originally approached him for an interview on clandestine religious groups in German concentration camps during the war. Corre's diary
is an important work that scholars have never adequately mined, perhaps
because it is replete with tales of the sexual exploits of Corre's "gros mem-
bre," as well as hundreds of perverse verses and couplets focused on female
anatomy and the sexual act that read more like the musings of an adolescent
boy than a grown man. (Only a sampling of these verses are reproduced by
Bernadac.) More than any other work on the Cagoule, however, Corre's diary gives a real sense of Cagoulard identity and the cultural mores of the
group. It is a marvelous day-by-day insider account of Cagoulard activity,
told by one of the group's key members. Scholars should take note that raw
material exists in *Les Carnets Secrets de la Cagoule* that, if properly mined,
would make a fascinating psychological study of the formation and demise
of a modern terrorist organization.[16]

Henry Charbonneau, a former low-level Cagoulard, published his recollections as *Les Mémoires de Porthos* (1967), but probably the best narrative
of the Cagoule is Philippe Bourdrel's *La Cagoule: 30 Ans de Complots* (1973),
later revised and expanded as *La Cagoule: Histoire d'une Société Secrète du
Front Populaire à la Ve République* (1992). Bourdrel's books have the merit
of incorporating much of the material that emerged in the postwar trials of
the members of the Cagoule and of pointing out how many former Cagoulards ended up as rehabilitated, prominent members of French government

and industry under De Gaulle. Bourdrel also interviewed top Cagoulard ringleaders, including Gabriel Jeantet and Jacques Corrèze, both of whom have since died. As a result, his book is a quite valuable source. Recently a few more Cagoulard biographies have begun to appear. Pierre Péan published a book about the most secretive of the Cagoulard chiefs, Félix Martin, *Le Mystérieux Docteur Martin (1895–1969)* (1993), using Martin's surviving private papers. Brigitte and Gilles Delluc have written a biography of the Cagoulard chief assassin, *Jean Filliol, du Périgord à la Cagoule, de la Milice à Oradour* (2005). While not a scholarly work, it does contain extensive information about Filliol, surely one of the most interesting, if homicidal, members of the infamous right-wing group.[17]

From time to time the CSAR is mentioned in some of the vast scholarly literature devoted to French fascism, although it is never a major focus of these works. Soucy's *French Fascism: The Second Wave* (1995), mentioned above, exemplifies the type of scholarly nod to the Cagoule that one finds in this literature. The present work on Laetitia Toureaux and the Cagoule is not preoccupied by the question of fascism, nor is it attempting to use the case-study of Toureaux as a way of trying to prove whether or not the French were fascists. In the scholarly literature, the definition of French fascism, as well as its roots, significance, and potential uniqueness, are deeply contested areas of debate. A whole generation of postwar French scholars developed an "immunity thesis," also referred to as the "consensus school of French historiography," arguing that the long post-Revolutionary history of French democratic ideals left most French men and women unresponsive to fascism's prewar appeal.[18] Because France never embraced a totalitarian regime in the 1930s, however, postwar scholars could contend in hindsight that the French experience was not really comparable with that of Germany and Italy and that the survival of the Third Republic until 1940 proved that France's steadfast fidelity to republicanism was the exception in interwar Continental Europe. As a further result, specialists on German and Italian fascism often overlooked the French experience because France produced no fascist state.

A revisionist school contested the immunity thesis, as scholars such as Robert Soucy, William Irvine, and Kevin Passmore attempted to analyze French fascism as a distinct phenomenon with a specific French history that was not necessarily connected to other fascist movements in Europe.[19] Zeev Sternhell, who iconoclastically viewed France as the seedbed of European fascism in his *Ni Droite ni Gauche: L'Idéologie Fasciste en France* (1983, reprinted in 2000), took the brunt of scholarly furor from historians who denied that "true" fascism was a significant force in France.[20] The French fascism debate has now grown stale, however, and current scholars appear to be more focused on contexts, processes, and nuances related to how fascism manifested itself in France, as opposed to debating French exceptionalism.[21] Two excellent attempts to synthesize much of the literature also can be found in the works edited respectively by Michel Dobry in French and Brian Jenkins in English, *Le Mythe de l'Allergie Française au Fascism* (2003) and *France in the Era of Fascism* (2005).[22] Current scholarship is focused on the exploration of the spectrum of right-wing nationalism during the Third Republic and the broader aspects of life—inclusive of gender, ideology, and masculinity—in interwar France. This attempt to move beyond categorizations of political ideologies is exemplified by the summer 2008 edition of *Historical Reflections/Réflexions Historiques*, edited by William Irvine, which is devoted to "Beyond Left and Right: New Perspectives on the Politics of the Third Republic."[23]

Our work has been heavily influenced by Kevin Passmore, who recognizes that in French political culture, far-right and fascists groups such as the Croix de Feu successfully engaged political debate in the prewar era to advance a conservative agenda. While these groups did not supplant the state, their paramilitary influence was not negligible. We have also been heavily influenced by Samuel Kalman's recent work, *The Extreme Right in Interwar France: The Faisceau and the Croix de Feu* (2008). Kalman starts with the idea that too much work on interwar right-wing groups has been focused on their organization and membership. He takes the two most successful right-wing groups from the period and explores their programs, ideologies, and, most significantly, plans for state transformation. He then connects their influence to Vichy and beyond. Kalman states, "Both groups aspired to the conquest of power in order to implement their transformative program. In the process, they prepared a generation of right-wing French men and women to support an authoritarian state, creating a substantial clientele for the Vichy Regime."[24]

We start with the idea that the CSAR leaders were fascists and drawn to many of the totalitarian and authoritarian ideals shared by Italian fascists, with whom they were closely tied. Yet the CSAR maintained links with less radical members of the far right in France who were clearly not fascists. Cagoulard devotion to secrecy meant that their influence extended to many right-wing people and organizations who may or may not have had a clear understanding of the CSAR's goals. Cagoule leaders were highly intelligent

men who espoused little in the way of a specific ideology beyond a vast hatred for all things on the left and a willingness to use violence to communicate with French society and thereby change it to their liking. More specifically, the Cagoule's leaders were not interested in any kind of mass appeal
to the French populace, preferring to work though a small elite to provoke
action that would destabilize France and ready the country for a coup. The
lack of a mass following, however, meant that these agents provocateurs
could never have been truly successful in overthrowing the French state;
and in a certain sense this fact underscores the resiliency of the Third Republic. The Cagoule was not a mass movement, but a conspiracy of terrorists inspired by fascism and nurtured by an unstable political climate that
was tied to the looming certainty of a coming war. The reach of the Cagoule
nevertheless extended well into the armed forces and probably to Pétain
himself. As a result, key members of the Cagoule were successful under
Vichy in helping to craft a government closely resembling the totalitarian
model they endorsed.

Although this book cannot rectify the lack of serious scholarship on the
CSAR, it demonstrates why scholars would profit from devoting more attention to the activities of the Cagoule in the late 1930s. The Cagoule deserves to be taken seriously even though it did not possess the capability
to topple the French government that its leaders so ardently desired, and it
failed to siphon off the membership of La Rocque's legitimate PSF. In many
ways, the Cagoule was a reaction to the rise of the left and the Popular Front
in 1936, and it essentially self-destructed after the fall of Blum's government
in 1937. The French police were probably aware of the Cagoule from the
very beginning and dismantled it efficiently after the November 1937 failed
coup. Regardless of the political danger the Cagoule may have posed—and
it is argued in this book that this danger was greater than many historians
have supposed—many influential people in the 1930s, including Léon Blum,
a target of Cagoule assassins, and Marx Dormoy, who investigated and exposed the organization but unfortunately fell victim to one of its bombs,
viewed it as a major threat. Many of the journalists who reported on the
Cagoule also perceived its plots as serious, even though those who wrote
for right-wing publications tended, like right-wing politicians, to play down
the group's importance in a sort of conservative damage-control maneuver
once the many connections linking the leaders of the Cagoule to prominent
politicians on the right and leaders of the army and French industry began
to emerge. And knowledge of these connections persisted into the postwar

period. On July 23, 1945, for example, in front of the High Court of Justice, the procureur-général, André Mornet, accused Marshal Pétain of having been the "standard-bearer of the Cagoule."[25] Mornet's evidence was based on government files that dated from 1936 to 1939. He may have exaggerated in an overt attempt to connect Pétain with rightist conspiracies during the final years of the Third République; nevertheless, Mornet perceived a close connection between the most famous Cagoulards and the men who surrounded Pétain during Vichy.[26]

Terrorism is a complicated attempt to communicate messages to and manipulate public opinion in society at large. This task is made easier in democratic societies because of the greater freedom of the press. On September 11, 2001, a mere nineteen terrorists succeeded in killing nearly three thousand people in the United States, certainly a tragedy but unlikely by itself a direct threat to the security and welfare of the vast majority of Americans. Nevertheless, that event dramatically changed American politics, culture, economy, society, and even the very nature of American democracy, perhaps forever. It is amazing to us that after the events of 9/11 the subject of the Cagoule did not become a more serious focus of scholarly investigation.[27] Perhaps a 2005 master's thesis from the University of Victoria by Valerie Deacon on the Cagoule is some indication that it is gaining visibility in graduate seminars on French history.[28]

In its bid to erect a right-wing conservative state, the Cagoule used violence as a means of promoting disorder in France in 1937. Joel Blatt has argued that the Cagoule plot to bring down the Popular Front marked the "climax of acute political and social ruptures."[29] Each message to the media that the CSAR sent, whether through an act of violence or through the publicity surrounding the arrest of its members, contributed to the social state of anxiety that engulfed France. Who knew what to believe by 1939? Through violent means, the Cagoule thus contributed seriously to the political discourse of the pre–World War II era. Their acts of terrorism, as well as the various interpretations of these acts in the French press, should be included in any understanding of the political discourse of interwar French society.[30] Perhaps Eugen Weber said it best in his 1962 *Action Française*, "Serious or childish, the plots of the Cagoule helped to convince both sides (right and left) that all such plots were real, with real arms and blood-curdling threats that one had to believe."[31]

NOTES

Introduction: Murder in the Métro

1. Maurice Pujo, *L'Action Française*, November 20, 1936, and November 18, 1937; Jean-Marc Berlière, *Les Policiers Français sous l'Occupation: D'Après les Archives Inédites de l'Épuration* (Paris: Perrin, 2001), 100 n. 1.

2. For more information on the historiography of the CSAR, see the appendix to this volume.

3. See, for example, Archives Nationales, F/7 14684, "Armes: Contrabande d'Armes à la Frontière Franco-Suisse, 1936–1939."

4. Michael Kronenwetter, *Terrorism: A Guide to Events and Documents* (Westport, Conn.: Greenwood Press, 2004), 26; Leonard Weinberg and Ami Pedahzur, *Political Parties and Terrorist Groups* (London: Routledge, 2003), 2.

5. Cited in Vincent Burns and Kate Dempsey Peterson, *Terrorism: A Documentary and Reference Guide* (Westport, Conn.: Greenwood Press, 2005), 10.

6. Uriel Rosenthal and Erwin Muller, *The Evil of Terrorism: Diagnosis and Countermeasures* (Springfield, Ill.: Charles C. Thomas, 2007), 6–7; Jeff Victoroff, "The Mind of a Terrorist: A Review and Critique of Psychological Approaches, *Journal of Conflict Resolution* 49, no. 1 (February 2005): 3–42.

7. For the best example of this literature, see Sean Kennedy, *Reconciling France against Democracy: The Croix de Feu and the Parti Social Français, 1927–1945* (Montreal: McGill-Queen's University Press, 2007). Also see Kevin Passmore, "Planting the Tricolor in the Citadels of Communism: Women's Social Action in the Croix de Feu and Parti Social Français," *Journal of Modern History* 71, no. 4 (Winter 1999): 814–52; Passmore, "The Croix de Feu: Bonapartism, National Populism, or Fascism?" *French History* 9 (1995): 67–92; Passmore, ed., *Women, Gender, and Fascism in Europe, 1919–45* (New Brunswick, N.J.: Rutgers University Press, 2003); Michel Dobry, ed., *Le Mythe de l'Allergie Française au Fascisme* (Paris: Albin Michel, 2003). See as well our appendix.

8. Dormoy was the minister in charge of investigating the Cagoule; ex-Cagoulards later assassinated him during the war. And in 1936 a member of the Cagoule, Jean Filliol, succeeded in putting Blum in the hospital. On February 13, 1936, Blum's motorcade by chance passed close by the funeral procession for the royalist historian Jacques Bainville. Ever the opportunist, Filliol led a group of Cagoulards in the procession in an impromptu attack on Blum's car. They broke the windshield and struck Blum on the head. A group of laborers at a nearby construction site drove off the attackers, but Blum was wounded badly enough to require treatment at the Hôtel-Dieu. Brigitte Delluc and Gilles Delluc, *Jean Filliol, du Périgord à la Cagoule, de la Milice à Oradour* (Périgord: Pilote 24 Éditions, 2005), 28–30.

9. Maurice Larkin, *France since the Popular Front: Government and People, 1936–1996* (Oxford: Oxford University Press, 1997), 6.

10. Richard Vinen, *France, 1934–1970* (New York: St. Martin's Press, 1996), 11.

11. This and the next paragraph come from Julian Jackson, *The Popular Front in France: Defending Democracy, 1934–38* (Cambridge: Cambridge University Press, 1988); Jackson, *France: The Dark Years, 1940–1944* (Oxford: Oxford University Press, 2001), 27–133; Antoine Prost, *Autour du Front Populaire: Aspects du Mouvement Social au XXe Siècle* (Paris: Seuil, 2006); Jacques Kergoat, *La France du Front Populaire* (Paris: Éditions La Découverte, 1986).

12. Jackson, *France: The Dark Years,* 72.

13. Quoted in Vinen, *France,* 15.

14. *Le Matin,* Paris, February 23, 1934, front-page headline "L'Assassinat du Conseiller Prince Demeure Toujours Aussi Mystérieux"; Karl Harr, *The Genesis and Effect of the Popular Front in France* (Lanham, Md.: University Press of America, 1987), 84–87; Georges Lefranc, *Le Front Populaire* (Paris: Presses Universitaires de France, 1965), 7–26; John Merriman, *A History of Modern Europe from the Renaissance to the Present* (New York: W. W. Norton, 1996), 1204–05; Eugen Weber, *The Hollow Years: France in the 1930s* (New York: W. W. Norton, 1994), 131–38.

15. Jackson, *France: The Dark Years,* 74–75.

16. Vinen, *France,* 15.

17. Jackson, *France: The Dark Years,* 76.

18. The quote is: "Contre les ouvriers, l'armée, Ils ne l'enverront pas en vain, Soldats brisez la croix gammée! Donnez-nous la main, camarades! Donnez-nous la main!" Reprinted in Serge Wolikow and Jean Vigreux, *1936 et les Années du Front Populaire* (Paris: Institut CGT d'Histoire Sociale et Musée de l'Histoire Vivante de Montreuil, 2006), 16.

19. Peter N. Stearns and Herrick Chapman, *European Society in Upheaval: Social History since 1750,* 3d ed. (New York: Macmillan, 1992), 324ff.

20. Quoted in Weber, *The Hollow Years,* 113.

21. Nathanael Greene, *Crisis and Decline: The French Socialist Party in the Popular Front Era* (Ithaca: Cornell University Press, 1969), 102, 138; Harr, *The Genesis and Effect of the Popular Front,* 96ff; Jackson, *The Popular Front in France,* 104ff; Lefranc, *Le Front Populaire,* 71–73, 102; Kennedy, *Reconciling France against Democracy,* 128–29.

22. Joel Blatt, "The Cagoule Plot, 1936–37," in *Crisis and Renewal in France, 1918–1963,* ed. Kenneth Mouré and Martin S. Alexander (New York: Berghahn Books, 2002), 87.

23. *Le Matin,* Paris, May 25, 1937.

24. Weber, *The Hollow Years,* 111ff.

25. Jacques Nobécourt, *Le Colonel de La Rocque, 1885–1946, ou les Pièges du Nationalisme Chrétien* (Paris: Fayard, 1996), 548, 552.

26. See, for example, Marthe Richard, alias Marthe Richer, *Mes Dernières Missions Secrètes: Espagne, 1936–1938* (Paris: Éditions de France, 1939). Two excellent studies of the fears haunting France in the interwar era are: Michael B. Miller, *Shanghai on the Métro: Spies, Intrigue, and the French between the Wars* (Berkeley: University of California Press, 1994) and Weber, *The Hollow Years,* 111ff.

27. Jackson, *The Popular Front in France,*104.

28. Archives Nationales, F7 14678, "Armes: Contrebande d'Armes à la Frontière Franco-Suisse: 1936–1939," clipping from *Le Populaire,* September 24, 1936.

29. For the history of Italian immigration to France, see especially Marie-Claude Blanc-Chaléard, *Les Italiens dans l'Est Parisien: Une Histoire d'Intégration (1880–1960)* (Rome: École Française de Rome, 2000); Judith Rainhorn, *Paris, New York: Des Migrants Italiens, Années 1880–Années 1930* (Paris: Éditions CNRS, 2005); and Pierre Milza, ed., *Les Italiens en France de 1914 à 1940* (Rome: École Française de Rome, 1986).

30. Pierre Milza, "L'Immigration Italienne en France d'une Guerre à l'Autre: Interrogations, Directions de Recherche, et Premier Bilan," in *Les Italiens en France*, ed. Milza, 1–42, 5–16; Gérard Noiriel, *Les Ouvriers dans la Société Française, XIXe–XX Siècle* (Paris: Seuil, 1986), 131–36.

31. Gary S. Cross, *Immigrant Workers in Industrial France: The Making of a New Laboring Class* (Philadelphia: Temple University Press, 1983), Table 8, p. 101; Pierre George, "L'Immigration Italienne en France de 1920 à 1939: Aspects Démographiques et Sociaux," in *Les Italiens en France*, ed. Milza, 45–67.

32. Elio Riccarand and Tullio Omezzoli, *Sur l'Emigration Valdôtaine, les Donneés Économiques et Socials, 1700–1939: Une Anthologie de la Presse (1913–1939)* (Aoste: Institute Historique de la Résistance en Vallée d'Aoste, 1975), 7–42. For the diaspora of workers from the Valle d'Aosta, see also Guiseppe Ciardullo, *Valdôtains à Paris: Le Rôle Joué par la Pro Schola de Champdepraz dans l'Émigration Valdôtaine à Paris (1919–1967)* (Quart, Valle d'Aosta: Musumeci, 1996).

33. Auguste Petigat, "L'Italianité de la Vallée d'Aoste," reprinted from *L'Echo de la Vallée d'Aoste*, December 30, 1938, in Ciardullo, *Valdôtains*, 212–23. For more on the languages of the Valle d'Aosta, see Jérôme-Frédéric Josserand, *Conquête, Survie et Disparition: Italien, Français et Francoprovençal en Vallée d'Aoste* (Stockholm: Uppsala Universitet, 2004).

34. Petigat, "L'Italianité," 212–13.

35. Riccarand and Omezzoli, *Sur l'Émigration Valdôtaine*, 44–52.

36. Cross, *Immigrant Workers in Industrial France*, 106–09; Caroline Wiegandt-Sakoun, "Le Fascisme Italien en France," in *Les Italiens en France*, ed. Milza, 430–69.

37. Cross, *Immigrant Workers in Industrial France*, 116–19; Rainhorn, *Paris, New York*, 151–54.

38. Rainhorn, *Paris, New York*, 139–44.

39. Riccarand and Omezzoli, *Sur l'Émigration Valdôtaine*, 43–62.

40. Association Valdôtaine Archives Sonores, *Émigration Valdôtaine dans le Monde: La Diaspora au Cours des Siècles: Histoire et Témoignages* (Aosta: Musumeci, 1986), 163.

41. The city of Paris is divided into twenty sections known as arrondissements, each of which is subdivided into four administrative quarters containing a police station.

42. Liliane Riou, "Le Crime du Metro Porte-Dorée," *Gavroche* 149, no. 3 (Janvier–Mars 2007): 28.

43. Eric Vial, "Le Casellario Politico Centrale: Source pour l'Histoire de l'Émigration Politique" in *Les Italiens en France*, ed. Milza, 155–67, esp. 160.

44. Cross, *Immigrant Workers in Industrial France*, 70; Paul Lawrence, "'Un Flot d'Agitateurs Politiques de Fauters de Désordes et de Criminals': Adverse Perceptions of Immigrants in France between the Wars," *French History* 14, no. 2 (2000): 201–21; Philip E. Ogden and Paul E. White, eds., *Population Mobility in the Later Nineteenth and Twentieth Centuries* (London: Unwin Hyman, 1989), 38–47; Robert Tomlinson, "The Disappearance of France, 1896–1940: French Politics and the Birth Rate," *Historical Journal* 28 (June 1985): 405–15.

45. Ralph Schor, *L'Opinion Française et les Étrangers en France, 1919–1939* (Paris: Publications de la Sorbonne, 1985), 653–54.

46. Michel Dreyfus, "Un Courant Socialiste Original: Les Maximalistes Italiens dans l'Émigration," in *Les Italiens en France*, ed. Milza, 169–93; Bruno Groppo, "La 'Propaganda Ouvrière' de Giustizia et Libertá et le Débat Politique au sein de l'Antifascisme Italien en 1931," in *Les Italiens en France*, ed. Milza, 257–83; Pierre Guillen, "Le Role Politique de l'Immigration Italienne en France dans l'Entre-Deux Guerres," in *Les Italiens en France*, ed. Milza, 324–41; Franco Ramella, "Biografia di un Operaio Antifascista: Ipotesi per una Storia Sociale

dell'Emigrazione Politica," in *Les Italiens en France,* ed. Milza, 385–406; Eric Vial, "La Ligue Italienne des Droits de l'Homme (LIDU), de sa Fondation à 1934," in *Les Italiens en France,* ed. Milza, 407–30.

47. Siân Reynolds, *France between the Wars, Gender and Politics* (London: Routledge, 1996), 63–64.

48. Ginette Vincendeau makes this observation about bals in French films produced in the 1930s. She also states, "The evocation by French films of the 1930s of warm, unified, communities entertaining themselves in cafés, bals, and guinguettes, undoubtedly had a basis in the social reality of the time, as confirmed by other documents (photographs, autobiographies, oral history). Ginette Vincendeau, "From the *Bal Populaire* to the Casino: Class and Leisure in French Films of the 1930s," *Nottingham French Studies* 31, no.2 (Autumn 1992): 60; Vincendeau, "French Cinema of the 1930s: Social Text and Context of a Popular Entertainment Medium" (Ph.D. diss., University of East Anglia, 1985).

49. Vincendeau, "From the *Bal Populaire* to the Casino," 59. One should note that there is very little scholarly literature available on the bals musette, and no book-length English work at all. Even in French, the amount of scholarly literature is negligible. In the area of popular culture, the bals musette deserve more scholarly attention. See: Louis Chevalier, *Montmartre du Plaisir et du Crime* (Paris: Éditions Robert Laffont, 1980); Claude Dubois, *La Bastoche: Bal-Musette, Plaisir et Crime 1750–1939: Paris entre Chiens et Loups* (Paris: Éditions du Félin, 1997). Photographs of bals musette can be found in Georges Brassaï, *Le Paris Secret des Années 30* (New York: Pantheon Books, 1976). There are also film evocations of the bals that were made in the 1930s. See, for example, *Sous les Toits de Paris,* directed by René Clair (1930); *Zouzou,* directed by Marc Allégret (1934); and *La Bête Humaine,* directed by Jean Renoir (1938). Finally, there are recordings of accordion music typical of the bals, such as Didier Duprat, *Paris Musette* (Paris: Just a Memory Records, 1990), 1 disc.

50. Pierre Mac Orlan, *Paris Vu par André Kertész* (Paris: Plon, 1934); Dudley Andrew and Steven Ungar, *Popular Front Paris and the Poetics of Culture* (Cambridge, Mass.: Harvard University Press, 2005), 251–52.

51. See Dubois, *La Bastoche.* This paragraph and the next are based on Dubois.

52. Ibid; Charles Rearick, *The French in Love and War: Popular Culture in the Era of the World Wars* (New Haven: Yale University Press, 1997), 108; Marcel Montarron, "Les Musettes de Paris," *Détective* 451 (June 17, 1937), 2.

53. Vincendeau, "From the *Bal Populaire* to the Casino," 55.

54. Montarron, "Les Musettes de Paris," 2; Carl Van Vechten, *Sacred and Profane Memories* (New York: Alfred A. Knopf, 1932), 43–57.

55. Couleur Lavande, "The Danced Musette: Musette Culture, Retro, Dance." Online at: pagesperso-orange.fr./musette.info/GB-General.htm (accessed August 25, 2009).

56. Quoted in Montarron, "Les Musettes de Paris," 2.

57. For an example of new work being done on the extreme right, other than Kennedy, *Reconciling France against Democracy,* see Samuel Kalman, *The Extreme Right in Interwar France: The Faisceau and the Croix de Feu* (Aldershot, Eng.: Ashgate, 2008).

1 / Le Crime du Métro: A Perfect Crime

1. Archives de la Préfecture de Police, Paris [hereafter APP], P. J. Assassinat 1937, "L'Affaire Laetitia Toureaux," Rapport Général, 7. Most of the account in this chapter of Laetitia Toureaux's final hours comes from the police report, Rapport Général, 3–99. Marcel Montarron,

"Les Musettes de Paris," *Détective* 451 (June 17, 1937); Claude Dubois, *La Bastoche: Bal-Musette, Plaisir et Crime 1750–1939: Paris entre Chiens et Loups* (Paris: Éditions du Félin, 1997). Even though Toureaux's murder was never officially solved, parts of the police dossier on her case still exist, although, as with most post–World War II documents, a dérogation is required to access them. Archives Nationales [hereafter AN], F/7 14816, "Meurtres Attribués au C.S.A.R.: Affaire c/x Meurtre Loetitia Toureaux." See also: APP, Ea III/137, "L'Affaire Laetitia Toureaux," which mostly contains newspaper clippings related to the crime and of interest to the police. All the newspapers in Paris, even those of the communists, reported on the murder. Because these files on Toureaux have only very recently been rediscovered and made accessible to scholars, their formal classification, organization, and title have changed several times since we first read them in 2002. Our citations use the most recent classifications and call numbers employed by the archives. Only a few writers have discussed Laetitia Toureaux, and fewer still have given her case any serious scholarly attention, despite the fascination it seems to hold for ordinary French people. As late as the 1970s, French television and radio aired documentaries on her life. For mention of her in secondary sources, see: Philippe Bourdrel, *La Cagoule: Histoire d'une Société du Front Populaire à la Ve République*, 2d ed. (Paris: Albin Michel, 1992); René Delpêche, *Affaires Classées: Crimes Prescrits, Crimes sans Châtiment* (Paris: Éditions du Dauphin, 1968); Lawrence Osborne, *Paris Dreambook: An Unconventional Guide to the Splendor and Squalor of the City* (New York: Vintage Books, 1990); Adrian Rifkin, *Street Noises: Parisian Pleasure, 1900–40* (Manchester: Manchester University Press, 1995); J. R. Tournoux, *L'Histoire Secrète: La Cagoule, le Front Populaire, Vichy, Londres, Deuxième Bureau, l'Agérie Française, l'O. A. S.* (Paris: Plon, 1973).

2. APP, P.J. Assassinat 1937, "L'Affaire Laetitia Toureaux," Les Sceaux, Lettre de Le Commissaire Principal Charles Badin, Attaché à la Direction de la Police Judicaire à Monsieur Bru, Juge d'Instruction au Première Instance du Département de la Seine dans une Affaire Suivie Contre: X Inculpé de Homicide Volontaire. There were twelve seals related to Laetitia Toureaux's murder, all items taken from her person after she died. These items are no longer in the police file. Nor is the original autopsy report, only a summary of it. Archivists informed us that the items either disappeared during World War II or were more probably sold off long ago as curiosities.

3. APP, P.J. Assassinat 1937, "L'Affaire Laetitia Toureaux," Rapport Général, 91. Statement Marceau Marnef made to the police.

4. Ibid., 94.

5. Ibid., 99. The following paragraphs, concerning the final hour of Toureaux's life and the events occurring immediately thereafter, are found in APP, P.J. Assassinat 1937, "L'Affaire Laetitia Toureaux," Rapport Général, 3–99.

6. *Paris Soir*, May 19, 1937; *La Liberté*, May 26, 1937; AN, F/7 14816, "Meurtres Attribués au C.S.A.R.," Report dated August 1, 1938.

7. APP, Ea/83/12, #21, *France-Soir*, June 1, 1937; Delpêche, *Affaires Classées*, 14–15.

8. APP, P.J. Assassinat 1937, "L'Affaire Laetitia Toureaux," Rapport Général, 6.

9. Throughout the text, if possible the first names of all persons mentioned have been provided when first introduced. It was common practice in many legal documents and newspaper articles to list people only by their last names. It was not always possible to identify first names of all persons cited. Agent Isambert was a "*gardien de la paix*," but his first name is not used in the documents.

10. APP Ea/83/12, #21, *France-Soir*, June 1, 1937; APP, P.J. Assassinat 1937, "L'Affaire Laetitia Toureaux," Rapport Général, 20–23; Delpêche, *Affaires Classées*, 19.

11. *Paris Soir,* May 20, 1937; *Ce Soir,* May 29, 1937; *Ce Soir,* May 29, 1937; Jean-Émile Né-aumet, *Les Grandes Enquêtes du Commissaire Chenevier de la Cagoule à l'Affaire Dominici* (Paris: Albin Michel, 1995), 125-27; "Le Crime du Métro," *Détective* 448 (May 27, 1937).

12. Ibid.

13. APP, P.J. Assassinat 1937, "L'Affaire Laetitia Toureaux," Rapport Général, May 31, 1938, 97-98, Audition de Pierrette Marnef.

2 / Police and Press on the Trail of an Assassin

1. Richard Frase, ed., *The French Code of Criminal Procedure,* rev. ed., trans. Gerald L. Kock and Richard Frase (Littleton, Colo.: Fred B. Rothman, 1988), 3-6; Benjamin F. Martin, *Crime and Criminal Justice under the Third Republic: The Shame of Marianne* (Baton Rouge: Louisiana State University Press, 1990), 82-124. The organization of the French police system in the 1930s was complex. We wish to thank the anonymous reader who contributed specific wording to clarify the content of this paragraph.

2. AN, F/7 14816, "Meurtres Attribués au C.S.A.R.: Affaire c/x Meurtre Loetitia Toureaux," "Monsieur Georges ALBAYEZ, Commissaire de Police Mobile à L'Inspection Générale des Services de Police Criminelle (Sûreté Nationale)," report dated August 1, 1938. See also APP, P.J. Assassinat 1937, "L'Affaire Laetitia Toureaux, 16 Mai 1937," Rapport Général, 20-30, 426-28. The Rapport Général is a 573-page dossier compiled by the police. It is dated March 31, 1938, and its contents cover the entire investigation of Toureaux's murder to that point.

3. The police tended to read the newspapers closely and to keep a file of articles pertaining to cases upon which they were working. Many of the newspaper articles cited below come from that file housed at the APP, under the code Ea III/137, which is the file for the Toureaux case. *Le Petit Parisien,* May 24, 1937. See also APP, P.J. Assassinat 1937, "L'Affaire Laetitia Toureaux," Rapport Général.

4. *Le Petit Parisien,* May 19, 1937.

5. AN, F/7 14816, Report dated August 1, 1938; *Le Petit Parisien,* May 17, 1937, and June 17, 1937.

6. *Le Petit Parisien,* May 17, 1937.

7. "Le Crime du Métro," *Détective* 448 (May 27, 1937), 1-5, 14-15 (quote, 14). By some accounts Sylvain "Jules" Toureaux died of tuberculosis, while other accounts indicate throat cancer.

8. APP, P.J. Assassinat 1937, "L'Affaire Laetitia Toureaux," Procès-Verbal 56, "Traductions de Lettres en Langue Italienne," letter dated July 14, 1929.

9. Ibid., "Traductions de Lettres en Langue Italienne," letter from Aoste, May 5, 1930.

10. In the interview he gave to the magazine *Détective,* Riton detailed her activities on the Sunday of her murder and made no mention of a trip to the cemetery. Henri Nourrissat, "Ma Dernière Danse avec Ma Soeur," *Détective* 449 (June 3, 1937), 4-5.

11. *France Soir,* July 2, 1962; *Paris-Soir,* May 22, 1937; APP, P.J. Assassinat 1937, "L'Affaire Laetitia Toureaux," Rapport Général.

12. *Le Petit Parisien,* May 19, 1937.

13. *Paris-Soir,* May 23, 1937.

14. For what follows, see AN, F/7 14816, Report dated August 1, 1938; Nourrissat, "Ma Dernière Danse avec Ma Soeur," 4-5; René Delpêche, *Affaires Classées: Crimes Prescrits, Crimes sans Chatiment* (Paris: Éditions du Dauphin, 1968), 13-46.

15. AN, F/7 14816, Report dated August 1, 1938. See also Claude Dubois, *La Bastoche: Bal-Musette, Plaisir et Crime, 1750-1939: Paris entre Chiens et Loups* (Paris: Éditions du Félin, 1997).

16. APP, P.J. Assassinat 1937, "L'Affaire Laetitia Toureaux," Renseignements sur la Famille Nourrissat, June 8, 1937; Rapport Général, March 31, 1938.

17. Ibid., Renseignements sur la Famille Nourrissat, June 8, 1937.

18. *Paris-Soir,* May 21, 1937. Her brother Virgile contradicted his father, saying that Toureaux had not visited Italy since 1930.

19. *Paris-Soir,* May 19, 1937.

20. Nourrissat, "Ma Dernière Danse avec Ma Soeur," 4.

21. "Le Crime du Métro, Le Double Assassinat de Notre Compatriote," *L'Écho de la Vallée d'Aoste,* June 4, 1937. The Valdôtaine paper also praised Toureaux and rejected negative newspaper reporting about her.

22. AN, F/7 14816, Note from the Contrôle Générale des Services de Police Criminelle, May 17, 1937, verifying the information about Laetitia Toureaux's relationship with Schramm, APP, P.J. Assassinat 1937, "L'Affaire Laetitia Toureaux," Rapport Général, 175; *Le Petit Parisien,* May 24, 1937; Delpêche, *Affaires Classées,* 23–24.

23. APP, P.J. Assassinat 1937, "L'Affaire Laetitia Toureaux," Rapport Général, 175–78, 252; Procès-Verbaux 5711; Folder #2, Copie de Rapports, #5; Folder, May–October, 1937, Interrogation of Le Boulanger. "Boulanger" is the word for "baker" in French, and "Petit Pain," or "Little Bread," was a play on the man's last name.

24. *Le Petit Parisien,* June 17, 1937.

25. AN, F/7 14816, Documents from Commissaire Georges Albayez, numbered 2 and 4, September 16, 1937, and September 30, 1937.

26. AN, F/7 14816, Report dated August 1, 1938. *Le Petit Parisien,* May 16, 1937, May 19, 1937; *L'Humanité,* May 25, 1937.

27. *Détective* 448 (May 27, 1937).

28. *Paris-Soir,* May 23, 1937.

29. *L'Humanité,* May 27, 1937.

30. *Paris-Soir,* May 22, 1937.

31. *La Liberté,* May 26, 1937.

32. Ibid.; Michael B. Miller, *Shanghai on the Métro: Spies, Intrigue, and the French between the Wars* (Berkeley: University of California Press, 1994), 69.

33. For an excellent description of the situation in 1930s France, see Eugen Weber, *The Hollow Years: France in the 1930s* (London: W. W. Norton, 1994).

34. *Paris-Soir,* May 26, 1937; Donald N. Baker, "The Surveillance of Subversion in Interwar France: The Carnet B in the Seine, 1922–1940," *French Historical Studies* 10 (Spring 1978): 3, 486–516, 507; Gary S. Cross, *Immigrant Workers in Industrial France: The Making of a New Laboring Class* (Philadelphia: Temple University Press, 1983), 106–07, 115–16.

35. *Le Petit Parisien,* May 22, 1937.

36. Ibid.

37. Quoted in Paul Bringuier and Marcel Montarron, "Le Crime du Métro," *Détective* 448 (May 27, 1937), 14.

38. *Paris-Soir,* May 27, 1937. If Toureaux actually did make such a claim, it seems unlikely to have been true, given the situation in Spain during 1937.

39. *Le Matin,* May 25, 1937.

40. This statement would also seem to suggest that Toureaux's sleuthing at the L'As-de-Coeur was for Rouffignac's firm, despite his secretary's avowal to the contrary. *Paris-Soir,* May 22, 1937.

41. *Le Matin,* May 25, 1937.

42. *Paris-Soir,* May 26, 1937; APP, P.J. Assassinat 1937, "L'Affaire Laetitia Toureaux," Rapport Général, 306.

43. *L'Intransigeant,* May 26, 1937.

44. This paragraph and previous two paragraphs come from APP, P.J. Assassinat 1937, "L'Affaire Laetitia Toureaux," Rapport Général, March 31, 1938, 310–27; ibid., "Rapport et les Renseignements Fournis par M. Rouffignac," May 28, 1938 (unpaginated procès-verbal).

45. AN, F/7 14816, Report dated August 1, 1938; APP, P.J. Assassinat 1937, "L'Affaire Laetitia Toureaux," Rapport Général, 306, and Interrogation 64/1, Victor Riou and Yvonne Cavret. Riou spoke with Badin about the Toureaux case in the stead of Cavret, who was in a maternity clinic, having just given birth to Riou's child. Cavret's daughter, Liliane Riou, recently published an article about her mother's relationship with Toureaux. Liliane Riou, "Le Crime du Métro Porte-Dorée," *Gavroche* 149, no. 3 (January–March 2007): 26–35. Unfortunately, Liliane Riou died before we were able to make contact with her.

46. AN, F/7 14816, Report dated August 1, 1938.

47. *Excelsior,* May 22, 1937; Nourrissat, "Ma Dernière Danse avec Ma Soeur," 4; *Paris-Soir,* May 23, 1937.

48. *Le Journal,* May 26, 1937; *Le Petit Parisien,* May 27, 1937.

49. The *Excelsior* broke this story, and within days Jean Martin was a celebrity, giving interviews to almost every newspaper in Paris. *Excelsior,* May 22, 1937; *Le Petit Parisien,* May 23, 1937; *L'Oeuvre,* May 25, 1937; *Le Populaire,* May 25, 1937.

50. Quoted in *Le Matin,* May 25, 1937.

51. Quoted in *Le Matin,* May 27, 1937.

52. AN, F/7 14816, Report dated April 12, 1938.

53. *L'Oeuvre,* May 29, 1937.

54. Quotes come from *L'Humanité,* May 25, 1937.

55. *Paris-Soir,* May 28, 1937.

56. Ibid.

57. *Le Petit Parisien,* May 27, 1937.

58. *Le Matin,* February 5, 1934, May 23, 1937; *L'Oeuvre,* May 25, 1937. For the story of the investigation of the death of Albert Prince, see Jean-Émile Néaumet, *Les Grandes Énquêtes du Commissaire Chenevier: De la Cagoule à l'Affaire Dominici* (Paris: Albin Michel, 1995), 41ff; for the Stavisky affair, see Paul Jankowski, *Stavisky: A Confidence Man in the Republic of Virtue* (Ithaca: Cornell University Press, 2002); William Wiser, *The Twilight Years: Paris in the 1930s* (New York: Carroll & Graf, 2000), 97ff; see also Weber, *The Hollow Years,* 131–40.

59. *Paris-Soir,* May 26, 1937.

60. AN, F/7 14816, Report dated August 1, 1938; *La Liberté,* May 26, 1937.

61. AN, F/7 14816, Report dated August 1, 1938.

62. *Paris-Soir,* May 23, 1937.

63. *L'Intransigeant,* June 6, 1937.

64. AN, F/7 14816, "Affaire Toureaux," "Affaire Navachine"; ADP, PEROTIN 212/79/3, "Affaire du C.S.A.R.—Comité Secret d'Action Révolutionnaire—et Autres Mouvements Nationalistes de Droite."

65. In his memoirs, Jean Belin, one of the inspectors on Toureaux's murder case, implied strongly that she was a police informant and that officers at the Sûreté were aware of this fact. He wrote in 1950, "I am not prepared to state that she had acted as an informer, although it seems likely such was the case. I mention this particular aspect of the case because it is quite possible that a number of police officers may have been in the know." Jean Belin, *Secrets of the Sûreté: The Memoirs of Commissioner Jean Belin* (New York: G. P. Putnam's Sons, 1950), 214. On police corruption, secrecy, and mistrust, see Martin, *Crime and Criminal Justice,* 102–06.

3 / Gentle Lamb or Wicked Sheep? Embodying Laetitia Toureaux

1. "Paris Was a Woman," DVD, directed by Greta Schiller (Paris: Arte/ZDF Feitgeist Films, 1995).

2. Sarah Maza, *The Myth of the French Bourgeoisie: An Essay on the Social Imaginary 1750–1850* (Cambridge, Mass.: Harvard University Press, 2003), 2, 4–5, 12–13, 158. See also Bertram Gordon's article, "The Bourgeoisie Reconstruction Problem in French History: A Kuhnian Paradigm," published on his website, www.mills.edu/academics/faculty/hist/bmgordon/bourgeoisie_reconstruction.pdf (accessed June 19, 2009); Theodore Zeldin, *France, 1848–1945* (Oxford: Clarendon Press, 1973), 1: 11–22.

3. Maza, *The Myth of the French Bourgeoisie*, 195.

4. Many of the newspaper clippings cited derive from the APP, P.J. Assassinat 1937, "L'Affaire Laetitia Toureaux, 16 Mai 1937," Dossier E/A 83/7–8; *L'Oeuvre*, May 25, 1937. Much of this chapter is taken from Annette Finley-Croswhite and Gayle K. Brunelle, "'Murder in the Métro': Masking and Unmasking Laetitia Toureaux in 1930s France," *French Cultural Studies* 14, no. 1 (2003): 53–80.

5. *Paris-Soir*, May 21, 1937.

6. *L'Humanité*, May 25, 1937.

7. *Paris-Soir*, May 19, 21, 1937; *France-Soir*, June 1, 1937; René Delpêche, *Affaires Classés: Crimes Préscrits, Crimes sans Chatiment* (Paris: Éditions du Dauphin, 1968), 26–28.

8. *Le Populaire*, May 25, 1937.

9. *Le Petit Parisien*, May 22, 1937; *Paris-Soir*, May 23, 31, 1937; *Le Populaire*, May 25, 1937; *Ce Soir*, May 29, 1937.

10. *Le Petit Parisien*, May 27, 1937

11. Oral interview the authors conducted with a former boyfriend of Laetitia Toureaux who wished to remain anonymous, Paris, France, August 3, 1997. He stated, "Laetitia was a beautiful woman, she had beautiful green eyes, but she was a bit odd. She kept to herself all the time. She was just too independent for her own good."

12. Henri Nourrissat, "Ma Dernière Danse avec Ma Soeur," *Détective* 449 (June 3, 1937), 4–5.

13. *Paris-Soir*, May 23, 1937.

14. For example, some of *Détective*'s most sensational reporting included: "L'Affaire de la Malle Sanglante," in 1929, "L'Affaire Violette Mozières," in 1933, and "L'Affaire Prince," in 1934.

15. *Le Matin*, May 2, 1934; *Paris-Soir*, May 23, 1937; June 1, 1937; *Le Petit Parisien*, May 27, 29, 31, 1937.

16. *Paris-Soir*, May 23, 1937; *L'Oeuvre*, May 27, 1937; *Le Populaire*, May 27, 1937.

17. Gaston Gallimard founded *Détective* in 1928 as a weekly magazine to exploit the public interest in crimes and scandals in interwar France. It was modeled on *Detective Fiction Weekly*, published in New York, and was similar to other French publications such as *Police et Reportage, Réalisme*, and *Scandales*. *Détective* enjoyed rapid success, tripling its readership in its first year of publication. By the end of its second year, it enjoyed a weekly circulation of 800,000. It ran until May 9, 1940, when most of its writing staff was mobilized for World War II. Catherine Maisonneuve, "Détective Le Grand Hebdomadaire des Faits Divers de 1928 à 1940" (thesis, Université de Droit, Économie, et Sciences Sociales de Paris, II, 1974). See also Claude Bellanger, Jacques Godechot, Pierre Guiral, and Fernand Terrou, eds., *Histoire Générale de la Presse Française*, Vol. 3, *De 1871 à 1940* (Paris: Presses Universitaires de France, 1972), 598–99; David Walker, "Cultivating the Fait Divers: *Détective*," *Nottingham French Studies* 31 (1992): 71–83; Robin Walz, *Pulp Surrealism: Insolent Popular Culture in Early Twentieth-Century Paris* (Berkeley: University of California Press, 2000), 148–49.

18. *Paris-Soir,* May 19, 1937.

19. For more discussion of the cultural readings of early twentieth-century French newspapers, see Walz, *Pulp Surrealism.*

20. Mary Louise Roberts, *Civilization without Sexes: Reconstructing Gender in Postwar France, 1917–1927* (Chicago: University of Chicago Press, 1994), 7. The literature on gender in the interwar period is still growing, but much of it focuses on Germany and Italy. For a general overview of the subject, see: Claudia Koonz, *Mothers in the Fatherland: Women, the Family, and Nazi Politics* (New York: St. Martin's Press, 1987); Robin Pickering-Iazzi, ed., *Mothers of Invention: Women, Italian Fascism, and Culture* (Minneapolis: University of Minnesota Press, 1995); Françoise Thébaud, ed., *A History of Women in the West,* vol. 5, *Toward a Cultural Identity in the Twentieth Century* (Cambridge, Mass.: Belknap Press, 1996); Victoria De Grazia, *How Fascism Ruled Women: Italy, 1922–1945* (Berkeley: University of California Press, 1992); Melanie Hawthorne and Richard Golsan, eds., *Gender and Fascism in Modern France* (Hanover, N.H.: University Press of New England, 1997); Martin Durham, *Women and Fascism* (London: Routledge, 1998); Kevin Passmore, *Women, Gender, and Fascism in Europe, 1919–1945* (New Brunswick, N.J.: Rutgers University Press, 2003); Passmore, "Femininity and the Right: From Moral Order to Moral Order," *Modern and Contemporary France* 8, no. 1 (2000): 55–69; Joachim Schlör, *Nights in the Big City: Paris, Berlin, London, 1840–1930* (London: Reaktion, 1998); Katharina von Ankum, ed., *Women in the Metropolis: Gender and Modernity in Weimar Culture* (Berkeley: University of California Press, 1997); Laurence Brown, "'Pour Aider Nos Frères d'Espagne': Humanitarian Aid, French Women, and Popular Mobilization during the Front Populaire," *French Politics, Culture, & Society* 25, no. 1 (Spring 2007): 30–48; Rifkin, *Street Noises;* Piers Brendon, *The Dark Valley: A Panorama of the 1930s* (New York: Alfred A. Knopf, 2000); Dudley Andrew and Steven Ungar, *Popular Front Paris and the Poetics of Culture* (Cambridge, Mass.: Harvard University Press, 2005); Miranda Pollard, *Reign of Virtue: Mobilizing Gender in Vichy France* (Chicago: University of Chicago Press, 1998), 9–41.

21. Jean Belin, *Secrets of the Sûreté: The Memoirs of Commissioner Jean Belin* (New York: G. P. Putnam's, 1950), 232; Raymond Manevy, *L'Évolution des Formules de Présentation de la Presse Quotidienne* (Paris: Éditions Estienne, 1956); Christian Delporte, *Les Journalistes en France (1880–1950): Naissance et Construction d'une Profession* (Paris: Seuil, 1999); Pierre Andreu, *Révoltes de l'Esprit: Les Revues des Années 30* (Paris: Éditions Kimé, 1991); Judith R. Walkowitz, *City of Dreadful Delight: Narratives of Sexual Danger in Late Victorian London* (Chicago: University of Chicago Press, 1992); Elizabeth Wilson, *The Sphinx in the City: Urban Life, the Control of Disorder, and Women* (Berkeley: University of California Press, 1991); Walz, *Pulp Surrealism.*

22. Delporte, *Les Journalistes en France,* 282–83, 314–18.

23. Walz, *Pulp Surrealism,* 79; Marcel Sicot, *Servitude et Grandeur Policières: Quarante Ans à la Sûreté* (Paris: Les Productions de Paris, 1949), 196–200.

24. Christopher Prendergast, *Paris and the Nineteenth Century* (Oxford: Blackwell, 1992).

25. Claude Dubois, *La Bastoche: Bal-Musette, Plaisir et Crime, 1750–1939: Paris entre Chiens et Loups* (Paris: Éditions du Félin, 1997).

26. Delporte, *Les Journalistes en France,* 229; Jacques Wolgensinger, *L'Histoire à la Une: La Grande Aventure* (Paris: Gallimard, 1989), 105–13.

27. Marcel Montarron, "Les Musettes de Paris," *Détective* 451 (June 17, 1937).

28. Walker, "Cultivating the *Fait Divers,*" 72.

29. Roberts, *Civilization without Sexes,* 5; Mary Jean Green, "Gender, Fascism, and the Croix de Feu: The Women's Pages of *Le Flambeau,*" *French Cultural Studies* 8 (1997), 229–39: Siân Reynolds, *France between the Wars: Gender and Politics* (London: Routledge, 1996).

30. Pollard, *Reign of Virtue*, 18, 10.

31. Anne-Marie Sohn, "Between the Wars in France and England," in *A History of Women*, 4: 94; Roberts, *Civilization without Sexes*, 46–62.

32. Hawthorne and Golsan, *Gender and Fascism*, 7.

33. *L'Humanité*, May 29, 1937

34. *L'Oeuvre*, May 29, 1937.

35. *Le Populaire*, May 28, 1937.

36. *Paris-Soir*, May 31, 1937.

37. August Petigat, "Le Crime du Métro: Le Double Assassinat de Notre Compatriote," *L'Écho de la Vallée d'Aoste*, June 4, 1937.

38. *Paris-Soir*, May 30, 1937.

39. *Paris-Soir*, May 19, 1937.

40. *Paris-Soir*, May 31, 1937.

41. *L'Oeuvre*, May 28, 1937; *L'Humanité*, May 29, 1937; *Paris-Soir*, May 30, 1937, June 1, 1937, June 6, 1937; *Le Journal*, June 6, 1937.

42. Female material consumption began to increase in the late nineteenth century. For more, see Michael B. Miller, *The Bon Marché: Bourgeois Culture and the Department Store, 1869–1920* (Princeton: Princeton University Press, 1981); Luisa Passerini, "The Ambivalent Image of Women in Mass Culture," in *A History of Women*, 4: 324–42; Rosalind Williams, *Dream Worlds: Mass Consumption in Late Nineteenth-Century France* (Berkeley: University of California Press, 1982); Charles Rearick, *The Pleasures of the Belle Epoque: Entertainment and Festivity in Turn-of-the-Century France* (New Haven: Yale University Press, 1986).

43. Helen Harden Chenut, *The Fabric of Gender: Working-Class Culture in Third Republic France* (University Park: Pennsylvania State University Press, 2005), 298–306, 310–18; Ralph Schor, "L'Image de l'Italien dans la France de l'Entre-Deux Guerres," in *Les Italiens en France*, 89–109, esp. 93.

44. Nourrissat, "Ma Dernière Danse," 4.

45. *Paris-Soir*, May 19, 1937.

46. Ibid.

47. Helen Harden Chenut, "The Gendering of Skill as Historical Process: The Case of French Knitters in Industrial Troyes, 1880–1939," in *Gender and Class in Modern Europe*, ed. Laura L. Frader and Sonya O. Rose (Ithaca: Cornell University Press, 1996), 77–107, especially 80–82.

48. Pollard, *Reign of Virtue*, 12.

49. APP, P.J. Assassinat 1937, "L'Affaire Laetitia Toureaux," Assassinat Laetitia Toureaux: Procès Verbaux, 72; APP, P.J. Assassinat 1937, "L'Affaire Laetitia Toureaux," Copies de Rapports, #67, Audition de Mlle. Landry.

50. Schlör, *Nights in the Big City*, 194.

51. Michael B. Miller, *Shanghai on the Métro: Spies, Intrigue, and the French between the Wars* (Berkeley: University of California Press, 1994), 226ff; Adrian Rifkin, *Street Noises: Parisian Pleasure, 1900–1940* (Manchester: Manchester University Press, 1995), 120ff; Roberts, *Civilization without Sexes*, 15.

52. Roberts, *Civilization without Sexes*, 158–59.

53. Laws in 1920 and 1923 attempted to ban contraception and abortion. Under Vichy, abortion was considered a crime against the state. Margaret Collins Weitz, *Sisters in the Resistance: How Women Fought to Free France, 1940–1945* (New York: John Wiley & Sons, 1995), 45.

54. Ibid., 159.

55. *Paris-Soir*, May 23, 1937.

56. *L'Humanité*, May 25, 1937.

57. *L'Oeuvre*, May 25, 1937.

58. Ibid.

59. This chapter does not seek to grapple with the literature on French fascism. The authors nonetheless take the position that the Vichy regime was fascist, at least by 1942. See Robert Soucy, *French Fascism: The Second Wave, 1933–39* (New Haven: Yale University Press, 1995), for a further discussion of French fascism in the 1930s. See as well the appendix of this book.

60. Bringuier and Montarron, "Le Crime du Métro," 4.

61. *France-Soir*, June 1, 1957, available in APP, EA/53/12, Paul Gordeaux, Images de Mant, "L'Assassinate 'Parfait' de Laetitia Toureaux."

62. Robert Maier, "Negotiation and Identity," *Amsterdam Studies in the Theory and History of Linguistic Science*, series 4, "Current Issues in Linguistic Theory," 214 (2001): 227.

63. APP, P.J. Assassinat 1937, "L'Affaire Laetitia Toureaux," Rapport Général, 332.

64. Although it deals with a much earlier period, John Jeffries Martin's *Myths of Renaissance Individualism* (Bastingstoke: Palgrave Macmillan, 2004) offers an excellent overview of a number of the questions historians have raised in recent years about the construction of identities, as well as a response in some ways to Stephen Greenblatt's seminal work on early modern identity. See Stephen Greenblatt, *Renaissance Self-Fashioning: From More to Shakespeare* (Chicago: University of Chicago Press, 1980). For work on more modern issues of identity, see the essays in Linda Marie Brooks, ed., *Alternative Identities: The Self in Literature, History, and Theory* (New York: Garland, 1995), especially Linda Maria Brooks, "Alternative Identities: Stating the Problem," 3–35; Riva Kastoryano, *Negotiating Identities: States and Immigrants in France and Germany*, trans. Barbara Harshav (Princeton: Princeton University Press, 2002); Aparna Nayak-Guercio, "The Project of Liberation and the Projection of National Identity: Aragon, Calvo, Jouhandeau, 1944–1945" (Ph.D. diss., University of Pittsburgh, 2006). Nayak-Guercio's findings are summarized in Aparna Nayak-Guercio, "The Project of Liberation and the Projection of National Identity: France, Literature and Politics, 1944–1945," *Contemporary French and Francophone Studies* 10, no. 2 (April 2006): 195–204. See also Virginia Yans-McLaughlin, "Metaphors of Self in History: Subjectivity, Oral Narrative, and Immigration Studies," in *Immigration Reconsidered: History, Sociology, and Politics*, ed. Virginia Yans-McLaughlin (New York: Oxford University Press, 1990), 254–90.

65. Miguel A. Cabrera, "On Language, Culture, and Social Action," *History and Theory*, 40, no. 4 (December 2001) 82–100 (quote, 94). See also Maier, "Negotiation and Identity," 225–38; Deborah Schiffrin, "The Transformation of Experience, Identity, and Context," *Amsterdam Studies in the Theory and History of Linguistic Science*, series 4, "Current Issues in Linguistic Theory," 128 (1997): 41–55; Joan W. Scott, "The Evidence of Experience," *Critical Inquiry* 17 (Summer 1991): 773–97; Lewis D. Wurgaft, "Identity in World History: A Postmodern Perspective," *History and Theory* 34, no. 2 (May 1995): 67–85.

66. APP, P.J. Assassinat 1937, "L'Affaire Laetitia Toureaux," Rapport Général, 462.

67. Kastoryano, *Negotiating Identities*, 4.

68. Brooks, "Alternative Identities," 4.

69. Maier, "Negotiation and Identity," 227.

4 / Provocations and Assassinations in 1937

1. AN, F/7 14816, "Meurtres Attribués au C. S. A. R."; Jean-Émile Néaumet, *Les Grandes Enquêtes du Commissaire Chenevier: De la Cagoule à l'Affaire Dominici* (Paris: Albin Michel, 1995), 125–27.

2. Archives de Paris [hereafter ADP], PEROTIN 212/79/3, carton 43, "Dossiers Relatifs au C.S.A.R., Agents d'Execution"; Rapport, "Le Commissaire de Police Mobile BELIN, Chef de la 1ère Section à Monsieur l'Inspecteur Général, Chargé des Services de Police Criminelle," Paris, July 17, 1937; Néaumet, *Les Grandes Enquêtes*, 44–45, 127.

3. AN, BB/18/3061/9, Report from M. Couve de Murville, Délégué du Gouvernment Proviso 1ère de la République Française au Conseil Consultatif pour les Affaires Italiennes to S. E. Monsieur Georges Bidault, Ministre des Affaires Étrangères, Paris, Rome, December 16, 1944; Frédéric Freigneaux, "Histoire d'un Mouvement Terroriste de l'Entre-Deux Guerres: 'La Cagoule'" (M.A. thesis, Université Toulouse, Mirail, 1991), 216–17.

4. Jean-Baptiste Duroselle, *La Décadence, 1932–1939* (Paris: Imprimerie National, 1979), 294–96, 389–91; Eugen Weber, *The Hollow Years: France in the 1930s* (London: W. W. Norton, 1994), 23–25.

5. *La Liberté*, June 16, 1937. "Ces Homicides Volontaires Avaient Été Commis par un Même Bande."

6. The principal works that discuss the Rosselli murders are: Mimmo Franzinelli, *Il Delitto Rosselli: 9 Giugno 1937, Anatomia di un Omicidio Politico* (Milano: Mondadori, 2007), and Franco Bandini, *Il Cono d'Ombra: Chi Armò la Mano degli Assassini dei Fratelli Rosselli* (Milan: Sugarco Edizioni, 1990). Bandini makes excellent use of the documents in Italian archives to demonstrate the culpability of the Italian fascists in the murders, using the Cagoule as their arm in France to commit this "imperfect crime." See also Philippe Bourdrel, *La Cagoule: Histoire d'une Société Secrète du Front Populaire à la Ve République*, 2d ed. (Paris: Albin Michel, 1992), 151ff; Freigneaux, "Histoire d'un Mouvement Terroriste de l'Entre-Deux Guerres," esp. 229–37; Frédéric Monier, *Le Complot dans la Républic: Stratégies du Secret, de Boulanger à la Cagoule* (Paris: Éditions La Découverte, 1998), 298–302; Stanislao G. Pugliese, *Carlo Rosselli: Socialist Heretic and Antifascist Exile* (Cambridge, Mass.: Harvard University Press, 1999). Pugliese is the foremost scholar on the Rosselli in the English-speaking world.

7. Much less is known about Dimitri Navachine than about the Rosselli brothers, despite the fact that he was a very high-profile figure in 1930s France. Most of the works that discuss him, including Bourdrel and Monier (cited above), glean their information from each other and from the press and police reports produced at the time of the murder. Not all of the information in these reports is reliable, based as it often was on hearsay generated by the many informers upon whom the police relied heavily. Moreover, during and after the Vichy regime, the more extravagant rumors tying Navachine's murder to the so-called Synarchie conspiracy accelerated, further obscuring the reality of the crime. For a well-reasoned discussion of the myth of the Synarchie, and Navachine's relationship to it, see Olivier Dard, *La Synarchie, ou le Mythe du Complot Permanent* (Paris: Perrin, 1998), esp. 107–10. For a discussion of the Synarchie and Navachine from the point of view of a true believer, see Henri Coston, *Les Technocrates et la Synarchie* (Paris: Lectures Françaises, 1962), 27–28. See also Bourdrel, *La Cagoule*, 125–28; Monier, *Le Complot dans la République*, 298; Pierre Péan, *Le Mystérieux Docteur Martin, 1895–1969* (Paris: Fayard, 1993), 125–35; Annie Lacroix-Riz, *Le Choix de la Défaite: Les Élites Françaises dans les Années 1930* (Paris: Armand Colin, 2006).

8. In recent years, Russian historians have begun to explore the role of Freemasons in the fall of the tsarist government during the early stages of the Russian Revolution. Although for many decades Russian scholars, following the orthodox Bolshevik line, denied vehemently that Freemasons might have played a role, in recent publications they have conceded that Freemasons were in fact prominent among supporters of Kerensky's 1917 provisional government. For the best introduction to this scholarship, see Barbara T. Norton, ed., *The Problem of Masonic Politics in Early Twentieth-Century Russia*, special ed. of *Russian Studies in History* 34, no. 4 (Spring 1996).

9. Dmitri Navachine, *La Crise et l'Europe Économique*, 2 vols. (Paris: Félix Alcan, 1932).

10. AN, F/7 14816, "Affaire Navachine," testimony of M. Jean Georges Wiart, accused of criminal association, January, 23, 1938.

11. Clifford Rosenberg, *Policing Paris: The Origins of Modern Immigration Control between the Wars* (Ithaca: Cornell University Press, 2006), 65ff.

12. Péan, Le Mystérieux Docteur Martin, 131–32.

13. For example, the police tracked down leads such as Navachine's friend Jérémie Rabbinovitch, a Russian Jew and Swiss citizen living in Versailles, who evidently tried to draw Navachine into an attempt to overthrow the French government with Moscow's support. Navachine seems to have found Rabbinovitch's plans ridiculous. Still, Rabbinovitch insisted that Navachine's break with Stalin was merely a pretext. Later it was revealed that Rabbinovitch was a police informant who spied on right-wing groups allied with Hitler. Lacroix-Riz, *Le Choix de la Défaite*, 302. AN, F/7 14816, "Affaire Navachine," 1938, paper stamped "Inconnu au Fichier Central" and "Sous Toute Reserve." See also J. R. Tournoux, *L'Histoire Secrète: La Cagoule, le Front Populaire, Vichy, Londres, Deuxième Bureau, l'Agérie Française, l'O. A. S.* (Paris: Plon, 1962), 62. Tournoux assumes that Navachine was a Soviet spy, whereas Philippe Bourdrel believes that he belonged to a mysterious secret organization called the Synarchie, which, like the Freemasons, was bent on dominating the world's economy. Bourdrel, *La Cagoule*, 127.

14. Déat originally was elected to the Chamber of Deputies, the French legislature, as a socialist. He became editor of *L'Oeuvre* in 1936. Déat had a rocky relationship with the socialists during the 1930s, however, and by the end of the decade had opted for a policy of appeasement of Germany and Italy. He joined the Vichy government during the war and, along with Pierre Laval and Eugène Deloncle, created a Nazi-approved collaborationist political movement based in Paris. He was tried by a French court in 1945 but fled to Italy. He died in Turin in 1955. See Harry Roderick Kedward, *Occupied France: Collaboration and Resistance, 1940–1944* (London: Blackwell, 1985), 41.

15. The Synarchie myth bears a strong resemblance to the present-day accusations of an anti-French, Anglo-Saxon plot for world dominance, as well as the fears of some in the United States of one world government. Proponents of the Synarchie myth believed (and still believe) that the Anglo-Saxon countries (notably England and the United States; curiously enough, Germany was omitted from the plot) sought to use their large and efficient corporations to impose a capitalist economy and technocratic culture on the world. Believers usually were not true socialists, however, despite their rejection of U.S.-style corporate capitalism. Rather, they resembled in some ways German romantic conservatives, in that they yearned nostalgically for the France of the past and an economy dominated by Catholic values, peasant agriculture, and small businesses. Hence the pro-Nazi stance of many of them during Vichy. The best academic study of the Synarchie myth is Dard, *La Synarchie*.

16. For more on the Synarchie, see the very controversial Lacroix-Riz, *Le Choix de la Défaite*. See also André Ulmann and Henri Azeau, *Synarchie et Pouvoir* (Paris: Julliard, 1968).

17. Jacob Katz, *Jews and Freemasons in Europe, 1723–1939*, trans. Leonard Oschry (Cambridge, Mass.: Harvard University Press, 1970), 1.

18. The Dreyfus affair erupted over the wrongful conviction for treason of Captain Alfred Dreyfus, a young officer in the Army general staff. Sentenced to life in prison on Devil's Island in French Guiana, Dreyfus was only exonerated and released after an outcry among intellectuals that included Émile Zola's famous 1898 essay "J'accuse." Although anti-Semitism played a central role in dividing the Dreyfusards from their opponents, the latter also tended to be strongly pro-military and nationalist Catholic conservatives, whereas the former tended to be

liberals or socialists with secular, internationalist views. For more on the Dreyfus affair, see Eric Cahm, *The Dreyfus Affair in French Society and Politics* (New York: Longman, 1996).

19. Ibid., 170–71, 174ff; Vicki Caron, "The Antisemitic Revival in France in the 1930s: The Socioeconomic Dimension Reconsidered," *Journal of Modern History* 70 (March 1998): 24–73; Dard, *La Synarchie*, 23ff.

20. AN, F/7 14816, "Affaire Navachine," Police report dated January 22, 1938.

21. Ibid.; Bourdrel, *La Cagoule*, 126–28; Fernand Fontenay, *La Cagoule contre la France: Ses Crimes, Son Organisation, Ses Chefs, Ses Inspirateurs* (Paris: Éditions Sociales Internationales, 1938), 157–58; Monier, *Le Complot dans la République*, 298–99; Robert H. Johnston, *"New Mecca, New Babylon": Paris and the Russian Exiles, 1920–1945* (Montreal: McGill-Queen's University Press, 1988), 25.

22. ADP, PEROTIN 212/79/3, carton 43, "Dossiers Relatifs au C.S.A.R.," "Le Commissaire de Police Mobile Belin à Monsieur l'Inspecteur Général," Paris, July 17, 1937; *France-Soir,* June 1, 1957, 13–14; Bourdrel, *La Cagoule*, 125–26.

23. ADP, PEROTIN 212/79/3, carton 43, "Dossiers Relatives au C.S.A.R.," "Le Commissaire de Police Mobile Belin á Monsieur l'Inspecteur Général," Paris, July 17, 1937.

24. Bourdrel, *La Cagoule*, 126.

25. AN, F/7 14816, "Affaire Navachine," Letter dated 13 January 1939, "Le Commissaire de Police Simon Louis Attaché à la Ville de Nantes à Monsieur l'Inspecteur Général Chargé des Services de Police Criminelle."

26. The police had been keeping a close eye on the Rosselli brothers and had listed Carlo in the Carnet B as a possible terrorist. ADP, PEROTIN 212/79/3, carton 37, Report from Police Commissioner Chenevier to the Commissaire de Police, Paris, June 13, 1937.

27. Rosenberg, *Policing Paris*, 67ff.

28. Pugliese, *Carlo Rosselli*, offers the most complete account of Carlo Rosselli's life and works. See also his article, "Death in Exile: The Assassination of Carlo Rosselli," *Journal of Contemporary History* 32 no. 3 (July 1997): 305–319, and Charles F. Delzell, "The Assassination of Carlo and Nello Rosselli, June 9, 1937: Closing a Chapter of Italian Anti-Fascism," *Italian Quarterly* 28 (1987): 47–64. In addition, see Giovanni Belardelli, *Nello Rosselli: Uno Storico Antifascista* (Firenze: Passigli Editori, 1992); Joel Blatt, "Carlo Rosselli's Socialism," in *Italian Socialism: Between Politics and History,* ed. Spencer M. Di Scala (Amherst: University of Massachusetts Press, 1996), 80–99; Gaetano Salvemini, *Carlo and Nello Rosselli: A Memoir* (London: Intellectual Library, 1937).

29. Belin, *Secrets of the Sûreté,* 229; Pugliese, *Carlo Rosselli,* 94–95.

30. Delzell, "The Assassination of Carlo and Nello Rosselli," 55–56; Pugliese, "Death in Exile," 306.

31. Delzell, "The Assassination of Carlo and Nello Rosselli," 57; Pugliese, "Death in Exile," 309.

32. The most complete general studies of the Spanish Civil War are Burnett Bolloten, *The Spanish Civil War: Revolution and Counterrevolution* (Chapel Hill: University of North Carolina Press, 1991) and Hugh Thomas, *The Spanish Civil War,* 3d ed. (New York: Harper & Row, 1977). See also George Esenwein and Adrian Shubert, *Spain at War: The Spanish Civil War in Context, 1931–1939* (London: Longman, 1995); Douglas Little, *Malevolent Neutrality: The United States, Great Britain, and the Origins of the Spanish Civil War* (Ithaca: Cornell University Press, 1985); Jean-François Berdah, *La Démocratie Assassinée: La République Espagnole et les Grandes Puissances, 1931–1939* (Paris: Berg International Éditeurs, 2000).

33. Pugliese, *Carlo Rosselli,* 198ff; Pugliese, "Death in Exile," 309–10; Berdah, *La Démocratie Assassinée,* 207ff, 255ff; Esenwein and Shubert, *Spain at War,* 155; Thomas, *The Spanish Civil*

War, 366–67, 381, 452–53; Freigneaux, "Histoire d'un Mouvement Terroriste de l'Entre-Deux Guerres," 230.

34. For details of the murder, see Jean Belin, *The Secrets of the Sûreté: The Memoires of Commissioner Jean Belin* (New York: G. P. Putnam, 1950), 228–31; Bourdrel, *La Cagoule,* 153–56, the reproduction of the police report on the murders, "Annexe No. 3," 362–67, and Marion Rosselli's statement, "Annexe No. 4," 368–72; Freigneaux, "Histoire d'un Mouvement Terroriste de l'Entre-Deux Guerres," 229–37; Pugliese, *Carlo Rosselli,* 218–19; Salvemini, *Carlo and Nello Rosselli,* 65–68.

35. There was no actual witness to the crime. The police learned the details through forensic work to reconstruct the crime and, later, the testimony of the assassins. Bourdrel, *La Cagoule,* 156–61; Testimony of Fernand Jakubiez as cited in J. R. Tournoux, *L'Histoire Secrète,* 308–12.

36. Ibid.

37. Belin, *The Secrets of the Sûreté,* 231.

38. ADP, PEROTIN 212/79/3, carton 34/1, Report dated March, 13, 1939, from Police Inspector Bascou, stating that the police suspected Huguet of committing armed robbery in 1936.

39. Pugliese, "Death in Exile," 313.

40. Quoted in Bourdrel, *La Cagoule,* 159.

41. Michael Alpert, *A New International History of the Spanish Civil War,* 2d ed. (Basingstoke: Palgrave, 2004), 41–46, 76–82, 150, 154, 172; John F. Coverdale, *Italian Intervention in the Spanish Civil War* (Princeton: Princeton University Press, 1975), 88–96; Duroselle, *La Décadence, 1932–1939,* 301–05, 318; Gerald Howson, *Arms for Spain: The Untold Story of the Spanish Civil War* (New York: St. Martin's Press, 1999), 114–19; H. Haywood Hunt, "The French Radicals, Spain, and the Emergence of Appeasement," in *The French and Spanish Popular Fronts: Comparative Perspectives,* ed. Martin S. Alexander and Helen Graham (Cambridge: Cambridge University Press, 1989), 38–49; Julian Jackson, *The Popular Front in France: Defending Democracy, 1934–1938* (Cambridge: Cambridge University Press, 1988), 201–09; Francisco J. Romero Salvadó, *The Spanish Civil War: Origins, Course, and Outcomes* (Basingstoke: Palgrave, 2005), 71–81.

42. The August 31, 1937, report of the *Procureur de la République de Versailles au Procureur Général près la Cour d'Appel de Paris,* which discusses in detail the sabotage at Toussus-le-Noble, can be found in AN, BB/18/3061/5. After the war, another report, dated October 23, 1946, was produced by the *Procureur de la République* for the *Procureur Général près la Cour d'Appel de Paris.* This can be found in Archives de Paris, 1320 W 119. The second report contains a slightly different version of events than the first. The following account is based on these reports as well as the discussion in Bourdrel, *La Cagoule,* 176–77; Brigitte and Gilles Delluc, *Jean Filliol, du Périgord à la Cagoule, de la Milice à Oradour* (Périgueux: Pilote 24 Éditions, 2005), 61–64; Freigneaux, "Histoire d'un Mouvement de l'Entre-Deux Guerres," 258–60; Monier, *Le Complot dans la République,* 301.

43. Bourdrel, *La Cagoule,* 165–79.

5 / Enter the Cagoule: Terrorists of the Extreme Right

1. AN, BB/18/3061/2, "État Actuel de l'Information au Regard des Divers Inculpations et des Différents Inculpés," 33–37.

2. AN, BB/18/3061/2, "État Actuel," 33–37. Some accounts say that the bombs contained thirty kilos of explosives, roughly fifteen kilos each. See Aristide Corre (pseud. Dagore), *Les Carnets Secrets de la Cagoule,* ed. Christian Bernadac (Paris: Éditions France-Empire, 1977), 140.

3. Corre (pseud. Dagore), *Les Carnets Secrets*, 137–38.

4. *Le Temps*, September 13, 1937.

5. *La Liberté*, September 14, 1937.

6. Robert Soucy, *French Fascism: The Second Wave, 1933–1939* (New Haven: Yale University Press, 1995), 50; *Candide*, June 18–25, 1962.

7. Quoted in Joel Blatt, "The Cagoule Plot, 1936–1937," in *Crisis and Renewal in France, 1918–1962*, ed. Kenneth Mouré and Martin S. Alexander (New York: Berghahn Books, 2002), 93. ADP, PEROTIN 212/79/3, carton 46, "Réquisitoire Definitive, L'Affaire de la Patrie Française." The quote is also found in an interview with Thomas Bourlier in AN, BB/18/3061/2.

8. Corre (pseud. Dagore), *Les Carnets Secrets*, 112; ADP, PEROTIN 212/79/3, carton 24.

9. Corre (pseud. Dagore), *Les Carnets Secrets*, 9–29, 91.

10. Blatt, "The Cagoule Plot," 87.

11. Pujo called upon members of the Action Française to "beware of these 'hooded' conspirators from a comic opera who claim to have the support of the Action Française when they have nothing of the kind." Quoted in Corre (pseud. Dagore), *Les Carnets Secrets*, 14.

12. For the complete archival collection on the Cagoule, see: ADP, PEROTIN 212/79/3, "Affaire du C.S.A.R.—Comité Secret d'Action Révolutionnaire—et Autres Mouvements Nationalistes de Droite." See also AN, BB/18/3061/2 to 3061/9, "Affaire de la Cagoule, 1937–1951." For more about the Cagoule, see: Frédéric Monier, *Le Complot dans la République: Stratégies du Secret de Boulanger à la Cagoule* (Paris: Éditions la Découverte, 1998); Philippe Bourdrel, *La Cagoule: Histoire d'une Société Secrète du Front Populaire à la Ve République* (Paris: Albin Michel, 1970); Henry Charbonneau, *Les Mémoires de Porthos* (Paris: Éditions du Clan, 1967); Fernand Fontenay, *La Cagoule contre la France: Ses Crimes, son Organization, ses Chefs, ses Inspirateurs* (Paris: Éditions Sociales Internationales, 1938); Pierre Péan, *Le Mystérieux Docteur Martin, 1895–1969* (Paris: Fayard, 1993); Franco Bandini, *Il Cono d'Ombra: Chi Armò la Mano degli Assassin dei Fratelli Rosselli* (Milan: Sugarco Edizioni, 1990). Joel Blatt is currently working on a study of the murder of the Rosselli brothers. His summary, cited above, is a good overview. For some of the better treatments of the French extreme right, see: Joel Blatt, "Relatives and Rivals: The Responses of the Action Française to Italian Fascism, 1919–1926," *European Studies Review* 2 (1981): 263–92; William D. Irvine, *French Conservatism in Crisis: The Republican Federation of France in the 1930s* (Baton Rouge: Louisiana State University Press, 1979); Irvine, "Fascism in France and the Strange Case of the Croix de Feu," *Journal of Modern History* 63 (June 1991): 271–95; Stanley G. Payne, *A History of Fascism, 1914–1945* (London: UCL Press, 1995); Robert Soucy, *French Fascism: The First Wave, 1924–1933* (New Haven: Yale University Press, 1986); Soucy, *French Fascism: The Second Wave, 1933–1939*; Zeev Sternhell, *Ni Droite ni Gauche: L'Idéologie Fasciste en France* (Paris: Seuil, 1983); Sternhell, *Naissance de l'Idéologie Fasciste* (Paris: Fayard, 1989); Eugen Weber, *The Hollow Years: France in the 1930s* (New York: W. W. Norton, 1994); Weber, *Action Française: Royalism and Reaction in Twentieth-Century France.* (Stanford: Stanford University Press, 1962); Martin Blinkhorn, ed., *Fascists and Conservatives: The Radical Right and the Establishment in Twentieth-Century Europe* (London: Unwin Hyman, 1990); René Rémond, *Les Crises du Catholicisme en France dans les Années Trente* (Paris: Éditions Cana, 1979, reprinted in 1996); Jean Belin, *Secrets of the Sûreté: The Memoirs of Commissioner Jean Belin* (New York: G. P. Putnam's Sons, 1950), 210.

13. D. L. L. Parry, "Counter Revolution by Conspiracy, 1935–37," in *The Right in France, 1789–1997*, ed. Nicholas Atkin and Frank Tallett (London: I. B. Tauris, 1998), 163; Malcolm Anderson, *Conservative Politics in France* (London: George Allen & Unwin, 1974), 59–60.

14. Parry, "Counter Revolution by Conspiracy," 161–81; Blatt, "The Cagoule Plot," 86–104.

15. Blatt, "The Cagoule Plot," 92; Georges André Groussard, *Chemins Secrets* (Paris: Bader-Dufour, 1948), 108. Groussard went on to have notable relationships with former Cagoulards during Vichy, when both he and Méténier worked for Pétain.

16. AN, BB/18/3061/3 "Interrogatoire de Eugène Deloncle," April 7, 1938.

17. Monier, *Le Complot dans la République*, 280–81; Parry, "Counter Revolution by Conspiracy," 184; Anderson, *Conservative Politics in France*, 226.

18. Jean-Claude Valla, *La Cagoule, 1936–1937* (Paris: Éditions de la Librarie Nationale, 2000), 40–41.

19. Corre (pseud. Dagore), *Les Carnets Secrets*, 257.

20. AN, BB/18/3061/6, Deposition de Raymond Lainey; Gabriel Jeantet, *Pétain contre Hitler* (Paris: La Table Ronde, 1966). Throughout his book, Jeantet emphasizes that he was against terrorism.

21. Parry, "Counter Revolution by Conspiracy," 164; Monier, Le Complot dans la République, 289; AN, BB/18/3061/6, Déposition de Raymond Lainey, 2; AN, BB/18/3061/2, "Direction des Affaires Criminelles 1er Bureau No. 26437, Parquet du Tribunal de Première Instances du Departement de la Seine. Contrôle des Informations, N. 3762 bis. C.A.D. Lettre du Procureur de la République à Monsieur le Procureur Générale." The CSAR's small membership is one reason why historians have underestimated its influence. It is obviously hard to believe how seventy to a hundred of even the most determined men could have orchestrated the overthrow of the French government. See also Soucy, *French Fascism: The Second Wave*, 47.

22. AN, BB/18/3061/6, Déposition de Raymond Lainey. Lainey's deposition was given to police on April 4, 1938, during the prewar investigation of the Cagoule. Each new recruit swore, "Je jure fidélité et obeisance à le C.S.A.R. et à ses chefs. Tout manquement à votre règle, j'en ai été averti et j'en mesure les conséquences, entraîne ma condamnation à mort." Translated: "I swear fidelity and obedience to the CSAR and its leaders. I have been informed that if I fail to uphold your rules, I will bear the consequences and I will be condemned to death."

23. Corre (pseud. Dagore), *Les Carnets Secrets*, 16.

24. AN, BB/18/3061/6, Déposition de Raymond Lainey.

25. Ibid.; AN, BB/18/3061/2, Procès-Verbal de Paul Pourcher.

26. AN, BB/18/3061/2, "État Actual de l'Information au Regard des Divers Inculpations et des Différents Inculpés," 4, and untitled document beginning, "L'Affaire du CSAR," 2.

27. AN, BB/18/3061/2, "État Actuel de l'Information au Regard des Divers Inculpations et des Differents Inculpés," 58–59. Information taken from police informant Thomas Bourlier cites the following: Deloncle was the head of the organzation. Martin was involved in the organization of the Cagoule. Those associated with the "attentats" of the Cagoule were: Méténier, Locuty, Corre, Moreau de la Meuse, Macon, Filliol, Jakubiez, Puireux, Fauran, Bouvyer, and Tenaille. Roidot, Sauvage, and Billecocq prepared executions. Jean-Baptiste, Juif, Barbier, Duchamp, Jeantet, and Crespin were leaders of the gunrunning operation. Jeantet took over for Juif after the latter's death. Another group is referred to as "delinquents," who transported arms into France: Jakubiez, Macon, Gauville, Charles Tenaille, Harispe, Vauclard, Van de Kerkove, Mathieu, Rouel, Desmoulins, Dallet, René, Dallet, Paul, Sourciat, Borot, Vogel, Moreau de la Meuse, Benoit, and Méténier. Boulier identified another group who kept the weapons in depots: Juchereau, Mauler, Laromiguière-Lafont, Harispe, Parent, Jeanniot, Hasenfuss, Gaudiot, Cretet, Henri Deloncle, Corrèze, Moreau de la Meuse, and Proust. Others possessed a few arms to use or give to others: Renne, Fautre, Percheron, Billecocq, Sauvage, Durand, Allo, Roidot, Vauclard, Van de Kerkove, Marminat, Mathieu, Valery, Chauche, Desmoulins, Vernadet, Dallet Paul, Dallet, Valet, Védrine, Vogel, Maron, Mandereau, and Fustier. Another group made or kept explosives: Juchereau, Laromiguière-Lafont, Harispe, Parent, Jeanniot,

Fautre, Hasenfuss, Sapin, Gaudin, Cretet, Méténier, Corrèze, and Moreau de la Meuse, Proust, Henri Deloncle, and the Tenaille brothers. The women of the Cagoule will be discussed later in this chapter.

28. When preparing the case against the CSAR in 1939, juge d'instruction Béteille commented on the differences inside the organization's membership, particularly with regard to those he termed the "agents d'exécution." Freigneaux, "Histoire d'un Mouvement Terroriste de l'Entre-Deux Guerres," 71–72; ADP, Perotin 212/79/3, carton 43, "Interrogatoire Récapitulatif de Eugène Deloncle, le 30 mars 1939."

29. AN, BB/18/3061/3, "L'Affaire, Dite du CSAR, pour la Commodité de la Conversation, A Donné jusqu'ici à une Inculpation Générale d'Association de Malfaiteurs, Envertu de l'Article 265," 21–27.

30. Ibid., dossier 22, Déposition de Louis Boucher, le 13 Janvier 1938, and Déposition du Professeur Iwo Lominsky, le 25 Février 1938.

31. Freigneaux, "Histoire d'un Mouvement Terroriste de l'Entre-Deux Guerres," 118–36; Jean-Claude Valla, *La Cagoule, 1936–1937* (Paris: Éditions de la Librairie Nationale, 2000), 26; Brigitte Delluc and Gilles Delluc, *Jean Filliol, du Périgord à la Cagoule, de la Milice à Oradour* (Périgueux: Pilote 24 Éditions, 2005); Jacques Delperrie de Bayac, *Histoire de la Milice, 1918–1945* (Paris: Fayard, 1994), 10–26; Henry Coston, *Dictionnaire de la Politique Française* (Paris: Publications Henry Coston, 1967), 331; APP, PJ/52, "Complot du CSAR," File on Gabriel Jeantet; AN, BB/18/3061/6, dossier 38, Sous-dossier Jeantet; ADP, Perotin 212/79/3, cartons 17, 21; AN, BB/18/3061/3, Interrogatoire de Georges Cachier and Interrogatoire de Lainey; AN, BB/18/3061/5, Interrogatoire de Gabriel Jeantet; AN, F/7 14816, "Meurtres Attribués aux CSAR." The entire section on Cagoulard profiles is derived from these sources.

32. Deloncle's connection to the Synarchie is very controversial, as is the group itself. See chapter 4 for a brief discussion of it. Annie Lacroix-Riz, *Le Choix de la Défaite: Les Élites Françaises dans les Années 1930* (Paris: Armand Colin, 2006). Many conspirarcy theorists, like Lacroix-Riz, argue that when the 1937 Cagoule coup d'état failed, the Synarchists opted for the defeat of the Third Republic through German intervention.

33. Groussard, *Chemins Secrets,* 109–10.

34. APP, PJ/52, "Complot du CSAR," dossier 38, Sous-dossier Jeantet.

35. Corre (pseud. Dagore), *Les Carnets Secrets,* 114.

36. This and the following paragraphs, unless otherwise indicated, come from a reading of Corre's diary.

37. Thirza Vallois, *Around and About Paris, New Horizons: Haussmann's Annexation, The 13th, 14th, 15th, 16th, 17th, 18th, 19th, and 20th Arrondissements* (London: Iliad Books, 1997), 112.

38. ADP, Perotin 212/79/3, carton 43.

39. Vallois, *Around and About Paris, New Horizons,* 112–19, 148–49.

40. Addresses for the Cagoulards come from the various interrogations found in ADP, Perotin 212/79/3.

41. Corre (pseud. Dagore), *Les Carnets Secrets,*177 .

42. Marquise de Rochegude, *Promenades dans Toutes les Rues de Paris par Arrondissements, XVIe Arrondissement* (Paris: Hachette, 1910), 72. Benjamin Franklin lived on the rue Raynouard in 1776. Information on various locales in the 16th arrondissement comes from Corre (pseud Dagore), *Les Carnets Secrets.*

43. ADP, Perotin 212/79/3, 21, carton 38, Sous-dossier Jeantet, carton 43.

44. For more on the mind of a terrorist, see Jeff Victoroff, "The Mind of the Terrorist: A Review and Critique of Psychological Approaches," *Journal of Conflict Resolution* 49, no. 1 (February 2005): 5.

45. Ibid., 12–14.

46. Corre (pseud. Dagore), *Les Carnets Secrets*, 445.

47. Frédéric Monier, *Le complot dans la République, Stratégies du secret, de Boulanger à la Cagoule* (Paris: Éditions de la Découverte, 1998), 297. See as well, Valerie Deacon, "The Art of Secrecy and Subversion: The Cagoule and French Politics in the 1930s" (M.A. thesis, University of Victoria, 2005), 107.

48. Quoted in Georges Loustaunau-Lacau, *Mémoires d'un Français Rebelle, 1914–48* (Paris: Robert Laffont, 1958), 115.

49. Groussard, *Chemins Secrets*, 110. Also quoted in Bertram M. Gordon, "The Condottieri of the Collaboration: Mouvement Social Révolutionnaire," *Journal of Contemporary History* 10, no. 2 (April 1975): 264.

50. Information on Cagoulard women comes from Corre (pseud. Dagore), *Les Carnets Secrets*.

51. Ibid., 95. Corre states, "Ces histoires en marge de notre grande affaire, ces histoires parasites ne sont pas sans intérêts."

52. Ibid., 125.

53. Ibid., 94–95.

54. Ibid., 119.

55. AN, F/7 14816, "Affaire Navachine," Letter dated March 3, 1939, "Enquête Faisant suite à Deux Rapports de M. Simon, Louis, Commissaire de Police à Nantes."

56. Corre (pseud. Dagore), *Les Carnets Secrets*, 124. Corre is later frustrated by the fact that he never acted on his instincts and nothing sexual happened on his trip to St. Malo with Massolles.

57. ADP, Perotin 212/79/3, carton 43.

58. See, for example, Corre (pseud. Dagore), *Les Carnets Secrets*, 135,

59. Ibid., 120.

60. Ibid., 95.

61. Alain-Bertrand-Marie-Gaston D'Humières was actually a brigadier general and commanding officer of the 2nd Cavalry Brigade. He and Colonel Bellefond (also spelled Bellefon) were killed in action in 1940. Lieutenant General Léon-Benoit de Fornel de La Laurencie was the commanding officer of the 1st Cavalry Division in the 1930s. Interned during Vichy, he died in 1958. Ibid., 151–52.

62. Ibid., 266.

63. Joseph Désert, *Toute la Vérité sur l'Affaire de la Cagoule: Sa Trahison, Ses Crimes, Ses Hommes* (Paris: Librairie des Sciences et des Arts, 1946), 56.

64. Not much had changed for women in clandestine operations since the early modern period or before. See Annette Finley-Croswhite, "Engendering the Wars of Religion: Female Agency during the Catholic League in Dijon," *French Historical Studies* 20, no. 2 (April 1997): 127–54.

65. Henri Coston, ed., *Dictionnaire de la Politique Française* (Paris: Publications Henri Coston, 1967), 455.

66. Corre (pseud. Dagore), *Les Carnets Secrets*, 151. Corre wrote on September 27, 1937: "J'ai vu ce soir mes femmes comme l'on dit ici et là: Marie de Massolles et Nicole de Monteynard." Translated: "This evening I saw my women, as they say, 'here and there': Marie de Massolles and Nicole de Monteynard."

67. Ibid., 109.

6 / Planning the Apocalypse: Arms Trafficking in 1930s France

1. Julian Jackson, *The Popular Front in France: Defending Democracy, 1934–38* (Cambridge: Cambridge University Press, 1988), 201–08; Nathanael Greene, *Crisis and Decline: The French Socialist Party in the Popular Front Era* (Ithaca: Cornell University Press, 1969), 164ff; William I. Shorrock, *From Ally to Enemy: The Enigma of Fascist Italy in French Diplomacy, 1920–1940* (Kent, Ohio: Kent State University Press, 1988), 196ff.

2. Donald J. Stoker Jr., and Jonathan A. Grant, "Introduction," in *Girding for Battle: The Arms Trade in a Global Perspective, 1815–1940,* ed. Donald J. Stoker Jr. and Jonathan A. Grant (Westport, Conn.: Praeger, 1999), xiv.

3. Ibid.

4. Georges Lefranc, *Le Front Populaire* (Paris: Presses Universitaires de France,1965), 78–80; Ed Westermann, "The Most Unlikely of Allies: Hitler and Haile Selassie and the Defense of Ethiopia, 1935–1936," in *Girding for Battle,* ed. Stoker and Grant, 155–76; J. Calvitt Clarke III, "Italo-Soviet Military Cooperation in the 1930s," in *Girding for Battle,* ed. Stoker and Grant, 177–200.

5. Greene, *Crisis and Decline,* 167ff; Jackson, *The Popular Front in France,* 201–208; Lefranc, *Le Front Populaire,* 81–85; John Merriman, *A History of Modern Europe from the Renaissance to the Present* (New York: W. W. Norton, 1996), 1222–30.

6. AN, BB/18/3061/3, dossier 12, "Déposition de Louis Boucher, le 13 Janvier 1938."

7. AN, F/7 14674, "Armes, Enquêts sur les Dépôts d'Armes, Consecutives à l'Affaire du C.S.A.R.—Seine (Affaire Harispe), 1936–1938," Letter transmitted December 29, 1938, to Monsieur Buissiere, Directeur Générale de la Sûreté Nationale; Pedro Barruso Barés, *El Frente Silencioso: La Guerra Civil Española en el Sudoeste de la Francia (1936–1940)* (Alegia: Hiria, 2001), 88ff; Jean-François Berdah, *La Démocratie Assassinée: La République Espagnole et les Grandes Puissances, 1931–1939* (Paris: Berg International Éditeurs, 2000), esp. 255ff; Gerald Howson, *Arms for Spain: The Untold Story of the Spanish Civil War* (New York: St. Martin's Press, 1999), 34, 50, 81ff; J. Martínez Parrilla, *Las Fuerzas Armadas Francesas ante la Guerra Civil Española (1936–1939)* (Madrid: Ediciones Ejército, 1987), 63; Michel Vincineau, "La Guerre Civile Espagnole: Les Exportations Belges d'Armes," *Revue Belge d'Histoire Contemporaine* 13, no. 1 (1987): 81–123. See also Catherine Breen, *La Droite Française et la Guerre d'Espagne (1936–1937)* (Genève: Éditions Médecine et Hygiène, 1973); Félix Luengo Teixidor, *Espías en la Embajada: los Servicios de Información Secreta Republicanos en Francia Durante la Guerra Civil* (Bilbao: Servicio Editorial, Universidad del País Vasco, 1996); Domingo Pastor Petit, *Espionaje (España, 1936–1939)* (Barcelona: Editorial Burguera, 1977); Pastor Petit, *Los Dossiers Secretos de la Guerra Civil* (Barcelona: Argos, 1978); Armando Paz, *Los Servicios de Espionajo en la Guerra Civil Española (1936–1939)* (Madrid: Libreria Editorial San Martin, 1976).

8. David Wingeate Pike, *Conjecture, Propaganda, and Deceit and the Spanish Civil War: The International Crisis over Spain, 1936–1939, as Seen in the French Press* (Stanford: Stanford University Press, 1968), 129–31. Pike views the Cagoule as having posed a serious, albeit short-lived, threat to the French government in 1937. See also Maura E. Mitchell, "Lessons from Spain: The Spanish Civil War as Propaganda in the Radical Right-Wing French Press, 1936–1939" (Ph.D. diss., Florida Atlantic University, 1989).

9. AN, F/7 14677, "Armes: Contrebande ou Traffic d'Armes à Destination de l'Espagne: Affaires Commencées à Partir de Janvier 1937 jusqu'à Juin 1938."

10. AN, F/7 14816, "Meurtres Attribués au C.S.A.R."

11. AN, F/7 14677, "Armes: Contrebande ou Traffic d'Armes à Destination de l'Espagne: Affaires Commencées à Partir de Janvier 1937 jusqu'à Juin 1938," for example, is entirely devoted to this traffic, which predated the creation of the Cagoule.

12. AN, BB/18/3061/2, "Cour d'Appel de Paris, Chambre des Mises en Accusation, Affaire du CSAR, Réquisitoire, 2 août 1939."

13. AN, F/7 14674, "Bordeaux, le 15 Janvier 1938, Le Commissaire Central à Monsieur le PREFET (Cabinet)." All quotes in this paragraph are from this source.

14. Ibid.

15. Ibid.

16. AN, F/7 14678, "Ministre de l'Interieur, Paris, le 15 Juin 1938, Liste de Suspects de nationalité espagnole." On p. 8 of the list is the name FILLIOL SERRATO, José, wanted for arms trafficking. Archives de Paris, PEROTIN, 212/79/3, "Dossier Filliol."

17. Martin S. Alexander, "Soldiers and Socialists: The French Officer Corps and the Leftist Government, 1935–7," in Martin S. Alexander and Helen Graham, ed., *The French and Spanish Popular Fronts: Comparative Perspectives* (Cambridge: Cambridge University Press, 1989), 76; Shorrock, *From Ally to Enemy*, 102ff.

18. For more on Ciano, see Ray Moseley, *Mussolini's Shadow: The Double Life of Count Galeazzo Ciano* (New Haven: Yale University Press, 1999).

19. AN, BB/18/3061/9, "Situation de l'Inculpé ANFUSO, Philippo," from an interrogation of Anfuso that took place after the war, on October 19, 1945, by the Parisian commissioner of police Dauzas.

20. AN, BB/18/3601/6, Interrogation de François Méténier (at his request) before Beteille, Juge d'Instruction. Méténier sought to make a statement regarding his alleged work on behalf of the French military in 1936 and 1937.

21. AN, BB/18/3061/2, "Cour d'Appel de Paris, Chambre des Mises en Accusation, Affaire du CSAR, Réquisitoire, 2 août 1939"; AN, BB/18/3061/9, "Situation de l'Inculpé ANFUSO, Philippo, 19 Octobre 1945."

22. Clifford Rosenberg, *Policing Paris: The Origins of Modern Immigration Control between the Wars* (Ithaca: Cornell University Press), 68.

23. Ibid., 66–70.

24. ADP, PEROTIN 212/79/3, carton 43, Police Report, July 8, 1937; Joel Blatt, "The Cagoule Plot, 1936–1937," in *Crisis and Renewal in France, 1918–1962*, ed. Kenneth Mouré and Martin S. Alexander (New York: Berghahn Books, 2002), 86–104, esp. 91; Frédéric Freigneaux, "Histoire d'un Mouvement Terroriste de l'Entre-Deux Guerres: 'La Cagoule'" (M.A. thesis, University of Toulouse, Mirail, 1991), 205–212, 339–340; Frédéric Monier, *Le Complot dans la République: Stratégies du Secret de Boulanger à la Cagoule* (Paris: Éditions La Découverte, 1998), 300, 308; Moseley, *Mussolini's Shadow*, 34–35; Stanislao Pugliese, "Death in Exile: The Assassination of Carlo Rosselli," *Journal of Contemporary History* 32 no. 3 (July 1997): 313–17.

25. We will explore in greater detail below Deloncle's effort to obtain support from Mussolini for the overthrow of the French government. See, however, AN, BB/18/3061/9, "Situation de l'Inculpé ANFUSO, Philippo," a report based on the testimony that Anfuso, head of Count Ciano's cabinet from 1936 to 1938, gave regarding the relationship between the Italian government and the Cagoule. See also Aristide Corre (pseud. Dagore), *Les Carnets Secrets de la Cagoule*, ed. Christian Bernadac (Paris: Éditions France-Empire, 1977), 83–88.

26. Evidence of the central role France hoped Italy would play as a counterweight to the Germans can be found in French diplomatic papers and correspondence from the period. See in particular the extensive correspondence between Jules Blondel, French ambassador in Rome, and Yvon Delbos, French foreign minister. Delbos looked to Count Gian Galeazzo

Ciano, Italian foreign minister and Mussolini's son-in-law, to be a moderate voice in the fascist government and help mediate between the French and Mussolini. The French were particularly concerned with the role of Italy in the Spanish Civil War. The Italians for their part were happy to string the French along, even while deepening their alliance with Germany. Commission de Publication des Documents Relatifs aux Origines de la Guerre 1939–1945, *Documents Diplomatiques Français 1932–1939, 2e série (1936–1939)*, vol. 5 (20 février–31 mai 1937) (Paris: Imprimerie National, 1968), #88, "M. Blondel, Chargé d'Affaires de France à Rome, à M. Delbos, Ministre des Affaires Étrangères," Rome, March 10, 1937, 142–44; ibid., # 89, Rome, March 10, 1937, 144–46; ibid., #141, Rome, March 20, 1937, 222–24; ibid., #142, Rome, March 20, 1937, 224–27; ibid., #278, Rome, April 15, 1937, 438–41; ibid., #427, Rome, May 14, 1937, 722–24; ibid., #475, Rome, March 30, 1937, 818–20; Commission de Publication des Documents Relatifs aux Origines de la Guerre 1939–1945, *Documents Diplomatiques Français 1932–1939, 2e série (1936–1939)*, vol. 6 (1 juin–29 septembre 1937) (Paris: Imprimerie Nationale, 1970), # 8, Blondel to Delbos, Rome, June 2, 1937, 11; ibid., #166, Rome, July 1, 1937, 264–65; ibid., #204, Rome, July 8, 1937, 337–39; M. Delbos, Ministre des Affaires Étrangères, aux représentants de France à Londres, Rome, #219, Paris, July 13, 1937, 369–70; Blondel to Delbos, #304, Rome, July 30, 1937, 533–38; ibid., #326, Rome, August 10, 1937, 573–79; ibid., #424, Rome, September 10, 1937, 740–41; ibid., #451, Rome, September 15, 1937, 787–88; M. Massigli, Délégué-Suppléant de France á la Conférence de Nyon, au Ministère des Affaires Étrangères, #452–454, Geneva, September 15, 1937, 788–90; ibid., # 455, 457, Geneva, September 16, 1937, 790–92; Blondel to Delbos, # 469, #470, Rome, September 19, 1937, 819–21; ibid., #477, Rome, September 21, 1937, 828–29; M. François-Poncet, Ambassadeur de France à Berlin, #488, Berlin, September 23, 1937, 857–61; M. Corbin, Ambassadeur de France à Londres, à M. Delbos, Ministre des Affaires Étrangères, #491, London, September 25, 1937, 864–67; Commission de Publication des Documents Relatifs aux Origines de la Guerre 1939–1945, *Documents Diplomatiques Français 1932–1939, 2e série (1936–1939)*, vol. 7 (29 septembre 1937–janvier 1938), Blondel to Delbos, #47, Rome, October 9, 1937, 90–91; ibid., #50, Rome, October 10, 1937, 97–98; ibid., #102, #103, Rome, October 18, 1937, 172–73; M. Corbin, Ambassadeur de France à Londres, à M. Delbos, Ministre des Affaires Étrangères, # 107, London, October 19, 1937, 178–79; ibid., #115, London, October 20, 1937, 191–92; Blondel to Delbos, #116, Rome, October 10, 1937, 193–96; Delbos to Corbin, #119, #120, Paris, October 21, 1937, 198–202; Blondel to Delbos, #121, Rome, October 21, 1937, 203; Corbin to Delbos, #125, London, October 22, 1937, 215; Corbin to Delbos, #129, London, October 22, 1937, 220–21; Corbin to Delbos, #222, London, November 12, 1937, 401–02; M. Charles-Roux, Ambassadeur de France à Rome Saint-Siège, à M. Delbos, Ministre des Affaires Étrangères, #288, Rome, November 29, 1937, 545–47; Blondel to Delbos, #292, Rome, November 30, 1937, 554–67; Blondel to Delbos, #334, Rome, December 10, 1937, 671–75; Blondel to Delbos, #338, #339, Rome, December 12, 1937, 677–79; M. François-Poncet, Ambassadeur de France à Berlin, à M. Chautemps, Ministre des Affaires Étrangères par Intérim, #342, Berlin, December 13, 1937, 684–86; Commission de Publication des Documents Relatifs aux Origines de la Guerre 1939–1945, *Documents Diplomatiques Français 1932–1939, 2e série (1936–1939)*, vol. 8 (17 janvier–20 mars 1938), Blondel to Delbos, #15, Rome, January 20, 1938, 23–31; M. Puaux, Ministre de France à Vienne, to Delbos, #18, Vienna, January 21, 1938, 34–37. For Count Ciano's perceptions of the relationship between France and Italy during this period, see Gian Galeazzo Ciano, *Diary, 1937–1943*, trans. Robert L. Miller (New York: Enigma Books, 2002). William I. Shorrock has also ably analyzed the vicissitudes of French-Italian diplomacy in *From Ally to Enemy*.

27. Commission de Publication des Documents Relatifs aux Origines de la Guerre 1939–1945, *Documents Diplomatiques Français 1932–1939, 2e série (1936–1939)*, vol. 8 (17 janvier–20

mars 1938), M. Coulondre, Ambassadeur de France à Moscou, à M. Delbos, Ministre des Affaires Étrangères, #30, Moscow, January 24, 1938, 53–56(quote, 54).

28. Commission de Publication des Documents Relatifs aux Origines de la Guerre 1939–1945, *Documents Diplomatiques Français 1932–1939, 2e série (1936–1939)*, vol. 8 (17 janvier–20 mars 1938), Blondel to Delbos, #369, Rome, March 11, 1938, 721; ibid., #388, Rome, March 12, 1938, 736–38; Charles-Roux to Delbos, #391, Rome, March 12, 1938, 741; ibid., #412, Rome, March 13, 1938, 765–66; Blondel to Delbos, #414, Rome, March 13, 1938, 767–68. On March 14, 1937, in a top-secret "Note du Chef d'État-Major Général de la Défense Nationale et de l'Armée sur les Conséquences de la Réalisation de l'Anschluss," General Maurice Gamelin stated, "As for Italy, she has not understood it, or more likely she pretends to accommodate it." #432, Paris, March 14, 1938, 786–803(quote, 802).

29. Franco Bandini, *Il Cono d'Ombra: Chi Armò la Mano degli Assassini dei Fratelli Rosselli* (Milan: Sugarco Edizioni, 1990), offers the most complete account of the entire affair, including the arrest and trials; see especially p. 375ff. Also see Moseley, *Mussolini's Shadow*, 34–35; Pugliese, "Death in Exile," 315–18.

30. Ibid.

31. Mimmo Franzinelli, *Il Delitto Rosselli: 9 Giugno 1937, Anatomia di un Omicidio Politico* (Milan: Mondadori, 2007); Bandini, *Il Cono d'Ombra*.

32. ADP, PEROTIN 212/79/3, cartons 15, 37, 43, Dossier Jeantet; Fernand Fontenay, *La Cagoule contre la France: Ses Crimes, son Organization, ses Chefs, ses Inspirateurs* (Paris: Éditions Sociales Internationales, 1938), 12–15, 91ff.

33. AN, BB/18/3061/2, "Affaire du CSAR, Réquisitoire, 2 août 1939," 4.

34. AN, BB/18/3061/2, Untitled document dated May 5, 1938.

35. Although Fontenay's *La Cagoule contre la France* is often sensationalist and sometimes inaccurate in details, it contains what is probably the best collection of detailed information regarding the location of the Cagoule's arms depots and their contents, including photos of the weapons themselves and the bunkers in which they were hidden.

36. Joseph Gollomb, *Armies of Spies* (New York: Macmillan, 1939), 114.

37. For this and the information in the following paragraphs on Juif and Jean-Baptiste, see AN, BB/18/3601/2, a report from the Procureur de la République to the Procureur Général, dated September 27, 1937, and a second report generated by the Cour d'Appel de Paris, Chambre des Mises en Accusation, entitled "Affaire du CSAR, Réquisitoire," dated August 2, 1939; ADP, PEROTIN 212/79/3, carton 46, "Réquisition Définitif au 1er Juillet 1939," 103–34. See also Bourdrel, *La Cagoule*, 128–32; Fontenay, *La Cagoule contre la France*, 122–28.

38. ADP, PEROTIN 212/79/3, carton 46, "Dossier Jeantet"; Philippe Bourdrel, *La Cagoule: Histoire d'une Société du Front Populaire (1936–1937) à la Ve République* (Paris: Albin Michel, 1970), 219–20.

39. The informant stated that weapons could be found "at Villeret, *chez* M. Plume (the farm of the Grand Priel), *chez* M. Deliniere, a farmer in Villeret, *chez* Fernand Anthénor, his domestic, *chez* M. Laurence, the manager of the canteen. It is at M. Deliniere's house that all of the PSF of the region hold their meetings. It is he who transports them to the meetings at Hargicourt, [held at the home of] Heitz, a baker in a cooperative." The police investigated the people named in this letter. It turned out that M. Plume in fact was a Dorgériste sympathizer, but as Plume himself pointed out, "It would have been foolish . . . to transport weapons to his new home during a period when his workers, who did not espouse his political views, had been alerted by the current events." AN, F/7 14673, "Armes: Enquêtes sur les Dépôts d'Armes, Consecutives à l'affaire du C.S.A.R., Ain à Haute Savoie, 1937–1938."

40. AN, F/7 14673, "Armes: Enquêtes sur les Dépôts d'Armes, Consecutives à l'affaire du

C.S.A.R., Ain à Haute Savoie, 1937–1938," letter from Paris, dated February 14, 1938, from Le Commissaire Divisionnaire, Chef de la 1ère Brigade Régionale de Police Mobile, á Monsieur L'INSPECTEUR GENERAL Chargé des Services de Police Criminelle á Paris.

41. AN, F/7 147673, "Armes: Enquêtes sur les Dépôts d'Armes, Consecutives à l'affaire du C.S.A.R., Ain à Haute-Savoie, 1937–1938," No. 3415, "Constate de Detention et d'Utilisation sans Autorisation, d'Appareils Émmeteurs de T.S.F.," and note dated March 25, 1938.

42. Ibid.

43. Ibid., Memo dated December 17, 1937, from the Commissariat Spécial de Laon, letter dated December 24, 1937, also from the Commissariat Spécial de Laon and addressed to "Monsieur le Préfet de l'Aisne," and a note dated March 25, 1938; AN, F/7 14774, "Armes: Enquêtes sur les Dépôts d'Armes, Consecutives à l'Affaire du C.S.A.R.—Seine (Affaire Harispe): 1936–1938," report dated October 19, 1938, from Le Commissaire Principal Charles Badin, Attaché à la Direction de la Police Judiciare, à Monsieur le Directeur de la Police Judiciare, 2e Section."

44. Martin S. Alexander, "Soldiers and Socialists: The French Officer Corps and Leftist Government," in *The French and Spanish Popular Fronts: Comparative Perspectives*, ed. Martin S. Alexander and Helen Graham (Cambridge: Cambridge University Press, 1980), 77; Jacques Nobécourt, *Le Colonel de La Rocque, 1885–1946, ou les Pièges du Nationalisme Chrétien* (Paris: Fayard, 1996), 551.

45. AN, BB/18/3061/4, "Affaire dite CSAR, Cour d'Appel de Paris, Chambre des Mises en Accusation," letter from Taittinger dated September 1, 1939; ibid., letter dated January 4, 1940; Nobécourt, *Le Colonel de La Rocque*, 545–46; Soucy, *French Fascism: The Second Wave*, 50–51. For more on financing the Cagoule, see ADP, PEROTIN 212/79/3, carton 10.

46. When police raided Deloncle's office in 1937 at La Caisse Hypothécaire et Fluvial, they took away a file cabinet full of compromising financial documents. Most of this documentation, however, relates to how much money Deloncle spent and not specifically where his money came from. Other information seems to have disappeared or have been destroyed during and after the war, so speculation still surrounds any discussion of how the Cagoule was financed. Aristide Corre claimed that he burned all of the CSAR's financial accounts on September 22, 1937, at the home of his mistress, Hélène d'Alton. Corre (pseud. Dagore), *Les Carnets Secrets*, 147.

47. Ibid., 67.

48. AN, BB/18/3061/6, Interrogatoire de Sieur Froment.

49. Information for this paragraph comes from Freigneaux, "Histoire d'un Mouvement Terroriste de l'Entre-Deux Guerres," 141–60.

50. William L. Langer, *Our Vichy Gamble* (New York: Alfred A. Knopf, 1947), 169–70.

51. Andre Géraud [pseud. Pertinax], *The Gravediggers of France, Gamelin, Daladier, Reynaud, Pétain, and Laval: Military Defeat, Armistice, Counterrevolution* (Garden City, N.Y.: Doubleday, Doran, 1944), 235–36; Philippe Bauchard, *Les Technocrates et le Pouvoir: X-Crise, Synarchie, C.G.T., Clubs* (Paris: B. Arthaud, 1966), 19, 47, 146–47. On Pucheu, see Annie Lacroix-Riz, *Le Choix de la Défaite: Les Élites Françaises dans les Années 1930* (Paris: Armand Colin, 2006). The opinions of Lacroix-Riz are highly politicized; however, she does have a good bit of documentation on Pucheu and Navachine. For more on Pucheu, see his 1944 prison diary, *Ma Vie* (Paris: Le Livre Contemporain, 1948). For more on Navachine see AN, F/7 14816 "Affaire Navachine," summary dated January 14, 1938.

52. For more on Cagoulard finances and activities, see Lacroix-Riz, *Le Choix de la Défaite*, 269–304.

53. AN, BB/18/3061/4 "Affaire dite CSAR, Cour d'Appel de Paris, Chambre des Mises en Accusation"; Soucy, *French Fascism: The Second Wave*, 50–51; Nobécourt, *Le Colonel de La Rocque (1885–1946)*, 545–46; D. L. L. Parry, "Counter Revolution by Conspiracy, 1935–37," in

The Right in France: 1789–1997, ed. Nicholas Alkin and Frank Tallett (London: I. B. Tauris, 1997) 172–73.

54. AN, BB/18/3061/6, letter from Le Commissaire de Police Mobile Duclos to le Commissaire de Police Criminelle.

55. Parry, "Counter Revolution by Conspiracy," 172–73; Jean Claude Valla, *La Cagoule, 1936–1937* (Paris: Éditions de la Librarie Nationale, 2000), 125–33.

56. AN, BB/18/3061/2, report from the Procureur de la République to the Procureur Général, dated September 27, 1937, especially 4ff. Also see above, note 38.

57. Steven Zdatny, "The Class That Didn't Bark: French Artisans in the Age of Fascism," in *Splintered Classes: Politics and the Lower Middle Classes in Interwar Europe*, ed. Rudy Koshar (New York: Homes & Meier, 1990), 121–22.

7 / Exposure and Dispersion of the Cagoule: November 1937–1948

1. AN, F/7 14816, "Déclarations de M. Wiart, Jean à Pierre Mace, Commissaire, 23 Janvier 1938." Aristide Corre also discusses the events of the night of November 15–16, although he was in Spain at the time of the attempted putsch. On December 13, Jacques Corrèze unexpectedly showed up in San Sebastian to join the little circle of Cagoule exiles there, and he filled them in on the debacle and its consequences. Aristide Corre (pseud. Dagore), *Les Carnets Secrets de la Cagoule*, ed. Christian Bernadac (Paris: Éditions France-Empire, 1977), 242–44. See also Philippe Bourdrel, *La Cagoule: Histoire d'une Société du Front Populaire à la Ve République* (Paris: Albin Michel, 1992), 210–13, 222–25; Frédéric Freigneaux, "Histoire d'un Mouvement Terroriste de l'Entre-Deux Guerres: 'La Cagoule'" (M.A. thesis, University of Toulouse, Mirail, 1991), 310–19.

2. AN, F/7 14816, "Déclarations de Wiart."

3. Ibid.

4. Ibid.

5. Ibid.

6. Corre (pseud. Dagore), *Les Carnets Secrets*, 189.

7. Henri Charbonneau, *Les Mémoires de Porthos* (Paris: Éditions du Clan, 1967), 202–04.

8. Corre (pseud. Dagore), *Les Carnets Secrets*, 194.

9. Ibid., 202.

10. *Le Matin*, August 27, 1941.

11. Freigneaux, "Histoire d'un Mouvement Terroriste de l'Entre-Deux Guerres," 318–19.

12. Extract from Georges Loustaunau-Lacau, *Mémoires d'un Français Rebelle* (Paris: Robert Laffont, 1948) as cited in Corre (pseud. Dagore), *Les Carnets Secrets*, 211.

13. Ibid., 205–11.

14. ADP, PEROTIN 212/79/3, "Affaire de C.S.A.R.," carton 43, Interview of Roger Illartheine. Filliol was prescient in this respect. The Gestapo indeed did shoot Deloncle in his Paris apartment in 1944

15. ADP, PEROTIN 212/79/3, "Affaire de C.S.A.R.," carton 43, Procès-verbal of Deloncle, 1938.

16. ADP, PEROTIN 212/79/3, "Affaire de C.S.A.R.," carton 43, Interview of Roger Illartheine by Pierre Mace, *Commissaire de Police Mobile*, January 22, 1938.

17. Corre (pseud. Dagore), *Les Carnets Secrets*, 202, and excerpts from Loustaunau-Laucau's memoirs cited ibid., 211.

18. AN, F/7 14816, "Déclarations de Wiart."

19. Boucher testified in his deposition that Roidot had given him a pistol and bullets as well as a flask containing typhoid bacteria and a photo of a suspected traitor to the Cagoule to

whom the bacteria was to be administered. Evidently Roidot was a fountain of creative plotting. Boucher also claimed that Roidot had ordered him to rob a bank and had provided him with a suitcase full of the necessary tools. In his December 1939 interrogation, Roidot denied Boucher's allegations, although he did admit that during a meeting in the garage of someone named Durand in 1937, "infuriated by the treason members of the organization were committing," he might have mentioned something about "making an example of someone." Roidot claimed he couldn't remember the occasion clearly enough to be sure of his exact words, but he professed surprise that Boucher took him seriously. AN, F/7 14674, "Armes, Enquêtes sur les Dépôts d'Armes, Consecutives à l'Affaire du C.S.A.R.—Seine (Affaire Harispe): 1936–1938," statement of Louis Boucher to the Commissaire de la Police Mobile, January 8, 1938; ibid., report addressed to Monsieur Mondanel, Inspecteur Général du Services de Police Criminelle, January 20, 1938; ibid., report from Paul Pourcher, Commissaire de la Police Mobile, March 8, 1938; ibid., report from Le Commissaire Principal Charles Badin, Attaché à la Direction de la Police Judiciare, à Monsieur le Directeur de la Police Judiciare, 2e section, October 19, 1938; ibid., letter transmitted December 29, 1938, to Monsieur Buissiere, Directeur Générale de la Sûreté Nationale; AN, BB/18/3061/5, "Affaire dite CSAR, Cour d'Appel de Paris, Chambre des Mises en Accusation," "Tribunal de Première Instance de la Seine, Procès-Verbal d'Interrogatoire, 12 Décembre, 1939." See also Bourdrel, *La Cagoule*, 133–34.

20. For the letters from JV.16 see AN, F/7 14674, "Armes, Enquêtes sur les Dépôts d'Armes, Consecutives à l'Affaire du C.S.A.R.—Seine (Affaire Harispe): 1936–1938." Anonymous letter sent to the Sûreté Nationale and stamped October 28, 1937. The letter is printed entirely in capital letters.

21. AN, F/7 14674, "Armes, Enquêtes sur les Dépôts d'Armes, Consecutives à l'Affaire du C.S.A.R.—Seine (Affaire Harispe): 1936–1938," letter from JV.16 stamped April 5, 1938.

22. Blatt, "The Cagoule Plot," 87, 90. See also Soucy, *French Fascism: The Second Wave*, 47; Parry, "Counter Revolution by Conspiracy," 161–81, esp. 163–64, 169; Freigneaux, "Histoire d'un Mouvement Terroriste de l'Entre-Deux Guerres," 119–38. For more on the army's supposed involvement with the Cagoule, see AN, BB/18/3061/6.

23. This is the conclusion of Nicolas Atkin. See Atkin, *Pétain* (London: Longman, 1998), 54.

24. Corre described the succession of police searches and arrests as news arrived to him in San Sebastian via the newspapers, which covered the events in detail. He also discussed his Spanish sources, and of course the Cagoulards who managed to reach Spain safely. See Corre (pseud. Dagore), *Les Carnets Secrets*, 212–67. The police investigations and their results can also be followed in ADP, PEROTIN 212/79/3, "Affaire de C.S.A.R." and AN, BB/18/3061/2–9, which contain a wealth of documents, including police reports and interviews with arrested Cagoulards, pertaining to the investigation. The newspapers also offer a rich source of material throughout late 1937 and 1938. See, for example, "Le Chiffre Secret du C.S.A.R. à Été Découvert," *Le Petit Parisien*, November 29, 1937; "On a Découvert les Assassins des Deux Frères Rosselli," *Le Journal*, January 13, 1938; "La 'Femme Blonde' Invitée de Méténier Tombe d'Accord avec Locuty sur le Menu du 11 septembre Partagé Place Gaillon avec les Deux Affiliés," *Le Petit Parisien*, January 21, 1938. Freigneaux, "Histoire d'un Mouvement Terroriste de l'Entre-Deux Guerres," 320–22, contains a timeline of the interrogations and arrests from June 1937, when the police first questioned Filliol about the Rosselli brothers' murder—they let him go for lack of evidence, but clearly had intelligence early on related to his involvement in the crime—through the end of 1939. Freigneaux also argues that the police were reluctant to act against the Cagoule until they absolutely had to do so out of concern about the reaction of the public. Freigneaux, ""Histoire d'un Mouvement Terroriste de l'Entre-Deux Guerres," 322, 325.

25. Corre (pseud. Dagore), *Les Carnets Secrets,* 310–11; Freigneaux, "Histoire d'un Mouvement Terroriste de l'Entre-Deux Guerres" 340–42.

26. Corre (pseud. Dagore), *Les Carnets Secrets,* 250–51.

27. Freigneaux, "Histoire d'un Mouvement Terroriste de l'Entre-Deux Guerres," 326.

28. Corre (pseud. Dagore), *Les Carnets Secrets,* 174.

29. Ibid., 245.

30. Ibid., 225; Freigneaux, "Histoire d'un Mouvement Terroriste de l'Entre-Deux Guerres," 324–25.

31. Corre (pseud. Dagore), *Les Carnets Secrets,* 251.

32. Marx Dormoy communication to the nation, November 23, 1937, as excerpted in Freigneaux, "Histoire d'un Mouvement Terroriste de l'Entre-Deux Guerres," 336–38.

33. *Le Populaire,* October 5, 1937.

34. *L'Humanité,* August 4, 1938.

35. Eugen Weber, *Action Française: Royalism and Reaction in Twentieth-Century France* (Stanford: Stanford University Press, 1961), 401–02.

36. See, for example, Maurice Pujo, "La Sûreté Générale et sa Cagoule," *L'Action Française,* September 19, 1937.

37. AN, BB/18/3061/5, letter from Pierre Taittinger to the Garde des Sceaux, June 18, 1937.

38. AN, BB/18/3061/6, Anonymous letter sent to the Garde des Sceaux, August 4, 1938.

39. Ibid., letter from Eugène Deloncle to *L'Oeuvre,* March 13, 1938.

40. Freigneaux, "Histoire d'un Mouvement Terroriste de l'Entre-Deux Guerres," 390.

41. Corre (pseud. Dagore), *Les Carnets Secrets,* 245.

42. Maurice Pujo, "La Sûreté Générale et sa Cagoule," *L'Action Française,* September 19, 1937.

43. *Petit Parisien,* November 29, 1937.

44. Freigneaux offers an excellent sampling of the types of articles the rightist press wrote about the Cagoule. Freigneaux, "Histoire d'un Mouvement Terroriste de l'Entre-Deux Guerres," 346–52.

45. Corre (pseud Dagore), *Les Carnets Secrets,* 239–40.

46. Freigneaux, "Histoire d'un Mouvement Terroriste de l'Entre-Deux Guerres," 353.

47. Ibid. Freigneaux has a table showing the various crimes with which the Cagoulards were charged. All were indicted for *association de malfaiteurs* and *complot.* Surprisingly, the third most common charge was tax evasion, ahead even of possession of illegal weapons. Only three were indicted for the l'Étoile bombings, and only five—Filliol, Jakubiez, Bouvyer, Purieux, and Fauran—were indicted for the murder of the Rosselli brothers. No indictments were handed down for either Navachine or the Toureaux case as, unlike in the case of the Rosselli brothers, no witnesses or hard evidence existed to place any Cagoulards at the scenes of those crimes.

48. Ibid., 353–59.

49. AN, BB/18/3061/4.

50. All of this correspondence can be found in AN, BB/18/3061/4.

51. Bourdrel, *La Cagoule,* 269–72; Freigneaux, "Histoire d'un Mouvement Terroriste de l'Entre-Deux Guerres," 370–72.

52. AN, F7/14816, March 15, 1938.

53. AN, BB/18/3061/2, letter from Senator Marx Dormoy, Paris, November 29, 1939.

54. For a good basic history of Vichy, see Julian T. Jackson, *France: The Dark Years, 1940–1944* (Oxford: Oxford University Press, 2001).

55. The participation of the Cagoulards in the war has been discussed in a variety of sources. Much of what follows can be found in: Bourdrel, *La Cagoule,* 275–323; Freigneaux, "Histoire

d'un Mouvement Terroriste de l'Entre-Deux Guerres," 373–90; J. R. Tournoux, *L'Histoire Secrète: La Cagoule* (Paris: Plon, 1973), 153ff.

56. Annie Lacroix-Riz, *Le Choix de la Défaite: Les Élites Françaises dans les Années 1930* (Paris: Armand Colin, 2006), 550.

57. Jeantet wrote about this period after the war, maintaining that he had always tried to guide Pétain toward the moderation to which the latter was naturally inclined, and against the collaborationist policy of Laval. Gabriel Jeantet, *Pétain contre Hitler* (Paris: La Table Ronde, 1966); Joel Blatt, "The Cagoule Plot, 1936–1937," in *Crisis and Renewal in France, 1918–1963*, ed. Kenneth Mouré and Martin S. Alexander (Oxford: Berghahn Books, 2002), 89.

58. Jean-Pierre Azéma, "Le Choc Armé et les Débandades," in *La France des Années Noires*, vol. 1, *De la Défaite à Vichy*, ed. Jean-Pierre Azéma and François Bédarida (Paris: Seuil, 2000), 134–35.

59. Quoted in Tournoux, *L'Histoire Secrète*, 153–54.

60. Paul Webster, *Pétain's Crime: The Full Story of French Collaboration in the Holocaust* (London: Papermac, 1992), 73–74; Nicholas Atkin, *Pétain* (London: Longman, 1998), 59–61, 176–77.

61. The dispatch is reproduced in Bourdrel, *La Cagoule*, 303.

62. Bourdrel, *La Cagoule*, 295–98; Freigneaux, "Histoire d'un Mouvement Terroriste de l'Entre-Deux Guerres," 377–81; Bertram M. Gordon, "The Condottieri of the Collaboration: *Mouvement Social Révolutionnaire*," *Journal of Contemporary History* 10, no. 2 (April 1975): 261–82.

63. Bourdrel, *La Cagoule*, 296–97; Gordon, "The Condottieri of the Collaboration," 272.

64. Owen Anthony Davey, "The Origins of the *Légion des Volontaires Français contre le Bolchevisme*," *Journal of Contemporary History* 6, no. 4 (1971): 29–45.

65. Bourdrel, *La Cagoule*, 301; Gordon, "The Condottieri of the Collaboration," 271–72; Tournoux, *L'Histoire Secrète*, 198–99.

66. Bourdrel, *La Cagoule*, 306–12; Gordon, "Condottieri of the Collaboration," 273–75.

67. Bourdrel, *La Cagoule*, 312–14; Gordon, Condottieri of the Collaboration," 275. Darlan's story can be found in George E. Melton, *Darlan: Admiral and Statesman of France, 1881–1942* (Westport, Conn.: Praeger, 1998).

68. AN, BB/18/3061/9, "Dossier Filliol, Jean Henri Robert, 35 ans, dit 'Chef Denis,'" November 9, 1944; Bourdrel, *La Cagoule*, 321–23; Freigneaux, "Histoire d'un Mouvement Terroriste de l'Entre-Deux Guerres," 389; ADP, PEROTIN 212/79/3, carton 25/1, Dossier Filliol, carton 34/1, Dossier Filliol. Filliol's story is told in Brigitte Delluc and Gilles Delluc, *Jean Filliol, du Périgord à la Cagoule, de la Milice à Oradour* (Périgueux: Pilote 24 Éditions, 2005). See esp. 123ff. For an excellent account of the massacre and the postwar struggles regarding how best to commemorate it and its meaning in French history, see Sarah Farmer, *Martyred Village: Commemorating the 1944 Massacre at Oradour-sur-Glane* (Berkeley: University of California Press, 1999). It is interesting to note that Farmer's account of the massacre and collective memory has very little to say about the role of the Milice and nothing about Jean Filliol, who played a central, if mysterious, part in choosing this village for reprisals on the part of his German masters.

69. AN, BB/18/3061/9, June 15, 1945, announcement from the Procureur Général of the Appeals Court of Riom announcing the death sentence pronounced against Filliol; Request for the Extradition from Spain of Guichard, Moynier, and Mourraille Presented to the Spanish Government on April 17, 1947, reproduced in Tournoux, *L'Histoire Secrète*, 461–62; Bourdrel, *La Cagoule*, 321.

70. Jules Roy, *The Trial of Marshal Pétain*, trans. Robert Baldick (New York: Harper & Row, 1966), 37; Fred Kupferman, *Le Procès de Vichy: Pucheu, Pétain, Laval* (Bruxelles: Édi-

tions Complexe, 1980), 77, 80, 117; ADP, PEROTIN 212/79/3, carton 38/5, "Document de Vichy."

71. A series of documents relating how the dossiers related to the Cagoule were recovered after the liberation is reproduced in Tournoux, *L'Histoire Secrète*, 463–75. See also Bourdrel, *La Cagoule*, 324–25.

72. This paragraph and the previous one are based on Bourdrel, *La Cagoule*, 325–33; Freigneaux, "Histoire d'un Mouvement Terroriste de l'Entre-Deux Guerres," 390–91; *Le Combat*, October 9, 1948.

73. AN, BB/18/3061/9, Direction des Affaires Criminelles, February 26, 1948.

8 / A Scenario for a Murder

1. Liliane Riou, "Le Crime du Métro Port Dorée," *Gavroche* 149 (Janvier–Mars 2007): 26–35.
2. Ibid., 30.
3. Archivio Centrale dello Stato, Rome, "Ministero dell'Interno Direzione Generale Pubblica Sicurezza, Divisione Polizia di Frontier e Transporti, Rubriche di Frontier (1929–1956), Cat. 11900-23, "Milizia Confinaria (1934–40); Cat. 11900-57/R, "Servizio Rubrica di Frontiera, Fascicoli Peronnali (1932–41)." These documents record persons monitored by the Italian police who crossed the French-Italian border. Laetitia Toureaux's name does not appear on the list, nor does the list register the names of Cagoulard leaders. This is not surprising, however. Toureaux was probably not an operative of high-enough rank to have warranted close examination, and the Cagoulards possessed multiple passports under a variety of names.
4. AN, F/7 14816, "Note," April 11, 1938, from Commissaire Albayez. This document is in a bad state of deterioration.
5. Riou, "Le Crime du Métro," 34.
6. APP, P.J. Assassinat 1937, "L'Affaire Laetitia Toureaux, 16 Mai 1937," Envelope 69, Interview with Henri Nourrissat, June 23, 1937.
7. AN, F/7 14816, "Déclaration de Locuty"; ADP PEROTIN 212/79/3, carton 49, Interrogatoire de Fernand Jakubiez, le 8 juin 1945.
8. AN, F/7 14816, August 1, 1938.
9. APP, "L'Affaire Laetitia Toureaux," Procès-Verbaux #35.
10. Ibid.
11. Jean-Claude Valla, *La Cagoule, 1936–1937* (Paris: Éditions de la Librairie Nationale, 2000), 94; Aristide Corre (pseud. Dagore), *Les Carnets Secrets de la Cagoule*, ed. Christian Bernadac (Paris: Éditions France-Empire, 1977), 180, 245; J. R. Tournoux, *L'Histoire Secrète: La Cagoule, Le Front Populaire, Vichy, Londres, Deuxième Bureau, L'Algérie Française, L'O.A.S.* (Paris: Plon, 1962), 38–86.
12. AN, BB/18/3061/5, Copy of a letter written by LOCUTY, Pierre, dated January 12, 1938, to M. Barrue, juge d'instruction.
13. Ibid.
14. APP, P.J. Assassinat 1937, "L'Affaire Laetitia Toureaux," 84/1, Verifications au CSAR des Personnes dont il est parlé dans l'Affaire Toureaux.
15. AN, BB/18/3061/5, Copy of a letter written by LOCUTY, Pierre, dated January 12, 1938, to M. Barrue, juge d'instruction.
16. Corre (pseud. Dagore), *Les Carnets Secrets*, 68.
17. Bourdrel, *La Cagoule*, 138–39.
18. Quoted in Riou, "Le Crime du Métro," 29.
19. APP, P.J. Assassinat 1937, "L'Affaire Laetitia Toureaux," Rapport Général, 469.
20. ADP, PEROTIN 212/79/3, carton 21 B/2, Dossier Jeantet.

21. Riou, "Le Crime du Métro" 34.

22. AN, F7/14816, "Meutres Attribués au C.S.A.R"; F7/15343, "Rapport Cagoule."

Conclusion: Who's Afraid of Laetitia Toureaux?

1. Joel Blatt, "The Cagoule Plot, 1936–37," in *Crisis and Renewal in France, 1918–1962*, ed. Kenneth Mouré and Martin S. Alexander (New York: Berghahn Books, 2002), 104 n. 101. The phrase is attributed to a talk Martin S. Alexander gave in 1998.

2. Pierre Péan, *Une Jeunesse Française: François Mitterrand, 1934–1947* (Paris: Fayard, 1994), 36–37, 105–08, 225–30, 548–55. See also Ronald Tiersky, *François Mitterrand: A Very French President* (Lanham, Md.: Rowman and Littlefield, 2003).

3. The full text of Mitterrand's article is reprinted in Emmanuel Faux, Thomas Legrand, and Gilles Perez, *La Main Droite de Dieu: Enquête sur François Mitterrand et l'Extrême Droite* (Paris: Seuil, 1994), 235–39.

4. Péan, *Une Jeunesse Française*, 269–70, 290–92, 558.

5. Thierry Meyssan, "Antisémitisme et Anti-Maçonnisme: Histoire Secrète de L'Oréal." Online at: www.voltairenet.org/article12751.html (accessed August 24, 2009).

6. Péan, *Une Jeunesse Française*, 556.

7. Eric Conan and Henry Rousso, *Vichy: An Ever-Present Past*, trans. Nathan Bracher (Hanover, N.H.: University Press of New England, 1998), 258.

8. Sophie Coignard and Marie-Thérèse Guichard, *French Connections: Networks of Influence*, trans. Keith Torjoc (New York: Algora Publishing, 2000), 230; Frédéric Freigneaux, "La Cagoule: Enquête sur une Conspiration d'Extrême Droite," in *La Droite depuis 1789: Les Hommes, les Ideés, les Réseaux*, ed. Michel Winock (Paris: Seuil, 1995), 229–31.

9. Gabriel Jeantet, *Pétain contre Hitler* (Paris: La Table Ronde, 1966).

10. "Pierre Jeantet élu president du directoire du Monde," lefigaro.fr/medias/2007/07/02/04002-20070702ARTWWW90387-Pierre_ Jeantet _elu_president du directoire_du_Monde .php (accessed August 24, 2009). Pierre Jeantet began his career at *l'Agence France Presse*, where, interestingly enough, Mitterrand's oldest son, Jean-Christophe Mitterrand, was employed as a journalist from 1973 to 1982.

11. Privacy laws do not allow us to name this person.

12. Meyssan, "Antisémitisme et Anti-Maçonnisme."

13. Robert O. Paxton, *Vichy France: Old Guard and New Order, 1940–1944* (London: Barrie & Jenkins, 1972); Robert O. Paxton and Claude Bertrand, *La France de Vichy, 1940–1944* (Paris: Seuil, 1973). See also Henry Rousso, *The Vichy Syndrome: History and Memory in France since 1944*, trans. Arthur Goldhammer (Cambridge, Mass.: Harvard University Press, 1991). For a good discussion of the historiography of the Vichy period, see Richard J. Golsan, *Vichy's Afterlife: History and Counter History in Postwar France* (Lincoln: University of Nebraska Press, 2000).

14. See our discussion of the literature in the Introduction. See also Sean Kennedy, *Reconciling France against Democracy: The Croix de Feu and the Parti Social Français, 1927–1945* (Montreal: McGill-Queen's University Press, 2007).

15. For example, see Marice Pujo, "La Sûreté Générale et sa Cagoule," *L'Action Française*, September 19, 1937.

16. Bertram M.Gordon, "The Condottieri of the Collaboration: Mouvement Social Revolutionnaire," *Journal of Contemporary History* 10, no. 2 (April 1975): 261–82.

17. Nehemia Friedland and Ariel Merari, "The Psychological Impact of Terrorism: A Double-Edged Sword," *Political Psychology* 6, no. 4 (December 1985): 591–604.

18. D. L. L. Parry, "Counter Revolution by Conspiracy, 1935–36," in *The Right in France: 1789–1997*, ed. Nicholas Atkin and Frank Tallett (London: I. B. Tauris, 1997), 177.

19. Jerome R. Corsi, "Terrorism as a Desperate Game: Fear, Bargaining, and Communication in the Terrorist Event," *Journal of Conflict Resolution* 25 (March 1981): 45–85, esp. 48–49; Y. Alexander, "Terrorism and the Media: Some Considerations," in *Terrorism: Theory and Practice*, ed. Yonah Alexander, David Carlton, and Paul Wilkinson (Boulder, Colo.: Westview, 1979), 159–74; Valdis E. Krebs, "Mapping Networks of Terrorist Cells," *Connections* 24, no. 3 (2001): 43–52.

Appendix: The Cagoule in Historiography

1. Léon Blum, *Le Populaire*, November 9, 1948. Quoted in Frédéric Freigneaux, "Histoire d'un Mouvement Terroriste de l'Entre-Deux Guerres: La 'Cagoule'" (M.A. thesis, Université de Toulouse, Mirail, 1991), 6.

2. Serge Berstein, *1936: Année Décisive en Europe* (Paris: Armand Colin, 1969). Berstein notes the assassination attempt (p. 75) but does not discuss the activities of the Cagoule in 1936. Eugen Weber, *The Hollow Years: France in the 1930s* (New York: W. W. Norton, 1994); Eugen Weber, *Action Française: Royalism and Reaction in Twentieth-Century France* (Stanford: Stanford University Press, 1962); Benjamin F. Martin, *France in 1938* (Baton Rouge: Louisiana State University Press, 2005); Jean-Baptiste Duroselle, *La Décadence, 1932–1939* (Paris: Imprimerie Nationale, 1979), 261; Brian Jenkins, "Conclusion: Beyond the Fascism Debate," in Brian Jenkins, ed., *France in the Era of Fascism: Essays on the French Authoritarian Right* (New York: Berghahn Books, 2005), 213–15.

3. Philippe Machefer, *Ligues et Fascismes en France (1919–1939)* (Paris: Presses Universitaires de France, 1974), 26; Olivier Dard, *Les Années 30: le Choix Impossible*, in series "La France Contemporaine" (Paris: Le Livre de Poche, 1999), 137–39; Robert Soucy, *French Fascism: The Second Wave, 1933–1939* (New Haven: Yale University Press, 1995); Jacques Nobécourt, *Le Colonel de La Rocque, 1885–1946, ou les Pièges du Nationalisme Chrétien* (Paris: Fayard, 1996), esp. chap. 41, "Cagoule contre PSF," 543–56; Sean Kennedy, *Reconciling France against Democracy*, 125.

4. Joel Blatt, "The Cagoule Plot, 1936–1937," in *Crisis and Renewal in France, 1918–1962*, ed. Kenneth Mouré and Martin S. Alexander (New York: Berghahn Books, 2002), 96.

5. D. L. L. Parry, "Counter Revolution by Conspiracy, 1935–37," in *The Right in France: 1789–1997*, ed. Nicholas Atkin and Frank Tallett (London: I. B. Tauris, 1997): 161–81.

6. Frédéric Monier, *Le Complot dans la République: Stratégies du Secret de Boulanger à la Cagoule* (Paris: Éditions La Découverte, 1998), esp. chap. 13, "La Cagoule: Réseaux et Organization," 271–96, and chap. 14, "Le CSAR, Terrorisme, et Tentative de Putsch," 297–319.

7. Bertram M. Gordon, "The Condottieri of the Collaboration: Mouvement Social Revolutionnaire," *Journal of Contemporary History* 10, no. 2 (April 1975): 261–82 (quote, 262).

8. Frédéric Freigneaux, "La Cagoule: Enquête sur une Conspiration d'Extrême Droit," *L'Histoire* 159 (October 1992): 6–17.

9. D. L. L. Parry, "Articulating the Third Republic by Conspiracy Theory," *European History Quarterly* 2, no. 2 (1998): 163–88.

10. Jean-Claude Valla, *La Cagoule, 1936–1937* (Paris: Librairie Nationale, 2000); William Karel, *La Cagoule: Enquête sur une Conspiration d'Extrême Droite* (Paris: La Sept Video, 1997).

11. Annie Lacroix-Riz, *Le Choix de la Défaite: Les Élites Françaises dans les Années 1930* (Paris: Armand Colin, 2006).

12. There are a number of works in Italian on the Rosselli brothers. Among the English-language scholarship on them, see: Joel Blatt, "The Battle of Turin, 1933–1936: Carlo Rosselli, Giustizia et Libertá, OVRA, and the Origins of Mussolini's Anti-Semitic Campaign," *Journal of Modern Italian Studies* 1, no. 1 (1995): 22–57; Charles F. Delzell, "The Assassination of Carlo and Nello Rosselli, June 9, 1937: Closing a Chapter of Italian Anti-Fascism," *Italian Quarterly* 28, no. 107 (1987): 47–64; Stanislao G. Pugliese, "Death in Exile: The Assassination of Carlo Rosselli," *Journal of Contemporary History* 32, no. 3 (July 1997): 305–19; Stanislao G. Pugliese, *Carlo Rosselli: Socialist Heretic and Antifascist Exile* (Cambridge, Mass.: Harvard University Press, 1999).

13. Jean-Marc Berlière, *Policiers Français sous l'Occupation d'après les Archives de l'Épuration* (Paris: Éditions Perrin, 2001, 2009), 100, 101, 103–04, 115–17, 120, 124.

14. Fernand Fontenay, *La Cagoule contre la France: Ses crimes, son Organization, ses Chefs, ses Inspirateurs* (Paris: Éditions Sociales Internationales, 1938).

15. Joseph Gollomb, *Armies of Spies* (New York: Macmillan, 1939); Joseph Désert, *Toute la Vérité sur l'Affaire de la Cagoule: Sa Trahison, ses Crimes, ses Hommes* (Paris: Librairie des Sciences et des Arts, 1946).

16. J. R. Tournoux, *L'Histoire Secrète: La Cagoule* (Paris: Plon, 1973); Aristide Corre (pseud. Dagore), *Le Carnets Secrèts de la Cagoule*, ed. Christian Bernadac (Paris: Éditions France-Empire, 1977). Bernadac recounts that he received ten notebooks from Father Fily containing over 3,000 handwritten pages, which translated into 609 typescript pages. Bernadac heavily edited the diary, however, and he admits to leaving out some of Corre's most vulgar erotic passages. He does not explain where the original manuscripts are housed. One assumes he kept them. Bernadac was a famous television journalist who died in 2003.

17. Henry Charbonneau, *Les Mémoires de Porthos* (Paris: Éditions du Clan, 1967); Philippe Bourdrel, *La Cagoule: 30 Ans de Complots* (Paris: A. Michel, 1970); Bourdrel, *La Cagoule: Histoire d'une Société du Front Populaire à la Ve République* (Paris: Albin Michel, 1992); Pierre Péan, *Le Mystérieux Docteur Martin (1895–1969)* (Paris: Fayard, 1993); Brigitte and Gilles Delluc, *Jean Filliol, du Périgord à la Cagoule, de la Milice à Oradour* (Périgueux: Pilote 24 Édition, 2005). Other works exist, but one must be extremely cautious given their pro-right stance. See, for example, Pierre Ordioni, *Le Pouvoir Militaire en France: De Charles VII à Charles de Gaulle*, 2 vols. (Paris: Albatros, 1981).

18. See René Rémond, *La Droite en France de 1815 à Nos Jours: Continuité et Diversité d'une Tradition Politque* (Paris: Aubien, 1954).

19. Soucy, *French Fascism: The Second Wave*; William Irvine, "Fascism in France and the Strange Case of the Croix de Feu," *Journal of Modern History* 63, no. 2 (June 1991): 271–95; Irvine, *French Conservatism in Crisis: The Republican Federation of France in the 1930s* (Baton Rouge: Louisiana State University Press, 1979); Kevin Passmore, *From Liberalism to Fascism: The Right in a French Province, 1928–1939* (Cambridge: Cambridge University Press, 1997); Passmore, "Planting the Tricolor in Citadels of Communism: Women's Social Action in the Croix de Feu and the Parti Social Français," *Journal of Modern History* 71 (1999): 814–51.

20. Zeev Sternhell, *Ni Droite ni Gauche: L'Idéologie Fasciste en France* (Paris: Seuil, 1983). See also Sternhell, *Naissance de l'Idéologie Fasciste* (Paris: Fayard, 1989).

21. Sean Kennedy's *Reconciling France against Democracy: The Croix de Feu and the Parti Social Français, 1927–1945* (Montreal: McGill-Queen's University Press, 2007) is a good example of the new literature on fascism. The scholarly work on fascism has been enormous. We list here other important titles: John Sweets, "Hold that Pendulum! Redefining Fascism, Collaboration, and Resistance in France," *French Historical Studies* 15, no. 4 (Fall 1988): 731–58;

Philippe Burrin, *La Dérive Fasciste: Doriot, Déat, Bergery, 1933–1945* (Paris: Seuil, 1986); Burrin, *Fascisme, Nazisme, Autoritarisme* (Paris: Seuil, 2000); Joel Blatt, ed., *The French Defeat of 1940: Reassessments* (New York: Berghahn, 1998); John Gingham, "Defining French Fascism, Finding Fascists in France," *Canadian Journal of History* 29 (1994): 525–43. Pierre Milza, *Fascisme Française: Passé et Présent* (Paris: Flammarion, 1987); Michel Winock, *Histoire de l'Extrême Droite en France* (Paris: Seuil, 1993).

22. Michel Dobry, *Le Mythe de l'Allergie Française au Fascism*; Jenkins, *France in the Era of Fascism*.

23. William Irvine, ed., "Beyond Left and Right: New Perspectives on the Politics of the Third Republic," *Historical Reflections/Réflexions Historiques* 34, no. 2 (Summer 2008): 1–146. In the 1990s much work connecting fascism and gender began to appear. See, for example, Mary Jean Green, "Gender, Fascism, and the Croix de Feu: The Women's Pages of *Le Flambeau*," *French Cultural Studies* 8 (1997): 29–39.

24. Samuel Kalman, *The Extreme Right in Interwar France: The Faisceau and the Croix de Feu* (Aldershot, Eng.: Ashgate, 2008), 4. Also see Kevin Passmore, "The Croix de Feu: Bonapartism, National Populism, or Fascism?" *French History* 9 (1995): 69–92.

25. Fred Kupferman, *Le Procès de Vichy: Pucheu, Pétain, Laval* (Bruxelles: Éditions Complexe, 1980), 77.

26. Ibid., 77, 80, 117.

27. For recent work on the impact of 9/11, see Andrew J. Perrin, "National Threat and Political Culture: Authoritarianism, Antiauthoritarianism, and the September 11 Attacks," *Political Psychology* 26, no. 2 (April 2005): 167–94; Walter Enders and Todd Sandler, "After 9/11: Is It All Different Now?" *Journal of Conflict Resolution* 49, no. 2 (April 2005): 259–77; Leonie Huddy, Stanley Feldman, Theresa Capelos, and Colin Provost, "The Consequences of Terrorism: Disentagling the Effects of Personal and National Threat," *Political Psychology* 23, no. 3 (September 2002): 485–509.

28. Valerie Deacon, "The Art of Secrecy and Subversion: The Cagoule and French Politics in the 1930s" (M.A. thesis, University of Victoria, 2005).

29. Blatt, "The Cagoule Plot," 95.

30. Deacon, "The Art of Secrecy," 33–53. Deacon's work has a chapter devoted to the press reaction to the Cagoule. Her thesis is also part of the new trend that views as unproductive any attempt to classify French right-wing groups as fascists.

31. Weber, *Action Française*, 402.

BIBLIOGRAPHY

Primary Sources

Allons au devant de la vie . . . Une Exposition de Photographies et de Documents autour du Front Populaire et des Premiers Congés Payés, 1934–1938. Exposition présentée du 5 octobre au 5 novembre 2006. Maison du Loir-et-Cher, Blois, France.

Archives de la Préfecture de la Police/Paris. P.J. Assassinat 1937. "L'Affaire Laetitia Toureaux, 16 Mai 1937." 2 cartons.

———. Ea III, File, "L'Affaire Laetitia Toureaux."

———. B/A 1903, "La Cagoule."

———. PJ/52, "Complot du CSAR."

———. D/B 536, "Coupures de Presse sur la Cagoule."

Archives de Paris. PEROTIN, 212/79/3, "Affaire du C.S.A.R.—Comité Secret d'Action Révolutionnaire et Autres Mouvements Nationalistes de Droite."

Archives Nationales. BB/18 3061/2 to 3061/9, "Affaire de la Cagoule. 1937–1951."

———. F/7 14673, "Armes: Enquête sur les Dépôts d'Armes, Consecutives à l'affaire du C.S.A.R., Ain à Haute Savoie, 1937–1938."

———. F/7 14677, "Armes: Contrebande ou Traffic d'Armes à Destination de l'Espagne: Affaires Commencées à Partir de Janvier 1937 jusqu'à 1938."

———. F/7 14678–14684, "Armes: Contrebande d'Armes à Frontière Franco-Suisse: 1936–1939."

———. F/7 14774, "Armes: Enquêtes sur les Dépôts d'Armes, Consecutives à l'Affaire du C.S.A.R.—Seine (Affaire Harispe): 1936–1938."

———. F/7 14815, "CSAR Dossiers Personnels dont Chefs, 1937–40."

———. F/7 14816, "Meurtres Attribués au C.S.A.R.: Affaire c/x Meurtre Loetitia Toureaux."

———. F/7 15343, "Synarchie, Études, Rapport Cagoule, 1941–48."

Archivo Centrale della Stato, Rome. Ministero dell'Interno Direzione Generale Pubblica Sicurezza. Divisione Polizia di Frontier e Transporti. Rubriche di Frontier (1929–1956). Consistenza 40bb. Strumenti di Recerca 13/169.

Association Valdôtaine, Archives Sonores. *Émigration Valdôtaine dans le Monde: La Diaspora au Cours des Siècles: Histoire et Témoignages.* Aosta: Musumeci, 1986.

Belin, Jean. *Secrets of the Sûreté: The Memoirs of Commissioner Jean Belin.* New York: G. P. Putnam's Sons, 1950.

Charbonneau, Henry. *Les Mémoires de Porthos*. Paris: Éditions du Clan, 1967.

Ciano, Gian Galeazzo. *Diary, 1937–1943*. Translated by Robert L. Miller. New York: Enigma Books, 2002.

Commission de Publication des Documents Relatifs aux Origines de la Guerre, 1939–1945. *Documents Diplomatiques Français, 1932–1939. 2e série, (1936–1939)*. Vol. 5 (20 Février–31 Mai 1937). Vol. 6 (1er Juin–29 Septembre 1937). Vol. 7 (29 Septembre 1937–Janvier 1938). Vol. 8 (17 Janvier–20 Mars 1938). Paris: Imprimerie National, 1970.

Corre, Aristide (pseud. Dagore). *Les Carnets Secrets de la Cagoule*. Edited by Christian Bernadac. Paris: Éditions France-Empire, 1977.

Denoyelle, Françoise, François Cuel, and Jean-Louis Vibert-Guigne. *La Front Populaires des Photographes*. Paris: Éditions Terre Bleue, 2006.

Fontenay, Fernand. *La Cagoule contre la France: Ses Crimes, son Organization, ses Chefs, ses Inspirateurs*. Paris: Éditions Sociales Internationales, 1938.

Groussard, Georges André. *Chemins Secrets*. Paris: Bader-Dufour, 1948.

Jeantet, Gabriel. *Pétain contre Hitler*. Paris: La Table Ronde, 1966.

Jeantet, Gabriel, and Cécil Saint-Laurent. *Année 40: Londres, De Gaulle, Vichy* (Paris: La Table Ronde, 1965).

Loustaunau-Lacau, Georges. *Mémoires d'un Français Rebelle, 1914–48*. Paris: Robert Laffont, 1958.

Navachine, Dmitri. *La Crise et L'Europe Économique*. 2 vols. Paris: Félix Alcan, 1932.

Pucheu, Pierre. *Ma Vie*. Paris: Le Livre Contemporain, 1948.

Richard, Marthe, alias Marthe Richer. *Mes Dernières Missions Secrètes: Espagne, 1936–1938*. Paris: Éditions de France, 1939.

Salvemini, Gaetano. *Carlo and Nello Rosselli: A Memoir*. London: Intellectual Library, 1937.

Sicot, Marcel. *Servitude et Grandeur Policières: Quarante ans à la Sûreté*. Paris: Productions de Paris, 1949.

Van Vechten, Carl. *Sacred and Profane Memories*. New York: Alfred A. Knopf, 1932.

Newspapers and Weekly Magazines

L'Action Française

Candide

Ce Soir

Le Combat

Détective: Le Grand Hebdomadaire des Faits Divers

L'Écho de la Vallée d'Aoste

Fait Divers

France-Soir

L'Humanité

L'Intransigeant

Le Journal
La Liberté
Le Matin
L'Oeuvre
Paris Matin
Paris-Soir
Le Petit Parisien
Police
Le Populaire

Secondary Sources

Alexander, Martin S. "Soldiers and Socialists: The French Officer Corps and Leftist Government, 1935–7." In *The French and Spanish Popular Fronts: Comparative Perspectives*, eds. Martin S. Alexander and Helen Graham. Cambridge: Cambridge University Press, 1989. 62–78.

Alexander, Yonah, David Carlton, and Paul Wilkinson, eds. *Terrorism: Theory and Practice*. Boulder, Colo.: Westview, 1979.

Alpert, Michael. *A New International History of the Spanish Civil War*, 2d ed. Bastingstoke: Palgrave, 2004.

Anderson, Malcolm. *Conservative Politics in France*. London: George Allen & Unwin, 1974.

Andreu, Pierre. *Révoltes de l'Esprit: Les Revues des Années 30*. Paris: Éditions Kimé, 1991.

Andrew, Dudley, and Steven Ungar. *Popular Front Paris and the Poetics of Culture*. Cambridge, Mass.: Harvard University Press, 2005.

Atkin, Nicholas. *Pétain*. London: Longman, 1998.

Atkin, Nicholas, and Frank Tallett, eds. *The Right in France, 1789–1997*. London: I. B. Tauris Publishers, 1998.

Azéma, Jean-Pierre, and François Bédarida, eds. *La France des Années Noires*. Vol. 1, *De la Défaite à Vichy*. Rev. ed. Paris: Seuil, 2000.

Baker, Donald N. "The Surveillance of Subversion in Interwar France: The Carnet B in the Seine, 1922–1940." *French Historical Studies* 10 (Spring 1978): 486–516.

Bandini, Franco. *Il Cono d'Ombra: Chi Armò la Mano Degli Assassini dei Fratelli Rosselli*. Milan: Sugarco Edizioni, 1990.

Barés, Pedro Barruso. *El Frente Silencioso: La Guerra Civil Española en el Sudoeste de Francia (1936–1940)*. Alegia: Hiria, 2001.

Bauchard, Philippe. *Les Technocrates et le Pouvoir: X-Crise, Synarchie, C.G.T., Clubs*. Paris: B. Arthaud, 1966.

Beech, Michael F. *Observing al Qaeda through the Lens of Complexity Theory: Recommendations for the National Strategy to Defeat Terrorism*. Carlisle Barracks, Pa.: U.S. Army War College, 2004.

Belardelli, Giovanni. *Nello Rosselli: Uno Storico Antifascista*. Firenze: Passigli Editori, 1982.

Bellanger, Claude, Jacques Godechot, Pierre Guiral, and Fernand Terrou, eds. *Histoire Générale de la Press Française*. Vol. 3, *De 1871 à 1940*. Paris: Presses Universitaires de France, 1972.

Berdah, Jean-François. *La Démocratie Assassinée: La République Espagnole et les Grandes Puissances, 1931–1939*. Paris: Berg International Éditeurs, 2000.

Berlière, Jean-Marc. *Policiers Français sous l'Occupation d'après les Archives de l'Épuration*. Paris: Perrin, 2001.

Berstein, Serge. *Léon Blum*. Paris: Fayard, 2006.

———. *1936: Année Décisive en Europe*. Paris: Armand Colin, 1969.

Blanc-Chaléard, Marie-Claude. *Les Italiens dans l'Est Parisien: Une Histoire d'Intégration (1880–1960)*. Rome: École Française de Rome, 2000.

Blatt, Joel. "The Battle of Turin, 1933–1936: Carlo Rosselli, Giustizia et Libertá, OVRA, and the Origins of Mussolini's Anti-Semitic Campaign." *Journal of Modern Italian Studies* 1, no. 1 (1995): 22–57.

———. "The Cagoule Plot, 1936–1937." In *Crisis and Renewal in France, 1918–1963*, ed. Kenneth Mouré and Martin S. Alexander. New York: Berghahn Books, 2002. 86–104.

———. "Carlo Rosselli's Socialism." In *Italian Socialism: Between Politics and History*, ed. Spencer M. Di Scala. Amherst: University of Massachusetts Press, 1996.

———, ed. *The French Defeat of 1940: Reassessments*. New York: Berghahn, 1998.

———. "Relatives and Rivals: The Responses of the Action Française to Italian Fascism, 1919–1926." *European Studies Review* 2 (1981): 263–92.

Blinkhorn, Martin ed. *Fascists and Conservatives: The Radical Right and the Establishment in Twentieth-Century Europe*. London: Unwin Hyman, 1990.

Bolloten, Burnett. *The Spanish Civil War: Revolution and Counterrevolution*. Chapel Hill: University of North Carolina Press, 1991.

Bonnefous, Édouard. *Histoire Politique de la Troisième République, Vers la Guerre, du Front Populaire à la Conference de Munich, 1936–1938*. Paris: Presses Universitaires de France, 2000.

Bourdrel, Philippe. *La Cagoule: Histoire d'une Société du Front Populaire à la Ve République*. 2d ed. Paris: Albin Michel, 1992.

Brassaï, Georges. *Le Paris Secret des Années 30*. New York: Pantheon Books, 1976.

Breen, Catherine. *La Droite Française et la Guerre d'Espagne (1936–1937)*. Genève: Éditions Médecine et Hygiène, 1973.

Brendon, Piers. *The Dark Valley: A Panorama of the 1930s*. New York: Alfred A. Knopf, 2000.

Brooks, Linda Marie, ed. *Alternative Identities: The Self in Literature, History, and Theory*. New York: Garland, 1995.

Brown, Laurence. "'Pour Aider Nos Frères d'Espagne': Humanitarian Aid, French Women, and Popular Mobilization during the Front Populaire." *French Politics, Culture, & Society* 5, no. 1 (Spring 2007): 30–48.

Brunet, Jean-Paul, *Histoire du Front Populaire (1934–1938)*. Paris: Presses Universitaires de France, 2001.

Brysac, Shareen Blair. *Resisting Hitler. Mildred Harnack and the Red Orchestra: The Life and Death of an American Woman in Nazi Germany.* Oxford: Oxford University Press, 2000.

Burns, Vincent, and Kate Dempsey Peterson. *Terrorism: A Documentary and Reference Guide.* Westport, Conn.: Greenwood Press, 2005.

Burrin, Philippe. *La Dérive Fasciste: Doriot, Déat, Bergery, 1933–1945.* Paris: Seuil, 1986.

———. *Fascisme, Nazisme, Autoritarisme.* Paris: Seuil, 2000.

Cabrera, Miguel A. "On Language, Culture, and Social Action." *History and Theory* 40, no. 4 (December 2001), 82–100.

Cahm, Eric. *The Dreyfus Affair in French Society and Politics.* New York: Longman, 1996.

Carle, Emmanuelle. "Women, Anti-fascism and Peace in Interwar France: Gabrielle Duchêne's Itinerary." *French History,* 18/3 (Spring 2004): 291–314.

Caron, Vicki. "The Anti-Semitic Revival in France in the 1930s: The Socioeconomic Dimension Reconsidered." *Journal of Modern History* 70 (March 1998): 24–73.

Chenut, Helen Harden. *The Fabric of Gender: Working-Class Culture in Third Republic France.* University Park: Pennsylvania State University Press, 2005.

Chevalier, Louis. *Montmartre du Plaisir et du Crime.* Paris: Éditions Robert Laffont, 1980.

Ciardullo, Guiseppe. *Valdôtains à Paris: Le Role Joué par la Pro Schola de Champdepraz dans l'Émigration Valdôtaine à Paris (1919–1967).* Quart, Valle d'Aosta: Musumeci, 1996.

Coignard, Sophie, and Marie-Thérèse Guichard. *French Connections, Networks of Influence.* Trans. Keith Torjoc. New York: Algora, 2000.

Conan, Éric, and Henry Rousso. *Vichy: An Ever-Present Past.* Trans. Nathan Bracher. Hanover, N.H.: University Press of New England, 1998.

Corsi, Jerome R. "Terrorism as a Desperate Game: Fear, Bargaining, and Communication in the Terrorist Event." *Journal of Conflict Resolution* 25 (March 1981): 45–85.

Coston, Henri. *Les Technocrats et la Synarchie.* Paris: Lectures Françaises, 1962.

———, ed. *Dictionnaire de la Politique Français.* Paris: Publications Henri Coston, 1967.

Couleur Lavande. "The Danced Musette: Musette Culture, Retro, Dance." Online at: pagesperso-orange.fr./musette.info/GB-General.htm (accessed August 25, 2009).

Coverdale, John F. *Italian Intervention in the Spanish Civil War.* Princeton: Princeton University Press, 1975.

Cross, Gary S. *Immigrant Workers in Industrial France: The Making of a New Laboring Class.* Philadelphia: Temple University Press, 1983.

Dard, Olivier. *La Synarchie, ou le Mythe du Complot Permanent.* Paris: Perrin, 1998.

Davey, Owen Anthony. "The Origins of the Légion des Volontaires Français Contre le Bolchevisme." *Journal of Contemporary History* 6, no. 6 (October 1971): 29–45.

Deacon, Valerie. "The Art of Secrecy and Subversion: The Cagoule and French Politics." M.A. thesis, University of Victoria, 2005.

De Grazia, Victoria. *How Fascism Ruled Women: Italy, 1922–1945.* Berkeley: University of California Press, 1992.

Delluc, Brigitte, and Gilles Delluc. *Jean Filliol, du Périgord à la Cagoule, de la Milice à Oradour.* Périgord: Pilote 24 Éditions, 2005.

Delpêche, René. *Affaires Classées: Crimes Prescrits, Crimes sans Châtiment.* Paris: Éditions du Dauphin, 1968.

Delperrie de Bayac, Jacques. *Histoire de la Milice, 1918–1945.* Paris: Fayard, 1994.

Delporte, Christian. *Les Journalistes en France (1880–1950): Naissance et Construction d'une Profession.* Paris: Seuil, 1999.

Delzell, Charles F. "The Assassination of Carlo and Nello Rosselli, June 9, 1937: Closing a Chapter of Italian Anti-Fascism." *Italian Quarterly* 28 (1987): 47–64.

Desanti, Dominique. *La Femme au Temps des Années Folles.* Paris: Pernoud, 1985.

Désert, Joseph. *Toute la Vérité sur l'Affaire de la Cagoule: Sa Trahison, ses Crimes, ses Hommes.* Paris: Librairie des Sciences et des Arts, 1946.

Dobry, Michel, ed. *Le Mythe de l'Allergie Française au Fascism.* Paris: Albin Michel, 2003.

Dubois, Claude. *La Bastoche: Bal-Musette, Plaisir et Crime, 1750–1939: Paris entre Chiens et Loups.* Paris: Éditions du Félin, 1997.

Duprat, Didier. *Paris Musette.* Paris: Just a Memory Records, 1990. 1 disc.

Durham, Martin. *Women and Fascism.* London: Routledge, 1998.

Duroselle, Jean-Baptiste. *La Décadence, 1932–1939.* Paris: Imprimerie Nationale, 1979.

Enders, Walter, and Todd Sandler. "After 9/11: Is It All Different Now?" *Journal of Conflict Resolution* 49, no. 2 (April 2005): 259–77.

Esenwein, George, and Adrian Shubert. *Spain at War: The Spanish Civil War in Context, 1931–1939.* London: Longman, 1995.

Farmer, Sarah. *Martyred Village: Commemorating the 1944 Massacre at Oradour-sur-Glane.* Berkeley: University of California Press, 1999.

Faux, Emmanuel, Thomas Legrand, and Gilles Perez. *La Main Droite de Dieu: Enquête sur François Mitterrand et l'Extrême-Droite.* Paris: Seuil, 1994.

Finley-Croswhite, Annette. "Engendering the Wars of Religion: Female Agency during the Catholic League in Dijon." *French Historical Studies* 20, no. 2 (April 1997): 127–54.

Finley-Croswhite, Annette, and Gayle K. Brunelle. "Murder in the Métro: Masking and Unmasking Laetitia Toureaux in 1930s France." *French Cultural Studies* 14, Part I (April 2003): 53–80.

———. "Murder in the Métro: Mysterious Death Leads to Scholarly Work on Gender and Fascism in 1937 France." *Quest: Old Dominion University's Research, Innovations, Breakthroughs* 9, no. 1 (Winter 2006): 19–23.

Frader, Laura L., and Sonya O. Rose, eds. *Gender and Class in Modern Europe.* Ithaca: Cornell University Press, 1996.

Franzinelli, Mimmo. *Il delitto Rosselli: 9 Giugno 1937, Anatomia di un Omicidio Politico*. Milan: Mondadori, 2007.

Frase, Richard., ed. *The French Code of Criminal Procedure*. Rev. ed. Trans. Gerald L. Kock and Richard Frase. Littleton, Colo.: Fred B. Rothman, 1988.

Freigneaux, Frédéric. "La Cagoule: Enquête sur Une Conspiration d'Extrême Droite." *L'Histoire* 192 (Octobre 1992): 6–17.

———. "Histoire d'un Mouvement Terroriste de l'Entre-Deux Guerres: 'La Cagoule.'" M.A. thesis, University of Toulouse, Mirail, 1991.

Friedland, Nehemia, and Ariel Merari. "The Psychological Impact of Terrorism: A Double-Edged Sword." *Political Psychology* 6, no. 4 (December 1985): 591–604.

Géraud, André [pseud. Pertinax]. *The Gravediggers of France: Gamelin, Daladier, Reynaud, Pétain, and Laval: Military Defeat, Armistice, Counter-Revolution*. Garden City, N.Y.: Doubleday, Doran, 1944.

Gingham, John. "Defining French Fascism, Finding Fascists in France." *Canadian Journal of History* 29 (1994): 525–42.

Godechot, Jacques, Pierre Guiral, and Fernand Terrou, eds. *Histoire Générale de la Press Française*. Tome III. *De 1871 à 1940*. Paris: Presses Universitaires de France, 1972.

Gollomb, Joseph. *Armies of Spies*. New York: Macmillan, 1939.

Golsan, Richard J. *Vichy's Afterlife: History and Counter History in Postwar France*. Lincoln: University of Nebraska Press, 2000.

Gordon, Bertram. "The Bourgeoisie Reconstruction Problem in French History: A Kuhnian Paradigm." www.mills.edu/academic/faculty/hist/bmgordon/bourgeoisie_reconstruction.pdf (accessed June 19, 2009).

———. "The Condottieri of the Collaboration: *Mouvement Social Revolutionnaire*." *Journal of Contemporary History* 10, no. 2 (April 1975): 261–82.

———. *The Fall of France: The Nazi Invasion of 1940*. Oxford: Oxford University Press, 2003.

Gottlief, Julie V. *Feminine Fascism: Women in Britain's Fascist Movement, 1923–1945*. London: I. B. Taurus, 2000.

Green, Mary Jean. "Gender, Fascism, and the Croix de Feu: The Women's Pages of *Le Flambeau*." *French Cultural Studies* 8 (1997): 29–39.

Greenblatt, Stephen. *Renaissance Self-Fashioning: From More to Shakespeare*. Chicago: University of Chicago Press, 1980.

Greene, Nathanael. *Crisis and Decline: The French Socialist Party in the Popular Front Era*. Ithaca: Cornell University Press, 1969.

Gunther, Irene. *Nazi Chic? Fashioning Women in the Third Reich*. Oxford: Berg, 2004.

Harr, Karl. *The Genesis and Effect of the Popular Front in France*. Lanham, Md.: University Press of America, 1987.

Hause, Steven, and Anne Kenney. *Women's Suffrage and Social Politics in the French Third Republic*. Princeton: Princeton University Press, 1984.

Hawthorne, Melanie, and Richard Golsan, eds. *Gender and Fascism in Modern France*. Hanover, N.H.: University Press of New England, 1997.

Homer-Dixon, Thomas. "The Rise of Complex Terrorism." *Foreign Policy* 128 (January 2002): 52–62.

Howson, Gerald. *Arms for Spain: The Untold Story of the Spanish Civil War.* New York: St. Martin's Press, 1999.

Huddy, Leonie, Stanly Feldman, Theresa Capelos, and Colin Provost. "The Consequences Of Terrorism: Disentangling the Effects of Personal and National Threat." *Political Psychology* 23, no. 3 (September 2002): 485–509.

Hunt, H. Haywood. "The French Radicals, Spain, and the Emergence of Appeasement." In *Crisis and Renewal in France, 1918–1963,* ed. Kenneth Mouré and Martin S. Alexander. Cambridge: Cambridge University Press, 1989. 38–49.

Irvine, William D. "Fascism in France and the Strange Case of the Croix de Feu." *Journal of Modern History* 63 (June 1991): 271–95.

———. *French Conservatism in Crisis: The Republican Federation of France in the 1930s.* Baton Rouge: Louisiana State University Press, 1979.

Jackson, Julian. *The Dark Years, 1940–1944.* Oxford: Oxford University Press, 2001.

———. *The Politics of Depression in France, 1932–1936.* Cambridge: Cambridge University Press, 1985.

———. *The Popular Front in France: Defending Democracy, 1934–38.* Cambridge: Cambridge University Press, 1988.

Janin, Bernard. *Une Région Alpine Originale de Val d'Aoste Tradition et Renouveau.* Grenoble: Imprimerie Allier, 1968.

Jankowski, Paul. *Stavisky: A Confidence Man in the Republic of Virtue.* Ithaca: Cornell University Press, 2002.

Jenkins, Brian, ed. *France in the Era of Fascism: Essays on the French Authoritarian Right.* New York: Berghahn Books, 2005.

Jensen, Richard Bach. "Daggers, Rifles, and Dynamite: Anarchist Terrorism in Nineteenth-Century Europe." *Terrorism and Political Violence* 16 (Spring 2004): 116–53.

Johnston, Robert H. *"New Mecca, New Babylon": Paris and the Russian Exiles, 1920–1945.* Montreal: McGill-Queen's University Press, 1988.

Josserand, Jerome-Frédéric. *Conquête, Survie et Disparition: Italien, Français et Francoprovençal en Vallée d'Aoste.* Stockholm: Uppsala Universitet, 2004.

Kalman, Samuel. *The Extreme Right in Interwar France; The Faisceau and the Croix de Feu.* Aldershot, Eng.: Ashgate, 2008.

Karel, William. *La Cagoule: Enquête sur Une Conspiration d'Extrême Droite.* Paris: La Sept Video, 1997.

Kastoryano, Riva. *Negotiating Identities: States and Immigrants in France and Germany.* Trans. Barbara Harshav. Princeton: Princeton University Press, 2002.

Katz, Jacob. *Jews and Freemasons in Europe, 1732–1939.* Trans. Leonard Oschry. Cambridge, Mass.: Harvard University Press, 1970.

Kedward, Harry Roderick. *Collaboration and Resistance, 1940–1944.* London: Blackwell, 1985.

Kennedy, Sean. *Reconciling France against Democracy: The Croix de Feu and the*

Parti Social Français, 1927–1945. Montreal: McGill-Queen's University Press, 2007.

Kergoat, Jacques. *La France du Front Populaire.* Paris: Éditions La Découverte, 2003.

Koonz, Claudia. *Mothers in the Fatherland: Women, the Family, and Nazi Politics.* New York: St. Martin's Press, 1987.

Koos, Cheryl. "Gender, Anti-Individualism, and Nationalism: the Alliance Nationale and the Pronatalist Backlash against the *Femme Moderne,* 1933–1940." *French Historical Studies* 19, no. 3 (Spring 1996): 699–725.

Krebs, Valdis E. "Mapping Networks of Terrorist Cells." *Connections* 24, no. 3 (2001): 43–52.

Kronenwetter, Michael. *Terrorism: A Guide to Events and Documents.* Westport, Conn.: Greenwood Press, 2004.

Kupferman, Fred. *Le Procès de Vichy: Pucheu, Pétain, Laval.* Brussels: Éditions Complexe, 1980.

Lacouture, Jean. *Léon Blum.* New York: Holmes & Meier, 1982.

Lacroix-Riz, Annie. *Le Choix de la Défaite: Les Élites Françaises dans les Années 1930.* Paris: Armand Colin, 2006.

Langer, William L. *Our Vichy Gamble.* New York: Alfred A. Knopf, 1947.

Larkin, Maurice. *France since the Popular Front: Government and People, 1936–1996.* Oxford: Oxford University Press, 1997.

Lawrence, Paul. "'Un Flot d'Agitateurs Politiques de Fauters de Désordres et de Criminels': Adverse Perceptions of Immigrants in France between the Wars." *French History* 14, no. 2 (June 2000): 201–21.

Lefranc, Georges. *Le Front Populaire.* Paris: Presses Universitaires de France, 1965.

Legrand, Thomas, Emmanuel Faux, and Gilles Perez. *La Main Droite de Dieu: Enquête sur François Mitterrand et l'Extrême Droite.* Paris: Seuil, 1994.

Lennon, Alexander T. *The Battle for Hearts and Minds: Using Soft Power to Undermine Terrorist Networks.* Cambridge, Mass.: MIT Press, 2003.

Little, Douglas. *Malevolent Neutrality: The United States, Great Britain, and the Origins of the Spanish Civil War.* Ithaca: Cornell University Press, 1985.

Luengo Teixidor, Félix. *Espias en la Embajada: Los Servicios de Información Secreta Republicanos en Francia Durante al Guerra Civil.* Bilbao: Servicio Editorial, Universidad del País Vasco, 1996.

Machefer, Philippe. *Ligues et Fascisms en France (1919–1939).* Paris: Presses Universitaires de France, 1974.

Mac Orlan, Pierre. *Paris vu par André Kertész.* Paris: Plon, 1934.

Maier, Robert. "Negotiation and Identity." *Amsterdam Studies in the Theory and History of Linguistic Science.* Series 4: *Current Issues in Linguistic Theory* 214 (2001): 225–38.

Maisonneuve, Catherine. "Détective Le Grand Hebdomadaire des Faits Divers de 1928 à 1940." Thesis, Université de Droit, Économie, et Sciences Sociales de Paris, II, 1974.

Manevy, Raymond. *L'Évolution des Formules de Présentation de la Presse Quotidienne.* Paris: Éditions Estienne, 1956.

Martin, Benjamin. F. *Crime and Criminal Justice under the Third Republic: The Shame of Marianne.* Baton Rouge: Louisiana State University Press, 1990.

——. *France in 1938.* Baton Rouge: Louisiana State University Press, 2005.

Martin, John Jeffries. *Myths of Renaissance Individualism.* Basingstoke: Palgrave Macmillan, 2004.

Martínez Parrilla, J. *Las Fuerzas Armadas Francesas ante la Guerra Civil Española (1936–1939).* Madrid: Ediciones Ejército, 1987.

Maza, Sarah. *The Myth of the French Bourgeoisie: An Essay on the Social Imaginary, 1750– 1850.* Cambridge, Mass.: Harvard University Press, 2003.

McMillan, James F. *Housewife or Harlot: The Position of Women in French Society.* New York: St. Martin's Press, 1980.

Melton, George E. *Darlan: Admiral and Statesman of France, 1881–1942.* Westport, Conn.: Praeger, 1998.

Merriman, John. *A History of Modern Europe from the Renaissance to the Present.* New York: W. W. Norton, 1996.

Meyssan, Thierry. "Antisémitisme et Anti-Maçonnisme: Histoirie Secrète de L'Oréal." Online at: www.voltairenet.org/article 12751.html (accessed 16 July 2007).

Miller, Michael B. *The Bon Marché: Bourgeois Culture and the Department Store, 1869–1920.* Princeton: Princeton University Press, 1981.

——. *Shanghai on the Métro: Spies, Intrigue, and the French between the Wars.* Berkeley: University of California Press, 1994.

Milza, Pierre. *Fascism Française: Passé et Present.* Paris: Flammarion, 1987.

——, ed. *Les Italiens en France de 1914 á 1940.* Rome: École Française de Rome, 1986.

Mitchell, Maura E. "Lessons from Spain: The Spanish Civil War as Propaganda in the Radical Right-Wing Press, 1936–1939." Ph.D. diss., Florida Atlantic University, 1989.

Monier, Frédéric. *Le Complot dans la République: Stratégies du Secret de Boulanger à la Cagoule.* Paris: Éditions La Découverte, 1998.

Moseley, Ray. *Mussolini's Shadow: The Double Life of Count Galeazzo Ciano.* New Haven: Yale University Press, 1999.

Nayak-Guercio, Aparna. "The Project of Liberation and the Projection of National Identity, Aragon, Calvo, Jouhandeau, 1944–1945." Ph.D. diss., University of Pittsburgh, 2006.

——. "The Project of Liberation and the Projection of National Identity: France, Literature, and Politics, 1944–1945." *Contemporary French and Francophone Studies* 10, no. 2 (April 2006): 195–204.

Néaumet, Jean-Émile. *Les Grandes Enquêtes du Commissaire Chenevier: De la Cagoule à l'Affaire Dominici.* Paris: Albin Michel, 1995.

Nobécourt, Jacques. *Le Colonel de La Roque, 1885–1946, ou les Pièges du Nationalisme Chrétien.* Paris: Fayard, 1996.

Noiriel, Gérard. *Les Ouvriers dans la Société Française, XIXe–XXe siècle.* Paris: Seuil, 1986.

Norton, Barbara T., ed. *The Problem of Masonic Politics in Early Twentieth-Century Russia.* Special edition of *Russian Studies in History* 34, no. 4 (Spring 1996).

Ogden, Philip E., and Paul E. White, eds. *Population Mobility in the Later Nineteenth and Twentieth Centuries.* London: Unwin Hyman, 1989.

Ordioni, Pierre. *Le Pouvoir Militaire en France: De Charles VII à la Cagoule, de la Milice à Charles de Gaulle.* 2 vols. Paris: Albatros, 1981.

Ory, Pascal. *La Belle Illusion: Culture et Politique sous le signe du Front populaire (1935–1938).* Paris: Plon, 1994.

Osborne, Lawrence. *Paris Dreambook: An Unconventional Guide to the Splendor and Squalor of the City.* New York: Vintage Books, 1990.

Parry, D. L. L. "Articulating the Third Republic by Conspiracy Theory." *European History Quarterly* 2, no. 2 (1998): 163–88.

———. "Counter Revolution by Conspiracy, 1935–37." In *The Right in France, 1789–1997,* ed. Nicholas Atkin and Frank Tallett. London: I. B. Tauris, 1997. 161–81.

Passmore, Kevin. "The Croix de Feu: Bonapartism, National Populism or Fascism?" *French History* 9 (1995): 67–92.

———. "Femininity and the Right: From Moral Order to Moral Order." *Modern and Contemporary France* 8, no. 1 (2000): 55–69.

———. *From Liberalism to Fascism: The Right in a French Province, 1928–1939.* Cambridge: Cambridge University Press, 1997.

———. "Planting the Tricolor in Citadels of Communism: Women's Social Action in the Croix de Feu and the Parti Social Français." *Journal of Modern History* 71 (1999): 814–51.

———. *Women, Gender, and Fascism in Europe.* New Brunswick, N.J.: Rutgers University Press, 2003.

Pastor Petit, Domingo. *Espionaje (España, 1936–1939).* Barcelona: Editorial Burguera, 1977.

———. *Los Dossiers Secretos de la Guerra Civil.* Barcelona: Argos, 1978.

Paxton, Robert O. *Vichy France: Old Guard and New Order, 1940–1944.* London: Barrie & Jenkins, 1972.

Paxton, Robert O., and Claude Bertrand. *La France de Vichy, 1940–1944.* Paris: Seuil, 1973.

Payne, Stanley G. *A History of Fascism, 1914–1945.* London: UCL Press, 1995.

Paz, Armando. *Los Servicios de Espionajo en la Guerra Civil Española (1936–1939).* Madrid: Libreria Editorial San Martin, 1976.

Péan, Pierre. *Le Mystérieux Docteur Martin, 1895–1969.* Paris: Fayard, 1993.

———. *Une Jeunesse Française: François Mitterrand, 1834–1947.* Paris: Fayard, 1994.

Perrin, Andrew J. "National Threat and Political Culture: Authoritarianism, Anti-authoritarianism, and the September 11 Attacks." *Political Psychology* 26, no. 2 (April 2005): 167–94.

Petro, Patrice. *Joyless Streets: Women and Melodramatic Representation in Weimar Germany.* Princeton: Princeton University Press, 1989.

Pickering-Iazzi, Robin, ed. *Mothers of Invention: Women, Italian Fascism, and Culture.* Minneapolis: University of Minnesota Press, 1995.

"Pierre Jeantet Élu President du Directoire du Monde." Online at: lefigaro.fr/medias/ 20070702. 000000387_Pierre_Jeantet_elu_president_du_directoire_du_Monde. html (accessed July 17, 2009).

Pike, David Wingeate. *Conjecture, Propaganda, and Deceit and the Spanish Civil War: The International Crisis over Spain, 1936–1939, as Seen in the French Press.* Stanford: Stanford University Press, 1968.

Pillitteri, Paolo. *Il Conformista Indifferente e il Delitto Rosselli.* Milan: Edizioni Bietti, 2003.

Pollard, Miranda. *Reign of Virtue: Mobilizing Gender in Vichy France.* Chicago: University of Chicago Press, 1998.

Prendergast, Christopher. *Paris and the Nineteenth Century.* Oxford: Blackwell, 1992.

Prost, Antoine. *Autour du Front Populaire: Aspects du Movement Sociale au XXème Siècle.* Paris: Seuil, 2006.

Pugliese, Stanislao G. *Carlo Rosselli: Socialist Heretic and Antifascist Exile.* Cambridge, Mass.: Harvard University Press, 1999.

———. "Death in Exile: The Assassination of Carlo Rosselli." *Journal of Contemporary History* 32, no. 3 (July 1997): 305–19.

Rainhorn, Judith. *Paris, New York: Des Migrants Italiens, Années 1880–Années 1930.* Paris: Éditions CNRS, 2005.

Rearick, Charles. *The French in Love and War: Popular Culture in the Era of the World Wars.* New Haven: Yale University Press, 1997.

———. *The Pleasures of the Belle Epoque: Entertainment and Festivity in Turn-of-the-Century France.* New Haven: Yale University Press, 1986.

Rémond, René. *La Droite en France de 1815 à Nos Jours: Continuité et Diversité d'une Tradition Politique.* Paris: Aubien, 1954.

———. *Les Crises du Catholicisme en France dans les Années Trente.* Paris: Éditions Cana, 1979, rpr. 1996.

Reynolds, Siân. *France Between the Wars, Gender and Politics.* London: Routledge, 1996.

Riccarand Elio, and Tullio Omezzoli, eds. *Sur l'Emigration Valdôtaine, les Donneés Économiques et Socials (1700–1939): Une Anthologie de la Presse (1913–1939).* Aoste: Institute Historique de la Résistance en Vallée d'Aoste, 1975.

Rifkin, Adrian. *Street Noises: Parisian Pleasure, 1900–40.* Manchester: Manchester University Press, 1995.

Riou, Liliane. "Le Crime du Métro Porte-Dorée." *Gavroche* 149, no. 3 (January–March 2007): 26–35.

Rioux, Jean-Pierre. *Au Bonheur la France: Des Impressionnistes à de Gaulle, Comment Nous Avons Su Être Heureux.* Paris: Perrin, 2004.

———. *La Front Populaire.* Paris: Tallandier, 2006.

Roberts, Mary Louise. *Civilization without Sexes: Reconstructing Gender in Postwar France.* Chicago: University of Chicago Press, 1994.

Rochegude, Marquise de. *Promenades dans Toutes les Rues de Paris par Arrondissements: XVIe Arrondissement.* Paris: Hachette, 1910.

Romero Salvadó, Francisco J. *The Spanish Civil War: Origins, Course, and Outcomes*. Bastingstoke: Palgrave, 2005.

Rosenberg, Clifford. *Policing Paris: The Origins of Modern Immigration Control between the Wars*. Ithaca: Cornell University Press, 2006.

Rosenthal, Uriel, and Erwin Muller. *The Evil of Terrorism: Diagnosis and Countermeasures*. Springfield, Ill.: Charles C. Thomas, 2007.

Rousso, Henry. *Le Syndrome de Vichy: De 1944 à Nos Jours*. Paris: Seuil, 1987.

———. *The Vichy Syndrome: History and Memory in France since 1944*. Trans. Arthur Goldhammer. Cambridge, Mass.: Harvard University Press, 1991.

Roy, Jules. *The Trial of Marshal Pétain*. Trans. Robert Baldick. New York: Harper & Row, 1966.

Schiffrin, Deborah. "The Transformation of Experience, Identity, and Context." *Amsterdam Studies in the Theory and History of Linguistic Science*. Ser. 4, "Current Issues in Linguistic Theory." 128 (1997): 41–55.

Schiller, Greta. "Paris was a Woman." Paris: ZDF/ARTE, VPRO, Eurimages, 1995.

Schlör, Joachim. *Nights in the Big City: Paris, Berlin, London, 1840–1930*. London: Reaktion, 1998.

Schor, Ralph. *L'Opinion Française et les Étrangers en France, 1919–1939*. Paris: Publications de la Sorbonne, 1985.

Scott, Joan W. "The Evidence of Experience." *Critical Inquiry* 17 (Summer 1991): 773–97.

Seidman, Michael. *Workers against Work: Labor in Paris and Barcelona during the Popular Fronts*. Berkeley: University of California Press, 1991.

Shorrock, William. *From Ally to Enemy: The Enigma of Fascist Italy in French Diplomacy, 1920–1940*. Kent, Ohio: Kent State University Press, 1988.

Smith, Paul. *Feminism and the Third Republic: Women's Political and Civil Rights in France, 1918–1945*. Oxford: Clarendon Press, 1996.

Soucy, Robert. *French Fascism: The First Wave, 1924–1933*. New Haven: Yale University Press, 1986.

———. *French Fascism: The Second Wave, 1933–1939*. New Haven: Yale University Press, 1995.

Stearns, Peter N., and Herrick Chapman. *European Society in Upheaval: Social History since 1760*. 3d ed. New York: Macmillan, 1992.

Sternhell, Zeev. *Naissance de l'Idéologie Fasciste*. Paris: Fayard, 1989.

———. *Ni Droite ni Gauche: L'Idéologie Fasciste en France*. Paris: Seuil, 1983.

Stoker, Donald Jr., and Jonathan A. Grant, eds. *Girding for Battle: The Arms Trade in a Global Perspective, 1815–1940*. Westport, Conn.: Praeger, 1999.

Sweets, John. "Hold That Pendulum! Redefining Fascism, Collaboration, and Resistance in France." *French Historical Studies* 15, no. 4 (Fall 1988): 731–58.

Thébaud, Françoise, ed. *A History of Women in the West*. Vol. 5: *Toward a Cultural Identity in the Twentieth Century*. Cambridge, Mass.: Belknap Press, 1996.

Thomas, Hugh. *The Spanish Civil War*. 3d ed. New York: Harper & Row, 1977.

Thomlinson, Robert. "The Disappearance of France, 1896–1940: French Politics and the Birth Rate." *Historical Journal* 28 (June 1985): 405–15.

Tiersky, Ronald. *François Mitterrand: A Very French President.* Lanham, Md.: Rowman and Littlefield, 2003.

Tompkins, Peter. *The Murder of Admiral Darlan: A Study in Conspiracy.* New York: Simon and Schuster, 1965.

Tournoux, J. R. *L'Histoire Secrète: La Cagoule, le Front Populaire, Vichy, Londres, Deuxième Bureau, l'Algérie Française, l'O.A.S.* Paris: Plon, 1973.

Ulmann, André, and Henri Azeau. *Synarchie et Pouvoir.* Paris: Julliard, 1968.

Valla, Jean-Claude. *La Cagoule, 1936–1937.* Paris: Éditions de la Librairie Nationale, 2000.

Vallois, Thirza. *Around and About Paris, New Horizons: Haussmann's Annexation, The 13th, 14th, 15th, 16th, 17th, 18th, 19th, and 20th Arrondissements.* London: Iliad Books, 1997.

Victoroff, Jeff. "The Mind of a Terrorist: A Review and Critique of Psychological Approaches." *Journal of Conflict Resolution* 49, no. 1 (February 2005): 3–42.

Vincendeau, Ginette. "French Cinema of the 1930s: Social Text and Context of a Popular Entertainment Medium." Ph.D. diss., University of East Anglia, 1985.

———. "From the *Bal Populaire* to the Casino: Class and Leisure in French Films of the 1930s." *Nottingham French Studies* 31, no. 2 (Autumn 1992): 52–69

Vincineau, Michel. "La Guerre Civile Espagnole: Les Exportations Belges d'Armes." *Revue Belge d'Histoire Contemporaine* 13, no. 1 (1987): 81–123.

Vinen, Richard. *France, 1934–1970.* New York: St. Martin's Press, 1996.

Von Ankum, Katharina, ed. *Women in the Metropolis: Gender and Modernity in Weimar Culture.* Berkeley: University of California Press, 1997.

Walker, David. "Cultivating the Fait Divers: Détective." *Nottingham French Studies* 31 (1992): 71–83.

Walkowitz, Judith R. *City of Dreadful Delight: Narratives of Sexual Danger in Late Victorian London.* Chicago: University of Chicago Press, 1992.

Walz, Robin. *Pulp Surrealism: Insolent Popular Culture in Early Twentieth-Century Paris.* Berkeley: University of California Press, 2000.

Weber, Eugen. *Action Française: Royalism and Reaction in Twentieth-Century France.* Stanford: Stanford University Press, 1962.

———. *The Hollow Years: France in the 1930s.* New York: W. W. Norton, 1994.

Webster, Paul. *Pétain's Crime: The Full Story of French Collaboration in the Holocaust.* London: Papermac, 1992.

Weinberg, Leonard, and Ami Pedahzur. *Political Parties and Terrorist Groups.* London: Routledge, 2003.

Weitz, Margaret Collins. *Sisters in the Resistance: How Women Fought to Free France, 1940– 1945.* New York: John Wiley & Sons, 1995.

Whitney, Susan B. "Embracing the Status Quo: French Communists, Young Women, and the Popular Front." *Journal of Social History* 30, no. 1 (1996): 29–53.

Williams, Rosalind. *Dream Worlds: Mass Consumption in Late Nineteenth-Century France.* Berkeley: University of California Press, 1982.

Wilson, Elizabeth. *The Sphinx in the City: Urban Life, the Control of Disorder, and Women.* Berkeley: University of California Press, 1991.

Winock, Michel, ed. *La Droite Depuis 1789: Les Hommes, les Idées, les Réseaux.* Paris: Seuil, 1995.

———. *Histoire de l'Extrême Droite en France.* Paris: Seuil, 1993.

Wiser, William. *The Twilight Years: Paris in the 1930s.* New York: Carroll & Graf, 2000.

Wolgensigner, Jacques. *L'Histoire à la Une: La Grande Aventure.* Paris: Gallimard, 1989.

Wolikow, Serge, and Jean Vigreux. *1936 et les Années du Front Populaire.* Paris: Institut CGT d'Histoire Sociale et Musée de l'Histoire Vivante de Montreuil, 2006.

Wurgaft, Lewis D. "Identity in World History: A Postmodern Perspective." *History and Theory* 34, no. 2 (May 1995): 67–85.

Yans-McLaughlin, Virginia, ed. *Immigration Reconsidered: History, Sociology, and Politics.* New York: Oxford University Press, 1990.

Zdatny, Steven. "The Class That Didn't Bark: French Artisans in the Age of Fascism." In *Splintered Classes: Politics and the Lower Middle Classes in Interwar Europe,* ed. Rudy Koshar. New York: Homes & Meier, 1990. 121–41.

Zeldin, Theodore. *France, 1848–1945.* 2 vols. Oxford: Clarendon Press, 1973.

INDEX